New Canadian Readings

PEOPLE PLACES PATTERNS PROCESSES

GEOGRAPHICAL PERSPECTIVES
ON THE CANADIAN PAST

Edited by
Graeme Wynn

Copp Clark Pitman Ltd.
A Longman Company
Toronto

ISBN 0-7730-4979-7

Executive editor: Brian Henderson
Editing: Camilla Jenkins
Design: Kathy Cloutier and Susan Coull
Cover: Liz Nyman, based on a detail from Carte de la Nouvelle France, Chatelain Z., *Atlas Historique*... Vol. VI. A. Amsterdam, Chez L'Honore & Chatelain, 1719, between pp. 90–91 (between sig. Z & Aa).
Typesetting: Carol Magee
Printing and binding: Alger Press Ltd.

Canadian Cataloguing in Publication Data

Main entry under title:

People, places, patterns, processes

(New Canadian readings)
Includes bibliographical references.
ISBN 0-7730-4979-7

1. Canada - Historical geography. I. Wynn, Graeme, 1946–   . II. Series.
FC179.P4 1990   911.71   C90-093987-7
F1027.5.P4 1990

Copp Clark Pitman Ltd.
2775 Matheson Blvd. East
Mississauga, Ontario
L4W 4P7

Associated companies:
  Longman Group Ltd., London
  Longman Inc., New York
  Longman Cheshire Pty., Melbourne
  Longman Paul Pty., Auckland

Printed and bound in Canada

FOREWORD

New Canadian Readings is an on-going series of inexpensive books intended to bring some of the best recent work by this country's scholars to the attention of students of Canada. Each volume consists of ten or more articles or book sections, carefully selected to present a fully-formed thesis about some critical aspect of Canadian development. Where useful, public documents or even private letters and statistical materials may be used as well to convey a different and fresh perspective.

The authors of the readings selected for inclusion in this volume (and all the others in the series) are all first-rank scholars, those who are doing the hard research that is rapidly changing our understanding of this country. Quite deliberately, the references for each selection have been retained, thus making additional research as easy as possible.

Like the authors of the individual articles, the editors of each volume are also scholars of note, completely up-to-date in their areas of specialization and, as the introductions demonstrate, fully aware of the changing nature of the debates within their professions and genres of research. The list of additional readings provided by the editor of each volume will steer readers to materials that could not be included because of space limitations.

This series will continue into the foreseeable future, and the General Editor is pleased to invite suggestions for additional topics.

J.L. Granatstein
General Editor

ACKNOWLEDGEMENTS

This volume is very much a collective effort. Every one of the authors whose articles fill these pages responded with surprising speed to my requests to review and comment on the revised versions of their essays included here; for that and their tolerance of my editorial interventions, as well as their general enthusiasm for the project I extend my wholehearted thanks.

Beyond this I gladly offer special acknowledgement to Cole Harris. His invaluable assistance in the translation of Serge Courville's article is recognized on the first page of that essay, but he has made a larger, if less visible, contribution to the whole by the admirable way in which he has combined the roles of colleague and friend with that of commentator on the shape and emphases of the developing volume.

Sandy Lapsky, Ray Schulte, and Paul Jance, indispensable members of the small but highly effective support staff of the Department of Geography at UBC, took good care of those technical tasks involved in completing the manuscript: typing, photography, and cartography. A small grant from the UBC Humanities and Social Sciences Research Committee met the costs of these services. The help of Geoffrey Matthews and John Glover of the University of Toronto in securing copies of some of the maps included here is also appreciated. I also thank Camilla Jenkins of Copp Clark Pitman, whose meticulous copy editing brought this book to its final, polished form.

I am especially grateful to the Killam Programme of the Canada Council for their award of a Killam Research Fellowship for 1988–90. Without it, this volume could not have been honed to its present shape, and my sense of the collective achievement of those historical geographers who have sought to understand this wide and fascinating country must have remained narrower. I would also like to take this opportunity to acknowledge the support, enthusiasm, insight, and advice, over the years, of my colleagues in geography in the University of British Columbia. Together they have provided a remarkably congenial and stimulating environment in which to grapple with the past, and present, of Canada.

Finally, but importantly, I thank Barbara (who has seen these essays occupy my thoughts and the floor of my study for far too long) for her continuing love and support, and Louise and Jonathan, for being wonderful children who understand that their Dad's work is not always, or easily, left at the office.

G.W.
Vancouver
April, 1990

CONTENTS

INTRODUCTION

Canada. The land. For Cartier, off the forbidding coast that we now call Labrador, it resembled the bleak territory that God gave to Cain. For most of its native inhabitants, the land was part of their sensate, animate world. Through the early history of New France, land was an important mediator of social relationships. In the middle of the nineteenth century, settlers in the rolling drumlin country north of Peterborough, Ontario, considered it a source of plenty and good prospects—"the true land of Goshen." A few decades later, the "Great Lone Land" west of the Great Lakes offered the promise of Eden to a generation of newcomers. Portrayed with bold strokes in vivid colours by the Group of Seven, the rugged north land provided Canadians with a symbolic escape from the cities and machines that grew in number and size through the early twentieth century. And when, in 1967, an overwhelmingly urban people celebrated a hundred years of nationhood, the land was the focus of one of the most striking and cherished commemorative products of that year: the National Film Board's *Canada: A Year of the Land*, an almost wordless collection of magnificent photographs portraying the diverse face of a vast country and the people who occupied it.[1]

In this northern realm, land and life, people and place, geography and history are inextricably intertwined. The story of the country is the story of people wrestling with a tough environment—confronting its climate, cultivating its often niggardly soils, altering its vegetation, hunting its fauna, adapting to its hugely varied terrain, spanning its great distances—and imprinting their mark upon it. Great themes of Canadian development—exploration, immigration, settlement, staple trades, and the National Policy—are as much geographical as they are historical. From one point of view, *exploration* was the source of stirring tales of "discovery," the record of the achievements of brave men who faced danger and endured severe hardships in the service of king or company. From another, it was the probing edge of cultural contact as Europeans encountered indigenous North Americans. From yet a third, exploration pushed back the European unknown and gave shape to a territory and its maps. *Immigration* was the source of population. It was also the process by which habits, customs, and ideas were carried from old worlds to new, the means by which practices as well as people were diffused across the globe. *Settlement*, the fixing of people in place and the increase of their numbers, presupposes the imposition of spatial order on the land (in the laying out of farms, the location of cities, and the alignment of roads) as well as the transformation of its appearance. *Staple trades* were the motors of economic growth and systems of resource use. Their central role in the development of British North America meant that the shape of the country and patterns of life within it were influenced by the character of its natural endowments. Finally, the *National Policy* was a political masterstroke predicated on the railroad's capacity to conquer distance and the growing ability of the nation state to integrate space.

Even the Laurentian thesis and the concept of "limited identities," historians' organizing principles that emphasize, respectively, Canadian economic and political unity, and regional, ethnic, and class diversity, rest heavily upon particular conceptions of geography. The Laurentian thesis takes the pulse of the country from the Great Lakes–St. Lawrence aorta; the limited identities principle acknowledges that the attenuated archipelago of Canadian settlement is far from homogeneous in ethnicity and class.[2] And so it goes. In Canada, as much as anywhere, history and geography are bound up together. Any thorough understanding of this complex place must rest upon the perspectives, insights, and conceptual apparatus of both disciplines.

For an earlier generation of Canadian historians, the links between history and geography were intuitive. Pioneering scholars writing about pioneering settlers were impressed by the achievements of their forebears, who had built a nation from the wilderness. Perhaps the backgrounds of these early scholars, more rural than urban, made them sensitive to the power of nature. To some extent, too, they inherited a turn-of-the-century conviction that the environment determined human destiny. The land therefore held a prominent place in their works. So A.R.M. Lower's sweeping, vigorous, and often overdrawn account of the timber trade that turned British North America into "Great Britain's Woodyard" attributed much the same transformative power to the assault on the forest as the great American frontier historian F.J. Turner ascribed to the settlement of free land in the United States.[3] So, too, Walter Sage wrote that the Prairie set "its mark upon all who… [came] to it." It was not always easy to analyse the effects of the environment, but there was no question in Sage's mind that no one had lived in the western interior and "remained the same as he [or she] was before… [coming] to that land of vast distances."[4]

Harold Innis also afforded geography and the environment significant roles in his interpretation of Canadian development. Because the beaver and the cod are the opening subjects of his two most important books, their distinctive habits and habitats give shape and substance to his interpretations of the trades in fish and fur. Scattered through Innis's writing, there is evidence of his fondness for the outdoors, of his travels along the canoe routes of the fur traders, and of his visits to the misty shorelines of the Atlantic. Time and again, and appropriately enough for a sometime lecturer in economic geography, Innis turned to ponder the spatial patterns, or geographical implications, of the economic activities whose histories he charted.[5] Similarly, geographer Marion Newbigin wove land and life together in her work. Her 1926 study of early European settlement along the St. Lawrence, *Canada: The Great River, the Lands and the Men*,[6] was written according to then current precepts that gave great weight to the influence of environment on people.

Since the 1940s, however, disciplinary specialization and the growing fragmentation of academic inquiry have almost everywhere tended to divide history and geography. In Canada, as historians turned from the broad, essentially economic histories of Innis and Lower to concentrate on biographical studies during the 1950s, the natural environment seemed irrelevant. Places became backdrops in the lives of biographers' subjects, and geography slipped to the margins of historical inquiry. Nor was this situation much changed in the 1960s and 70s by the great proliferation of "new" histories—social, labour, immigrant, ethnic, education, women's, family, urban, and so on. Although each of these new specialties is important and increasingly sophisticated in its own right, none has focussed very vigorously on questions that lead into geography. In ethnic and urban studies, in particular, this has been more a matter of choice than of necessity.[7]

Meanwhile, geographers tended to turn their backs on the past. According to most practitioners in the 1940s and 1950s, geography was the study of areal variation; its concern was space, not time. Despite a strong attachment to the idea that places differed and that uniqueness was a "special problem" of geography, it was generally agreed that the subject was an empirical science, its concern with observing and classifying spatial data a necessary prelude to the development of geographic laws and theories.

Fundamental contradictions in the philosophical underpinnings of this position were largely ignored until the rise of logical-positivist modes of explanation in the social sciences after World War II. Predicated on the twin convictions that all worthwhile knowledge about the world was verifiable and objective, logical positivism assumed a single basic model of explanation, in which events were explained, or predicted, by reference to initial, determining conditions and appropriate general laws. Building upon this foundation, a growing number of geographers defined their subject as "spatial analysis," and embraced new methods of statistical analysis in the quest for rigorous, objective explanation. At the end of the 1960s, those infatuated with "the fantastic power of the scientific method" lamented that "traditional geography" had somehow hedged itself about "with so many inhibiting taboos and restrictions that it could not hope to realise the aims and objectives it had set itself." Deductive models and abstract theories, the cornerstones of science, were heralded as the basis of geography's future.[8] Other approaches were considered imprecise, pedestrian, and incapable of producing results of more than local interest.

Then came reaction. The 1970s and 1980s have seen much questing for a new "humanistic" geography, and practitioners have borrowed methods and philosophies from many sources. Proponents of behaviouralism, phenomenology, structuralism, and Marxism have each urged their favoured perspective; European philosophers Habermas, Foucault, and Derrida, among others, have been hailed as keys to better geographical understanding. Entering the 1990s, geography is a strikingly pluralistic enterprise, far more open to the importance of contextual studies than it was twenty years ago.[9] Still, many geographers seek an explicit methodology with which to interpret the world. Their search carries them, and with them what is sometimes perceived as the cutting edge of the discipline, towards the approaches of anthropology, sociology, and linguistics more readily than it encourages cultivation of the historian's rather more flexible, elusive habit of mind.[10]

Historical geography, in its modern sense, is a product of these developments. Although the term was applied in the nineteenth century to the study of changes in political boundaries and also came to mean the investigation of geographical influences on history, the subject began to emerge as a distinct field of inquiry barely two generations ago, straddling the ground between history and geography. As recently as 1937, when French historian Marc Bloch reviewed one of the first products of the new discipline, H.C. Darby's edited collection of essays, *An Historical Geography of England before AD 1800*, he commented, "Our vocabulary is so imperfect that to entitle a book 'An historical geography' is to risk not giving in advance a very precise idea of its content."[11] Such uncertainty was quickly, if temporarily, dispelled by efforts to define the role of geographical studies of the past. Most geographers of the 1930s insisted that historical geography was "the reconstruction of the geographical conditions of past times."[12] As geographers described the contemporary scene, noting variations in the distribution of phenomena and identifying distinct regions, so historical geographers examined the patterns of the past. Their studies were thin slices through time, cross sections depicting the geography of an area at a particular moment.

Late in the decade, these ideas were codified in an extended and highly influential essay entitled *The Nature of Geography* (1939), by University of Wisconsin scholar Richard Hartshorne. Believing that geography was a field in which "time in general steps into the background," and claiming that there was probably more agreement among geographers on this than upon any other question of definition in the field, he argued that historical geography was "simply the geography of past periods." Geographers considered processes of development only to interpret cross-sectional patterns, not from any intrinsic interest in the processes themselves. Although historians and geographers shared the task of integrating knowledge, the former studied associations in time, the latter associations in space. If history sought to understand the character of different periods, geography sought to identify the character of different areas and places. *Choro*logical rather than *chrono*logical in approach, geography was, emphatically, the study of "spatial arrangement on the surface of the earth." From this it followed that historical geography did not "begin, proceed and end, according to a time sequence," and that its products were "essentially different in character" from the work that "any historian could or would...[produce]."[13]

Fully in accord with these ideas, the first important work of modern historical geography in North America, R.H. Brown's, *Mirror for Americans* (1943) offered a likeness of the eastern seaboard in 1810.[14] Artfully conceived and beautifully crafted, it remains a significant book. Confining himself to sources available in 1810, Brown wrote about the geography of the eastern United States from the vantage point and in the style of a literate and well-informed early nineteenth-century American. Indeed, he carried the fiction of contemporaneity to the point of including a brief preface, attributing authorship of *Mirror for Americans* to a fictional character, Thomas Pownall Keystone, purportedly a resident of Philadelphia and owner of an impressive library. The contents of this "library" were listed in lieu of a bibliography for the volume. There is charm in all of this, but there are also limits to such artifice. However detailed, however evocative, static regional descriptions and period pictures cannot address questions of process. In, rather than of, the past, they resemble still pictures, revealing what places were like but failing to explain how they came about.

Recognizing as much, Carl Sauer of the University of California, Berkeley, argued forcibly for a genetic geography concerned with processes. He accepted the view that human geography was concerned with "the areal differentiation of human activities," but maintained that geographers could not "study houses and towns, fields and factories, as to their where and why without asking... about their origins."[15] Leading by example although remaining somewhat apart from the mainstream of geography between 1925 and 1940, Sauer developed a distinctive "cultural geography" (also referred to at times as "culture history" and historical geography). Sauer's approach was sensitive to the "inherent pluralism and diversity of nature and culture." It was also heavily empirical, tied to observation in the field, and concerned less with what Sauer described as "this fearfully inclusive thing, man," than with *culture* and the *landscape*. Both of these terms were defined rather more narrowly than they are in the common-sense usage of our day. Following contemporary anthropologists, Sauer regarded culture as "the learned and conventionalized activity of a group" of people. He drew his conception of the landscape from the work of German geographers, and saw it as an amalgam of patterns and features, some of them "residues" of earlier phases of occupancy, that comprised the material evidence of human activity in particular areas.[16]

The essential outlines of this approach were sketched in 1925, when Sauer proposed that the appropriation and subsequent modification of the environment for human purposes were pivotal geographical concerns. From this position it made conceptual sense to distinguish natural landscapes from cultural landscapes.[17] In very simple terms, the natural landscape—that pristine complex of climate, rocks, soils, land forms, and vegetation developed by the operation of physical processes over time—is the stage on which people "act." In an equally basic sense, the cultural landscape is a complex of features—roads and bridges, farms and fields, towns and villages—erected upon the natural stage by people. The fundamental point here is that people inevitably change the natural landscape to some extent, according to their numbers and their needs and means, or broadly, their culture.

To clarify the matter, imagine a small, remote island, richly clothed with vegetation and supporting a diverse small fauna but never inhabited by humans. Then envisage two scenarios. In one, a wind-driven canoe bearing two families, a few goats, a handful of seed, and a rudimentary set of tools is driven ashore and wrecked on the island. The families, inhabitants of a distant but not dissimilar island whose people have no knowledge of the wheel or fire, manage to scramble ashore with the little they possess. In the second scenario, our hypothetical island is purchased by a wealthy group of late twentieth-century utopians intent on building a new technological society.

Struggling to survive, the first group might uproot a few small trees, erect simple shelters, plant their seeds in tiny clearings, and allow the animals to graze at will. The second might introduce backhoes and bulldozers, a nuclear power plant, and the latest in construction materials to realize their dream. Obviously, both groups would have an impact on the ecology and appearance of the island. Yet from a single natural landscape our two scripts produce markedly different cultural landscapes, each reflecting the endowment of nature, although in highly differing degrees, and deriving their character from the culture of those who made them.

Thus, the cultural landscape is seen to be shaped from the natural landscape by human actions over time (figure 1a). Should different cultural groups succeed one another in a particular area, new landscapes would be superimposed upon the remnants of older ones. The "catalytic relation of civilized... [human beings]

The "morphology" of the cultural landscape

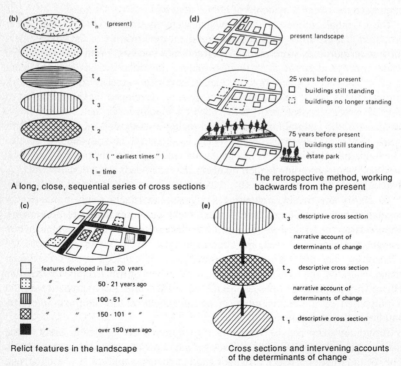

FIGURE 1 Approaches to the study of historical geography

to area" is inscribed on the ground. It was this record that Sauer believed historical geographers should seek to understand by examining its component forms.

With the alternatives defined by Hartshorne and Sauer before them, historical geographers of the 1940s and 1950s considered several strategies to incorporate the study of process within the narrow confines of geographical orthodoxy. Hartshorne envisaged the preparation of a long, close, sequential series of cross sections to illuminate the nature of change by providing "a motion picture of the geography of an area from the earliest times to the present" (figure 1b). Resembling the cinematic technique of animation, and later disparaged by a critical wit as the Mickey Mouse method, this theoretical possibility was neither practical nor especially pertinent to the problem at hand. Of a handful of studies of this sort completed before 1950, Alfred H. Meyer's four views of the Kankakee Marsh in northern Indiana and Illinois effectively reveal the character and limitations of the method. Meyer's study provided reconstructions of the area in the days of the Indian hunter and French trader (pre 1840), the pioneer trapper and frontier farmer (1840–1880), the stock farmer and sportsman fowler (1880–1910), and the Corn Belt farmer and river resorter (1910–1935). Although the study was undoubtedly geographic, it omitted "the compelling time sequence of related events ... the vital spark of history" that might have accounted for a century of rapid landscape transformation.[18] The several dioramas that constitute the Harvard Forest Models on display in Petersham, Massachusetts, provide another example of this approach, although here the cross sections are small-scale, three-dimensional reconstructions of part of the New England landscape (figure 2), rather than the textual and cartographic descriptions offered by Meyer.

Other scholars maintained that the past is relevant only if it has left vestiges in the present. In this view, geography deals with the current scene, and historical geography is limited to revealing the legacies of the past. Its practitioners might map relict features in the landscape (figure 1c); trace the origins of inherited cultural forms, such as the echo of earlier field systems in the layout of city streets; or work backwards from the present, drawing cross sections as one might separate the layers of an onion, to discover the origins of current patterns (figure 1d).[19] However it was approached, the task was simply to account for those elements in the contemporary scene that could not be explained by reference to current needs and processes.

More useful in carrying historical geography beyond description and providing it with an autonomous purpose were two models that resulted in several studies. The first combined descriptive cross sections of the sort advocated by Hartshorne with explanatory narratives that dealt with the stream of time and explained the changes that had occurred in the geography of the area under consideration. Perhaps the most frequently cited work of this type is J.O.M. Broek's study of the Santa Clara Valley, California, in which cross-sectional descriptions of the "primitive," "Spanish–Mexican," "early American," and "present" landscapes are separated, and their characteristics explained by, three intervening chapters treating the

Height of Cultivation, 1830

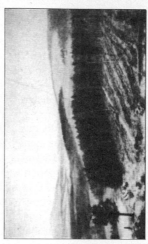

Abandoned Farm Produces White Pine Crop, 1910

Early Homestead Clearing, 1740

Farm Abandonment, 1850

FIGURE 2 Four of a series of three-dimensional models (dioramas) showing the New England landscape at different dates.

SOURCE: The Harvard Forest Models, Fisher Museum of Forestry, Harvard Forest, Harvard University, Petersham, Massachusetts.

socio-economic determinants of change (figure 1e). Some forty years after publication, it provided a model for the organization of H.C. Darby's *A New Historical Geography of England* (1973). The second approach simplified the task of treating changes in space and time together by focussing on the process most obviously responsible for the transformation of a particular landscape. Great vertical themes of geographical change, such as woodland clearing or wetland drainage, provided an organizing principle for studies that treated the changing form and character of sections of the earth's surface.[20]

In retrospect, much of the historical geography written during these years of debate and doubt appears blinkered in conception and hobbled by anxiety about its geographical virtue. The methodological debates about the relationship between geography and historical geography seem repetitive, tedious, and remarkably straitjacketed. For Carl Sauer, committed to letting inquiry range where the search for understanding took it, pedantry had won the day, and he spoke scathingly of "the pernicious anemia of the 'but-is-this-geography?' [mentality]" that he saw about him.[21] Yet the intellectual wriggling of the period was essential to legitimizing any study of the past in a subject both increasingly sensitive to the importance of defining its identity, and intent on claiming the study of area as its own distinct subject matter.[22]

English-language writing on the historical geography of Canada grew from these antecedents. Most instructors in the newly established geography departments of the universities of Toronto (1935), McMaster (1942), McGill (1945), Western Ontario (1949), Manitoba (1951), and British Columbia (1953) had received their post-graduate training in Britain or the United States, and a handful of scholars in these countries wrote on Canadian topics.[23] The studies were products of their times and thus it was not surprising that cross-sectional work was in vogue in the 1950s and early 1960s. T. L. Hills wrote "The St. Francis to the Chaudière, 1830," and J.D. Wood entitled a study of Dumfries Township, Upper Canada, in 1816 "The Stage is Set...." At Oxford University, W.H. Parker completed a doctoral thesis entitled "The Geography of the Province of Lower Canada in 1837." A few years later, J.H. Warkentin wrote "Western Canada in 1886," and R.L. Gentilcore, "The Niagara District of Robert Gourlay."[24] Also broadly in accord with prevailing ideas about the nature of geography during this period, others mapped population distributions and settlement patterns at several dates, studied spatial relationships between territories, examined changes in land use, and compared regional patterns of economic activity in the mid-twentieth century with those of the nineteenth century.[25]

By far the most important contribution to the field of historical geography and to the geographical literature on the Canadian past during these years, however, came from Andrew H. Clark.[26] While completing a Master's degree at the University of Toronto, Clark was influenced by H.A. Innis; he was also a graduate of the doctoral program in Sauer's department at Berkeley, and a colleague of Hartshorne at the University of Wisconsin. Shaped by these contacts, Clark struggled through the 1950s to develop an historical geography that combined a chorological focus with recognition that patterns were "constantly changing things."

This was no easy task. The result was an uneasy compromise described as the study of "geographical change."[27] Clark's method, which is discussed in several methodological articles, focussed on "the changing patterns of phenomena and relationships in and through area." Its essential characteristics are best revealed by Clark's own studies of the Maritimes, especially *Three Centuries and the Island.*

This book, the first and, for five years, the only English-language monograph in Canadian historical geography written by a Canadian, is an obvious product of the methodological concerns of its time. Published in 1959, it was described by Clark as self-evidently historical because it considered three hundred years of development. Yet its geographical pedigree was clear in the maps—well over a hundred of them—that summarized spatial patterns of settlement and land use in Prince Edward Island. Their depictions of "likenesses and differences from place to place" were central to the study; although seen as "reflections of the momentary character of constantly changing distributions," they imparted a clear cross-sectional emphasis to the book. Furthermore, *Three Centuries* reflected a good deal of Sauer's influence in its explicit comparisons of the agricultural practices of Prince Edward Island's four major ethnic groups. Bearers of different cultures, they were expected (and shown) to act rather differently in their appropriation of this territory to their needs. For all the relative homogeneity of its natural environment, the island past and present offered several examples of "uneconomic geographies" attributable to "cultural drives or prejudices." So, for example, the cultivation of wheat in some heavily Acadian areas, long after production elsewhere on the island had fallen precipitously in the face of Prairie competition, marked the triumph of inheritance over economics, of tradition over environment.[28] From this insight, revealed by his sequential series of maps, Clark hoped that geographers would learn that the contemporary scene often reflects what has gone before; in it, he implied, historians might discover a "broad new vista of interpretation."

Here, in a nutshell, were exposed some of the limitations of Clark's work. Despite their substantial empirical foundations and distinctive emphases, his studies of geographical change suffered from an arbitrary division of labour between geographers and historians. Holding that it was the task of the former to examine the *geography* of change, and of the latter to explore changes in economy, culture, and society, Clark treated culture, or ethnicity, as something static and given, rather than dynamic and reflexive. His work paid far more attention to patterns on maps than to people in places, and it revealed the facts of change far more fully than it accounted for the processes that lay behind them. Although he attempted, in his final years, to develop a broadly integrative perspective on "the interwoven phenomena of the [human] world," he was unable to transcend the dogma of his times in his two books and half dozen articles on the Maritimes.[29] Nonetheless, his leading role in training graduate students (many of them Canadian) in historical geography, his insistence upon the fundamental importance of archival research, and his spirited defence of an historical perspective in geography, give him an important place among the early builders of his subject in Canada.

In 1967, when one of Clark's first Canadian graduate students assessed the state of historical geography in this country, the discipline remained a fledgling. "There are," wrote R. Cole Harris, "few trained historical geographers in Canada, and they have done little research."[30] A comprehensive inventory identified approximately fifty graduate theses and fewer than a hundred publications in the field. Many of the theses, including twelve of the fourteen doctoral studies, had been completed at British and American universities. The articles were extremely diverse in subject, method, and quality, and were scattered through a wide range of journals. There was enormous potential for future work, but that which had been done was difficult to describe. Much of it focussed on tiny tracts of territory—the Ile d'Orléans, this or that county, a particular valley—dotted across the continent from Bonavista Bay to the Bow Valley and from the Erie Triangle to the Arctic waters. Topics ran the gamut from pioneer settlement to the growth of Edmonton, from migration to transportation, from environmental response to landscape change, and there had been "little attempt to relate individual studies to previous work."

Many geographers in the late 1960s loudly condemned these characteristics as symptomatic failings of historical geography, as social science, with its promises of cumulative inquiry, generalization, and relevance to planning seized their imaginations. Publication of A.H. Clark's *Acadia: The Geography of Early Nova Scotia to 1760* in 1968, provided a convenient lightning rod for such criticism. One especially acerbic critic lamented the book's lack of "a consistent focus and purposeful internal organization," and claimed that its author's principal contribution lay in "gathering information about a little known area previously neglected by historical geographers." In this view, the study of geographical change was a cul-de-sac. There was an intellectual crisis in historical geography; its practitioners clung to the archaic notion that "all the facts must be ordered before generalization can begin," and their only salvation lay in adopting the new conceptual frameworks, models, and techniques of social scientific geography.[31]

Such conviction produced converts. Amid the flurry of methodological pronouncements, redefinitions of the subject, and calls to consummate the marriage of history and theory in geography, the late 1960s saw a number of Canadian geographers turning new tools on the past. C.J.B. Wood developed a probabilistic model of settlement expansion in the Long Point region of Ontario in a 1966 M.A. thesis. Six years later, at the International Geographical Union meeting in Montreal, John Clarke reported on his trend-surface analysis of rural settlement patterns in Canada West. In 1973, Hayward and Osborne used content analysis—a supposedly objective procedure for tabulating the content of a text or assessing the balance of opinions expressed in it—to demonstrate that an 1847 Toronto newspaper considered immigration to that city a local problem. A year later, diffusion theory enabled David Wood to simulate pre-census population distributions in certain Upper Canadian townships.[32]

Through the last decade or so, the strongest champion of such approaches, among Canadian geographers, has been William Norton of the University of Manitoba. A firm advocate of an historical geography devoted to understanding the evolution of spatial form, Norton has made his case in *Historical Analysis in Geography* (1984), and in substantive studies of agricultural settlement patterns in Ontario. In essence, he identifies three broad streams of historical geographical work. The first, the study of geographical change through time, he associates with A.H. Clark. The second, concerned with the development of landscapes, is seen to follow Sauer's ideas. The third, quite distinct strand draws inspiration and approaches from those who see geography as a spatial-analytical, socio-scientific discipline, as well as from modern economic history.

This last type of work is described as the study of spatial form evolution and is, in Norton's words, concerned with "the temporal or historical analysis of process to form relationships." Quantitative hypothesis testing and explicit use of theory are integral parts of this approach, which is said to rest upon rigorous analysis of cause-and-effect relationships. It proceeds, characteristically, through a series of steps: problem definition, hypothesis specification, identification of a putative causal process, expression of this process as a set of variables, use of the process to generate spatial forms, comparison of actual and generated forms, and refinement of the process model. Counterfactual propositions, which ask what would have happened had certain conditions or preconditions been different, are seen as valuable aids to the identification of cause-and-effect relationships. Simulation techniques provide the operational basis of many process models. In sum, Norton's work is explicitly positivist in approach and quantitative in execution. It seeks to develop theories to account for change by hypothesizing form and deducing process.[33]

Yet on balance, calls for a social-scientific, spatial-analytical historical geography had limited impact upon the field in Canada. Many Canadian historical geographers shared a growing dissatisfaction with "the level of understanding achieved in the application of statistical techniques and a priori models to geographic phenomena."[34] Insisting, with colleagues in other branches of geography, that human behaviour reflects human decision making and that people are not simple pawns of the market, some historical geographers sought a better understanding of spatial behaviour (such as the choice of settlement site) by investigating contemporary images and perceptions of particular locales.[35] At times, this work has simply added another variable to those included in the spatial analysts' equation. Yet at best it has illuminated the processes of settlement and development by revealing the impact of ideas and images on the actions of settlers, explorers, promoters, and politicians.

More characteristically though, historical geographers have firmly asserted that the social scientific critique of the field was misguided, and that the subject involves more than applying current geographical techniques to old data. From this perspective, historical geography offers a distinctive way of thinking about and studying the world. In contrast with much contemporary geography, which is still closely tied to explicit methodologies and specific research techniques, the methods of historical geography are "open, eclectic and curiously undefinable"; they constitute a habit of mind rather than a set of formal research procedures. Oriented towards synthesis, the practice of seeing things together and in context, this habit of mind depends upon judgment and learning, and is not unlike that often ascribed to historians.[36]

Yet historical geography stands apart from history because its fundamental concern is with the settings in which people lived. At its base lies an interest in the interaction between human beings and their physical environment, and a fascination with the landscapes (broadly defined) produced by this process. If there is no longer much truth to the old adage that "history is about chaps and geography is about maps," the two subjects remain distinct even as they explore much common ground. At the risk of giving short shrift to both disciplines, and certainly ignoring the emphases of much modern social history, this distinction can be suggested epigrammatically as follows: historical geographers are more interested in the ways in which people make places than are most historians, and historians, generally, pay more attention to the play of character and circumstances upon events than do historical geographers.[37]

Both the approach and the focus of historical geography so conceived imply certain scales and types of inquiry that distinguish the subject from its neighbouring disciplines. Because data are understood in context, and because the face of the earth is richly diverse, studies in this mode tend to be particularistic. Their compass is typically local or regional rather than national, continental, or global, and their authors are generally more cautious than many geographers about the possibilities of identifying laws or even broad generalizations that explain the patterns of human life. Yet because their studies of places and the processes that created them point a little more directly to the possibilities of comparison than do some of the characteristic concerns of history, historical geographers may be more inclined to generalize the results of their inquiries than are most historians. In any event, it is clear that Canadian historical geography emerged from the intellectual tumult of the late 1960s and early 1970s as a singular, vigorous, and increasingly secure field of inquiry. The recent publication of volume 1 of the *Historical Atlas of Canada* is perhaps the best single measure of this achievement. It is ambitious in both chronological and spatial scope, and impressive for the way that it carefully combines rich local detail and wider interpretations of regional and subcontinental development. As well, at least one historian has identified a lengthy honour roll of first-rate scholarship by geographers on early Canada in the work of the last twenty-five years.[38]

Any comprehensive review of Canadian historical geography since 1967 is nevertheless likely to raise echoes of Charles R. Dryer's claim, in 1920, that "the earth is a ball filled inside with dirt and worms and covered all over on the outside with nothing but geography."[39] The range of places and subjects studied is enormous, reflecting the growth of Canadian universities in the 1960s and 1970s, and a corresponding increase in the number of scholars publishing and supervising work in historical geography. As even the limited selection of work in this volume reveals, the analysis of many themes familiar in 1967 has been extended—migration, settlement, and cultural transfer (Harris, Hornsby),[40] the historical geography of particular locales (Courville, Mannion, Ross, Wynn),[41] the development of urban places,[42] the distribution of specific activities or groups of people (Lehr),[43] survey systems, vernacular buildings, and the look of the land (Ennals and

Holdsworth).[44] New, broadly theoretical insights and an understanding of processes, built from the evidence of earlier studies, have been brought to bear on hitherto neglected areas. New topics have also drawn attention—among them, native peoples (Heidenreich, Moodie),[45] ecological impacts and environmental conservation (Kelly),[46] the internal geography of cities (Gad and Holdsworth, McCririck and Wynn),[47] communications (McIlwraith),[48] urban system development (McCann),[49] and the fundamental patterns of the country (Harris).[50]

Methodologies have multiplied in tandem with topics.[51] Because no single definition of geography now holds sway, as the doctrine of spatial differentiation did in the 1950s and 60s, historical geographers are no longer constrained to cloak their studies in the mantle of disciplinary orthodoxy. So cross sections continue to be drawn, but less frequently, and they take their place, with other strategies developed in the 1940s and 50s, alongside approaches untried in 1967.[52] To the techniques of content analysis and simulation have been added quantification and data manipulation on a scale unimagined before the computer revolution. Although the use of maps and a tendency to think about problems in spatial terms remain integral parts of the historical geographer's arsenal, approaches are now characteristically fitted to the topic and data at hand, rather than shaped by an overarching and almost inevitably restricting concern for geographical purity.

As the selections that follow suggest, values, ideologies, and beliefs,[53] the state, demographic, economic, and social forces,[54] and kinship, land speculation, technology, and the law[55] have all been invoked by historical geographers in the last two decades to further understanding of the Canadian past. If anything, these developments tend to make the recent literature in historical geography appear even more diffuse than it did in 1967. Now, as then, this impression is heightened by the number of careful empirical studies (many of them substantial M.A. theses) that remain unconnected in any explicit way to larger interpretive themes.

Yet for all its particularity, this literature is far from atomistic. It has grown between the mainstreams of geographical and historical writing about Canada, and has benefited from this. From its geographical roots it has drawn interest in the organization of space, the modification of the environment, and the look of the land. From its historical ones have come a concern to understand the ways in which people have made sense of their settings and conducted themselves within them, as well as an interest in the pressures, tensions, opportunities, and aspirations from which the nation and its regions and communities were forged.[56]

Combined in various ways and to various degrees, these emphases have yielded a literature focussed on people, places, patterns, and processes that bears directly upon our understanding of a country largely shaped by the relatively recent encounter of migrant peoples with a vast and often difficult land. Because its most characteristic scales of inquiry are close to those at which lives were lived and communities created, this literature reveals a good deal about the economic, social, and material circumstances confronted by the majority of British North Americans/Canadians. It puts us in touch with the everyday. Yet it also recognises that however multiform the places occupied by our forebears, those places were always the products of local and individual responses to more general processes, and that from these interactions broad patterns emerged.

Much recent writing in historical geography therefore bears on pivotal themes in the development of this country. Some of these form the subsections of the following selection of essays. Considered against such a framework, this is a more coherent body of work than it first seems, and can justifiably claim to lie near the heart of the Canadian studies enterprise. The separate introductions to each of the subsections of this collection seek to distill some of the more general implications of the whole for an understanding of the settlement and development of this country.

Any selection of seventeen articles from so broad a literature inevitably involves hard choices and difficult omissions. Individual quality must be weighed against the need for a cohesive volume. Although Canadian historical geographers have made several vigorous and distinguished contributions to methodological and philosophical debates about the nature of historical geography and its relationship to geography and history, none of these appear here.[57] This is a volume of substantive essays, studies of the past rather than discussions of how to study the past. More than this, the volume focusses upon real patterns and places, shaped by real people and real processes. Studies either devoted to modelling or simulating distributions, or embodying technical analyses of aggregate numerical data are omitted from this collection, not for want of high-quality examples of work of this type[58] but because of two convictions: first, that the omission would yield a better integrated volume; and second, that an important distinguishing feature of Canadian historical geography has been its respect for reality.

Finally, any geographer contemplating a Canadian collection of articles is forced to confront the question of regional equity in the favoured selection. There is no easy way around this one. The historical geographical literature on British Columbia, for example, remains woefully thin, and the outstanding article in this meagre field, "Industry and the Good life around Idaho Peak," by Cole Harris, has already been reprinted in an earlier volume of the New Canadian Readings series.[59] But for the report upon McCririck's investigation of early suburban Vancouver, the province from which I write largely falls from sight in what follows. More serious is the substantial neglect of the considerable and distinctive French-language literature on the historical geography of Quebec,[60] a lack entailed by the orientation of this series to the English-language market. Drawing inspiration from sources very different from those behind most English-Canadian historical geography (among which are French geography and its links to the *Annales* school of French historians), and addressed to the special concerns of the Quebec past, this work surely warrants more serious attention than it receives here. It is nonetheless a real pleasure to include in this volume an English translation of an article first published in *Revue d'histoire de l'Amérique française*, by Serge Courville of Université Laval. Clearly, no single, short piece can represent a large and diverse literature but the essay effectively suggests something of this distinctive body of work. It is part of a substantial series of publications on the eighteenth- and early nineteenth-century Quebec countryside by one of that province's most productive historical geographers.

Subject to these caveats, the articles reprinted here reveal a great deal about the range, scales, emphases, approaches, and achievements of the work undertaken by the still relatively small band of publishing historical geographers in this country. The studies have been drawn from a wide selection of journals and books published in the last two decades. Almost all of them have been revised for this publication to take into account recent work on their topics, to improve the coherence of the collection, and in some cases to allow abbreviation and, thus, the inclusion of additional material in the volume.

Reviewing the whole, one is struck by the catholic compass and general concreteness of these historical geographers' concerns, as well as with their ingenuity in marshalling and using the evidence needed to address them. Here we find resort to the evidence of archives, interviews, and the field. Ecological insights are often fundamental, in particular for Heidenreich and Ray in dealing with facets of the indigenous peoples' past and for Kelly in assessing the effect of farm clearing upon the land of Ontario. They also underpin other writing less explicitly, for example the studies by Ross and Mannion. Ennals and Gad, and their common collaborator, Holdsworth, offer us keys to the interpretation of countryside and townscape but are not content to deal with façades alone. In their quest for understanding, they cross the thresholds of the buildings they describe, to explore some of the connections between form and function. McIlwraith revises popular perceptions about the difficulties of overland movement in early British North America by asking how and when ordinary settlers travelled. He turns the scattered evidence of their everyday behaviour against the comments of visitors, officials, and those with special interests, from which "standard" interpretations have been drawn. As they deal with the basic issue of immigration and settlement, Harris, Hornsby, and Lehr employ dramatically different scales of inquiry. Although their conclusions vary in generality, they are not incongruent, and all help the reader to grasp what crossing an ocean to settle the new world meant to those who did it. In revealing the sophisticated geographical understanding possessed by native inhabitants of the western interior early in the nineteenth century, Moodie demonstrates that groups and individuals may hold very different conceptions of particular territories. His work reminds us how important it is to "see the land with the eyes of its former occupants, from the standpoint of their needs and capacities,"[61] if we are to understand their actions and the geographies they created. Indeed this point is implicit in the radically different treatments Mannion and Ross give to two of the many highly distinctive places that helped constitute the complex, changing face of British North America, and then Canada.

Yet historical geographers have always sought to explain as well as describe the fascinating diversity of early Canada. In one way and another they have endeavoured to show how and why the country took shape as it did. Gad and Holdsworth continue and extend this tradition by exploring some of the fundamental forces that transformed Canadian cities, and the buildings that imparted character to their central districts. Although their concern is with a small, peripheral area of rapidly growing Vancouver, McCririck and Wynn throw light on the process of suburban development which reshaped Canadian cities during the great transformation of an essentially rural people into an urban commercial-industrial society in the late nineteenth and early twentieth centuries. Knowledge of this process is central to understanding the segregation of urban residential space along economic or class lines. Similarly, in discussing what he felicitously calls the "sting of the metropolis" upon the Maritimes, McCann identifies a process that did much to forge the pattern of modern Canada. Finally, Harris illustrates just how fully modern Canada is a product of its complex past and argues that a clear understanding of its developing human geography is essential to a full appreciation of its distinctive character.

Taken together, these essays offer a unique and fresh set of perspectives on the Canadian past. Yet they are, realistically, only stepping stones to further work. To date, Canadian historical geographers have given a great deal more attention to the countryside than to towns; we know far more about rural settlement and farm making than we do about suburban lives and landscapes.[62] There is far too little good work on the geography of commercial intercourse and the resulting development of closely integrated clusters or systems of cities.[63] Basic, systematic information about the means and efficiency of transport and communication in many parts of the developing country is wanting. So too are sophisticated studies of the local and geographical implications of changes in transport or communications technology.[64]

It is also clear that the places of our literature, if not our past, have been overwhelmingly male products. To be sure, the camps that were such a characteristic early Canadian workplace were largely staffed by men, and it was almost always men who wielded the axes that wrought the most visible transformation of the eastern Canadian landscape. But as Margaret Atwood's short poem "The Planters" so starkly reminds us, this was only part of the story.[65] The optimistic energy of pioneering men contrasted sharply with the dark doubts that surrounded women in these circumstances. There is need and scope for geographers to investigate further the role of women in shaping past places and the impact of those places upon women's lives.

By the same token, few Canadian historical geographers have given much explicit attention to questions of class.[66] The omission stems in part from a focus upon rural and pre-industrial life, but also owes something to the argument that, in contrast to Europe, the opportunity of new world land pared extremes of wealth and poverty from the Canadian countryside.[67] If most would concede that such pruning rarely, if ever, produced thoroughly egalitarian communities, and hardly any would deny the existence of some economic stratification in the nineteenth century, few scholars have been inclined to ponder the implications of this for the economic independence and consciousness of early Canadians. In studies of the urban past, especially, the geographer's predisposition to think about problems in spatial terms is surely full of potential insight into the making, meaning, and persistence of class divisions. Were there marked patterns of spatial segregation between rich and poor, workers and bosses, in Canada's developing cities? Did residential neighbourhoods define territories of social or ethnic interaction?

More attention is also due to questions of power. They are, of course, implicit in any discussion of class but can be conceived more broadly—as the power of guns versus arrows, of access to markets versus isolation in the fishery, of the community patriarch versus the transient, and of the state and all its works versus local life. These issues are fundamental to understanding the dynamics of communities and places. Insofar as they point to questions about the consolidation of hegemony, they are likely to lead into exploration of the channels through which authority was deployed, resisted, and accepted. Further consideration of all these matters and others is essential if we are to develop the well-rounded understanding of land and life in early Canada so vital to gaining perspective on the present and to shaping a future that respects the achievements of the past.

Canadian historical geographers therefore contemplate a full, challenging, and very enticing agenda for the 1990s. As they have in the past, they will find almost innumerable topics to occupy their attention. Twenty years from now, it is entirely likely that a commentator on the field will reflect, again, on the diversity of the historical geographical enterprise. Even more probable is the prospect that she or he will identify substantial differences between the literature of the early twenty-first century and that of the 1970s and 1980s. Changes in the global economy, in patterns of international migration, in Canada's relationship with the United States, and within the political, economic, and social fabric of this country, will more or less decisively transform the face of Canada. Those who experience these changes will need to learn about their own present by asking new questions of the past. They will do so with new insights and new concerns generated by new currents of thought running through contemporary geography and modern scholarship in the social sciences and humanities.

In the early 1990s, at least, the most pertinent of these currents of thought appears to be the broad stream of "social theory." For all the debate going on among social theorists about the appropriate orientation, subject matter, focus, and procedures of their study, it seems certain that the new perspectives raised by scholars such as Anthony Giddens and Immanuel Wallerstein will have a substantial impact on the nature of human geography through the next decade.[68] They promise the development of a more integrated subject, one conscious of the impact of the past on the present, concerned with "knowledgeable and capable human subjects" shaping lives within the contingencies of their settings, and therefore thoroughly congenial to the traditions of historical geography. They also offer historical geographers frameworks against which to set their inquiries. Because these frameworks raise conceptual issues of wide intellectual interest, they should both sharpen the focus of specific investigations and encourage the use of broader interpretation in local and regional studies, without jeopardizing the traditional strengths and distinctive emphases of historical inquiry.

In these developments there surely lie prospects of an even more vital, exciting historical geography than that represented in this volume. Although few historical geographers claim any special skill in the art of prediction, it seems safe to say that in the next two decades their studies will build upon the subject's substantial record of empirical accomplishment and break new ground by bringing fresh, theoretically informed insights to the task of finding out how, when, and why places developed as they did. The results will almost certainly be rather different from those most characteristic of the last twenty years. Yet there is no doubt that with the fascinating challenge of understanding the settlement and development of a vast and varied country before them, Canadian historical geographers will continue to produce books, articles, and theses that reveal how places and patterns are created by people and processes operating at a variety of scales.

Notes

1. G. Wynn, "Notes on Society and Environment in Old Ontario," *Journal of Social History* 13 (1979): 49–65; D. Owram, *Promise of Eden: The Canadian Expansionist Movement and the Idea of the West* (Toronto: University of Toronto Press, 1980); R. Cook, "Landscape Painting and National Sentiment in Canada," *Historical Reflections/Reflexions historiques* 1 (1974): 263–83; National Film Board of Canada, *Canada: A Year of the Land* (Ottawa: Queen's Printer, 1967).

2. J.M.S. Careless, "Frontierism, Metropolitanism, and Canadian History," in *Approaches to Canadian History*, ed. C.C. Berger (Toronto: University of Toronto Press, 1967), 63–83; J.M.S. Careless, "'Limited Identities' in Canada," *Canadian Historical Review* 50 (1969): 1–10; R.C. Harris, "Regionalism and the Canadian Archipelago," in *Heartland and Hinterland: A Geography of Canada*, ed. L.D. McCann (Scarborough, Ont.: Prentice-Hall Canada, 1987), 532–59.

3. A.R.M. Lower, *"Great Britain's Woodyard" : British America and the Timber Trade, 1763–1867* (Montreal: McGill-Queen's University Press, 1973); A.R.M. Lower, *Settlement and the Forest Frontier in Eastern Canada* (Toronto: University of Toronto Press, 1936). In his most famous article, the young Frederick Jackson Turner argued, "The existence of an area of free land, its continuous recession, and the advance of American settlement westward, explain American development." This argument was advanced in "The Significance of the Frontier in American History," American Historical Association, *Annual Report for 1893* (Washington, 1894): 199–227. It became the basis for the powerful "frontier school" of American history. A useful compilation and assessment of the influence of these ideas on the writing of Canadian history is *The Frontier Thesis and the Canadas: The Debate on the Impact of the Canadian Environment*, ed. M.S. Cross (Toronto: Copp Clark, 1970), which reprints Turner's article and many other relevant works.

4. W.N. Sage, "Geographic and Cultural Aspects of the Five Canadas," Canadian Historical Association, *Report* (1937), 28–34.

5. H.A. Innis, *The Fur Trade in Canada: An Introduction to Canadian Economic History* (Toronto: University of Toronto Press, [1962]); H.A. Innis, *The Cod Fisheries: The History of an International Economy* (New Haven: Yale University Press, 1940). C.C. Berger, *The Writing of Canadian History: Aspects of English Canadian Historical Writing since 1900* (Toronto: University of Toronto Press, 1986) treats both Innis and Lower, 85–111 and 112–36.

6. M.I. Newbigin, *Canada: The Great River, the Lands and the Men* (London: Christophers, 1926).

7. Berger, *The Writing of Canadian History*, 259–320, provides a summary of developments in Canadian history since the mid-1960s. For some suggestion of the overlap between history and geography in ethnic studies see H-G. Slichtmann, "Ethnic Themes in Geographical Research on Western Canada," *Canadian Ethnic Studies/Études ethniques du Canada* 9 (1977): 9–41; and G. Wynn, "Ethnic Migrations and Atlantic Canada: Geographical Perspectives," *Canadian Ethnic Studies/Études ethniques du Canada* 18 (1986): 1–15. For urban questions see J.U. Marshall, "Geography's Contribution to the Historical Study of Urban Canada," *Urban History Review* 1 (1973): 15–23 and J.T. Lemon, "Approaches to the Study of the Urban Past: Geography," *Urban History Review* 2 (1973): 13–19.

8. The quotation is taken from D. Harvey, *Explanation in Geography* (London: Edward Arnold, 1969), *vi*. For commentary on the developments summarized in this paragraph, see L.T. Guelke, "Geography and Logical Positivism," in *Geography and the Urban Environment. Progress in Research and Applications*, ed. D.T. Herbert and R.J. Johnston (Toronto: John Wiley and Sons, 1978), 1:35–61.

9. R.J. Johnston, *Geography and Geographers: Anglo-American Human Geography since 1945* (London: Edward Arnold, 1979) summarizes developments through the 1960s. For a review of more recent developments, and of the incorporation of different "philosophies" into geography, see R.J. Johnston, *Philosophy and Human Geography: An Introduction to Contemporary Approaches* (London: Edward Arnold, 1986).

10. See, for example, P.J. Jackson and S. Smith, *Exploring Social Geography* (London: George Allen and Unwin, 1984); R. Ellen, "Persistence and Change in the Relationship between Anthropology and Human Geography," *Progress in Human Geography* 12 (1988): 229–62.

11. E.A. Freeman, *The Historical Geography of Europe* (London: Longmans, Green and Co., 1881); G.A. Smith, *The Historical Geography of the Holy Land* (London: Hodder and Stoughton, 1894); M. Bloch, "En Angleterre: l'histoire et le terrain," *Annales d'histoire, économique et sociale* 9 (1937): 208. For a Canadian example of work in this older tradition, see N.L. Nicholson's useful *The Boundaries of the Canadian Confederation* (Toronto: McClelland and Stewart, 1979).

12. E.W. Gilbert, "What is Historical Geography?" *Scottish Geographical Magazine* 48 (1932): 129–36; "What is Historical Geography?" *Geography* 17 (1939): 39–44; W.G. East, "A Note on Historical Geography," *Geography* 18 (1933): 282–92. See also R.A. Butlin, "Theory and Methodology in Historical Geography," in *Historical Geography: Progress and Prospect*, ed. M. Pacione (Wolfboro, NH: Croom Helm, 1987), 16–45. R.A. Butlin, *Historical Geography: Retrospects, Context and Prospect* (London: Edward Arnold, forthcoming) promises a thorough general review of the development of historical geography.

13. R. Hartshorne, *The Nature of Geography: A Critical Survey of Current Thought in the Light of the Past* (Lancaster, PA: Association of American Geographers, 1939), quotations from 184–87.

14. R.H. Brown, *Mirror for Americans: Likeness of the Eastern Seaboard, 1810* (New York: American Geographical Society, 1943).

15. C.O. Sauer, "Foreword to Historical Geography," in *Land and Life: A Selection from the Writings of Carl Ortwin Sauer*, ed. J. Leighly (Berkeley and Los Angeles: University of California Press, 1967), 351–88, quotations from 359, 360.

16. J.N. Entrikin, "Carl O. Sauer, Philosopher in Spite of Himself," *The Geographical Review* 74 (1984): 387–408, quotations from 389, 405. For more on Sauer, see M. Solot, "Carl Sauer and Cultural Evolution," *Annals of the Association of*

American Geographers 76 (1986): 508–20; M. Williams, "'The Apple of My Eye, Carl Sauer and Historical Geography," *Journal of Historical Geography* 9 (1983): 1–28; J. Leighly, "Carl Ortwin Sauer, 1889–1975," in *Geographers: Biobibliographic Studies,* ed. T.W. Freeman and P. Pinchemel (London: Mansell, 1976), 2: 99–108; D. Hooson, "Carl O. Sauer," and W.W. Speth, "Berkeley Geography, 1923–33," in *The Origins of Academic Geography in the United States,* ed. B.W. Blouet (Hamden, CT: Archon Books, 1981), 165–74 and 211–44; and M. Kenzer, ed., *Carl O. Sauer, A Tribute* (Corvallis, OR: Oregon State University Press, 1986).

17.   C.O. Sauer, "The Morphology of Landscape," in *Land and Life,* ed. Leighly, 315–50.

18.   Hartshorne, *Nature,* 188; A.H. Meyer, "The Kankakee Marsh of Northern Indiana and Illinois," *Papers of the Michigan Academy of Science, Arts, and Letters* 21 (1935): 359–96; D. Whittlesey, "The Horizon of Geography," *Annals of the Association of American Geographers* 35 (1945): 1–36.

19.   Reviews of these possibilities are provided in H.C. Darby, "The Problem of Geographical Description," *Transactions of the Institute of British Geographers* 30 (1962): 1–14; H.C. Darby, "On the Relations of Geography and History," *Transactions of the Institute of British Geographers* 19 (1954): 1–11; H.C. Darby, "Historical Geography," in *Approaches to History,* ed. H.P.R. Finberg (London: Routledge and Kegan Paul, 1962), 127–56; and H.C. Darby, "Historical Geography in Britain, 1920–1980: Continuity and Change," *Transactions of the Institute of British Geographers* n.s. 8 (1983): 421–28. For an example of the relict features approach, see J.W. Watson, "Relict Geography in an Urban Community," in *Geographical Essays in Memory of Alan G. Ogilvie,* ed. R. Miller and J.W. Watson (London: Nelson, 1959). For a study of inherited cultural forms, see D. Ward, "The Pre-Urban Cadaster and the Urban Pattern of Leeds," *Annals of the Association of American Geographers* 52 (1962): 150–65.

20.   J.O.M. Broek, *The Santa Clara Valley, California: A Study in Landscape Change* (Utrecht: Oosthoek, 1932); H.C. Darby, *A New Historical Geography of England* (Cambridge: Cambridge University Press, 1973); H.C. Darby, *The Draining of the Fens* (Cambridge: Cambridge University Press, 1940); H.C. Darby, "The Clearing of the English Woodlands," *Geography* 36 (1951): 71–83; H.C. Darby, "The Clearing of the Woodland in Europe," in *Man's Role in Changing the Face of the Earth,* ed. W.L. Thomas Jr. (Chicago: University of Chicago Press, 1956), 183–216; M. Williams, *The Draining of the Somerset Levels* ([London]: Cambridge University Press, 1970). For an assessment of Darby's work, see P.J. Perry, "H.C. Darby and Historical Geography: Survey and Review," *Geographische Zeitschrift* 57 (1969): 161–78. The *Journal of Historical Geography* 15, 1 (1989): 5–13 includes a full bibliography of Darby's writing as well as essays of appreciation by R. Lawton and R. Butlin (14–19) and D.W. Meinig (20–23).

21.   Sauer, "Foreword," 355.

22.   R. Hartshorne, *Perspective on the Nature of Geography* (Chicago: Rand McNally and Co. for Association of American Geographers, 1959) reassessed the field, with little more openness to a truly historical geography than twenty years before. See also P.E. James and C.F. Jones, eds., *American Geography: Inventory and Prospect* (Syracuse: Association of American Geographers, 1954).

23.   Assigning dates to the beginnings of university geography in Canada is a rather arbitrary exercise. There was a professorship in commercial geography in the University of Montreal in 1910, and a joint Department of Geology and Geography existed at U.B.C. from 1922. Single courses in commercial (or economic) geography were taught at Toronto in 1906 and in several universities through the 1920s. The dates given in the text mark the establishment of distinct departments of geography. The

history of Canadian geography remains to be written; such beginnings as there have been are limited in scope and concentrate heavily on "founding fathers" H.A. Innis and T.G. Taylor, who established the Toronto Department. See G.S. Tomkins, *Griffith Taylor and Canadian Geography* (Ann Arbor: University Microfilms, 1967); M. Sanderson, "Griffith Taylor: A Geographer to Remember," *Canadian Geographer* 26 (1982): 293–97; M. Sanderson, *Griffith Taylor: Antarctic Scientist and Pioneer Geographer* (Ottawa: Carleton University Press, 1987); G.S. Dunbar, "Harold Innis and Canadian Geography," *Canadian Geographer* 29 (1985): 159–64; I. Parker, "Harold Innis as a Canadian Geographer," *Canadian Geographer* 32 (1988): 63–69. General surveys are provided by J.L. Robinson, "The Development and Status of Geography in the Universities and Government in Canada," *Yearbook, Association of Pacific Coast Geographers* 13 (1951): 3–13; [J.L. Robinson],"Geography (in Canada)," *The Canadian Encyclopedia* (Edmonton: Hurtig, 1985), 2: 725–26; and [J.W. Watson], "Geography. Study and Teaching," *Encyclopedia Canadiana* (Toronto: Grolier of Canada, 1975), 339–43.

24.   T.L. Hills, "The St. Francis to the Chaudière, 1830: A Study in the Historical Geography of Southeastern Quebec," *Canadian Geographer* 6 (1955): 25–36; J.D. Wood, "The Stage is Set: Dumfries Township, 1816," *Waterloo Historical Society Annual Volume* 48 (1960): 40–50; W.H. Parker, "The Geography of the Province of Lower Canada in 1837" (D.Phil. thesis, Oxford University, 1958); J.H. Warkentin, "Western Canada in 1886," *Papers Read before the Historical and Scientific Society of Manitoba*, series III, 19 (1963–64): 85–116; R.L. Gentilcore, "The Niagara District of Robert Gourlay," *Ontario History* 54 (1962): 228–36.

25.   M.E. Crawford, "A Geographic Study of the Distribution of Population Change in Alberta, 1931–61" (M.A. thesis, University of Alberta, 1962); J.B. Bird, "Settlement Patterns in Maritime Canada, 1687–1786," *Geographical Review* 45 (1955): 385–404; H.B. Johnson, "French Canada and the Ohio Country: A Study in Early Spatial Relationships," *Canadian Geographer* 12 (1958): 1–10; P.B. Clibbon, "The Evolution and Present Pattern of Land-use in Terrebonne County, Quebec" (M.A. thesis, Université de Montréal, 1962), and "Changing Land Use in Terrebonne County, Quebec," *Cahiers de géographie du Québec* 8 (1964): 5–40; L.G. Reeds, "Agricultural Regions of Southern Ontario, 1880 and 1951," *Economic Geography* 35 (1959): 219–27.

26.   For fuller assessments of Clark's career and contributions, see D.W. Meinig, "Prologue: Andrew Hill Clark, Historical Geographer," in *European Settlement and Development in North America: Essays on Geographical Change in Honour and Memory of Andrew Hill Clark*, ed. J.R. Gibson (Toronto: University of Toronto Press, 1978), 3–26; and G. Wynn, "W.F. Ganong, A.H. Clark and the Historical Geography of Maritime Canada," *Acadiensis* 10 (1981): 5–28.

27.   A.H. Clark, "Geographical Change: A Theme for Economic History," *Journal of Economic History* 20 (1960): 607–13; A.H. Clark, "Historical Geography," in *American Geography*, ed. James and Jones, 71–105.

28.   A.H. Clark, *Three Centuries and the Island: A Historical Geography of Settlement and Agriculture in Prince Edward Island, Canada* (Toronto: University of Toronto Press, 1959), quotations from 218–23.

29.   A.H. Clark, "First Things First," in *Pattern and Process: Research in Historical Geography*, ed. R.E. Ehrenberg (Washington, DC: Howard University Press, 1975), 12. Perhaps the most heartfelt statement of Clark's attachment to the broad view is his "Honing the Edge of Curiosity: The Challenge of Historical Geography in Canada," in *Occasional Papers in Geography*, ed. W.G. Hardwick and J.D. Chapman (Vancouver, 1963), 4:1–12. In addition to *Three Centuries*, Clark published *Acadia. The Geography*

of Early Nova Scotia to 1760 (Madison, WI: University of Wisconsin Press, 1968). His articles on the Maritimes are: "Acadia and the Acadians: The Creation of a Geographical Entity," in *Frontiers and Men*, ed. J.D. Andrews (Melbourne: F.W. Cheshire, 1966), 90–119; "New England's Role in the Underdevelopment of Cape Breton Island during the French Regime, 1713–1758," *Canadian Geographer* 9 (1965): 1–12; "Old World Origins and Religious Adherence in Nova Scotia," *Geographical Review* 50 (1960): 317–44; "Contributions of its Southern Neighbours to the Underdevelopment of the Maritime Provinces Area of Present Canada, 1710–1867," in *The Influence of the United States on Canadian Development*, ed. R.A. Preston (Durham, NC: Duke University Press, 1972), 164–84; "The Sheep/Swine Ratio as a Guide to a Century's Change in the Livestock Geography of Nova Scotia," *Economic Geography* 38 (1962): 38–55; "South Island, New Zealand and Prince Edward Island, Canada: A Study of Insularity," *New Zealand Geographer* 3 (1947): 137–50; "Titus Smith Junior and the Geography of Nova Scotia in 1801 and 1802," *Annals of the Association of American Geographers* 44 (1954): 291–314.

30.   R.C. Harris, "Historical Geography in Canada," *Canadian Geographer* 11 (1967): 235–50.

31.   W.A. Koelsch, "Review of *Acadia*," *Economic Geography* 46 (1970): 201–2.

32.   C.J.B. Wood, "Settlement of the Long Point Region" (M.A. thesis, McMaster University, 1966); J. Clarke, "Spatial Variations in Population Density: Southwestern Ontario in 1851," in *International Geography*, ed. W.P. Adams and F.M. Helleiner (Toronto: University of Toronto Press, 1972), 1: 408–11; R. Hayward and B.S. Osborne, "The 'British Colonist' and the Immigration to Toronto of 1847: A Content Analysis Approach to Newspaper Research in Historical Geography," *Canadian Geographer* 17 (1973): 391–402; J.D. Wood, "Simulating Pre-Census Population Distribution," *Canadian Geographer* 18 (1974): 250–64. Content analysis has also been advocated and employed in D.W. Moodie, "Content Analysis: A Method for Historical Geography," *Area* 4 (1969): 146–49; A.J.W. Catchpole, D.W. Moodie, and B. Kaye, "Content Analysis: A Method for Identification of Dates of First Freezing and First Breaking from Descriptive Accounts," *Professional Geographer* 22 (1970): 252–57; A.J.W. Catchpole, D.W. Moodie, and D. Milton, "Freeze-up and Break-up of Estuaries on Hudson Bay in the Eighteenth and Nineteenth Centuries," *Canadian Geographer* 20 (1976): 279–96; D.W. Moodie and A.J.W. Catchpole, *Environmental Data from Historical Documents by Content Analysis: Freeze-up and Break-up of Estuaries on Hudson Bay, 1714–1871*, Manitoba Geographical Studies no. 5 (Winnipeg: Department of Geography, University of Winnipeg, 1975); and R.S. Dilley, "British Travellers in Early Upper Canada: A Content Analysis of Itineraries and Images," *Canadian Papers in Rural History* 5 (1986): 198–223.

33.   W. Norton, *Historical Analysis in Geography* (London: Longman Group Ltd., 1984); see also his "Historical Geography as the Evolution of Spatial Form," in *Period and Place: Research Methods in Historical Geography*, ed. A.R.H. Baker and M. Billinge (Cambridge: Cambridge University Press, 1982): 251–57. Among Norton's articles are "The Process of Rural Land Occupation in Upper Canada," *Scottish Geographical Magazine* 91 (1975): 145–52; "Constructing Abstract Worlds of the Past," *Geographical Analysis* 8 (1976): 269–88; "Some Comments on Late Nineteenth Century Agriculture in Areas of European Overseas Expansion," *Ontario History* 74 (1982): 113–17; and, with E.C. Conkling, "Land-use Theory and the Pioneering Economy," *Geografiska Annaler* 56B (1974): 44–56. An early example of the use of a non-quantitative counterfactual proposition is in Andrew Clark's reflection on the possible consequences of the discovery of the mouth of the Hudson River by Samuel Champlain, in "The Conceptions of 'Empires' of the St. Lawrence and the Mississippi:

An Historio-geographical View with Some Quizzical Comments on Environmental Determinism," *American Review of Canadian Studies* 5 (1975): 4–27.

34. Guelke, "Geography and Logical Positivism," quotation from 53.

35. The notes to this essay cannot provide a complete inventory of recent work in Canadian historical geography but they do offer a reasonably comprehensive survey of writing by geographers on this country's past, published in the last two decades. Inevitably, the categories used to list this work below are somewhat arbitrary; where several different types of work are included in a single note the references are broadly divided accordingly.

The **perception** literature is perhaps especially diverse. Examples include J. Warkentin, "The Geography of Franklin and Long: A Comparison," in *The West and the Nation: Essays in Honour of W.L. Morton*, ed. C.C. Berger and R. Cook (Toronto: McClelland and Stewart, 1976), 33–71; D.W. Moodie, "Science and Reality. Arthur Dobbs and the Eighteenth Century Geography of Rupert's Land," *Journal of Historical Geography* 2, 4 (1976): 293–310; D.W. Moodie, "Early British Images of Rupert's Land," in *Man and Nature on the Prairies*, ed. R. Allen (Regina: Canadian Plains Research Center, 1976), 1–20; J. Warkentin, "Steppe, Desert and Empire," in *Prairie Perspectives*, ed. A.W. Rasporich and H.C. Klassen (1973), 2:102–36; F.J. Jankunis, "Perception, Innovation and Adaption: The Palliser Triangle of Western Canada," *Yearbook of the Association of Pacific Coast Geographers* 39 (1977): 63–76; K. Kelly, "The Changing Attitude of Farmers to Forest in Nineteenth Century Ontario," *Ontario Geography* 8 (1974): 64–77; O.F.G. Sitwell, "Pioneer Attitudes as Revealed by the Township of Strathcona, Alberta," in *The Settlement of Canada: Origins and Transfers*, ed. B.S. Osborne (Kingston: Queen's University Press, 1976): 236–37; H.E. Parson, "Settlement Policy and Land Evaluation at the turn of the Twentieth Century in Quebec," *Area* 9 (1977): 290–92; H.E. Parson, "An Overview of Landscape Assessment and Settlement Policy on the Southern Ontario Section of the Canadian Shield in the Nineteenth Century," *Ontario Geography* 22 (1983): 15–28; B.S. Osborne, "Frontier Settlement in Eastern Ontario in the Nineteenth Century: A Study in Changing Perceptions of Land and Opportunity," in *The Frontier*, ed. D.H. Miller and J.O. Steffen (Norman, OK: University of Oklahoma Press, 1977): 201–26; C.J. Tracie, "Land of Plenty or Poor Man's Land: Environmental Perception and Appraisal Respecting Agricultural Settlement in the Peace River Country, Canada," in *Images of the Plains*, ed. B.W. Blouet and M.P. Lawson (Lincoln, NB: University of Nebraska Press, 1973): 115–22; J.C. Lehr, "Propaganda and Belief, Ukrainian Emigrant Views of the Canadian West," in *New Soil–Old Roots: The Ukrainian Experience in Canada*, ed. J. Rozumnyj (Winnipeg: Ukrainian Academy of Arts and Sciences in Canada, 1983), 1–17.

Artists' perceptions are treated in R. Rees, "Images of the Prairie: Landscape Painting and Perception in the Western Interior of Canada," *Canadian Geographer* 20 (1976): 259–78; R. Rees, *Land of Earth and Sky: Landscape Painting of Western Canada* (Saskatoon: Western Producer Prairie Books, 1984). **Photographers' perceptions** are examined by J.M. Schwartz, "The Photographic Record of pre-Confederation British Columbia," *Archivaria* 5 (1977–1978): 17–44; J.M. Schwartz and L. Koltun, "A Visual Cliché: Five Views of Yale," *BC Studies* 52 (1981–1982): 113–28; G. Wynn, " 'Images of the Acadian Valley': The Photographs of Amos Lawson Hardy," *Acadiensis* 15 (1985): 59–83; and M.T. Hadley, "Photography, Tourism and the CPR. Western Canada, 1884–1914," in *Essays on the Historical Geography of the Canadian West: Regional Perspectives on the Settlement Process*, ed. L.A. Rosenvall and S.M. Evans (Calgary: Department of Geography, University of Calgary, 1987), 48–69. See also J.M. Schwartz, "The Past in Focus.

Photography and British Columbia, 1858–1914," *BC Studies* 52 (1981–1982): 5–15. For **surveyors' and cartographers' perceptions**, see J.C. Tyman, "Subjective Surveyors: The Appraisal of Farm Lands in Western Canada, 1870–1930," in *Images of the Plains*, ed. Blouet and Lawson, 75–97; R.I. Ruggles, "The West of Canada in 1763: Imagination and Reality," *Canadian Geographer* 15 (1971): 235–61; R.I. Ruggles, "Mapping the Interior Plains of Rupert's Land by the Hudson's Bay Company to 1870," and J.M. Richtík, "Mapping the Quality of Land for Agriculture in Western Canada," both in *Mapping the North American Plains*, ed. F.C. Luebke, F.W. Kaye, and E. Moulton (Norman, OK: University of Oklahoma Press, 1987), 145–60 and 161–72. For a wide-ranging **assessment** of this approach, see R.W. Chambers, "Images, Acts and Consequences: A Critical Review of Historical Geosophy," in *Period and Place*, ed. Baker and Billinge, 197–204.

    36.   R.C. Harris, "The Historical Mind and the Practice of Geography," in *Humanistic Geography*, ed. D. Ley and M.S. Samuels (Chicago: Maroufa Press, 1978), 123–37; For other strands of this reaction, see: L.T. Guelke, "Problems of Scientific Explanation in Geography," *Canadian Geographer* 15 (1971): 38–53; "An Idealist Alternative in Human Geography," *Annals of the Association of American Geographers* 64 (1974): 193–202; and "On Rethinking Historical Geography," *Area* 7 (1975): 135–38; D.W. Moodie and J.C. Lehr, "Fact and Theory in Historical Geography," *Professional Geographer* 28 (1976): 132–35; and R.C. Harris, "Theory and Synthesis in Historical Geography," *Canadian Geographer* 19 (1971): 157–72.

    37.   Thus, for example, the title of *Character and Circumstance: Essays in Honour of Donald Grant Creighton*, ed. J.S. Moir (Toronto: Macmillan, 1970).

    38.   R.C. Harris, *The Historical Atlas of Canada*, vol.1, *From the Beginning to 1800* (Toronto: University of Toronto Press, 1987); J.M. Bumsted, "Putting it on the Map," *The Beaver* (April–May 1988), 54. Two earlier, rather different, historical atlases are R.L. Gentilcore and C.G. Head, *Ontario's History in Maps* (Toronto: University of Toronto Press, 1984); and J. Warkentin and R.I. Ruggles, *Historical Atlas of Manitoba* (Winnipeg: Historical and Scientific Society of Manitoba, 1970), both of which reproduce a wide selection of the early cartography of their territories.

    39.   C.R. Dryer, quoted in J.O. Wheeler and F.M. Sibley, *Dictionary of Quotations in Geography* (Westport, CT: Greenwood Press, 1986), 7.

    40.   On the patterns and processes of **migration** see J.M. Cameron, "Scottish Emigration to Upper Canada, 1815–55: A Study of Process," in *International Geography*, ed. Adams and Helleiner, 404–6; J.M. Cameron, "The Role of Shipping from Scottish Ports in Emigration to the Canadas, 1815–1855," *Canadian Papers in Rural History* 2 (1980): 135–54; R.C. Harris, "The French Background of Immigrants to Canada before 1700," *Cahiers de géographie du Québec* 37 (1972): 313–24; W.G. Handcock, "English Migration to Newfoundland," and A.G. Macpherson, "A Modal Sequence in the Peopling of Central Bonavista Bay, 1676–1857," both in *The Peopling of Newfoundland: Essays in Historical Geography*, ed. J.J. Mannion (St. John's: ISER, 1977), 15–48 and 102–35; W.G. Handcock, "The West Country Migrations to . Newfoundland," *Bulletin of Canadian Studies* 5 (1981): 5–24; C.J. Houston and W.J. Smyth, *Irish Emigration and Canadian Settlement: Patterns, Links, and Letters* (Toronto: University of Toronto Press, 1990); C.J. Houston and W.J. Smyth, "Irish Emigrants to Canada: Whence They Came," in *The Untold Story: The Irish in Canada*, ed. R. O'Driscoll and L. Reynolds (Toronto: Celtic Arts of Canada, 1988), 1: 27–36; S.J. Hornsby, "Migration and Settlement: The Scots of Cape Breton," in *Geographical Perspectives on the Maritime Provinces*, ed. D. Day (Halifax: St. Mary's University Press, 1988), 15–24; G. Wynn, "A Share of the Necessaries of Life: Remarks on Migration, Development and Dependency in Atlantic Canada," in *Beyond Anger and*

Longing: Community and Development in Atlantic Canada, ed. B. Fleming (Fredericton: Acadiensis Press, 1988), 17–52; A.L. Kobayashi, "Emigration to Canada, Landholding, and Social Networks in a Japanese Village, 1885 to 1950," in *Japanese Studies in Canada*, ed. M. Soga and B. Saint-Jaques (Ottawa: Canadian Asian Studies Association, 1985), 162–86.

On **settlement** see J.M. Cameron, "An Introduction to the Study of Scottish Settlement of Southern Ontario: A Comparison of Place Names," *Ontario History* 61 (1969): 167–72; S.J. Hornsby, "Staple Trades, Subsistence Agriculture, and Nineteenth Century Cape Breton Island," *Annals of the Association of American Geographers* 79 (1989): 411–34; C.W. Sanger, "The Evolution of Sealing and the Spread of Settlement in Northeastern Newfoundland," P.A. Thornton, "The Demographic and Mercantile Bases of Initial Permanent Settlement in the Strait of Belle Isle," and F.W. Remiggi, "Ethnic Diversity and Settler Location on the Eastern Lower North Shore of Quebec," all in *The Peopling of Newfoundland*, ed. Mannion, 136–51, 152–83, and 184–211; R.C. Harris, "Of Poverty and Helplessness in Petite-Nation," *Canadian Historical Review* 52 (1971): 23–50; R.C. Harris, P. Roulston, and C. De Freitas, "The Settlement of Mono Township," *The Canadian Geographer* 19 (1975): 1–17; H.E. Parson, "The Colonization of the Southern Canadian Shield in Ontario: Hastings Road," *Ontario History* 74 (1987): 263–73; D.W. Moodie, "The Trading Post Settlement of the Canadian North West, 1774–1821," *Journal of Historical Geography* 13 (1987): 360–74; J.D.R. Holmes, "The Canmore Corridor, 1880–1914. A Case Study of the Selection and Development of a Pass Site," in *Essays on . . . the Canadian West,* ed. Rosenvall and Evans, 27–47; J.M. Richtik, "Settlement Process in the 1870s: An Example from Manitoba's Pembina Mountain," in *Building Beyond the Homestead: Rural History on the Prairies*, ed. D.C. Jones and I. MacPherson (Calgary: University of Calgary Press, 1985), 7–28; J.C. Lehr, " 'The Peculiar People': Ukrainian Settlement of Marginal Lands in Southeastern Manitoba," in *Building*, ed. Jones and MacPherson, 29–48; G. Cho and R. Leigh, "Patterns of Residence of the Chinese in Vancouver," in *Peoples of the Living Land: Geography of Cultural Diversity in British Columbia*, ed. J.V. Minghi (Vancouver: Tantalus Research Ltd., 1972), 67–84; J.L. Robinson, "Vancouver: Changing Geographical Aspects of a Multicultural City," *BC Studies* 79 (1988): 59–80; P.M. Koroscil, "Boosterism and the Settlement Process in the Okanagan Valley 1890–1914," *Canadian Papers in Rural History* 5 (1985): 73–103.

On **cultural transfer** see J.J. Mannion, *Irish Settlements in Eastern Canada: A Study of Cultural Transfer and Adaptation* (Toronto: University of Toronto Press, 1974); R.S. Dilley, "Migration and the Mennonites: Nineteenth Century Waterloo County, Ontario," *Canadian Papers in Rural History* 4 (1984): 108–29; L.A. Rosenvall, "The Transfer of Mormon Culture to Alberta," *American Review of Canadian Studies* 12 (1982): 51–63, reprinted in *Essays on . . . the Canadian West,* ed. Rosenvall and Evans, 122–44; C.J. Tracie, "Ethnicity and the Prairie Environment: Patterns of Old Colony Mennonite and Doukhobor Settlement," in *Man and Nature on the Prairies*, ed. Allen, 46–65; S.M. Evans, "The Hutterites of Alberta. Past and Present Settlement Patterns," in *Essays on. . . the Canadian West*, ed. Rosenvall and Evans, 145–71.

More **general items** include R. Rees, "In a Strange Land . . . Homesick Pioneers on the Canadian Prairie," *Landscape* 26 (1982): 1–9; H.W. Taylor, J. Clarke, and W.R. Wightman, "Contrasting Land Development Rates in Southern Ontario to 1891," *Canadian Papers in Rural History* 5 (1986): 50–72; K.S. Sandhu, "Indian Immigration and Racial Prejudice in British Columbia: Some Preliminary Observations," in *People of the Living Land*, ed. Minghi, 29–40; D.C. Lai, *Chinatowns: Towns within Cities in Canada* (Vancouver: University of British Columbia Press, 1988); and a series of short pieces in the *Canadian Geographer* 32 (1988): 351–62, organized by A. Kobayashi under the title "Focus: Asian Migration to Canada." They are: D.Vibert, "Asian

Migration to Canada in Historical Context"; K.J. Anderson, "Community Formation in Official Context: Residential Segregation and the 'Chinese' in Early Vancouver"; A. Kobayashi, "Regional and Demographic Aspects of Japanese Migration to Canada."
    41. Other studies of **particular locales** include C.G. Head, *Eighteenth Century Newfoundland* (Toronto: McClelland and Stewart, 1976); W.G. Handcock, "The Poole Mercantile Community and the Growth of Trinity, 1700–1839," *Newfoundland Quarterly* 80, 3 (1985): 19–30; G. Wynn, "A Province Too Much Dependent on New England," *Canadian Geographer* 31, 2 (1987): 98–113; G. Wynn, "A Region of Scattered Settlements and Bounded Possibilities: Northeastern America, 1775–1800," *Canadian Geographer* 31 (1987): 319–38, reprinted in this volume; E. Ross, "The Rise and Fall of Pictou Island," in *People and Place: Studies of Small Town Life in the Maritimes*, ed. L.D. McCann (Fredericton: Acadiensis Press, 1987), 161–88; Harris, "Of Poverty and Helplessness"; R.L. Gentilcore and D. Wood, "A Military Colony in a Wilderness: The Upper Canada Frontier," in *Perspectives on Landscape and Settlement in Nineteenth Century Ontario*, ed. J.D. Wood (Toronto: McClelland and Stewart, 1975), 32–50; A.G. Brunger, "Early Settlement in Contrasting Areas of Peterborough County, Ontario," *Perspectives on Landscape and Settlement*, ed. Wood, 117–40; J. Clarke and K. Skof, "Social Dimensions of an Ontario County, 1851–52," in *Our Geographic Mosaic: Research Essays in Honour of G.C. Merrill*, ed. D.B. Knight (Ottawa: Carleton University Press, 1985), 107–36; R.L. Gentilcore, "The Beginnings: Hamilton in the Nineteenth Century," and H.A. Wood, "Emergence of the Modern City: Hamilton 1891–1950," both in *Steel City: Hamilton and Region*, ed. M.J. Dear, J.J. Drake, and L.G. Reeds (Toronto: University of Toronto Press, 1987), 99–118, 119–37; B. Kaye, "The Red River Settlement: Lord Selkirk's Isolated Colony in the Wilderness," *Prairie Forum* 11 (1986): 1–20; J. Warkentin, "Time and Place in the Western Interior," *Arts Canada* 20 (1972): 20–38.
    42. Among studies of the **development of urban places**, see J.D. Wood, "Grand Designs for the Fringes of Empire. New Towns for British North America," *Canadian Geographer* 26 (1982): 243–55; B.S. Osborne, "Kingston in the Nineteenth Century: A Study in Urban Decline," in *Perspectives on Landscape and Settlement*, 159–82; B.S. Osborne and D. Swainson, *Kingston: Building on the Past* (Westport, Ont.: Butternut Press, 1988); P.M. Ennals, "Cobourg and Port Hope; The Struggle for the Control of 'The Back Country,' " in *Perspectives on Landscape and Settlement*, ed. Wood, 183–96; L.D. McCann, "Staples and the New Industrialism in the Growth of post-Confederation Halifax," *Acadiensis* 8 (1979): 47–79; L.D. McCann, "The Mercantile-Industrial Transition in the Metal Towns of Pictou County 1857–1931," *Acadiensis* 10 (1981): 29–64; L.D. McCann, "Urban Growth in a Staple Economy: The Emergence of Vancouver as a Regional Metropolis, 1886–1914," in *Vancouver: Western Metropolis*, ed. L.J. Evenden, Western Geographical Series (Victoria, BC: University of Victoria, 1978), 16: 17–41.
    43. Studies treating the **distribution of specific activities or groups of people** include J.M. Gilmour, *Spatial Evolution of Manufacturing: Southern Ontario, 1851–1891* (Toronto: University of Toronto Press, 1972); W.R. Bland, "The Location of Manufacturing in Southern Ontario in 1881," *Ontario Geography* 8 (1974): 9–39; W.R. Bland, "The Changing Location of Metal Fabrication and Clothing Industries in Southern Ontario, 1881–1932," *Ontario Geography* 9 (1975): 34–57; D.F. Walker, "The Energy Sources of Manufacturing Industry in Southern Ontario, 1871–1921," *Ontario Geography* 6 (1971): 56–66; H. Millward, "The Development, Decline, and Revival of Mining on the Sydney Coalfield," *Canadian Geographer* 28 (1984): 180–85; H. Millward, "A Model of Coalfield Development: Six Stages Exemplified by the Sydney Field," *Canadian Geographer* 29 (1985): 234–48; H. Millward, "Mine Locations and the Sequence of Coal Exploitation on the Sydney Coalfield,

1720–1980," in *Cape Breton at 200: Historical Essays in Honour of the Island's Bicentennial, 1785–1985*, ed. K. Donovan (Sydney: University College of Cape Breton Press, 1985), 183–202; R. Ommer, "Anticipating the Trend: The Pictou Ship Register, 1840–1889," *Acadiensis* 10 (1980): 67–89; R. Ommer, "The Decline of the Eastern Canadian Shipping Industry, 1880–95," *Journal of Transport History* 3d ser., 5 (1984): 25–44; R. Ommer, "The Cod Trade of the New World," in *A People of the Sea: The Maritime History of the Channel Islands*, ed. A.G. Jamieson (London: Methuen, 1986), 245–68; C.G. Head, "An Introduction to Forest Exploitation in Nineteenth Century Ontario," in *Perspectives on Landscape and Settlement*, ed. Wood, 78–112; A.G. Brunger, "Geographical Propinquity among pre-Famine Catholic Irish Settlers in Upper Canada," *Journal of Historical Geography* 8 (1982): 265–82; A.G. Brunger, "The Distribution of English in Upper Canada, 1851–71," *Canadian Geographer* 30, 4 (1986): 337–42; J. Clarke and P.K. MacLeod, "Concentration of Scots in Rural Southern Ontario," *Canadian Cartographer* 11 (1974): 107–13; J.D. Wood, "Population Change on an Agricultural Frontier: Upper Canada 1796 to 1841," in *Patterns of the Past. Interpreting Ontario's History*, ed. R. Hall, W. Westfall, and L.S. MacDowell (Toronto: Dundurn Press, 1988), 55–77. Several studies of the settlement of particular groups of people, listed in note 40, are also relevant here.

44. For examples of work on **survey systems**, see R.L. Gentilcore, "Lines on the Land: Crown Survey and Settlement in Upper Canada," *Ontario History* 61 (1969): 57–73; J. Clarke and G.F. Finnegan, "Colonial Survey Records and the Vegetation of Essex County, Ontario," *Journal of Historical Geography* 10 (1984): 119–38; R.G. Ironside and E. Tomasky, "Agriculture and River Lot Settlement in Western Canada: The Case of Pakan (Victoria) Alberta," *Prairie Forum* 1 (1976): 3–18.

For **vernacular building** in the **Atlantic region**, see D.S. Mills, "The Development of Folk Architecture in Trinity Bay," in *Peopling of Newfoundland*, ed. Mannion, 77–101; P.M.Ennals, "The Yankee Origins of Bluenose Vernacular Architecture," *American Review of Canadian Studies* 12 (1982): 5–21; for **Ontario**, see P.M. Ennals, "Nineteenth-Century Barns in Southern Ontario," *Canadian Geographer* 16 (1972): 256–70; B. Coffey, "Building Materials in Early Ontario. The Example of Augusta Township," *Canadian Geographer* 32 (1988): 150–59; W.R. Wightman, "Construction Materials in Colonial Ontario, 1831–1861," *Aspects of Nineteenth Century Ontario*, ed. F.H. Armstrong, H.D. Stevenson, and J.D. Wilson (Toronto: University of Toronto Press, 1974), 114–34; B. Coffey, "Factors Affecting the Use of Construction Materials in Early Ontario," *Ontario History* 77 (1985): 301–18; D.A. Norris and V. Konrad, "Time, Context, and House Type Validation: Euphrasia Township, Ontario," *Canadian Papers in Rural History* 3 (1982): 50–83; D.A. Norris, "Vetting the Vernacular. Local Varieties in Ontario's Housing," *Ontario History* 74 (1982): 66–94; T.F. McIlwraith, "Altered Buildings. Another Way of Looking at the Ontario Landscape," *Ontario History* 75 (1983): 110–34.

For the **Prairie region**, see J.C. Lehr, "Ukrainian Houses in Alberta," *Alberta Historical Review* 21 (1973): 9–15; J.C. Lehr, "The Log Buildings of Ukrainian Settlers in Western Canada," *Prairie Forum* 5 (1980): 183–96; J.C. Lehr, "Colour Preferences and Building Decoration among Ukrainians in Western Canada," *Prairie Forum* 6 (1981): 203–6; R. Rees and C.J. Tracie, "The Prairie House," *Landscape* 22 (1978): 26–32; W.C. Wonders and M. Rasmussen, "Log Buildings of West Central Alberta," *Prairie Forum* 5 (1980): 1–18; W.C. Wonders, "Log Dwellings in Canadian Folk Architecture," *Annals of the Association of American Geographers* 69 (1979): 187–207.

For **British Columbia**, see D.W. Holdsworth, "House and Home in Vancouver: Images of West Coast Urbanism, 1886–1929," in *The Canadian City. Essays in Urban History*, ed. G.A. Stelter and A.F.J. Artibise (Toronto: McClelland and Stewart, 1977): 186–211; D. Holdsworth, "Regional Distinctiveness in an Industrial Age: Some

California Influences on British Columbia Housing," *American Review of Canadian Studies* 12 (1982): 64–81; D.W. Holdsworth, "Cottages and Castles for Vancouver Home-Seekers," *BC Studies* 69–70 (1986): 11–32; E.G. Mills and D.W. Holdsworth, "The BC Mills Prefabricated System: The Emergence of Ready-Made Buildings in Western Canada," Canadian Historic Sites, *Occasional Papers in Archeology and History* 14 (Ottawa, 1974): 127–69.

On **the look of the land,** see A.G. Brunger, "The Development of the Cultural Landscape of Peterborough and the Kawarthas," in *Peterborough and the Kawarthas,* ed. P. Adams and C. Taylor (Peterborough: Trent University Geography Department, 1985), 95–116; P. Ennals and D. Holdsworth, "The Cultural Landscape of the Maritime Provinces," in *Geographical Perspectives on the Maritime Provinces,* ed. Day, 1–14; C.J. Houston and W.J. Smyth, "The Impact of Fraternalism on the Landscape of Newfoundland," *Canadian Geographer* 29 (1985): 59–65.

Among **other studies** are J.J. Jackson, "Houses as Urban Artifacts: A Case Study of London, Ontario, 1845–1915," *Ontario Geography* 12 (1978): 49–68; and M.J. Doucet and J.C. Weaver, "Material Culture and the North American House: The Era of the Common Man, 1870–1920," *Journal of American History 72 (1985): 560–87, a sweeping exploration of some facets of this topic, written collaboratively by a geographer and an historian.*

45.   **General reviews** of this topic are provided by A.J. Ray, "When Two Worlds Met," in *The Illustrated History of Canada,* ed. R.C. Brown (Toronto: Lester and Orpen Dennys, 1987), 17–104; C.E. Heidenreich, "Mapping the Location of Native Groups, 1600–1760," *Mapping History* 2 (1981): 6–13; C.E. Heidenreich and A.J. Ray, *The Early Fur Trades: A Study in Cultural Interaction* (Toronto: McClelland and Stewart, 1976); as well as *The Historical Atlas of Canada,* ed. Harris.

Most work is more regional and centred on either **Ontario**: J.G. Cruickshank and C.E. Heidenreich, "Pedological Investigations at the Huron Indian Village of Cahiagué," *Canadian Geographer* 13 (1969): 34–46; C.E. Heidenreich, *Huronia. A History and Geography of the Huron Indians, 1600–1650* (Toronto: McClelland and Stewart, 1971); C.E. Heidenreich, "A Relict Indian Corn Field near Creemore, Ontario," *Canadian Geographer* 18 (1974): 379–94; C.E. Heidenreich and S. Navratil, "Soil Analysis at the Robitaille Site: Determining the Perimeter of the Village," *Ontario Archeology* 20 (1973): 25–32; V. Konrad, "An Iroquois Frontier: The North Shore of Lake Ontario during the Late 17th Century," *Journal of Historical Geography* 7 (1981): 129–44; V.A. Konrad, "Distribution, Site and Morphology of Prehistorical Settlements in the Toronto Area," in *Perspectives on Landscape and Settlement,* ed. Wood, 6–31; or on the **Prairies**: D.W. Moodie and B. Kaye, "The Northern Limit of Indian Agriculture in North America," *Geographical Review* 59 (1969): 513–29; D.W. Moodie and B. Kaye, "Indian Agriculture in the Fur Trade Northwest," *Prairie Forum* 11 (1986): 171–84; D.W. Moodie and B. Kaye, "The Ac Ko Mok Ki Map," *The Beaver* (1977), 5–15; A.J. Ray, *Indians in the Fur-Trade: Their Role as Hunters, Trappers, and Middlemen in the Lands Southwest of Hudson Bay 1660–1870* (Toronto: University of Toronto Press, 1974); A.J. Ray, Jr., "Indian Adaptations to the Forest–Grassland Boundary of Manitoba and Saskatchewan, 1656–1821: Some Implications for Interregional Migration," *Canadian Geographer* 16 (1972): 103–18; A.J. Ray, "The Northern Great Plains: Pantry of the Northwestern Fur Trade, 1774–1885," *Prairie Forum* 9 (1984): 263–80. Another facet of the fur trade is presented in J.F. Decker, "Scurvy at York: A Dread Affliction Lingered at the Bay," *The Beaver* (Feb./Mar. 1989), 42–48. For a brief essay on **British Columbia,** see P.L. Wagner, "The Persistence of Native Settlement in Coastal British Columbia," in *People of the Living Land,* ed. Minghi, 15–28. On **Indian reserves,** see D.A. McQuillan, "Creation of Indian Reserves on the Canadian Prairies 1870–1885," *Geographical*

Review 70 (1980): 379–96; S. Raby, "Indian Land Surrenders in Southern Saskatchewan," *Canadian Geographer* 17 (1973): 36–52; C. Notzke, "The Past in the Present. Spatial and Land-use Change on Two Indian Reserves," in *Essays on . . . the Canadian West,* ed. Rosenvall and Evans, 95–121.

46. **Ecological impacts** are considered in K. Kelly "Damaged and Efficient Landscapes in Rural Southern Ontario 1880–1900," *Ontario History* 66 (1974): 1–14, reprinted in this volume; K. Kelly, "The Impact of Nineteenth Century Agricultural Settlement on the Land," in *Perspectives on Landscape and Settlement,* ed. Wood, 64–77; K. Kelly, "Artificial Drainage of Land in Nineteenth Century Ontario," *Canadian Geographer* 19 (1975): 279–98; J.G. Nelson, "Man and Landscape in the Western Plains of Canada," *Canadian Geographer* 11 (1967): 251–64; J.G. Nelson and R.E. England, "Some Comments on the Causes and Effects of Fire in the Northern Grasslands Area of Canada and the nearby United States ca. 1750–1900," *Canadian Geographer* 15 (1971): 295–306.

Conservation and resource management, broadly defined, are addressed in A.J. Ray, "Some Conservation Schemes of the Hudson's Bay Company, 1821–50: An Examination of the Problems of Resource Management in the Fur Trade," *Journal of Historical Geography* 1 (1975): 49–68; R.C.A Johnson, "Resource Management in Canada's National Parks, 1885–1911," *Alberta Geographer* 15 (1979): 19–36; C. Norbeck and J.G. Nelson, "Canadian Conservation and the Cypress Hills," *Prairie Forum* 1 (1976): 9–15; B.S. Osborne and D. Swainson, *Dividing the Waters: A Preliminary Overview of Water Management on the Rideau, 1832 to 1972* (Ottawa: Parks Canada, 1985).

47. On the **internal geography of cities**, see P.W. Moore, "Zoning and Neighbourhood Change. The Annex in Toronto, 1900–1970," *Canadian Geographer* 26 (1982): 21–36; P.W. Moore, "Zoning and Planning: The Toronto Experience," in *The Usable Urban Past,* ed. A.F.J. Artibise and G.A. Stelter (Toronto: Macmillan, 1979), 316–41; I. Ganton, "The Subdivision Process in Toronto, 1851–1883," in *Shaping the Urban Landscape: Aspects of the Canadian City Building Process,* ed. G. Stelter and A. Artibise (Toronto: Oxford University Press, 1982), 200–31; M.J. Doucet, "Working Class Housing in a Small Nineteenth Century Canadian City: Hamilton, Ontario 1852–1881," in *Essays in Working Class History,* ed. G.S. Kealey and P. Warrian (Toronto: McClelland and Stewart, 1976), 83–105; I. Davey and M. Doucet, "The Social Geography of a Commercial City ca. 1853," in M. Katz, *The People of Hamilton, Canada West* (Cambridge, MA: Harvard University Press, 1975), 319–42; G. Gad and D.W. Holdsworth, "Building for City, Region and Nation. Offices in Toronto 1834–1984," in *Forging a Consensus. Historical Essays on Toronto,* ed. V.L. Russell (Toronto: University of Toronto Press, 1984), 272–319; G. Gad and D.W. Holdsworth, "Looking inside the Skyscraper. Size and Occupancy of Toronto Office Buildings, 1890–1950," *Urban History Review* 16, 2 (1987): 176–89; G. Gad and D.W. Holdsworth, "Large Office Buildings and their Changing Occupancy, King Street, Toronto, 1880–1950," *Bulletin. Society for the Study of Architecture in Canada* 10 (1985): 19–26; G. Gad and D.W. Holdsworth, "Streetscape and Society: The Changing Built Environment of King Street, Toronto," in *Patterns of the Past,* ed. Hall et al., 174–205; D. Hanna and S. Olson, "Métiers, loyers et bouts de rues: l'armature de la société montréalaise 1881 à 1901," *Cahiers de géographie du Québec* 27 (1983): 255–75; D.G. Janelle, "Urban Land Use Changes: London, Ontario, 1850–1960," *Ontario Geography* 7 (1972): 66–86; J.C. Everitt and C. Stadel, "Spatial Dimensions of the Urban Growth of Brandon, Manitoba, 1882–1982," *Bulletin of the Association of North Dakota Geographers* 35 (1985): 1–32; J.C. Everitt, M. Westenberger, and C. Stadel, "The Development of Brandon's Social Areas, 1881–1914," *The Alberta Geographer* 21 (1985): 79–95.

48. **Communications:** T.F. McIlwraith, "Transportation in the Landscape of Early Upper Canada," in *Perspectives on Landscape and Settlement*, ed. Wood, 51–63; T.F. McIlwraith, "Transportation in Old Ontario," *American Review of Canadian Studies* 14 (1984): 177–92. The closest parallel to McIlwraith's work outside Ontario is probably P.L. McCormick, "Transportation and Settlement Problems in the Expansion of the Frontier of Saskatchewan and Assiniboia in 1904," *Prairie Forum* 5 (1980): 1–18. See also T.F. McIlwraith, "Freight Capacity and Utilization of the Erie and Great Lakes Canals before 1850," *Journal of Economic History* 36 (1976): 852–77; A.F. Burghardt, "Transportation in Early Canada," in *The Shaping of Ontario: From Exploration to Confederation*, ed. N. Mika (Belleville, Ont.: Mika Publishing, 1985), 210–19; B.S Osborne, "The Canadian National Postal System, 1852–1914: An Examination of a Regional Communication System," in *Regionalism and National Identity*, ed. R. Berry and J. Acheson (Christchurch, New Zealand: ACSANZ, 1985), 227–40; B.S. Osborne and R. Pike, "Lowering 'The Walls of Oblivion': The Revolution in Postal Communications in Central Canada, 1851–1911," *Canadian Papers in Rural History* 4 (1984): 200–25. See also three articles by B.S. Osborne and R.M. Pike: "The Postal Service and Canadian Postal History," in *Postal Historical Society of Canada Journal* 41 (1955): 11–14, 42 (1985): 21–27, and "From 'A Cornerstone of Canada's Social Structure' to 'Financial Self-Sufficiency.' The Transformation of the Canadian Postal Service 1852–1987," *Canadian Journal of Communications* 13 (1987): 1–26. As well, see G. Wall, "Transportation in a Pioneer Area: A Note on Muskoka," *Transport History* 5 (1972): 54–66. See also note 64.

49. **Urban systems:** J.U. Marshall and W.R. Smith, "The Dynamics of Growth in a Regional Urban System in Southern Ontario, 1851–1971," *Canadian Geographer* 22 (1978): 22–40; L.H. Russwurm and B. Thakur, "Hierarchical and Functional Stability and Change in a Strongly Urbanizing Area of Southwestern Ontario, 1871–1971," *Canadian Geographer* 25 (1981): 149–66; C.F.J. Whebell, "Corridors. A Theory of Urban Systems," *Annals of the Association of American Geographers* 59 (1969): 1–26; D. Kerr, "Metropolitan Dominance in Canada," in *Canada: A Geographical Interpretation*, ed. J. Warkentin (Toronto: Methuen, 1968), 531–55. A more general commentary is provided by P. Goheen, "Some Aspects of Canadian Urbanization from 1850–1920," in *Urbanization in the Americas*, ed. W. Borah, J. Hardoy, and G. Stelter (Ottawa: History Division, National Museum of Man, 1980), 77–84. See also Yeates, notes 58 and 63 below.

50. See also C. Harris, "Within the Fantastic Frontier: A Geographer's Thoughts on Canadian Unity," *Canadian Geographer* 23 (1979): 197–200; D.W. Holdsworth, "Dependence, Diversity and the Canadian Identity," *Journal of Geography* 83 (1984): 199–204, and the items listed in note 56 below.

51. P.G. Goheen, "Methodology in Historical Geography: The 1970s in Review," *Historical Methods* 16 (1983): 8–15.

52. This point can be exemplified by comparison of the several books produced by historical geographers since 1967: Clark, *Acadia*; E. Ross, *Beyond the River and the Bay* (Toronto: University of Toronto Press, 1970) from which 109–18 are excerpted in this text; P.G. Goheen, *Victorian Toronto 1850–1900*, Department of Geography research paper (Chicago: University of Chicago, 1970); J.L. Tyman, *By Section, Township and Range Studies in Prairie Settlement* (Brandon, Man.: Assiniboine Historical Society, 1972); Gilmour, *Spatial Evolution of Manufacturing*; Heidenreich, *Huronia*; R.C. Harris and J. Warkentin, *Canada before Confederation* (New York: Oxford University Press, 1974); Ray, *Indians in the Fur Trade*; Mannion, *Irish Settlements*; W.G. Ross, *Whaling and Eskimos: Hudson Bay, 1860–1915*, Publications in Ethnology no. 10 (Ottawa: National Museum of Man, 1975); Head, *Eighteenth Century Newfoundland*; D.B. Knight, *A Capital for Canada: Conflict and Compromise*

in the Nineteenth Century, Department of Geography research paper (Chicago: University of Chicago, 1977); C.J. Houston and W.J. Smyth, *The Sash Canada Wore: A Historical Geography of the Orange Order in Canada* (Toronto: University of Toronto Press, 1980); G. Wynn, *Timber Colony: A Historical Geography of Early Nineteenth Century New Brunswick* (Toronto: University of Toronto Press, 1981); W.R. Smith, *Aspects of Growth in a Regional Urban System: Southern Ontario 1851–1951*, Geographical Monographs no. 12 (Downsview, Ont.: Atkinson College, 1982); Rees, *Land of Earth and Sky*; J.T. Lemon, *Toronto since 1918. An Illustrated History* (Toronto: J. Lorimer, 1985); W.G. Ross, *Arctic Whalers, Icy Seas: Narratives of the Davis Strait Whale Fishery* (Toronto: Irwin, 1985); R. Rees, *New and Naked Land. Making the Prairies Home*, (Saskatoon: Western Producer Prairie Books, 1988); Lai, *Chinatowns*; Houston and Smyth, *Irish Emigration*.

53.   Studies considering the impact of **values, ideologies, and beliefs** include G. Wynn, "'Deplorably Dark and Demoralized Lumberers'? Rhetoric and Reality in Early Nineteenth Century New Brunswick," *Journal of Forest History* 24 (1980): 168–87; R.C. Harris et al., "The Settlement of Mono Township"; Houston and Smyth, *The Sash Canada Wore*; C.J. Houston and W.J. Smyth, "The Orange Order and the Expansion of the Frontier in Ontario, 1830–1900," *Journal of Historical Geography* 4, 3 (1978): 231–50; K.J. Anderson, "The Idea of Chinatown: The Power of Place and Institutional Practice in the Making of a Racial Category," *Annals of the Association of American Geographers* 77 (1987): 580–98; K.J.Anderson, "Cultural Hegemony and the Race-Definition Process in Chinatown, Vancouver: 1880–1980," *Environment and Planning D: Society and Space* 6 (1988): 127–50; P.J. Smith, "The Principle of Utility and the Origins of Planning Legislation in Alberta, 1912–1975," and O. Saarinen, "The Influence of Thomas Adams and the British New Towns Movement in the Planning of Canadian Resource Communities," both in *The Usable Urban Past*, ed. Artibise and Stelter, 196–225 and 268–92; P.J. Smith, "American Influences and Local Needs: Adaptations to the Alberta Planning System in 1928–1929," and O. Saarinen, "Single Sector Communities in Northern Ontario: The Creation and Planning of Dependent Towns," both in *Power and Place. Canadian Urban Development in the North American Context*, ed. G.A. Stelter and A.F.J. Artibise (Vancouver: University of British Columbia Press, 1986), 109–32 and 219–64; C.F.J. Whebell, "Why Pembroke? The Politics of Selecting a County Capital in the mid-Nineteenth Century," *Ontario History* 78 (1986): 127–56. Somewhat different in emphasis is G. Wynn, "New England's Outpost in the Nineteenth Century," in *The Northeastern Borderlands: Four Centuries of Interaction*, ed. S.J. Hornsby, V.A Konrad, and J.J. Herlan (Fredericton: Acadiensis, 1989), 64–90.

54.   Examples of the **influence of the state** (broadly conceived) include J.W. Simmons, "The Impact of the Public Sector on the Canadian Urban System," in *Power and Place*, ed. Stelter and Artibise, 21–50; J.C. Lehr, "Governmental Coercion in the Settlement of Ukrainian Immigrants in Western Canada," *Prairie Forum* 8 (1983): 179–94; M. Sundstrom, "Geographical Aspects of Dominion Government Creameries in the Northwest Territories, 1897–1905," *Prairie Forum* 10 (1985): 129–46; W. Carlyle, "The Changing Geography of Administrative Units for Rural Schooling and Local Government on the Canadian Prairies," *Prairie Forum* 12 (1987): 5–30; P.W. Moore, "Public Services and Residential Development in a Toronto Neighbourhood 1880–1915," *Journal of Urban History* 9 (1983): 445–72; C.F.J. Whebell, "The Upper Canada District Councils Act of 1841 and British Colonial Policy," *Journal of Imperial and Commonwealth History* 17 (1989): 185–209.

Studies of **demographic forces** include P.A. Thornton, "The Problem of Out-Migration from Atlantic Canada, 1871–1921: A New Look," *Acadiensis* 15 (1985): 3–34; P.A. Thornton, "Some Preliminary Comments on the Extent and

Consequences of Out-Migration from the Atlantic Region, 1870–1920," in *Merchant Shipping and Economic Development in Atlantic Canada*, ed. L.R. Fischer and E.W. Sager (St. John's: Memorial University of Newfoundland, 1982): 187–218. **Economic influences** are examined in R. Ommer, "'All the Fish of the Post': Resource Property Rights and Development in a Nineteenth-Century Inshore Fishery," *Acadiensis* 10 (1981): 107–23; J.J. Mannion, "Settlers and Traders in Western Newfoundland," in *Peopling of Newfoundland*, ed. Mannion, 234–74; C.W. Sanger, "The Dundee–St John's Connection: Nineteenth Century Interlinkages between Scottish Arctic Whaling and the Newfoundland Seal Fishery," *Newfoundland Studies* 4 (1988): 1–26; J.J. Mannion, "The Waterford Merchants and the Irish-Newfoundland Provisions Trade, 1770–1820," *Canadian Papers in Rural History* 3 (1982): 178–203; G. Wynn, "Industrialism, Entrepreneurship, and Opportunity in the New Brunswick Timber Trade," in *The Enterprising Canadians: Entrepreneurs and Economic Development in Eastern Canada, 1820–1914*, ed. L.R. Fischer and E.W. Sager (St. John's: Maritime History Group, Memorial University of Newfoundland, 1979): 5–22; F.W. Remiggi, " 'La lutte du clerge contre le marchand de poisson': A Study of Power Structures on the Northern Gaspé Coast in the Nineteenth Century," in *The Enterprising Canadians*, ed. Fischer and Sager, 183–200; R. Ommer, "The Trade and Navigation of the Island," in *Volumes not Values*, ed. D. Alexander and R. Ommer (St. John's: Memorial University of Newfoundland, 1979), 33–55; D.W. Holdsworth and J.C. Everitt, "Bank Branches and Elevators: Expressions of Big Corporations in Small Prairie Towns," *Prairie Forum* 13, 2 (1988): 173–90. **Social forces** play a significant part in the following analyses: L.D. McCann and J. Burnett, "Social Mobility and the Ironmasters of Late Nineteenth Century New Glasgow," in *People and Place*, ed. McCann, 59–77; L.D. McCann, " 'Living the Double Life': Town and Country in the Industrialization of the Maritimes," in *Geographical Perspectives on the Maritime Provinces*, ed. Day, 93–113; D.G. Cartwright, "Institutions on the Frontier: French Canadian Settlement in Eastern Ontario in the Nineteenth Century," *Canadian Geographer* 21 (1971): 1–21; and M.J. Doucet and J.C. Weaver, "Town Fathers and Urban Continuity: The Roots of Community Power and Physical Form in Hamilton, Upper Canada, in the 1830s," *Urban History Review* 13 (1984): 75–90.

55. **Kinship** is to the fore in R. Ommer, "Highland Scots Migration to Western Newfoundland: A Study of Kinship," in *Peopling of Newfoundland*, ed. Mannion, 212–33; R. Ommer, "Primitive Accumulation and the Scottish Clann in Old World and New," *Journal of Historical Geography* 12 (1986): 121–41.

Speculation is a prominent theme in J. Clarke, "The Role of Political Position and Family and Economic Linkage in Land Speculation in the Western District of Upper Canada, 1788–1815," *Canadian Geographer* 19 (1975): 18–34; J. Clarke, "Aspects of Land Acquisition in Essex County, Ontario," *Histoire sociale/Social History* 11 (1978): 98–119; J. Clarke and D.L. Brown, "Pricing Decisions for Ontario Land: The Farm Community and the Speculator in Essex County during the First Half of the Nineteenth Century," *Canadian Geographer* 31 (1987): 169–76; J. Clarke and D.L. Brown, "Land Prices in Essex County, Ontario, 1798 to 1852," *Canadian Geographer* 26 (1982): 300–17; J. Clarke, "The Activity of an Early Canadian Land Speculator in Essex County, Ontario: Would the Real John Askin Please Stand up?" *Canadian Papers in Rural History* 3 (1982): 84–109; R.W. Widdis, "Motivation and Scale: A Method of Identifying Land Speculators in Upper Canada," *Canadian Geographer* 23 (1979): 337–51; R.W. Widdis, "Speculation and the Surveyor: An Analysis of the Role Played by the Surveyors in the Settlement of Upper Canada," *Histoire sociale/Social History* 15 (1982): 443–58; D.A. McNabb, "The Role of the Land in Settling Horton Township, Nova Scotia, 1766–1830," in *They Planted Well. New England Planters in*

Maritime Canada, ed. M. Conrad (Fredericton: Acadiensis Press, 1988), 151–60;
M. Doucet, "Speculation and the Physical Expansion of Mid-Nineteenth Century
Hamilton," in *Shaping the Urban Landscape*, ed. Stelter and Artibise, 173–99.
Technology is a factor in M.J. Doucet, "Politics, Space and Trolleys: Mass Transit in
Early Twentieth-Century Toronto," in *Shaping the Urban Landscape*, ed. Stelter and
Artibise, 356–81.
    The law is considered in J.M. Richtik, "The Policy Framework for Settling the
Canadian West, 1870–1880," *Agricultural History* 49 (1975): 613–28; G. Wynn,
"Administration in Adversity: Deputy Surveyors and Control of the New Brunswick
Crown Forest before 1844," *Acadiensis* 7 (1977): 49–65. See also Moore, note 47, and
Smith, note 53, above.
    56.   Perhaps the best illustration of this point comes from the several broad **historical
geographical syntheses** written in the last fifteen years, although these were written for
different purposes, at different scales, and with different audiences in mind. They also,
of course, reflect the distinct interests and approaches of their authors. Nonetheless,
comparison is instructive. Harris and Warkentin, *Canada before Confederation*; R.C.
Harris, "France in North America," T.F. McIlwraith, "British North America,
1763–1867," and G. Wynn, "Forging a Canadian Nation," all in R.D. Mitchell and P.A.
Groves, *North America: The Historical Geography of a Changing Continent* (Totawa,
NJ: Rowman and Littlefield, 1987): 65–92, 220–52 and 373–409; G. Wynn, "On the
Margins of Empire, 1760–1840," in *The Illustrated History of Canada*, ed. Brown,
189–278. These treatments might also be compared with a series of shorter regional
essays for the British *Geographical Magazine* 45, 2–7 (1972–73), namely, R.I.
Ruggles, "Westward Thrust in a New World" (Nov., 1972), 116–25; A.H. Clark,
"Acadian Heritage in Maritime 'New France'" (Dec., 1972), 219–27; F.C. Innes,
"Heartbreak of Former New France" (Jan., 1973), 277–84; R.L. Gentilcore, "Ontario
Emerges from the Trees" (Feb., 1973), 383–92; J. Warkentin, "Dry Farmers on the
Canadian Plains" (Mar., 1973), 443–50; and T.R. Weir, "Road Back from the Prairie"
(Apr., 1973) 506–10. They can also be compared with R.L. Gentilcore, "The Making
of a Province: Ontario to 1850," *American Review of Canadian Studies* 14 (1985):
137–56; with A.H. Clark, "Geographical Diversity and the Personality of Canada," in
Land and Livelihood: Geographical Essays in Honour of George Jobberns, ed. M.
McCaskill (Christchurch: New Zealand Geographical Society, 1962), 23–47; and with
Harris, "Pattern of Canada," in this text. For a yet broader canvas, see R.C. Harris, "The
Historical Geography of North American Regions," *American Behavioural Scientist* 22
(1978): 115–30.
    57.   For **methodology/philosophy,** see: note 36, above; L.T.Guelke, *Historical
Understanding in Geography: An Idealist Approach* (New York: Cambridge
University Press, 1982); and L.T. Guelke, "Historical Geography and Collingwood's
Theory of Historical Knowing," in *Period and Place*, ed. Baker and Billinge, 189–96.
Often substantial **commentaries on method and data sources** are also excluded. See
O.F.G. Sitwell, "Difficulties in the Interpretation of the Agricultural Statistics in the
Canadian Censuses of the Nineteenth Century," *Canadian Geographer* 13 (1969):
72–76; G.J. Levine, "Criticising the Assessment: Views of the Property Evaluation
Process in Montreal, 1870–1920 and Their Implications for Historical Geography,"
Canadian Geographer 28 (1984): 276–84; B. Coffey, "The Canadian Inventory of
Historic Building as a Basis for House Type Classification: An Example from Southern
Ontario," *Canadian Geographer* 28 (1984): 83–89; and R.W. Widdis, "Tracing
Property Ownership in Nineteenth Century Ontario. A Guide to the Archival Sources,"
Canadian Papers in Rural History 2 (1980): 83–102.
    58.   In addition to the **quantitative-theoretical** work of W. Norton listed in note 33
above, examples include: M. Yeates, "Urbanization in the Windsor–Quebec City Axis

1921–1981," *Urban Geography* 5 (1984): 2–24; M. Yeates, "The Core/Periphery Model and Urban Development in Central Canada," *Urban Geography* 6 (1985): 101–21; J. Clarke, H.W. Taylor, and W.R. Wightman, "Areal Patterns of Population Change in Southern Ontario 1831–1891: Core, Frontier and Intervening Space," *Ontario Geography* 12 (1978): 27–48; D.G. Janelle, "Scale Components in the Descriptive Analysis of Urban Land Use Change, London, Ontario, 1850–1960," *Ontario Geography* 7 (1972): 66–86; J.P. Wiesinger, "Modelling the Agricultural Settlement Process of Southern Manitoba, 1872–1891: Some Implications for Settlement Theory," *Prairie Forum* 10 (1985): 83–104. See also Janelle (note 47), Marshall and Smith, and Russwurm and Thakur (note 49), and E.G. Moore and B.S. Osborne, "Marital Fertility in Kingston 1861–1881: A Study of Socio-Economic Differentials," *Histoire sociale/Social History* 20 (1987): 9–28, for examples.

59.   R.C. Harris, "Industry and the Good Life Around Idaho Peak," *Canadian Historical Review* 56 (1985): 315–43 and in *Canadian Labour History: Selected Readings*, ed. D.J Bercuson (Toronto: Copp Clark Pitman, 1987), 62–84.

60.   Far too extensive to detail here, the **literature on Quebec in French** can be approached through the *Cahiers de géographie du Québec*. For example, vol. 28 (1984) is a special issue devoted to "Rangs et villages du Québec. Perspectives géohistorique," and vol. 24 (1980) includes an extended two-part article on "La crise agricole du Bas Canada" by S. Courville. Among more recent publications by Courville elsewhere are "Un monde rural en mutation: le Bas Canada dans la première moité du XIXe siècle," *Histoire sociale/Social History* 20, 40 (1987): 237–58, and "Le marché des «subsistances». L'exemple de Montréal au début des années 1830: une perspective géographique," *Revue d'histoire de l'Amérique française* 42 (1988): 193–239. See also S. Courville and N. Seguin, *Rural Life in Nineteenth Century Quebec*, Canadian Historical Association Historical Booklet no. 47 (Ottawa: Canadian Historical Association, 1989) for a recent summary of some of this material in English.

61.   Sauer, "Foreword," in *Land and Life*, ed. Leighly, 362.

62.   Reflecting the diversity of work on **agriculture** are J. O'Mara, "The Seasonal Round of Gentry Farmers in Early Ontario: A Preliminary Analysis," *Canadian Papers in Rural History* 2 (1980): 103–12; S. Courville, "Villages and Agriculture in the Seigneuries of Lower Canada: Conditions of a Comprehensive Study of Rural Quebec in the First Half of the Nineteenth Century," *Canadian Papers in Rural History* 5 (1986): 121–49; G. Wynn, "Late-Eighteenth Century Agriculture on the Bay of Fundy Marshlands," *Acadiensis* 8 (1979): 80–89; R. Mackinnon and G. Wynn, "Nova Scotian Agriculture in the 'Golden Age': A New Look," in *Geographical Perspectives on the Maritime Provinces*, ed. Day, 47–59; K. Kelly, "Wheat Farming in Simcoe County in the Mid-Nineteenth Century," *Canadian Geographer* 15 (1971): 95–112; K. Kelly, "Notes on a Type of Mixed Farming Practised in Ontario during the Early Nineteenth Century," *Canadian Geographer* 17 (1973): 205–19; K. Kelly, "The Transfer of British Ideas on Improved Farming to Ontario during the First Half of the Nineteenth Century," *Ontario History* 63 (1971): 103–11; B. Kaye, " 'The Settlers' Grand Difficulty': Haying in the Economy of the Red River Settlement," *Prairie Forum* 9 (1984): 1–12; B. Kaye, "The Trade in Livestock between the Red River Settlement and the American Frontier, 1812–1870," *Prairie Forum* 6 (1981): 163–82; S.M. Evans, "Stocking the Canadian Range," *Alberta History* 26 (1978): 1–8; S.M. Evans, "American Cattlemen on the Canadian Range, 1874 to 1914," *Prairie Forum* 4 (1979): 121–36; S.M. Evans, "The End of the Open Range Era in Western Canada," *Prairie Forum* 8 (1983): 71–88; S.M. Evans, "The Origin of Ranching in Western Canada," in *Essays on…the Canadian West*, ed. Rosenvall and Evans, 70–94.

Among studies of **suburban development**, see McCririck, "Opportunity and the Workingman: A Study of Land Accessibility and the Growth of Blue Collar Suburbs in

Early Vancouver" (M.A. thesis, University of British Columbia, 1981); D. Hanna, "The Creation of an Early Victorian Suburb in Montreal," *Urban History Review* 2 (1980): 38–64; R. Paterson, "The Development of an Interwar Suburb: Kingsway Park, Etobicoke," *Urban History Review* 13 (1985): 225–35; M.J. Doucet, "Urban Land Development in Nineteenth-Century North America," *Journal of Urban History* 8 (1982): 299–342; and M.J. Doucet and J. Weaver "The North American Shelter Business, 1860–1920: A Study of a Canadian Real Estate and Property Management Agency," *Business History Review* 58 (1984): 234–62.

63. On **commercial intercourse and city systems** see, in addition to the works listed in notes 48 and 49 above, B.S. Osborne, "Trading on a Frontier: The Function of Peddlers, Markets, and Fairs in Nineteenth Century Ontario," *Canadian Papers in Rural History* 2 (1980): 59–81; K. Kelly, "The Development of Farm Produce Marketing Agencies and Competition between Marketing Centres in Eastern Simcoe County, 1850–1875," *Canadian Papers in Rural History* 1 (1978): 67–88; P. Goheen, "Communications and Urban Systems in Mid-Nineteenth Century Canada," *Urban History Review* 14 (1986): 235–46; P.G. Goheen, "Canadian Communications circa 1845," *Geographical Review* 77 (1987): 35–51; J.W. Simmons, "The Evolution of the Canadian Urban System," in *The Usable Urban Past*, ed. Artibise and Stelter, 9–33; and a series of papers by F.A. Dahms, namely "Regional Urban History: A Statistical and Cartographical Survey of Huron and Southern Bruce Counties, 1864–1981," *Urban History Review* 15 (1987): 254–68; "The Evolution of Settlement Systems. A Canadian Example, 1851–1970," *Journal of Urban History* 7 (1981): 169–204; "The Changing Function of Villages and Hamlets in Wellington County, 1881–1891," *Urban History Review* 8 (1980): 3–19; and "The Process of Urbanization in the Countryside: A Study of Huron and Southern Bruce Counties, Ontario, 1891–1981," *Urban History Review* 12 (1984): 1–18.

64. Facets of **transport and communication** are treated in A.F. Burghardt, "The Origin and Development of the Road Network of the Niagara Peninsula, Ontario, 1770–1851," *Annals of the Association of American Geographers* 59 (1969): 417–40; R.C. Harris, "Moving Amid the Mountains 1870–1930," *BC Studies* 58 (1983): 3–39; G. Wynn, "Moving Goods and People in Mid-Nineteenth Century New Brunswick," *Canadian Papers in Rural History* 6 (1988): 226–39; P. Darby, "From River Boat to Rail Lines: Circulation Patterns in the Canadian West during the Last Quarter of the Nineteenth Century," in *Essays on ... the Canadian West*, ed. Rosenvall and Evans, 7–26; and B.S. Osborne and D. Swainson, *The Rideau Navigation 1832–1972: Its Operation, Maintenance and Management* (Ottawa: Parks Canada, 1985). See also Doucet, note 55 and items in note 48.

65. M. Atwood, *The Journals of Susanna Moodie. Poems by Margaret Atwood* (Toronto: Oxford University Press, 1970), 16–17.

66. There are exceptions to the general lack of attention to **class**, including S. Hertzog and R.D. Lewis, "A City of Tenants: Homeownership and Social Class in Montreal, 1847–1881," *Canadian Geographer* 30 (1986): 316–23; R. Harris, B. Osborne, and G. Levine, "Housing Tenure and Social Classes in Kingston, Ontario, 1881–1901," *Journal of Historical Geography* 7 (1981): 271–89; and G.J. Levine, "Class, Ethnicity and Property Transfer in Montreal, 1907–1909," *Journal of Historical Geography* 14 (1988): 342–80. See also R. Harris, "Residential Segregation and Class Formation in Canadian Cities. A Critical Review," *Canadian Geographer* 28 (1984): 186–96. Compare also R. Harris, "The Unremarked Homeownership Boom in Toronto," *Histoire sociale/Social History* 18 (1986): 433–37; and R. Harris, "Working-Class Home Ownership and Housing Affordability across Canada in 1931," *Histoire sociale/Social History* 19 (1986): 121–38.

67. This **"simplification"** argument was first adumbrated in R.C. Harris and L.T. Guelke, "Land and Society in Early Canada and South Africa," *Journal of Historical Geography* 3 (1977): 135–53; and in R.C. Harris, "The Extension of France into Rural Canada," in *European Settlement and Development in North America*, ed. J.R. Gibson (Toronto: University of Toronto Press, 1978), 27–45. For further statements, see R.C. Harris, "The Simplification of Europe Overseas," *Annals of the Association of American Geographers* 67 (1977): 468–82; and C. Harris, "European Beginnings in the Northwest Atlantic: A Comparative View," in *Seventeenth Century New England*, ed. D.D. Hall and D.G. Allen (Boston: The Colonial Society of Massachusetts, 1985), 119–52.

68. Useful summaries and introductions to recent developments in the various branches of **social theory** are provided by A. Giddens and J. Turner, eds., *Social Theory Today* (Stanford, CA: Stanford University Press, 1987); and T.Skocpol, ed., *Vision and Method in Historical Sociology* (Cambridge: Cambridge University Press, 1984). A. Callinicos, *Making History* (Cambridge and Oxford: Polity Press and Basil Blackwell Ltd., 1987) offers a perspective on the roles played by social structure and human agency in history. Recent years have seen a considerable outpouring of commentary and enthusiasm for social theory in geography; much of this can be found in *Environment and Planning D: Society and Space*. Of special interest to historical geographers is N. Gregson, "Structuration Theory: Some Thoughts on the Possibilities for Empirical Research," *Environment and Planning D: Society and Space* 5 (1987): 73–91, but see also N. Thrift, "Bear and Mouse or Bear and Tree? Anthony Giddens' Reconstitution of Social Theory," *Sociology* 19 (1985): 609–23. For a wide-ranging "conversation" on historical geography in the 1980s, see A.R.H. Baker and D. Gregory, "Some *Terra Incognitae* in Historical Geography: An Exploratory Discussion," in *Explorations in Historical Geography: Interpretive Essays*, ed. A.R.H. Baker and D. Gregory (Cambridge: Cambridge University Press, 1984), 180–93. C. Earle et al., "Historical Geography," in *Geography in America*, ed. G.L. Gaile and C.J. Willmott (Columbus, OH: Merrill Publishing Company, 1989), 156–91, assesses current and prospective research trends in the field.

SECTION 1

A NATIVE REALM

Late in the fifteenth century, Europeans again began to explore the northeastern edges of the American hemisphere visited by Norse adventurers from Greenland almost five hundred years before. As they coasted its shores and made their first, halting penetration inland, the newcomers initiated contact with a few of the 300 000 or so indigenous inhabitants of the northern reaches of the continent. These "Indians," as Europeans characterized them, comprised a rich, complex, and dynamic mosaic of peoples. Native Canadians spoke numerous dialects of a dozen major languages, possessed an intimate knowledge of the resources of their particular territories, and supplemented local production of the goods they needed for subsistence by trading with their neighbours. They had shaped an intricate and distinctive set of geographies in the territory that we now call Canada.

All this was changed by the coming of Europeans. The fur trade drew native peoples into an international trading system; missionaries entered their camps and villages; new ideas, new technologies, new desires, new rivalries, and devastating new diseases forever changed the native world. By 1820, there were only 175 000 indigenous people in British North America and in some areas, where over-trapping and over-hunting had destroyed the bases of traditional economies, small groups struggled to survive.

Recovering the details of pre-contact native life and its subsequent transformation is no easy task. Native societies left no written records, and their strongly developed oral traditions were intended mainly to convey moral and social lessons. Although these traditions also recall events in the native past, they are difficult to date, and because so many of them were recorded long after European influences had begun to alter native life, they often fuse aboriginal and post-contact experience. The archeological record is also both limited and incomplete because only certain kinds of material survive the centuries and many sites remain unexcavated. European explorers, missionaries and traders recorded a good deal of information about the people with whom they came in contact but this, too, is problematic. In many areas, European goods and diseases preceded the arrival of European people among the Indians and significantly affected the societies they encountered. Confronting ways of life and languages dramatically different from their own, newcomers saw and heard them through the filters of their own experience and expectations. Moreover, their contacts with native peoples, whose lives followed complex rhythms of seasonal movement and resource exploitation, were often fleeting. Little wonder that debate about the precise character of aboriginal Canada continues, or that caution is essential in the interpretation of evidence relating to the native past of the country.

Our knowledge of the native past comes from a wide range of research techniques: archeological excavation, soil and pollen analysis, field survey, oral history, and close scrutiny of the written record. By combining the many types of evidence thus produced in a manner long characteristic of their discipline, geographers have made several significant contributions to the task of understanding the complex, rapidly changing panorama of native life in the Americas since the eve of contact.

Much of this work has drawn inspiration from the leadership of Carl O. Sauer, who long urged his colleagues to investigate the far reaches of human time and wrote extensively and provocatively on the indigenous people of early America. (For a discussion of Sauer's work, see the general introduction to this text.) Although none of the essays that follow presses as far beyond the existence of written records as Sauer was prepared to do, each addresses a topic that he held important. The first explores patterns of native life at the very beginning of European–Indian contact in the Great Lakes lowland, the second seeks to understand the land as it appeared to its original inhabitants, and the third deals with one facet of the appalling story of Indian population decline. If, in the end, these essays lack the powerful sweep of Sauer's writing,* they nonetheless effectively demonstrate the range, importance, and distinctiveness of geographical perspectives on indigenous life in early Canada.

The first contribution to this section, by Conrad Heidenreich, a long-time member of the Department of Geography at York University and a prominent contributor to volume 1 of the *Historical Atlas of Canada*, is drawn from his larger, prize-winning study of Huronia. This essay offers a vivid sketch of the ways in which early seventeenth-century inhabitants of the relatively small area between modern lakes Simcoe and Huron in Ontario interacted with each other and with their environment. Here, fragments of evidence from anthropology, archeology, botany, economics, history, and zoology are combined with an understanding of ecology and the landscape to compose a complex yet essentially geographical picture. The study thus reveals much about the settings, rhythms, and demands of life among a people who had felt and responded to European influences but whose existence had not yet been radically disrupted by them. This is historical geography broadly conceived, addressed to the traditional task of reconstructing and interpreting past landscapes, but using synthesis to carry understanding beyond the limits of more narrowly defined approaches.

In very different vein, Wayne Moodie of the University of Manitoba examines two of the fascinating maps collected by fur traders from native informants. In doing so, he demonstrates the detailed geographical knowledge possessed by native people and reminds us of the extent to which European exploration of North America depended upon their wisdom. The maps are remarkable documents— artifacts of the mind, in a sense—that reveal their native authors' perceptions and intellectual ordering of the landscapes around them. Consider the range and detail of these maps, and ask whether you could come close to producing similarly useful charts of your own province, or of the area within fifty kilometres of your home. Then remember that the authors of these maps had never had the benefit of seeing

---

* Sauer's powerful writing style is demonstrated most clearly in *The Early Spanish Main* (Berkeley: University of California Press, 1966), an elegaic account of the effects of European contact on the aboriginal societies of that region. The work is full of moral indignation at the fate of the indigenous peoples of the Caribbean and Central America.

the territory they charted from memory laid out before them in the way that atlases, road maps, and satellite pictures on televised weather reports outline our surroundings for us.

The final essay of this section clarifies how and why newly introduced diseases spread rapidly yet unevenly through scattered indigenous populations involved in the European trading system. Written by Arthur Ray, a member of the History Department in the University of British Columbia who trained as an historical geographer with Andrew H. Clark at the University of Wisconsin, it is a piece of detective work. Often faint clues, such as the dates and descriptions of "sickness" and "pestilence" in traders' journals, are combined with scientific knowledge about the symptoms and contagious periods of particular diseases, and brought into focus by the author's understanding of spatial patterns and the processes of geographical diffusion. The result is an intriguing story. In a few pages, we are brought to understand the sweep of contagious diseases through the mid-nineteenth-century western interior, although the progress of these diseases surely appeared providential or inexplicable to many of those afflicted by them. This is also a story full of poignant reverberations. Its account of populations ravaged by two decades of repeated epidemics, against which they had few defences and of which they had little understanding, reveals much of the process by which European introductions altered forever the fabric of native life throughout the length and breadth of the continent.

The Natural Environment of Huronia and Huron Seasonal Activities*

CONRAD E. HEIDENREICH

Today, Huronia is best known as a tourist area encompassing most of Simcoe County, Ontario. In the early part of the 17th century, the northern part of this area was the territory of the Huron Confederacy, a group of semi-sedentary, agricultural Indians belonging to the larger family of Iroquoian speaking peoples. With a population estimated at 21 000, in a territory of some 340 square miles, Huronia was perhaps the most densely settled area of aboriginal Canada.

When French traders arrived in the St. Lawrence valley early in the 17th century, the Huron were joined with the Montagnais and Algonquin bands of the Canadian Shield and the Petun Indians of the Collingwood area in a loose military and trading alliance against the powerful Iroquois Confederacy located south of Lake Ontario. Together the Huron, Montagnais and Algonquins controlled access to the lands north of the Great Lakes and in particular to the fur resources of the Canadian Shield. As well, the Montagnais controlled access to the lower St. Lawrence valley. Realizing this, the French committed themselves to the Montagnais–Huron–Algonquin alliance. Soon after initial French–Huron contact, the Huron began to take over the Algonquin's role as major suppliers of fur to the French traders in the upper St. Lawrence area. They thus became the most important early commercial allies of French trading interests in North America.

With their large semi-sedentary agricultural population, housed in villages of up to several thousand people, the Huron offered an unusual opportunity for missionary ambitions, and several Récollet, and later Jesuit, missions were established among them. Inspired by genuine religious zeal, these initiatives were intended to bring native peoples into the Catholic Christian community and to cement the French–Huron alliance. In the end, they failed in the face of European diseases,

---

* From *Beitrage zur Kulturgeographie von Kanada*, ed. C. Schott (Marburg: Marburger Geographische Gesellschaft e.V., 1971), 103–16.

trade rivalries and the age old rancours of inter-tribal warfare. But until the late 1630s, when disasters began to overtake the Huron, their territory was a relatively stable one that offers the geographer a good opportunity to study significant aspects of the aboriginal geography of Canada. Basic research material on the Huron, as well as other Indian groups in eastern Canada, is in some respects fairly good. Tribal areas can be delimited quite accurately from a number of early maps;[1] contemporary travellers' descriptions of Indian life can be found in the writings of the Jesuits,[2] the explorer Champlain[3] and the Récollets Sagard,[4] and Le Clercq.[5] Until recently, archaeological work has been confined primarily to the pre-European period and much of the potentially useful material on 17th century Huronia has not yet been published. Palaeoecological studies have begun in Huronia, but only the broadest outlines of the climatic and vegetation patterns of the area have been determined.[6] The only studies that have attempted a more or less complete reconstruction of the Huron are by Trigger and Heidenreich;[7] the former are primarily anthropological studies of Huron history and society, and the latter essentially a historical geography of Huronia and adjacent areas.

This paper describes the natural environment of Huronia and indicates how the Huron utilized and modified it. Attention is focussed on activities related to the operation of a Huron village rather than on those of a tribe or the Confederacy as a whole. The logic behind this approach is that Huron villages, made up of a number of closely co-operating lineages or extended families, were economically, and to a large degree also politically, autonomous. The tribe was essentially a socio-political unit with little economic importance and the Confederacy was a loose military alliance. The impact of tribal or Confederacy decisions on the landscape was negligible; resource utilization and landscape change emanated from the village.

The Natural Landscape

From 17th century ethnohistorical descriptions, and pollen, soils, and snails studies, the climate of Huronia seems to have been very similar to that of the present.[8] Winters may have been slightly longer and the frost-free season slightly shorter but if so, these differences were insufficient to hinder Huron agriculture. The growing season in Huronia is about 140 days; Huron corn matured in 90–120 days. Summer droughts, which were carefully recorded by Jesuit missionaries, occurred with about the same frequency as they do today, namely about twice every ten years.

Although the extent of the forest cover has changed greatly since the Huron occupation, the dominant species are the same. The dominant association throughout the area is maple (*Acer saccharum*), beech (*Fagus grandifolia*) and basswood (*Tilia americana*). In some areas, beech drops out of the association and is replaced by elm (*Ulmus americana*) and hemlock (*Tsuga canadensis*). White pine (*Pinus strobus*) is found throughout Huronia and may be considered a secondary dominant. On very droughty soils, oak (*Quercus rubra, Q. alba, Q. macrocarpa*) and white pine are prevalent almost to the exclusion of all the other species. Poplar (*Populus sp.*), ash (*Fraxinus sp.*) and balsam fir (*Abies balsamea*) are also fairly common throughout Huronia. In poorly drained areas and swamps, the most abundant species are cedar (*Thuja occidentalis*), alder (*Alnus rugosa*) and in open areas, willow (*Salix sp.*) and dogwood (*Cornus sp.*). Tamarak (*Larix laricina*) is scattered throughout most of the swamps; black spruce (*Picea mariana*) occurs only rarely.

Between 1811 and 1822, Huronia was surveyed for European settlement. Because the natural vegetation growing along the survey lines had to be described in some detail, the original field notes of the surveyors allow one to make a fairly accurate map of the pre-settlement vegetation of the area (figure 1, strongly generalized). Without the survey reports, such a reconstruction would be impossible or at best a very rough guess. Relicts of the original forest in Huronia are rare and tell us almost nothing of the species distribution. The same is true of drainage conditions before and after European settlement. Some of the creeks and springs present in the 17th and 19th century are gone today, as well as at least four small lakes. In some cases, old drainage channels have been obliterated; in other cases, water has been diverted; and throughout the area, swamps have been drained and the water table has dropped.

In considering Indian occupancy, it is particularly important to delimit the extent of the swamps and poorly drained areas. Although these were not used for agriculture, the height of the water table was of some importance to the raising of corn, particularly during periods of growth when rains failed, and the presence of water at a village was, of course, absolutely essential. Judging from excavations at Ste. Marie near Midland, Ontario, the water level in Georgian Bay stood at 578.4 feet (176.3m) above mean sea level in the middle of the 17th century, or about the same as it is today.[9] Swamps were more extensive and surface water in the upland areas more abundant. Today many archaeological sites are beside dry springs and creek beds that held water in the 17th century. Since the Huron did not drain swamps or for that matter use any soils that were not well drained, one can assume that the descriptions of the early 19th century surveyors mirror 17th century conditions. These indicate that Huronia was almost an island, with the water of Nottawasaga Bay, Georgian Bay and Lake Couchiching along the western, northwestern and eastern frontiers (figure 1). Vast swamps stretched along the contact line between the Canadian Shield and the arable uplands of Huronia along the northeastern frontier, while the swampy Nottawasaga lowlands, dotted by numerous ponds, closed off the southwestern frontier. Only along the southeastern borders of Huronia between Orr Lake and Lake Couchiching were the swamps more discontinuous. It is small wonder that the Huron called themselves Ouendat or dwellers of "The Island" or "The-Land-Apart."

The occupied portion of Huronia consisted of four major upland areas separated from each other by small rivers, with floodplains of poorly drained soils occupied by a heavy growth of cedar, alder and in places hemlock, elm, pine and maple. Except for one of the upland areas, which was shared by two tribes, each of the

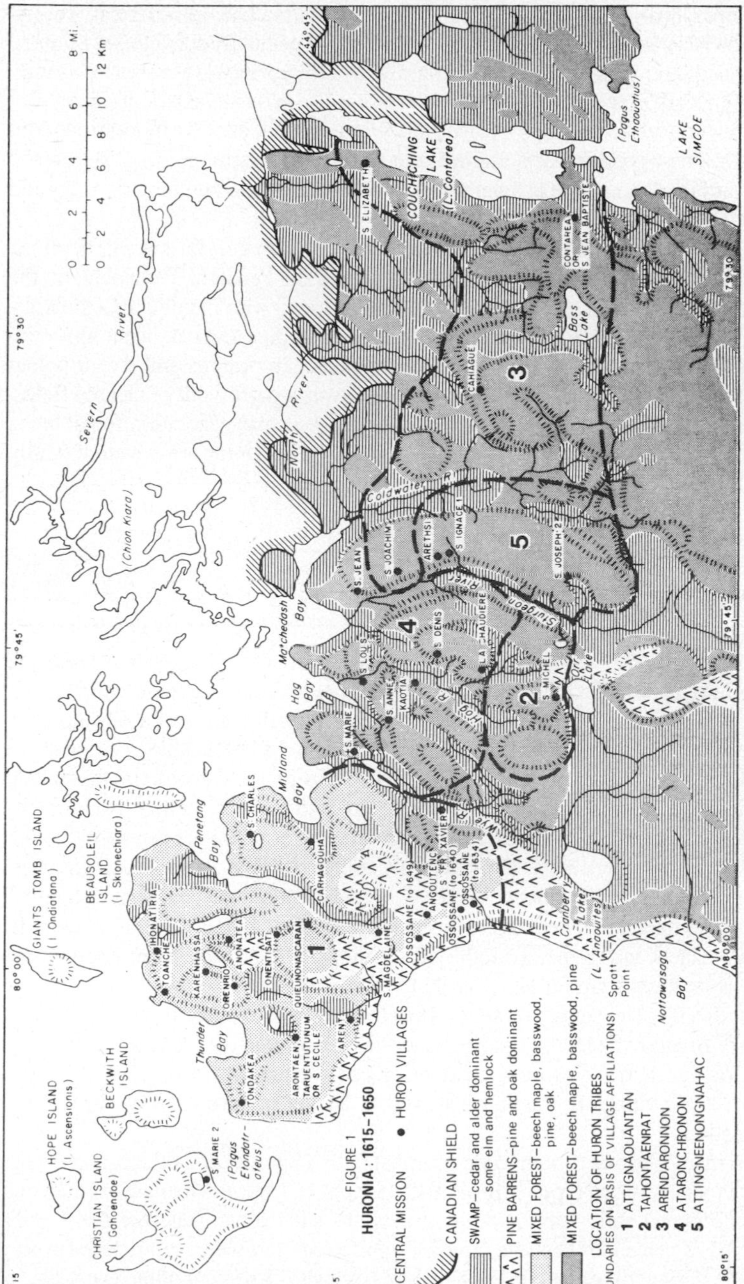
FIGURE 1
HURONIA : 1615–1650
CENTRAL MISSION
HURON VILLAGES
CANADIAN SHIELD
SWAMP–cedar and alder dominant some elm and hemlock
PINE BARRENS–pine and oak dominant
MIXED FOREST–beech maple, basswood, pine, oak
MIXED FOREST–beech maple, basswood, pine
LOCATION OF HURON TRIBES (BOUNDARIES ON BASIS OF VILLAGE AFFILIATIONS)
1 ATTIGNAOUANTAN
2 TAHONTAENRAT
3 ARENDARONNON
4 ATARONCHRONON
5 ATTINGNEENONGNAHAC
CHRISTIAN ISLAND (I. Gahoendoe)
HOPE ISLAND (I. Ascensionis)
BECKWITH ISLAND
GIANTS TOMB ISLAND (I. Ondiatana)
BEAUSOLEIL ISLAND (I. Skionechiara)
S. MARIE 2
(Pagus Etondatrateus)
Thunder Bay
Penetang Bay
Midland Bay
Hog Bay
Matchedash Bay
Nottawasaga Bay
Spratt Point
Cranberry Lake
(L. Anaouites)
Orr Lake
Bass Lake
COUCHICHING LAKE
(L. Contarea)
LAKE SIMCOE
(Pagus Cthaouatius)
Severn River
(Chion Kiara)
North River
Coldwater R.
Sturgeon River
Hog R.
Wye R.
TONDAKEA
ARONTAEN, TARUENTUTUNUM OR S. CECILE
ARENT
S. MAGDELAINE
QUIEUNONASCARAN
ONENTISATI
ANONATEA
ORENRIO
KARENHASSA
TOANCHE
IHONATIRIA
CARHAGOUHA
S. CHARLES
OSSOSSANE (to 1649)
ANGOUTENC
S. FR. XAVIER
OSSOSSANE (to 1640)
OSSOSSANE (to 1634)
S. MARIE
S. ANNE
KAOTIA
S. LOUIS
S. DENIS
LA CHAUDIERE
S. MICHEL
S. JEAN
S. JOACHIM
ARETHSI
S. IGNACE 1
S. JOSEPH 2
CAHIAGUE
CONTAREA OR S. JEAN BAPTISTE
S. ELIZABETH
0 2 4 6 8 Mi.
0 2 4 6 8 10 12 Km
80°15'
80°00'
79°45'
79°30'
44°45'

FIGURE 1

other three areas coincided with Huron tribal districts. The upland areas were at one time islands in glacial Lake Algonquin and are generally surrounded by steep abandoned shorelines. Most of the surface area of the uplands is covered by a sandy till and in some places sandy outwash deposits. These form the parent material of the brown podzolic and grey-brown podzolic soils that are common throughout Huronia. These soils are well drained and of fair to moderate fertility. Below the sandy surface deposits are heavier clays, accounting for the numerous springs and the considerable amount of surface water in the area.

The original forest of the upland areas was beech, maple, basswood, hemlock and pine. Towards the western end of Huronia in the Penetang Peninsula, on the sandier soils, pine and oak appear as dominants along with the ubiquitous maple, beech and basswood. In a few areas, on gravel soils, pine and oak occur almost to the exclusion of the other species. Contemporary descriptions and recent pollen studies show that during Huron times this area was a patchwork of cleared fields, abandoned fields in grasses, and various stages of second-generation forest interspersed with mature stands on the heavier soils. The low-lying areas were virtually untouched.

Factors in Village Site Selection

The Huron exercised considerable care in the selection of village sites. Each site had to have a combination of specific physical requirements among which proximity to a source of water, a hinterland of arable soils, an available source of firewood, proximity to a young secondary forest, and a defendable position seem to have been the most important. The one socio-political requirement for site selection was that no village could locate on land actively farmed by a neighbouring village. Land abandoned in the process of village movement could, however, be taken by others. The same rule operated within a village. All land was common property until someone decided to farm it. Since land could not be bought, sold or inherited, it reverted to common land as soon as a family ceased to work it.

A permanent and readily available water supply was of paramount importance. There is no known site in Huronia that is not immediately adjacent to a spring, creek or some other supply of water. Proximity to a permanent water supply was essential because the Huron did not have the technology to store much water, dig wells, or transport water over great distances. Water had to be carried by the women to the village in fragile earthenware, leather or bark vessels whenever it was needed.

Like many slash-and-burn agriculturalists, the Huron exhibited a marked preference for certain soil types.[10] In all, 94.5 percent of 139 known village sites occur on well-drained soils ranging from gravels to silt loams. Together these soils comprise 75 percent of Huronia. The soils preferred most were well-drained sandy loams, covering 40 percent of Huronia and having 68.5 percent of the sites. These were among the more fertile soils within the capabilities of the Huron digging-stick technology, but they tend to have a low moisture-holding capacity and are deficient in phosphorus, potassium and nitrogen. Once depleted through over-use, their recovery rate is extremely slow. A young secondary forest might take 30 to 60 years to become established; soil profile development takes more than 400 years. Although they are more fertile, silt and clay loams were generally avoided, probably because of their heavier forest growth, the Huron's lack of drainage techniques, and the fact that once these soils become dry they are extremely difficult to work with a digging stick.

Although certain species of trees were preferred as building material and firewood, macro-vegetational patterns seem to have no obvious relation to the distribution of village sites. Tree species commonly used were cedar, birch, elm, pine and oak and all five are widely distributed in Huronia. Cedar and elm bark were essential for the building of longhouses. Birch bark was used in small quantities for the manufacture of utensils and canoes and could be transported easily over some distance if it was scarce near a village.

Pine, a preferred source of resin, firewood and palisade posts is more common in the western end of Huronia, but there does not seem to be any obvious relationship between the location of village sites and the occurrence of stands of pine. Areas of pure pine were avoided, but this can be related to the coarse sands, gravels and lack of surface water in these areas. Oak is also concentrated on the droughtier soils in western Huronia, but apart from their acorns, which were eaten in times of famine, oaks did not have any particular value to the Huron.

Far more important than any single species or association of species, was the actual size composition of a particular timber stand. Huron technology was inadequate to cope with large trees, and the construction of Huron villages demanded enormous quantities of logs under twelve inches in diameter. The amount of wood needed for a large village of, for example, six acres, housing 1 000 people in 36 longhouses surrounded by a single palisade, can be roughly calculated:

Palisade — 3 600 posts, 5 ins. diameter, 30 ft. long
Longhouses (exterior walls) — 16 000 poles, 3–5 ins. diameter, 10–30 ft. long
Longhouses (interior support posts) — 250 posts, 10 ins. diameter, 15–20 ft. long
Longhouses (elm or cedar bark for roofing) — 162 000 sq. ft., 4 500 sq. ft. per longhouse

These estimates are conservative since most villages of this size had double- or triple-rowed palisades, and large villages of 15 acres such as Cahiague or St. Joseph had 80 to 120 longhouses with three- to five-rowed palisades. At Cahiague some 24 000 posts were used in the palisade alone. Even the bark for the longhouses could be obtained from small trees, since an elm or cedar ten inches in diameter could furnish a piece of bark 30 inches by at least five to eight feet. A mature forest might furnish enough building material if only the branches from large trees were used, but the job of first cutting down the large trees and then stripping them of their branches would be enormous, and the often crooked tree limbs were inferior to young trees and saplings as palisade and longhouse material. Moreover, the bark from a mature elm or cedar is difficult to remove and not very pliable. By necessity, therefore, the Huron located their villages in areas of secondary forest growth—areas of long-abandoned cornfields that contained a good stand of trees under twelve inches in diameter. Because Huronia was fairly densely settled and had been occupied by agriculturalists for several hundred years prior to the 17th century, there was probably no shortage of immature forest. Archaeological surveys in Huronia have often revealed pre-European village sites in close proximity to sites that were in existence during the French period. Many of the former pre-date the latter by 50 to 80 years, approximately the time required for the development of an immature forest cover.

The criteria by which the Huron chose a defensive position are more difficult to establish. Judging from statements made by the missionaries, the Huron made an effort to locate their villages on sites that had reasonably good natural defences such as a break-in-slope. However, Iroquois methods of warfare depended for their success not on a prolonged siege but rather on a surprise attack. A break-in-slope alone was no major obstacle to the successful conquest of a village. Protection required a palisade, and since not all villages were palisaded, one would suspect that many occurred on breaks-in-slope simply because a spring or creek happened to issue there. The absence of palisades at many otherwise defendable sites would tend to support this view. In general, only the largest villages and especially those of the historic period seem to have been located with an eye to defence. Villages such as Ossossane, Cahiague, St. Joseph, St. Louis and St. Ignace each have their natural defences developed to an unusually high degree; that is, breaks-in-slope occur on two or three sides of the village.

In summary, the ideal Huron village site seems to have been a fairly level area next to a permanent water supply with a large hinterland of sandy loams. A defendable position was desirable, but only a necessity in the case of the larger villages, which seemed to have acted as regional strongholds—places where people from the smaller villages could flee in times of enemy attack. Due to the difficulty of clearing a mature forest and because construction material was needed, the villages were placed in or near areas of young timber stands.

The Seasonal Cycle of Village Activities

The activities of Hurons in and around their villages, their interaction with their natural surroundings and their general spatial behaviour can be illustrated through a reconstruction of their seasonal round, beginning with the spring (figure 2).

Early in March, some of the men went deer hunting in places where deer had congregated to escape deep snow or where their movement had been impeded by the dangerous icy crusts that form on the snow in the late winter. On returning from the hunt, some of the men went fishing until the end of May to take advantage of the spring spawning runs. Small weedy bays, creeks, and rivers were closed off

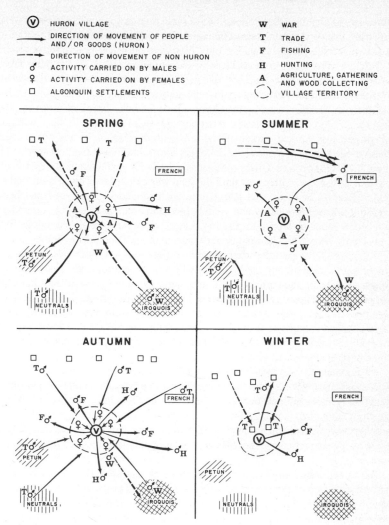

FIGURE 2   Spatial Aspects of the Huron Seasonal Cycle

with nets and weirs, and yielded pike (*Esox lucius*), walleye (*Stizostedion vitreum*) and sucker (*Catostomus commersonii*). Sturgeon (*Acipenser fulvescens*) and maskinonge (*Esox masquinongy*) were speared in shallow waters where they had come to lay their eggs. The fish were smoked or reduced to oil and stored in bark casks in the longhouses.

The first major task for the women in the early spring was to tap the maple trees for sap. Next the women tried to get in the season's supply of firewood, which was stored in and about the longhouses. At the same time as some of the women were gathering firewood, others helped the men who had stayed home from fishing to prepare the fields for planting. The old fields were burned over to remove weeds and the previous year's corn stalks. New clearings were made by the men. Trees were chopped down a few feet above the ground, some of the wood was taken away for firewood and the rest piled against the stumps and burned. The resulting ash was the only fertilizer used by the Huron. Once the heavy work of preparing the fields was completed, the women took over and began planting. In the new fields the ground was worked into small mounds with digging sticks and crude hoes. These mounds were as a rule about three feet across and four to five feet apart, with about 2 000 hills per acre. On the old fields the previous year's mounds were rebuilt and thus re-used year after year until the land was exhausted. Towards the end of May a handful of seeds was placed into each mound. All the seed had been carefully selected for quality and yield beforehand and was often pre-germinated in a bed of moist bark prior to planting. Later, when the corn was about one foot high, beans, squash and pumpkins were planted in the same hills with the corn.

Meantime, some men departed on raids against the New York Iroquois, while others left to trade among the Petun in the Collingwood hills, the Neutral in the Niagara Peninsula and various Algonquin bands along the shore of Georgian Bay and in the Lake Nipissing–upper Ottawa River area. The village chiefs designated a number of men to stay behind to protect the village from possible enemy raids. They engaged in summer fishing, odd jobs around the village and some work in the fields. If the Huron had news of a large impending raid, more men would stay home until the threat had passed.

Throughout the summer the women lived in the fields, hoeing the corn, pulling weeds and chasing pests from the crops. During this time, the village was virtually deserted. Keeping animals out of the fields was a particularly difficult job. Mice, raccoons and birds such as the grackle (*Quiscalus quiscula*), crow (*Corvus brachyrynchos*), sandhill crane (*Grus canadensis*) and blackbirds (*Euphagus carolinus*) were particularly troublesome and probably took up to 20 percent of the corn crop.

Their trade with the Algonquins complete by midsummer, Huron men began to make their way down the Ottawa to the French trading posts on the St. Lawrence, which were reached towards the end of July or early in August. Along the way, they ran the gauntlet of Iroquois war parties who were out to take captives and Huron furs. Back at home, small Iroquois war parties made surprise raids on unsuspecting women and children working in the fields, or men hunting and fishing away from the village. Similar raids were carried out by the Huron in the territory of their enemies.

Towards the end of August and through September, the corn was harvested by the women, dried, and stored in the longhouses. Average yields appear to have been in the order of 25 to 28 bushels per acre. Each family tried to plant enough corn to give them a return of about 9 bushels per person, which was enough to meet their yearly corn requirements.

Because they opened and then abandoned clearings in the forest, the Huron created a favourable habitat for a variety of fruit bearing plants. During the summer, especially June and July, adults and children gathered strawberries, raspberries, cherries and wild peas. These were dried and stored for the winter. Indian hemp (*Apocynum cannabium* and *A. androsaemifolium*) also grew as a weed on the abandoned fields and was used to make twine and fishnets. Clams, crabs and turtles were gathered in shallow waters throughout the summer, but none of the gathered produce figured very heavily in the Huron diet. It was a welcome supplement to the ubiquitous corn and fish soup.

Shortly after the harvest was complete, the men returned from trading and war. In late September, some departed again to go on the large autumn deer hunts. The most successful way of hunting deer was in organized mass drives in the acorn-producing areas of Southern Ontario, where the deer gathered for the rutting season. Apart from the late winter, this was the only time of the year that the Huron ate large amounts of meat. Because Huronia was densely settled and its game was much hunted, it was only in the late winter and fall that deer gathered in large enough numbers to make hunting worthwhile. Other sources of meat were dogs, bear and the occasional moose.

November, when the rutting season ended, was the best time of the year for fishing. The three most important fall fish were whitefish (*Coregonus culpeaformis*), lake trout (*Salvelinus namaycush*) and the cisco (*Coregonus artedii*). All three school in large numbers in shallow waters and are easily caught in seine nets and weirs. Trips were undertaken to the islands in Georgian Bay, and to the shores of Lakes Simcoe and Couchiching. The narrows between the latter two lakes were a particularly good place to fish. Weirs and nets blocked off the entire channel between the two lakes and villagers could easily take their winter's supply of fish in a few weeks. As in the spring, the fish were dried or smoked and stored in bark casks.

As a source of food, fishing had several advantages over hunting. Pound for pound, fish were more plentiful, easier to catch and more predictable in their habitat and habits than deer or moose. Moreover, fish could be dried and stored. There is no evidence that the Huron had the ability to preserve and store meat for any length of time. Meat was regarded as a feast food, and invariably eaten immediately after the animal was killed. Fish and corn were staples, while meat was a seasonal supplement. The Huron subsistence economy was an agriculturefishing complex rather than an agriculture–hunting complex.

During the late fall, various Algonquin bands settled near the Huron villages to spend the winter. The Nipissings usually settled in western Huronia and various Ottawa Valley Algonquins in the east. Similarly, the Cheveux-Relevés (Ottawas) wintered among the Petun. On their way to Huronia, the Algonquins would lay in a supply of fish and furs to barter for corn and other items such as fishnets. Much of Huron–Algonquin trade was probably carried out in the winter months. As soon as the ice was out of the lakes and streams in the spring, the Algonquins would again depart for the north.

By late November and early December, everyone was back in the village. This was a period for socializing. A variety of feasts took place to celebrate successes in the harvest, hunting, fishing and trading. These feasts were accompanied by gambling and gift exchanges. If war had been successful, captives were tortured to highlight the social activities. Few economic activities took place in the winter. Women wove mats, manufactured fishnets and prepared corn for the following season's trade, and there was some ice-fishing and trade with the Algonquins.

Roughly every eight to fifteen or more years this cycle of seasonal activities would be modified through village relocation. Prior to a move all the people who had died during the existence of the village would be buried in a large common grave during the great "feast-of-the-dead." Sometimes only one village was involved, but most commonly several villages would engage in these activities together. Relocation precipitated both social realignments, as larger villages were split up, and social reaffirmations, as smaller villages were temporarily united.

Village movement resulted from a combination of factors. Chief among these was soil depletion in the fields closest to the village and the resultant scattering of a limited number of women over a great number of small, family-sized corn patches spread across a large area. This also made the task of protecting fields from birds and animals more difficult. Iroquois raids were a constant summer threat; rarely were there enough Huron men near the villages to protect the women in the fields. As long as the women were within the shadow of the village they could flee there for protection. Once they moved away from the closest fields they could no longer be adequately guarded. The exhaustion of firewood within carrying distance of a village was another factor sometimes cited in village abandonment. Other causes were fires, fear of enemy attacks (especially on frontier villages) and internal social strife.

Social strife was probably the major reason why only a few villages exceeded populations of 1 000. Of 46 villages whose sizes are known, only nine were over six acres (circa 1 000 people) and only thirteen over five acres (circa 900 people). The majority of the villages were about four acres (circa 700 people) or less in size. From historical documents, one is led to the conclusion that the large villages had leaders of unusual abilities, leaders whose decisions were respected and followed. Since the Huron chiefs and councils did not have coercive institutions such as a police or army at their disposal, their decisions were only followed if they met with village approval. Dissenting village factions could, and did, move out of villages and erect their own. By the time villages neared populations of 1 000, they were difficult to control and usually split into two or more smaller villages, unless a person or persons of unusual ability could prevent serious village strife and keep the village together.

The successive movement of villages is extremely difficult to trace. Only three historical cases are known and in no case was the new site more than three miles from the old. The Huron only moved far enough to find fresh soils, firewood and building materials. If palisade posts and houses from the old site were still useable, these were taken along.

Modification of the Natural Environment

As agriculturalists, the Huron changed the natural environment they occupied, but none of these changes was long lasting. Large clearings were created with the axe and fire, and planted with corn. Abandoned fields were colonized by grasses, shrubs and finally by trees, only to be removed again as the agricultural cycle was repeated. Soils were depleted of nutrients and there was some soil erosion. The beaver population was decimated in and about Huronia as a result of the fur trade, and deer were more plentiful outside the area than within it. In the 170 years between the final dispersal of the Huron by the Iroquois in 1649, and the beginning of European settlement in 1820, however, a closed forest was re-established over Huronia. Few visible remnants of the Huron corn fields remained.[11] The beaver colonies and deer returned so quickly that forty years after the Huron occupation the Iroquois were using the area as a hunting ground. The only remnants of the former village sites visible in the present landscape are small ash deposits marking Huron middens or refuse dumps, and a surface scatter of broken pottery. Soil analysis reveals considerably higher concentrations of phosphorus, magnesium, calcium and other elements in the top 20 inches of the soil profiles of village sites than in those of natural soils in the area, but these concentrations have had no visible effect on present vegetation patterns.[12] In valleys adjacent to some of the larger villages there is evidence of soil erosion caused by the Indian presence, but today it is detectable only through soil analysis.[13] The original impact of the Huron on the landscape they inhabited lasted only as long as it took the forest to reclaim the abandoned villages and cornfields. At most this took about 100 years.

Conclusions

The spatial behaviour and annual cycle of activities of the Huron were more or less what one would expect from a society with a subsistence technology such as theirs. They reflect an intimate knowledge of, and close adjustment to, the natural environment, an adjustment shaped largely by the technological and sociological aspects of Huron culture. Huron technology limited Huron agriculture to certain soil types; Huron social organization and values determined the patterns of fields and the work in them. Together these cultural factors exposed limitations in the natural environment that resulted in declining yields over time, fuel exhaustion and village relocation, limitations that could have been avoided with a readjustment of social values and technology.

Huron technology applied to fishing and fish preservation was considerably more efficient than hunting. Due to the limitations in the carrying capacity of the physical environment, it is difficult to see how yields of hunted meat could have been very much improved. Preservation techniques could have assured a more even yearly meat supply but this would have necessitated not only a change in technology, but also a change in cultural attitudes which regarded meat primarily as a feast food. The lack of potential domesticates in the area (except the turkey) precluded the invention of a mixed farm economy.

Huron technology severely limited the society in its choice of building materials. Until the introduction of the iron axe, the Huron had no means of coping with a mature forest. If large trees were chopped down there was no method by which they could be utilized. Technological limitations in the use of building materials, the Huron agricultural system and endemic warfare resulted in transitory villages that were regularly shifted and rebuilt.

In the main, the Huron occupied and moved within a tightly circumscribed territory. In this they were similar to other shifting cultivators. Most of the women never left Huronia or even their tribal district. A few accompanied the men on hunting and fishing expeditions as far as 50 miles or so from their village. Only a few men travelled any great distances. Before the French contact period, some men went approximately 300 miles from Huronia to trade or fight. But for them, Huron contact was limited to those who came to the Huron villages. First-hand knowledge of other tribes was largely confined to those that bordered Huronia. After French contact, however, Huron traders travelled 600 miles or more to the St. Lawrence and intercourse with foreign tribes broadened extensively in all directions.

For all the apparent limitations of Huron technology, this group operated a very efficient subsistence economy that allowed them to achieve population densities ranging from a low of 50 to 60 people per square mile in eastern and western Huronia, to 150 people per square mile in areas of central Huronia. If only arable soils are taken into account, densities ranged up to 230 people per square mile. The factors responsible for this were first, a highly developed form of corn cultivation, involving intensive care of the fields by closely co-operating groups of women, and secondly, a highly developed fishing technology. The most serious limitations in an otherwise bountiful environment were the modestly fertile soils and the slow soil recovery rates. Yet there was enough land to ensure that these soil conditions did not hinder agricultural efficiency or restrict the movement of the villages. Only about 40 percent of the arable soils in Huronia were in use at any one time (fields and fallow); the rest was in forest.

In 1650, the Huron disappeared as a viable cultural group. Their failure lay not in their subsistence economy or in any known environment constraints. Ravaged by epidemic diseases, especially the smallpox attacks in the 1630s that cut their population by at least 60 percent, and hampered by an inefficient political system, they could not meet the challenges posed by European cultural values and the Iroquois armies. Like so many other North American Indian groups, they finally ceased to exist.

Notes

1. C.E. Heidenreich, "Maps Relating to the First Half of the 17th Century and their Use in Determining the Location of Jesuit Missions in Huronia," *The Cartographer* 3, 2 (1966): 103–26; National Archives of Canada, Map Division, Ottawa.

2. R.G. Thwaites, ed., *The Jesuit Relations and Allied Documents*, 73 vols. (New York, 1959); P.J. Robinson and J.B. Conacher, *Du Creux: History of Canada or New France*, 2 vols. (Toronto, 1951–1952).

3. H.P. Biggar, ed., *The Works of Samuel de Champlain*, 6 vols. (Toronto, 1922–1926).

4. G.M. Wrong, ed., *Sagard: The Long Journey to the Country of the Hurons* (Toronto, 1939).

5. J.G. Shea, ed., *Le Clercq: First Establishment of the Faith in New France*, 2 vols. (New York, 1881).

6. W.M. Hurley and C.E. Heidenreich, "Palaeoecology and Ontario Prehistory," Research Report nos. 1 and 2 (Department of Anthropology, University of Toronto, 1969, 1971); C.E. Heidenreich, *Huronia: A History and Geography of the Huron Indians, 1600–1650* (Toronto, 1973).

7. B.G. Trigger, *The Huron: Farmers of the North* (New York, 1969); B.G. Trigger, *The Children of Aataentsic*, 2 vols. (Montreal, 1976); Heidenreich, *Huronia*.

8. Hurley and Heidenreich, "Palaeoecology and Ontario History," Research Report nos. 1 and 2.

9. C.T. Bishop, *Great Lakes Water Levels: A Review for Coastal Engineering Design*, National Water Research Institute, Environment Canada, no. 87-18 (Burlington, 1987).

10. J.G. Cruickshank and C.E. Heidenreich, "Pedological Investigations at the Huron Indian Village of Cahiague," *The Canadian Geographer* 13, 1 (1969): 34–46.

11. C.E. Heidenreich, "A Relict Indian Cornfield near Creemore, Ontario," *The Canadian Geographer* 18, 4 (1974): 379–94.

12. C.E. Heidenreich and S. Navratil, "Soil Analysis at the Robitaille Site: Determining the Perimeter of the Village," *Ontario Archeology* no. 20 (1973): 25–32.

13. Cruickshank and Heidenreich, "Pedological Investigations"; Hurley and Heidenreich, "Palaeoecology and Ontario Prehistory," Research Report no. 2.

INDIAN MAP-MAKING: TWO EXAMPLES FROM THE FUR TRADE WEST*

D. WAYNE MOODIE

Map-making is among the oldest of the graphic arts and appears to have preceded writing in most of the early cultures for which any significant knowledge has survived. Insofar as the North American record allows, it would seem to have been a well-established art among most, if not all, of the native peoples of this continent on the eve of European contact. Clearly, this was the case in Western Canada, as is evident in the relatively large number of maps drawn by Indians for the early explorers, fur traders and other Europeans who were among the first to travel in the vast uncharted spaces of the West.

Unfortunately, very few of the maps actually drawn by Indians have survived. Rather, most of the artifactual evidence for Indian cartography has been preserved in the form of copies of Indian maps made by Europeans. This is hardly surprising, as most Indian maps were sketched on the ground or in the snow. Indians also drew maps on other media, such as bark, skins and even paper, but almost all of the maps of this nature known from historical accounts have been lost. The graphical evidence for Indian map-making is thus largely confined to the charts that Europeans found of sufficient interest or value to copy and preserve. Although some of these maps may have been altered or influenced in different ways by the Europeans who solicited or copied them, they can with little qualification be considered as bona fide examples of Indian map-making.

In Western Canada, most of the maps of Indian origin that have survived were copied by servants of the Hudson's Bay Company and are preserved today in the

* Association of Canadian Map Libraries and Archives, *Bulletin* 55 (June 1985): 32–43. The author gratefully acknowledges the assistance and advice given to him by Dr. Alan Catchpole, Department of Geography, University of Manitoba, in the course of writing this paper. Acknowledgements are also owing to the Hudson's Bay Company Archives, Provincial Archives of Manitoba, for permission to consult their records and to publish the two Indian maps presented here. It should be pointed out that both maps have been redrafted and re-arranged from the originals for legibility and to fit the format required for publication.

Hudson's Bay Company Archives, Winnipeg. As a group, they bespeak an impressive knowledge of geography among the nomadic Indian nations of the West, and a well-developed ability to convey this knowledge to others in cartographic form. In communicating geographical information in map form, the Indians performed a fundamental, if still largely unappreciated, role in facilitating European travel and expansion, not only in the West, but also in other unexplored or little known parts of the continent. This paper examines two such maps which in different ways contributed to European exploration and map-making in the western interior of the continent. Known as the Cot aw ney yaz zah and Ak ko mok ki maps, after the Chipewyan and Blackfoot Indians who drew them for the Hudson's Bay Company fur trader and surveyor, Peter Fidler, they are also representative of the two major types of Indian maps: general or area maps, and route maps. Area maps were drawn to depict the geography of a region and generally portray those features of the area deemed distinctive or significant by the map-maker. Route maps, in contrast, were drawn specially to make a section of country navigable to the map user. Only the features of the route thought to be essential to the intending traveller are shown. All else is generally omitted as extraneous or as clutter irrelevant to, or detracting from, the purpose of the map. By contrast with maps drawn in the European tradition, which include as many features as can possibly be shown at a given scale, both types of Indian maps appear as simple, unelaborated sketches.

This contrast reflects the circumstances in which Indian maps were most often employed. Sketched to aid navigation or to clarify the character of a particular territory, their creation was accompanied by verbal descriptions, and even dialogues, among those involved about the nature of the country being mapped. The maps were mnemonic devices, graphic displays that reinforced and made more memorable the verbal accounts. They were spatial schema to be fixed in the mind of the map user and to be recalled when the occasion demanded.

The Cot aw ney yaz zah map depicts a route across almost three hundred miles of complex, Canadian Shield country (figure 1). Despite the maze of lakes and streams in the area it covers, the map shows no details of the landscape other than those necessary to navigate by canoe from the Churchill River to Lake Athabasca. Cot aw ney yaz zah not only confined his mapping to the route, but drew only those features of it that he considered necessary for successful navigation. Of all the details on the map, only three trading posts—two on present Cree Lake, and the other on Weitzel Lake—are irrelevant to its way-finding purpose. They were almost certainly included at the request of Peter Fidler, who was interested in learning of the activities of rival fur traders from Montreal in this region.

One of the most distinctive cartographic properties of Indian maps is their treatment of scale. Shape is generally well preserved, but scale frequently varies greatly from one part of the map to another. This has often been described as a defect in Indian map-making attributable to the lack of survey instruments. Certainly the preservation of true scale on maps drawn from memory and embracing hundreds and often thousands of square miles was impossible. Nonetheless, many Indian maps show relatively constant scale over huge areas, and most scale variations

FIGURE 1   The Cot aw nez yaz zah Map. The water route from Lake Athabasca to the mouth of the Deers River.

SOURCE: Redrawn from Public Archives of Manitoba, HBC Archives E3/4 fo 14d. Courtesy of G.J. Matthews.

'Days going down from Indian to Black Lake
ever ascend it in Canoes so very rapids —
So from Black ¦ Lake¦ 1 Day & arrive at mouth of the
river B & so up it 6 Days & carry into Trout
Lake — being much the first way — The
Trout river is remarkably crooked but
large Current. — No Carrying places in the
Indian River. B ul ti ah wooz ze dey za
1 Day from mouth of Trout river to
Black Lake; against the Current.

Drawn by Cot. aw ney yaz zah.
a Young Man. Ispowyan July 17: 1810

within them reflect purposeful distortions, rather than inadequate knowledge or
faulty memory. Not only was the Indian draftsman unfettered by the European
concept of a constant scale but, as is clearly evident in the Cot aw ney yaz zah map,
he manipulated it to suit his purposes. Viewed in this way, the flexible use of scale
can be seen as a great strength of Indian map-making, and not the fundamental
weakness that a purely Eurocentric view implies.

The overall scale of the Cot aw nez yaz zah map is consistent with that of a
modern survey map. Yet there are great variations in scale within the Cot aw nez
yaz zah chart. The most conspicuous of these occurs in the section of the route
between the Churchill River and Cree Lake. The distance up the present Mudjatik

River from the Churchill River to Loon Mud Lake is very much condensed on the Cot aw nez yaz zah map, although the small lines or strokes across this stretch of the Mudjatik River indicate seven days' travel time to ascend to Loon Mud Lake. As there was little possibility of error in navigating this section of the route, it was given little prominence in the map. In contrast, the relatively short stretch of country between the upper waters of the Mudjatik River and Cree/Indian Lake was the most critical and potentially confusing section of the entire route. It entailed a complex set of portages following small streams and lakes to cross the height of land between waters flowing into Hudson Bay and those draining into the Arctic Ocean. This is clearly shown on the map by drawing the connecting rivers, lakes and portages at a scale many times larger than that used in the map as a whole. Thus, Cot aw nez yaz zah adjusted the scale to suit his purposes and was able to construct a single chart that provided all the information necessary for navigation in a simple but memorable manner.

Cot aw nez yaz zah's intimate knowledge, but highly selective portrayal, of the hydrography of the region is further manifest in his depiction of the streams to be followed in travelling between Cree Lake and Lake Athabasca. Fidler's written directions relating to this section of the map were undoubtedly added to his copy from the descriptions given him by Cot aw nez yaz zah. They indicate that the route from Cree Lake is down the Cree River to Black Lake and that, despite the great distance to Black Lake, this part of the route can be travelled in one day because of the swift current in the Cree River. Significantly, the directions also state that the traveller is not to ascend the Cree River in returning to Cree Lake. Rather the return journey is to follow the series of small streams and lakes that Cot aw nez yaz zah has elaborated to the west of Cree River. Such an alternative route was a common feature of Indian travel, and is known in the Cree language as an *otahkwahikan*, which might best be translated into English as a "backway,"[1] Generally otahkwahikan offered less difficult passages, by avoiding rapids or other navigational dangers, or routes that could be travelled more quickly. Here Cot aw nez yaz zah has shown what might be called a double backway, and has greatly increased the scale of this sector of his map to clarify the connections and portages required to follow it. So the returning traveller is directed to leave the swiftly flowing Cree River just south of Black Lake to travel west up the smaller, more gently flowing Pipestone River. Because the Pipestone River is "crooked" and therefore consuming of travel time, a second backway is to be followed by Hunter Creek. The traveller is then to follow the succession of lakes, creeks and portages that Cot aw nez yaz zah has been at pains to elaborate to eventually reach the northwest shore of Cree Lake. Thus, despite his obviously detailed knowledge of the country, this Chipewyan Indian cartographer depicted only the information that he regarded as essential for successful travel. He also skilfully and accurately accomplished this task by manipulating scale in a manner foreign to European cartography but admirably suited to his task.

The Ak ko mok ki map depicts a huge portion of Western North America extending from the Red Deer River of Alberta in the north to the Rattlesnake Mountains of Central Wyoming in the south, and encompassing the western half of the continent between the Big Bend of the Missouri River in the east and the shores of the Pacific Ocean in the west (figure 2). The most ambitious of several maps that Ak ko mok ki drew for Fidler while the latter was stationed at Chester-field House on the South Saskatchewan River, it depicts an area of approximately 1 000 000 square miles. It is a remarkable testament to the geographical knowledge of the native peoples of the plains that this Blackfoot Indian Chief was able, at the request of a fur trader, to conceive of and sketch out the main features of an area similar to that of Western Europe in extent.

The major scale variation on the Ak ko mok ki map occurs along the line of the Rocky Mountains. The country lying to the west of the Rockies has been greatly reduced in width compared to the area of plains environment shown to the east. In consequence, as comparison with any modern map will reveal, the east–west dimension of Ak ko mok ki's map is significantly distorted. The only other scale variation of note occurs within the plains section of the map. The grasslands to the north of the Missouri River have been drawn at a larger scale than those to the south, and have thus been given more prominence on the map. Otherwise, scale is well preserved and relative distances between locational features display little distortion.

The Ak ko mok ki map is centred upon the line of the Missouri River and, perhaps at Fidler's request, elaborates the entire drainage network of the river from its sources in the Rockies to its Big Bend in North Dakota. In the north, it shows the height of land separating the waters of the Missouri, which flow into the Gulf of Mexico, from those draining into Hudson Bay via the headwater tributaries of the South Saskatchewan River. It also identifies the most remarkable mountain features that occur along the eastern flank of the Rockies. In addition, most of the hill lands and mountain outliers that extend into the plains to the east are shown, and are well placed in relation to the Rocky Mountain front and the drainage network of the plains.

In contrast to his depiction of the plains, Ak ko mok ki's rendition of the much greater expanse of country between the Rockies and the Pacific affords little detail and is severely reduced in scale. Whether this was a matter of choice or a reflection of more limited knowledge of this complex region is unknown but the latter seems more likely. Other than the coastline and the eastern limits of the Rockies, the only landscape features shown in this area are the two rivers traversing the country between the Rockies and the sea. The northernmost of these is identified as the Big River, which is most likely the Columbia River, the largest stream draining to the Pacific in this region. The other, which is described as the Red Deers River, is probably the Snake River, which is a south bank tributary of the Columbia. Ak ko mok ki was probably familiar with the headwater region of the Snake, but on his map he has erroneously shown the river as flowing directly into the Pacific. Although Ak ko mok ki would have known much more about the country to the west of the Rockies than is shown on his map, this confusion, together with the highly schematic manner in which the rivers are drawn, suggest that his knowledge of the region was limited and that this influenced, at least in part, both the detail and scale of his mapping of this area.

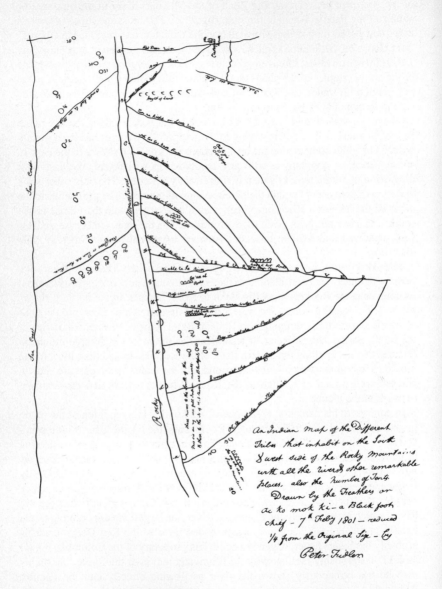

FIGURE 2   The Ak ko mok ki Map

SOURCE: Redrawn from Public Archives of Manitoba, HBC Archives G 1/25.
Courtesy of G.J. Matthews.

Explanation   Tents

1 Cho. que – Mud House Indians — 150
4 Sip. pe tā ke – The wrinkled Indians 90
2 Is sap poo – Crow mountain Indians 200
5 Kix tā ka tap pee – Beaver Indians 50
3 Ams cope sox sue – Sessew's Ind⁰ –70
6 Cho. que. they go to war with N°1 –160
7 Nee koo chis ak kā – Tattoo'd Inds –80
8 Sin ne po tup pe — Grey Fox Inds –40
9 Ke ta Kap sum – Garter Inds – 30
10 So hoo is too ye – Hairy or Beard Inds –50
11 Ak ken nix sa tuppee   40
13 Oo aps sex sa tuppee–Thigh Inds — 20
12 Pik et a tuppee – Rib Inds ——100
14 Oc sa tup pee – Scabby Inds ——100
15 Mak que a tuppee – Wolf Inds —— 200
16 Mak ta yo que – Grass Tent Ind —180
17 Mem me ow you – Fish eating Ind — 20
18 Ne chick a pā soy – a Particular root – 60
19 Nis che tap pe — Wood Indians ——100
20 Sox sue chicks sin na tappee–Sussew Snake Inds. 50
21 Poo can nam a tappee — Pearl shell Inds 70
22 Six too k tappee – Black Inds — 200
23 Cut tux pee too pin — Flatt heads — 50
24 Cum mun na tappee Blue Mud Ind. 60
25 Ap pa tuppee – Ermin or White Inds 80
32 Pun nus pee tup pin – Long hair Inds 100
27 Ac cook sa tappee — Padling Inds – 80
26 To kee pee tup pee – those that collect shells
28 at cha tappee – Snair Indians — 18
29 Cut tux in nā mi – Weak bow Inds —18
30 Patch now ———————— 10
31 Cotton nā ————————— 22

Explanation

a Devils head – or Omoch cow wat che mooks as o'd
B King – Wini made tok zue.
C Heart – us te chip.
D Pop – Cut to yio.
Y Bears Tooth – ki as te kid
E the Belt – Ma-pis, sees it k g:
26 the Rattle – owwan nax.
Y the Heart – us te chik.
S Snow mountain – Com is tak.
K Bad mountain – Pauk sis tok zue.
L Bulls nose – Sommis mook sis sa zue.
M the Owl head – see pis too tuck caw

B to C ——— 2   numberg
C to D ——— 5   nights
D to Y ——— 3   the snos
Y to E ——— 3   stops w
E to 26 ——— 1
26 to Y ——— 1   going from
Y to S ——— 2   one place
S to K ——— 1   to the
K to L ——— 5   other.
L to M ——— 9

These are remarkable & high places at the mountain that the Indians fancy has the same appearance as the names given.

From a to M 33 Days walk for young man, no Blackfeet has been there, only a chance Fall Indian, that has been that great Distance.

The Mountain to the South of the Missoury River inclines almost East – or between E & S & is considerably lower & not so far across as in Lat. 53° to 49°

Even in the plains area, the map embraces a far greater sweep of country than Ak ko mok ki appears to have visited. In one of several annotations on the map Fidler indicated that young men required 33 days to walk from A to N, the full north–south extension of the map along the line of the Rockies, and added that "no Blackfoot has been there, only a chance Fall Indian has been there." Elsewhere on the map Fidler noted that "these rivers to the South of Mis sis ou ry are Fall Indian names & those to N[orth] are Blackfoot." These two comments suggest that the Blackfoot, and Ak ko mok ki in particular, were not as familiar with the country to the south of the Missouri as that to the north. At this time, all of the Blackfoot tribes, or the Blood, Piegan and Blackfoot proper, lived and hunted to the north of the Missouri River.

Blackfoot Indians did, to be sure, journey to the south of the Missouri occasionally. Fidler's own earlier journal of exploration indicates that the Piegan, the southernmost of the Blackfoot tribes, travelled considerable distances south of the river on trading, warfare and horse-stealing expeditions. And the Blackfoot proper were part of a war party that, in the autumn of 1800, travelled south of the Missouri and into the Rocky Mountains in search of their enemies, the Snake Indians. The route taken by this expedition is shown in Fidler's notebook copy of Ak ko mok ki's map, suggesting that Ak ko mok ki himself had taken part in this campaign.[2] But Ak ko mok ki's depiction of the war track makes it apparent that these warriors penetrated no more than seventy-five miles south of the Missouri to the Musselshell River of Western Montana.

The Blackfoot proper, or the Siksika as they called themselves, were the most northerly of the Blackfoot tribes and, for this reason, were probably not as familiar with the country to the south as were the Blood and especially the Piegan. Because Ak ko mok ki identified the rivers to the south of the Missouri by their Fall Indian names, it seems reasonable to assume that much of his knowledge of this country was communicated to him by the Fall Indians, who were also known to the fur traders as Gros Ventres, but called themselves Atsina. They bordered upon the Blackfoot to the south and east and, at the beginning of the nineteenth century, were middlemen in the trade with plains peoples such as the Arapahoe to the south.[3]

Indian maps have usually been described as cognitive maps based upon personal observation and travel, but these details indicate that Ak ko mok ki was capable of mapping large areas of which he had no experience and in which he had not travelled. Ak ko mok ki was clearly able to take knowledge communicated to him by neighbouring Atsina Indians, probably using maps as well as verbal descriptions, and to integrate it into his own perceptual framework derived from observation to produce the map that Fidler copied.

Taken as a whole, this map is one of the most impressive surviving examples of a general or area map constructed by North American Indians. Sketched from memory, integrating information from his own travels with that provided by others, and abstracting only the main identifying features of the landscape to provide a rational ordering of the geography of 300 000 square miles of the western plains, Ak ko mok ki's map was a remarkable achievement that testifies to an outstanding ability to represent, not just the features that establish the spatial sequence of a route, but the basic geographical organization of an entire landscape, with each identifying component placed in its proper relative position within the whole.

In addition to portraying the main hydrographic framework of the region and its most remarkable topographic features, the Ak ko mok ki map also identifies the different native peoples inhabiting this huge area and provides a census of their numbers. It shows the locations of over thirty different Indian nations as perceived by the Blackfoot and Atsina Indians. Estimates of the populations of almost all these peoples are given in terms of the number of tents or lodges comprising each group. Of the thirty-one different peoples identified, only two had visited Hudson's Bay Company trading posts before 1801.

Finally, the Ak ko mok ki map highlights the importance of the Indian in expediting European exploration, mapping and geographical expansion on the continent. Drawn for Fidler in February of 1801, it was dispatched to England in the summer of 1802. Together with Fidler's report and other Indian maps, it arrived in London on the Hudson's Bay Company's ship *King George* on 23 October. Shortly thereafter it was in the hands of the London cartographer, Aaron Arrowsmith. On 17 December, the Hudson's Bay Company secretary wrote to both the Admiralty and the Royal Society informing them that the Arrowsmith firm considered the Indian maps sent by Fidler "important in ascertaining, with some degree of certainty, the sources of the Missisoury." He also observed that they "convey much curious information respecting the face of many countries unknown to Europeans."[4]

The information on the Ak ko mok ki map enabled Arrowsmith to publish the first map containing an outline of the Missouri drainage system. This information appeared almost immediately on the 1802 edition of his map of British North America, and was of more than academic interest in the United States. American President Thomas Jefferson, and his Secretary of State, Albert Gallatin, had long regarded the Missouri River as a potential pathway to American empire in the Pacific Northwest, but virtually nothing was known of the course of the river beyond its Big Bend in present North Dakota. Its portrayal for the first time on the 1802 Arrowsmith map was timely indeed, for by 1803 Jefferson had negotiated the Louisiana Purchase. In 1804, he dispatched Lewis and Clark on the first government expedition to explore the Louisiana Territory along the line of the Missouri River. Not only did the Ak ko mok ki map help fuel the American design to expand into the Pacific Northwest, but as depicted on the 1802 Arrowsmith map, it was also the only cartographic guide available to Lewis and Clark when they set out from St. Louis in 1804 to follow the Missouri River to its sources in the Rocky Mountains.[5]

Notes

1. David H. Pentland, "Cartographic Concepts of the Northern Algonquians," *The Canadian Geographer* 12 (1975): 158.

2. For an account of these events, as well as additional information on Ak ko mok ki, see Judith Beattie, "Indian Maps in the Hudson's Bay Company Archives: A Comparison of Five Area Maps Recorded by Peter Fidler, 1801–1802," *Archivaria* 21 (1985–1986): 166–75 (an earlier version of which was presented at the 11th International Conference on the History of Cartography, Ottawa, 8–12 July 1985 as "The Indian Maps Recorded by Peter Fidler, 1801–1810"). For a comprehensive analysis and identification of the individual features shown on the Ak ko mok ki map, see D.W. Moodie and Barry Kaye, "The Ak ko mok ki Map," *The Beaver* (Spring 1977): 4–15.

3. The Ak ko mok ki map is one of the few historical documents that records the Atsina language, which is preserved in the names of the south bank tributaries of the Missouri, communicated to Fidler by Ak ko mok ki.

4. Alice M. Johnson, ed., *Saskatchewan Journals and Correspondence* (London, 1967), 319n–320n.

5. D.W. Moodie, "Indian Maps," Plate 59 of *From the Beginning to 1800,* vol. 1 of *Historical Atlas of Canada,* ed. R.C. Harris (Toronto, University of Toronto Press, 1987), includes copies of both these maps, with a third by Ki oo cus (1802) and a map of Western North America showing the approximate areas covered by the Indian maps.

DIFFUSION OF DISEASES IN THE WESTERN INTERIOR OF CANADA, 1830–1850*

ARTHUR J. RAY

Much has been written about the effects of certain European diseases, most notably smallpox, on Indian populations; yet few scholars have attempted to assess the impact that a series of epidemics had on Indian life in various areas of North America. According to the anthropologist John C. Ewers, the paucity of such studies has probably led scholars to underestimate the havoc that diseases wrought. He contends that scholars should consider the cumulative effects that these visitations of death had on population trends, band sizes and structures, tribal movements, balances of power, and the customs of Indians.[1] For most areas of North America, however, before these questions can be dealt with effectively the historical record must be examined to construct an inventory of diseases. Also, the geography of epidemics must be worked out in as much detail as possible to determine the frequency with which diseases occurred regionally, the origins and patterns of dispersals of the various epidemics, and the diffusion processes that produced these spatial patterns. This paper focuses on a portion of the Western Interior of Canada between 1830 and 1850 and attempts to achieve these latter objectives. It should also illustrate the type of work that can be done and should be a useful building block for further studies in the historical population geography of western Canada.

The area chosen for examination comprises the former Northern Department of the Hudson's Bay Company. This department covered a vast territory and was

* *Geographical Review* 66 (April 1976): 139–57. The author wishes to thank the Hudson's Bay Company for permitting him to consult and quote from its microfilm collection in the Public Archives of Canada, in Ottawa; the Canada Council, for defraying his travel and research expenses; and C.F. Godfrey, M.D. and the late Andrew H. Clark, for their comments and suggestions on earlier drafts of this paper. He would also like to thank the York University cartographic office, particularly Robert P. Ryan, for drafting the maps.

divided into eighteen districts for administrative convenience (figure 1). The physical and cultural geography of the department was highly varied. The central and southern portions of the Red River, Swan River, and Saskatchewan districts were grassland areas, home of nomadic, bison-hunting Indian groups such as the Blackfoot, Plains Assiniboine, Cree, and Ojibwa. Arching from the east bank of the Red River northwestward across the northern sections of the Swan River and Saskatchewan districts was a transitional vegetational zone known as the parklands. Here prairie meadows were interspersed with sections of woodlands. The vast boreal forests of the subarctic stretched east of Lake Winnipeg and north of the Swan River and Saskatchewan River districts. These lands were inhabited by Woodland Indians such as the Ojibwa, Cree, Assiniboine, and Chipewyan. In the northern section of the Churchill District and the northeastern portion of the Great Slave District, the forest yielded to open tundra. This region came to be known as

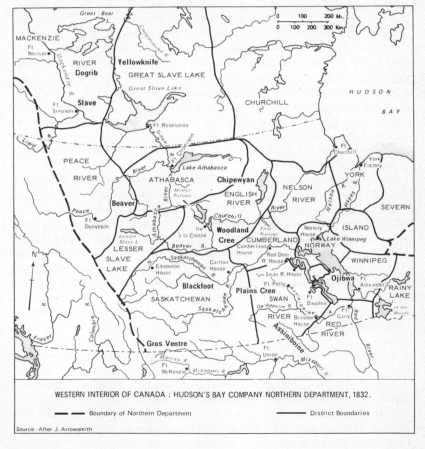

WESTERN INTERIOR OF CANADA : HUDSON'S BAY COMPANY NORTHERN DEPARTMENT, 1832.

▬ ▬ Boundary of Northern Department   ▬▬▬ District Boundaries

Source : After J. Arrowsmith

FIGURE 1

the barren lands. An analysis of the diffusion of diseases in the Northern Department thus affords an opportunity to consider how a variety of physical and cultural ecological factors may have influenced patterns of dispersal.

Population movements significantly affected the spread of disease (figure 2). In the Saskatchewan, Swan River, and Red River districts, Plains Indians such as the Assiniboine, Cree, and Ojibwa passed the winters in the sheltered river valleys and forested portions of the parklands. They spent the summers in the open grasslands, hunting the massive bison herds and travelling south to trade with horticultural Indians and American Fur Company traders in the Missouri River valley. Their Woodland Cree, Ojibwa, and Assiniboine relatives inhabited the woodlands during the warmer months of the year but often joined the Plains groups in the parklands during the middle and late winter in order to hunt bison.[2] Large-scale seasonal shifts of population also took place in the vicinity of the boreal forest–tundra zone, where bands of Chipewyan Indians followed the migratory barren-ground caribou. These caribou passed the summer grazing in the open tundra and retreated to the shelter of the northern edges of the forest in winter.

The spatial concentration of Indian populations also varied seasonally. In all areas Indian groups came together in the summer to form large villages. In the woodlands, fishing encampments of two or three hundred were common; in the grasslands, bison camps of one to four thousand were frequently reported. In the grassland and woodland areas, the Indians dispersed into smaller bands during the winter. These bands varied greatly in size depending on local resources. In the woodlands they often consisted of twenty to thirty individuals; in the parklands some camps of up to a thousand people were reported, but most were probably much smaller.[3]

Many non-Indian inhabitants of the Northern Department were also highly mobile. Hudson's Bay Company posts were linked together by boat, canoe, and cart brigades largely manned by Métis (figure 2). Although letters were exchanged among traders via the so-called winter express, there were relatively few couriers and the possibility of disease transmission during the winter was limited. Almost all traffic between posts occurred during the summer. But with spring breakup, boat brigades were usually dispatched from the various district headquarters to Norway House and/or to York Factory. The latter was the chief port of entry for the Northern Department and a terminal point for brigades of the Rainy Lake, Winnipeg, Island, Swan River, and Cumberland districts. Traffic volume peaked between mid-June and mid-August and was heaviest between York Factory and Norway House because of the key functions they served in the trading network. These two posts also had frequent contacts with the Red River Colony in the vicinity of Fort Garry.

Because of the relatively short open-water season, boat transport operated on a tight schedule and every effort was made to avoid delays. The late dispatch of a brigade often meant that a district ran the risk of not receiving critical winter supplies. This was particularly the case with more northerly Mackenzie River and Great Slave Lake districts, where brigades often did not complete their return voyage until late autumn or early winter.

In southern Manitoba and the adjacent portions of Saskatchewan, the Red River cart brigades carried a considerable volume of trade between the various posts during the summer season. These cart trains, consisting of horse-drawn two-wheeled carts, followed well-established routes (figure 2) and played an increasingly important role in the company's transport business as time passed.

In short, during the period between 1830 and 1850 there was a considerable amount of interaction among the populations of the various sections of the

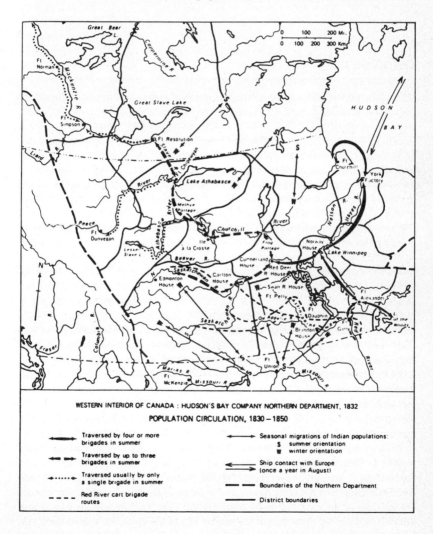

WESTERN INTERIOR OF CANADA : HUDSON'S BAY COMPANY NORTHERN DEPARTMENT, 1832

POPULATION CIRCULATION, 1830 – 1850

←→ Traversed by four or more brigades in summer	←— Seasonal migrations of Indian populations: **S** summer orientation **W** winter orientation
←🢒 Traversed by up to three brigades in summer	← Ship contact with Europe → (once a year in August)
•••••→ Traversed usually by only a single brigade in summer	— — Boundaries of the Northern Department
– – – Red River cart brigade routes	—— District boundaries

FIGURE 2

Northern Department. This interaction was facilitated by the migratory habits of certain Indian groups, by their trade at Hudson's Bay Company posts, and by the movement of men and material between the various posts by boat, canoe, and Red River cart. Furthermore, there was a marked seasonality to these patterns of interaction. Interregional Indian–European and Indian–Indian contacts were all more intensive during the summer, and the possibilities of transmitting diseases were therefore greatest at that time.

Influenza

During the period under consideration, a series of major and minor outbreaks of contagious diseases occurred.[4] Epidemics of influenza, most frequently reported, were recorded in 1835, 1837, 1843, 1845, 1847, and 1850. Influenza is a viral infection, with an incubation period of one to four days. Symptoms vary, but individuals generally experience a fever during the first twenty-four hours and suffer from inflammation of the respiratory and/or alimentary canal. General body aches and weakness are common. Significantly, since the disease usually affects primarily the respiratory passages, the first appearance of the illness may lead an untrained observer to diagnose it as a bad cold.

The influenza epidemic of 1835 was first reported almost simultaneously at Norway House and York Factory (figure 3). The journal entry for Norway House for June 22 reads, "Several of the people laid up with a most severe cold." The following day, Don Ross, chief trader at the post, added, "The whole establishment...[was] much afflicted with sickness, somewhat resembling a cold but of a much more serious nature."[5] On the 26th, the disease was said to be spreading in every direction. On June 29, Ross wrote, "We are all severely affected with the prevailing sickness, Influenza, no one escapes it: there are now upwards of 120 individuals young and old, including Indians, labouring under it at and about the Establishment."[6] Ross was the first to diagnose the disease as influenza.

At York Factory the first man to be reported sick was one of the crewmen of the Red River boat brigade. On June 21, this brigade departed for Norway House, but the sick man remained at York Factory. Five days later, chief trader James Hargrave said that six men were suffering from severe colds and sore throats. The number of men sick continued to increase, and on July 5, Hargrave wrote, "Severe colds, sore throats, pains in the breast, headaches, etc. still prevail very generally both in the establishment among the crews of the inland brigade and also among the Natives."[7] Hargrave never indicated that the disease was influenza, but his men were suffering from the same symptoms as those of the people at Norway House. On the basis of the information contained in the York Factory and Norway House journals, it therefore appears that the source area of the epidemic was in the York, Island, Nelson River, and Norway districts.

Illness spread quickly to other brigades that arrived at Norway House or York Factory from the interior. For instance, on July 1 and 2, the Red River and Rainy Lake brigades arrived at York Factory healthy, but three days later many of the crewmen were sick. The tight time constraints under which the company operated made it necessary to dispatch the boats anyway, and the sick crews were sent into the interior on July 5.[8] Because of their weakened condition they took twenty-seven days to reach Norway House.[9] On arriving at this post they reported that

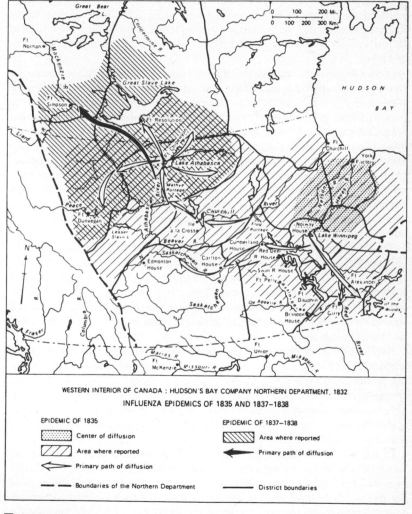

WESTERN INTERIOR OF CANADA : HUDSON'S BAY COMPANY NORTHERN DEPARTMENT, 1832
INFLUENZA EPIDEMICS OF 1835 AND 1837–1838

EPIDEMIC OF 1835

Center of diffusion

Area where reported

Primary path of diffusion

EPIDEMIC OF 1837–1838

Area where reported

Primary path of diffusion

Boundaries of the Northern Department

District boundaries

FIGURE 3

most of the other inland brigades were laid up along the route to York Factory. Among these were the crews from the Swan River and English River districts, who had been forced to stop at Oxford House.

Meanwhile, on July 12, the Athabasca brigade of four boats arrived at Norway House in good health. Eight days later they were ready to head inland again, but many of the boatmen and Edward Smith, who was in charge of the brigade, were too sick to proceed.[10] They finally departed on July 23, with many of the crewmen still suffering from the effects of influenza.[11] Although the Athabasca brigade was thus a carrier of the disease, as were the other brigades, the epidemic apparently preceded the brigade as far to the northwest as Ile à la Crosse. According to Roderick Mackenzie, "the few Indians that we found at the Establishment [Ile à la Crosse] on arrival were laid up with Influenza; which broke out among them early in August."[12]

Farther to the north, the Indians did contract the disease from the Athabasca brigade, which arrived at Fort Chipewyan on October 3. Smith wrote, "Shortly after our arrival at this station Influenza broke out among the people that pass the summer inland and the families. The Indians being all about us at this season did not escape the effects of the disease."[13] By October 12, the sickness was reported to be raging throughout the country. The rapid spread of the epidemic to the Chipewyan Indians in the hinterland of Fort Chipewyan was apparently a consequence of the fact that when the brigade arrived at the post, 162 Indians were waiting to trade. They bartered their furs for the goods they wanted and then dispersed to their winter hunting grounds, inadvertently carrying the disease with them. On January 22, 1836, Smith learned the illness had reached the "Caribou" Indians in the forest–tundra zone.[14]

The diffusion of influenza to the north and west of Fort Chipewyan seems to have been the result of dispatching company men and supplies in those directions. So, on October 3, men departed from Fort Chipewyan for Forts Vermilion and Dunvegan, in the Peace River District. Three days later crews departed for Fort Resolution and the Mackenzie River District. On December 19, Smith received a letter from the Peace River brigade informing him that the influenza epidemic had broken out in that region.[15]

Although the Mackenzie River brigade no doubt carried the disease with them when they left Fort Chipewyan on October 6, influenza apparently did not break out in the Mackenzie River Valley during the winter. No references to the contagion are found in the journals of posts located in that district. The late arrival of the disease-carrying brigades may account for the failure of the epidemic to spread; by the time the crews arrived, the Indians had already scattered to their winter hunting grounds.

Farther to the southwest, the epidemic seems to have been spread to the Saskatchewan District by brigades from that area which arrived at Norway House between June 25 and August 2, 1835. Like the other inland crews, they contracted the disease at the post and left before they were fully recovered. All of the Saskatchewan boats embarked for the trip home by August 3. Unfortunately, the records for the Edmonton District for this period are incomplete, and no journals have survived for this year for Edmonton House. Thus it is difficult to obtain a clear picture of the diffusion of disease in this quarter. Nonetheless, judging from the information contained in a letter addressed to Governor George Simpson by John Rowand at Edmonton House on December 31, 1835, it is clear that the epidemic broke out during the summer. Apparently it affected only the Woodland Assiniboine and Cree.[16] The Plains Indians may have avoided exposure because most of them were farther south in the open grasslands.

In 1837, influenza broke out again in the Northern Department (figure 3). Although information concerning this epidemic is less complete than was the case with the preceding one, its diffusion can be outlined. The 1837 epidemic seems to have erupted in the Athabasca and Peace River districts. On December 30, 1837, Alexander McLeod informed Governor Simpson from Fort Chipewyan that "a bad cough or Influenza afflicted the Natives all over this District, since the middle of summer."[17] A journal entry for Fort Dunvegan for May 29, 1837, states that most of the Indians living in the district were ill. As late as February 28, 1838, the post journal indicates that many Indians were still suffering from the "prevailing illness."[18]

The records from York Factory, Norway House, and Fort Edmonton contain no references to influenza during the summer and autumn of 1837, suggesting that the epidemic did not spread southward. Rather, it seems to have diffused northward, into the Mackenzie District. For instance, the journal for Fort Resolution for the summer of 1837 indicates that on several occasions company men suffered from bad coughs. Also, one of the Indian crewmen of the Mackenzie River brigade became ill on July 3 and was left at Fort Resolution to recuperate. Considering that the brigade had just come from the Athabasca District, where influenza was widespread, it seems highly likely that the Indian was suffering from the same illness. Unfortunately, no diagnosis was offered in this case, or for the "bad cough" suffered by the other men at the post. In any event, although influenza may have been present at Fort Resolution, it did not spread to the adjacent parts of the district as no contagion was reported among the Indians.

The epidemic did reach the Mackenzie River District, however. The timing of its appearance there suggests that the Mackenzie brigade which passed Fort Resolution on July 3 was the carrier. A letter dispatched to Governor Simpson from Fort Simpson on November 27, 1837, states that, "a kind of Epidemic disease or Influenza got among the Indians towards the latter end of summer, and still continues."[19] Assuming that "latter end of summer" was August, the disease broke out after the Mackenzie brigades arrived home.

Although the epidemic spread to Indians in the vicinity of Fort Simpson, it does not appear to have reached much farther down the Mackenzie River Valley or east of the Coppermine River area. Not one of the dispatches from Fort Norman includes any references to influenza or to any other diseases. Thus, as figure 3 shows, the influenza epidemic of 1837 was apparently more localized than was that of 1835.

Six years later, in 1843, yet another epidemic of influenza occurred. Initial reports of the disease came almost simultaneously from York Factory and Norway

House. Letters from these two posts indicate that it broke out in July and persisted through August. During the late summer and autumn, Indians in the vicinity of Fort Alexander were said to be sick with influenza.[20] To the northwest, the epidemic spread as far as Ile à la Crosse, in the English River District. It apparently reached that area in September, for between the 21st and the 26th the Ile à la Crosse journal indicates that many Indians were sick and refused to leave the post.[21] The records from Forts Chipewyan, Dunvegan, and Edmonton contain no references to widespread sickness during the summer, autumn, or winter, so the epidemic does not seem to have extended beyond the English River District.

During the summer of 1845, influenza hit sections of the Northern Department for the fourth time in ten years (figure 4). According to the York Factory journals, the disease was first contracted by the boat crews of the Red River colony in the spring. These crews carried it northward to Norway House and York Factory. Influenza was widespread in the vicinity of Norway House by mid-July, and an Indian died from the illness at that post on the 21st of that month. From then until August 29 the disease is mentioned frequently in the journal. That no reference is made to it thereafter suggests the epidemic had subsided.

Influenza apparently did not reach York Factory until mid-July, for it was first mentioned in the post journal on the 17th of the month: "In the afternoon four Oxford House boats received cargoes [they had arrived on the 15th]... and took their departure.... The Crews of these boats are generally affected with Influenza, a disease prevalent this summer among the Natives and servants in the low country."[22] On July 19, just four days after this Oxford House brigade arrived, a servant at York Factory was reported sick with influenza. Two days later, four more were sick; the disease began to spread. The rapidity with which this epidemic diffused to the area around the post led Hargrave to write: "The disease,—Influenza—broke out...and although on two previous occasions of a similar nature I had witnessed more mortality, at no time within these last twenty years did the contagion spread so widely or produce such effects upon the physical strength of the convalescents."[23] Not until the first week of September did the outbreak begin to subside in the area around York Factory.[24]

Although the debilitating effects of the epidemic brought the freighting business between York Factory and Norway House to a virtual standstill in late July and August, Hargrave indicated that the sickness did not interfere with the inland brigades.[25] The fact that most of the brigades had left for the interior before the disease reached epidemic proportions may explain why it does not appear to have spread to the English River area or to other districts to the northwest. Why the epidemic did not spread to the Saskatchewan District is not clear, however. One Saskatchewan brigade left Norway House on July 28, and many of the crewmen were sick. Thus the disease was carried into the district, even though it did not cause an epidemic.

In 1846, influenza was reported again in the English River, Athabasca, and Great Slave districts, but the symptoms that fur traders diagnosed as influenza may have been complications resulting from measles, which was prevalent that year. The following year, however, influenza did make its appearance once more, this time primarily in the Saskatchewan Valley and the lands to the south (figure 4). According to Ross, a "severe" epidemic broke out in the Norway District in the autumn.[26] From there it spread to the west and southwest. William Todd reported that influenza was also widespread around Fort Pelly in the Swan River District in autumn, affecting Plains and Woodland Indians alike.[27] A letter from John Harriott at Edmonton House indicates the epidemics reached that area in early winter and that its effects were felt most strongly in the parkland area. No other posts reported the disease, so it appears to have been confined to the area shown in figure 4.

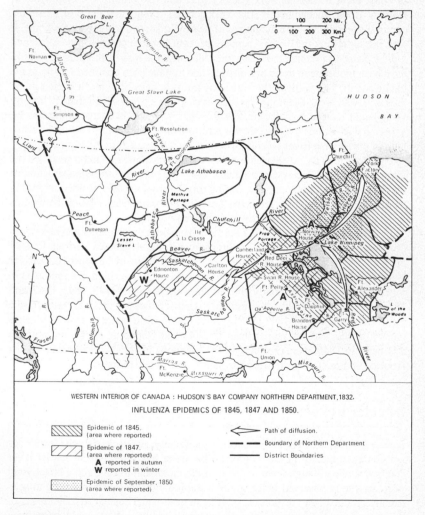

WESTERN INTERIOR OF CANADA : HUDSON'S BAY COMPANY NORTHERN DEPARTMENT, 1832.

INFLUENZA EPIDEMICS OF 1845, 1847 AND 1850.

Epidemic of 1845.
(area where reported)

Epidemic of 1847.
(area where reported)
A reported in autumn
W reported in winter

Epidemic of September, 1850
(area where reported)

Path of diffusion.

Boundary of Northern Department

District Boundaries

FIGURE 4

In the autumn of 1850, the sixth outbreak of influenza in twenty years took place. As on three preceding occasions, it appeared almost simultaneously at York Factory and Norway house in the month of September.[28] Like the epidemic of 1847 it was relatively localized and seems to have been confined mostly to the York, Norway, and contiguous districts (figure 4). The epidemic probably did not spread more widely because it broke out in autumn, after most of the transport business had been completed.

The mortality rates from the various influenza epidemics varied considerably. In 1835, eight Indians at York Factory died and two children of employees at Norway House succumbed.[29] The York journal reveals that the post's medical doctor made daily visits to the lodges of nearby Indians to administer medicine. It adds that his efforts and the food supplies sent out from the post to aid the weakened Indians helped to reduce the death toll. Although the loss of life thus appears to have been moderate in these two districts and to have been confined mostly to the young and the old, particularly women, it seems to have been much greater in the Saskatchewan area. There the "prevalent sickness carried off so many," mostly Woodland Cree and Assiniboine, that Rowand, who was in charge of the district, expected it to seriously reduce the fur returns from the region.[30] The toll was also high in the English River District, where at least forty or fifty Indians perished.[31] The loss of life in the Athabasca and Peace River districts, said to be great, led the journalist of Fort Chipewyan to remark that "the present distressing situation of the Indians is without parallel during my thirty-six years residence among them."[32] Even though the record of fatalities is incomplete, most of the victims again appear to have been women and children.

The influenza epidemic of 1837 seems to have been much milder and reportedly produced no fatalities around Fort Simpson or in the Athabasca District. Loss of life was widespread only in the vicinity of Fort Dunvegan, in the upper Peace River Valley.[33] The toll there may have been boosted by malnutrition, for food was in short supply that year. Similarly, the influenza epidemics of 1843, 1845, 1847, and 1850 were relatively mild and caused few deaths. However, the death rates for the influenza epidemics of 1843 and 1845 may have been underestimated, because other illnesses, such as scarlet fever in 1843 and whooping cough and perhaps dysentery in 1845, were prevalent in the Manitoba lowlands. Most of the deaths reported in those two years were attributed to these other illnesses.

Scarlet Fever

Scarlet fever is caused by streptococci. Significantly, an attack of scarlet fever does not confer immunity to the victim; on the other hand, the typical scarlet fever symptoms of early high fever, redness of the throat and tonsils, and a blotchy red rash, are rarely observed twice in the same individual. Rather, repeated attacks usually produce other responses, such as strep throat. Thus the first outbreaks of the disease in the early nineteenth-century Canadian West could have been identified easily, but subsequent visitations of the fever would be more difficult to diagnose and thus may not have been recorded. Also, although scarlet fever is communicable, it rarely occurs in epidemic form.[34]

The epidemic of 1843 was probably the first occurrence of scarlet fever in the Canadian West for at least a generation, because most of the people afflicted by it had readily identifiable symptoms. The disease seems to have appeared first among the Red River colonists in mid-summer and to have persisted there until December.[35] By late summer, it had spread among the Indians along the lower Winnipeg River in the vicinity of Fort Alexander. In October, it broke out among the Indians along the Berens River on the eastern shore of Lake Winnipeg when they came to pick up their winter supplies.[36] Whether the disease reached the Norway or Island Lake districts is not clear. Ross's letters from Norway House to Governor Simpson indicate that influenza was common in his district as well as to the south and to the northeast. He also mentioned the scarlet fever epidemic in the Red River and Berens River areas. Presumably, if the fever had been present in his district he would have said so. Given the lack of references to scarlet fever and given the fact the disease is less contagious than influenza or measles, it was probably localized in the Red River and Winnipeg districts of southeastern Manitoba. Even so, loss of life was reportedly heavy among Indians and Europeans alike in the affected area. Mortality rates were not spread evenly over the population, however, and the victims were usually children.[37]

Measles

The epidemic of measles that began in 1846 lasted almost a year in the Northern Department (figure 5). Like the influenza epidemic of 1835, its effects were widely felt. Measles is a viral disease, one of the most communicable known.[38] The disease causes an inflammation of the mucous membrane of the nose and air passages within ten days of contact. Three or four days after these symptoms are manifest, a rash appears on the face, abdomen, and extremities. It generally attacks children under the age of fifteen, but when the disease is introduced into a population not previously exposed, an extremely high proportion of people of all ages, often more than 90 percent, will contract it.[39]

The measles epidemic of 1846 first appeared in the Red River area in the early summer. Again the boat brigades seem to have been the primary carriers. On June 7, four boats arrived at Norway House from Red River, and Ross reported that the crews were sick with measles.[40] He quickly loaded their canoes and sent them on to York Factory, hoping to avoid the contagion. The same day, the Methey Portage brigade arrived from Ile à la Crosse and remained for two days. On the 9th, boats from Rainy Lake arrived. All of these crews were healthy. On the 13th, all of the district Indians arrived to trade and in the afternoon, a boat came in from the Berens River. On June 17, Ross reported that several of his men were sick with measles.

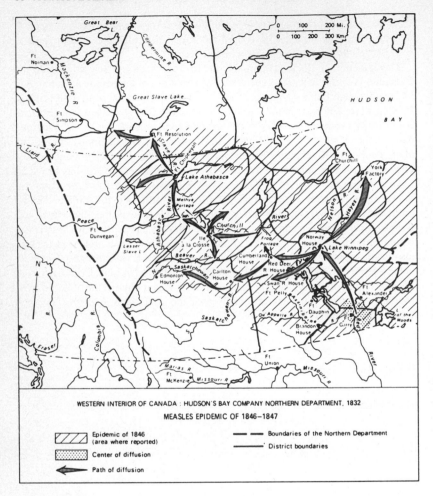

WESTERN INTERIOR OF CANADA : HUDSON'S BAY COMPANY NORTHERN DEPARTMENT, 1832

MEASLES EPIDEMIC OF 1846-1847

FIGURE 5

This happened ten days after their first exposure to the disease and thus corresponds closely to the normal incubation period for the illness.[41] The same day, the English River brigade arrived at Norway House and informed Ross that eighteen of the men of the Methey Portage brigade, which they had passed on the way, were sick with measles.

Measles were now widespread from Norway House to York Factory and southward to the Red River colony. Meanwhile, other brigades continued to arrive at Norway House: the Saskatchewan on June 26, the Swan River on July 8, the Athabasca on July 15, and two more from the Red River on July 25 and August 4.

All were exposed to the disease for varying lengths of time and then departed for home, usually with some of the men suffering from the illness.

Initially the disease appears to have spread most rapidly northeastward. This is not surprising. Until midsummer, most crews were heading for Norway House and/or for York Factory. Westward and northwestward expansion of the epidemic accelerated as the crews left for home. As the arrival–departure information for Norway House indicates, this began in mid-July. On July 29, half of the men stationed at Cumberland House were said to be sick from measles.[42] Considering the incubation period for the disease, the post would have been exposed as early as July 19, perhaps by the Athabasca brigade that had left Norway House on July 16. By August 9, measles was widespread around Carlton House, suggesting that the population had been exposed at least as early as the first of the month.

Because of the greater travel distances, the disease spread to the north of the Saskatchewan River more slowly. Roderick Mackenzie indicated that the outfit from York Factory did not arrive at Ile à la Crosse until September 10. This was later than normal, owing to the debilitating effects which the measles had on the crews. When the brigade arrived, he reported, "We found nearly the whole of our Chipewyans in camp here apparently in good health." But, "early in October the Measles and Influenza broke out violently among our unfortunate Indians."[43] Mackenzie's observations thus leave little doubt that the Ile à la Crosse brigade carried the disease into the English River District.

Farther to the north, the Athabasca brigade arrived at Fort Chipewyan on September 17. Measles among the crews was again cited as the reason for their late arrival.[44] On September 29, boats were dispatched to Forts Vermilion and Dunvegan in the Peace River Valley to the west and to Forts Resolution and Simpson to the north. On December 3 some of the men at Fort Chipewyan were sick with the measles and influenza. A week earlier a Chipewyan had complained that sickness was widespread among them in their winter camps. The disease was not specified, but in all probability the Indians were suffering from measles.

Measles apparently did not spread westward to the Peace River area that winter, for a letter from Fort Chipewyan dated December 24 stated that everyone there was enjoying good health. Similarly, the epidemic does not seem to have diffused northward to the Indians in the upper Mackenzie District. A probable explanation is that the disease had so delayed the crews that they did not arrive at Fort Simpson until after the Indians had completed their autumn trading and had scattered to their winter camps. Somewhat surprisingly, it does not appear to have affected the men at Fort Simpson either that winter or the following summer.

The measles epidemic of 1846–1847 was not only widespread but also took a heavy toll of life among all ages. On August 10, Hargrave reported that thirty-one Indians had died around York Factory, including "only those in the immediate vicinity and buried by the company's Servants."[45] Nicol Finlayson dispatched a letter to Governor Simpson from Fort Alexander on August 3 in which he remarked that "sickness had made such ravage among the natives this summer, and the last which has more the appearance of a pestilence than an epidemic."[46] Similar reports came from the Red River, Norway House, and Oxford House. The loss of life and the debility of the survivors was such that the company was unable to find enough able-bodied men to take the boats to the Red River, Norway, Oxford, and York districts.[47] The disease had equally devastating results in other areas, and with the exception of the smallpox epidemic of 1838, the measles epidemic seems to have produced the highest mortality rate.

Judging from the information provided by Hargrave at York Factory, it may be that many of the deaths resulted not directly from measles but from subsequent complications. Commenting on the heavy loss of life, he observed that "inflammation of the heart and of the chest generally followed the disease that originally attacked them, and the greatest mortality resulted from that cause."[48] Measles can produce serious consequences that affect the respiratory system, the ears, and the brain.[49] Hargrave's observation indicates that the Indians were prone to the first of these sequelae. As has been noted, the records of Ile à la Crosse, Fort Chipewyan, and Fort Resolution all reveal that influenza broke out along with measles in 1846. The coughing and respiratory troubles reported as influenza may well have been complications associated with the measles.

Smallpox

Smallpox was undoubtedly one of the most dreaded of all European diseases to which the Indians were exposed. It broke out in the Northern Department in 1837 (figure 6). Initial symptoms of smallpox are fever, chills, headaches, and prostration, which continue for three or four days. The temperature then begins to fall, and a rash appears and evolves into a number of pustules. Crusts form and the scabs finally fall off about the end of the third week. Smallpox varies from a mild disease with a fatality rate of less than 1 percent to a severe condition with a fatality rate of 30 percent or more. The severity of a given epidemic is directly proportional to the residual immunity of the population and therefore decreases over time after exposure.[50] The epidemic of 1837 was the first major outbreak in the Northern Department since 1780. Consequently, it is not surprising that many of the Indian groups who contracted the disease suffered terrible losses. The fur traders estimated that the Indians, chiefly Assiniboine, Sarsee, Piegan, Blackfoot, and Gros Ventre, lost up to three-quarters of their populations.[51]

Figure 6 traces the diffusion of the epidemic. Significantly, the pattern is similar in most respects to two other smallpox epidemics that struck the Northern Department in 1780 and 1869.[52] Furthermore, it contrasts sharply with the patterns outlined for the influenza, scarlet fever, and measles epidemics. The smallpox epidemic first broke out in June 1837, at Fort Union. The source of the contagion was an American Fur Company supply boat that had been dispatched from St. Louis. When it arrived at Fort Union, one man on board was suffering from smallpox. Although the American Fur Company traders attempted to prevent the

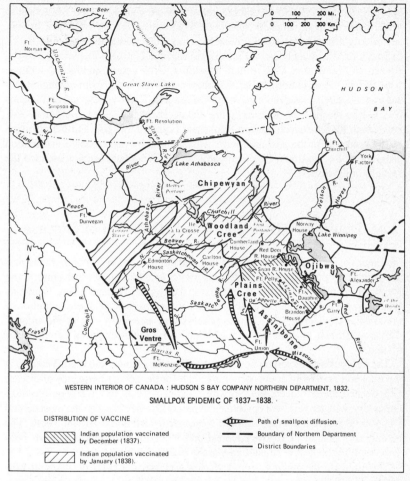

WESTERN INTERIOR OF CANADA : HUDSON S BAY COMPANY NORTHERN DEPARTMENT, 1832.

SMALLPOX EPIDEMIC OF 1837–1838.

DISTRIBUTION OF VACCINE

Indian population vaccinated
by December (1837).

Indian population vaccinated
by January (1838).

Path of smallpox diffusion.

Boundary of Northern Department

District Boundaries

FIGURE 6

spread of the disease in the vicinity of the post, their efforts failed. A party of more than 1 000 Indians ignored warnings to stay away from the fort, and they contracted smallpox soon after their arrival. Only 150 survived.[53]

The epidemic was transmitted farther up the Missouri River valley by another supply boat of the American Fur Company. Shortly after the steamboat had arrived at Fort Union, a longboat was sent on to Fort McKenzie, on the Marias River a short distance upstream from its confluence with the Missouri River. The crew of the longboat became ill shortly after leaving Fort Union, and an attempt was made to quarantine them in the vicinity of the Judith River. However, a party of more than five thousand Blackfoot and Piegan, who were waiting at Fort McKenzie to trade, insisted that the supply boat proceed. Trade began as soon as the boat arrived, and shortly thereafter the Blackfoot and Piegan fell victim to the epidemic.[54]

Smallpox was quickly carried northward into the Northern Department by the equestrian Assiniboine, Cree, Blood, Blackfoot, Gros Ventre, and Piegan Indians, who fled in the misguided belief that they could run away from contagion. By autumn, the disease was reported in the Qu'Appelle River valley, and by November, it had reached the Indians living in the parklands along the North Saskatchewan River between Carlton House and Edmonton House. Further diffusion of the epidemic to the east and north was arrested by an extensive vaccination program of the Hudson's Bay Company, so the Woodland Indians escaped the ravages of the disease.[55]

The Trading Network and the Diffusion of Disease

Outbreaks of contagious diseases that affected populations in two or more districts occurred nine times between 1830 and 1850. In addition, several other, more localized epidemics occurred.[56] In most instances the Hudson's Bay Company boat brigades served as the primary carriers of the diseases. With the exception of the smallpox epidemic of 1837, the process was essentially one of hierarchical diffusion, similar to what one would expect in a well-developed central place system.[57]

The key position of certain posts, such as Norway House and York Factory, in the transport system no doubt accounts in part for the greater frequency of disease experienced there. Indeed, the Norway District appears to have been the most unhealthy, with ten different epidemics. Norway District was also the most central location, in frequent contact with the west, northwest, northeast, and south. The ecological situation of Norway House and York Factory may also have been important, for both were situated in marshy lowland areas.

The timing of the outbreak of a disease was clearly critical in determining how widely it diffused. Generally, epidemics that began in midwinter remained relatively localized because the Indians had little contact with the posts, because they were widely dispersed, and because traffic between districts was minimal. On the other hand, if an epidemic erupted in midsummer it generally spread rapidly, especially if it was highly contagious. At this time of the year, Indians gathered together in larger encampments, visited the trading houses frequently, and there was high volume of boat and canoe traffic between districts.

Diseases were less frequent in the peripheral areas, such as the Mackenzie River and Great Slave Lake districts, which were so distant from the usual point of origin in Manitoba that the brigades did not arrive until early winter, or later in epidemic years owing to the debilitating effects of disease on the crews. By that time, the local Indians often had already dispersed to their winter camps. Thus the timing of transmission also helped to reduce the prevalence of disease in the northernmost areas. Elsewhere, large trading parties of Indians would await the arrival of the supply boats. During the trading that followed, the Indians often contracted disease and spread it to the hinterlands of the posts as they fanned out to their winter hunting grounds.

The smallpox epidemic of 1837–1838 was an exception to the general pattern. Rather than breaking out in the York Factory–Norway House–Red River area, it erupted in the Missouri River valley. Initial transmission was via American Fur Company supply boats, but subsequent dispersal was caused by the northward flight of Indians who sought to escape from the dreaded disease. The disease failed to diffuse through the network of woodland posts of the Hudson's Bay Company because of the vaccination program that the company carried out as a counter-measure.

Assessments of the impact of these repeated epidemics on the population of the various districts remains impressionistic. Clearly, however, the epidemics of influenza in 1835, of smallpox in 1837, and of measles in 1846–1847 caused heavy losses in areas affected; most other epidemics were said to have taken light to moderate tolls. Verification or refinement of these general statements, however, must await meticulous analysis of the population estimates and tallies taken at various times.

Notes

1. John C. Ewers, "The Influence of the Fur Trade on Indians of the Northern Plains," in *People and Pelts: Selected Papers of the Second North American Fur Trade Conference*, ed. Malvina Bolus (Winnipeg: Peguis Publishers, 1972), 1–26, reference on 20.

2. Arthur J. Ray, *Indians in the Fur Trade: Their Role as Trappers, Hunters, and Middlemen in the Lands Southwest of Hudson Bay, 1660-1870* (Toronto and Buffalo: University of Toronto Press, 1974), 166–81.

3. Charles A. Bishop, *The Northern Ojibwa and the Fur Trade: An Historical and Ecological Study* (Toronto: Holt, Rinehart and Winston, 1974), 277–89.

4. The Hudson's Bay Company records are an excellent source of information regarding diseases and the general health of the Indians. The traders in charge of the various districts of the Northern Department generally wrote two to four letters a year to Governor George Simpson, in which they reported on the general state of the fur trade in their respective areas. Since epidemics almost always disrupted trade, they were usually reported. Frequently these reports include accounts of when and where a disease broke out. Supplementing the correspondence are the journals of the posts. The daily entries in many of these journals make it possible to pinpoint the date on which an epidemic erupted and the length of time it lasted.

The principal difficulty with the data relates to the fact that many of the posts lacked trained medical personnel to diagnose illnesses. Compounding the problem is the fact that some diseases, such as smallpox and measles, have similar symptoms in their early stages and that others produce classic symptoms in an individual only once, making subsequent attacks of the illness hard to diagnose. Finally, in some years, such as in 1843, several diseases reached epidemic proportions at almost the same time. For these reasons, the traders' diagnoses of illnesses must be viewed with caution, particularly when the epidemics were localized. Generalized outbreaks afford an opportunity to do more cross-checking of sources, so that correct diagnoses are more likely.

5.   Norway House Journal, 1835, B154/a/26, p. 6, Public Archives of Canada, Hudson's Bay Company Collection (microfilm) (hereinafter HBC).

6.   Ibid., 8.

7.   York Factory Journal, 1834–1835, 239/a/148, p. 60, HBC.

8.   Ibid.

9.   Norway House Journal, 1835, B154/a/26, p. 12, HBC.

10.   Ibid.

11.   Ibid., 13.

12.   Governor George Simpson, Letters Inward to Simpson (hereinafter Simpson Inward), Roderick Mackenzie, Ile à la Crosse, 10 Jan. 1836, D5/4, p. 152, HBC.

13.   Simpson Inward, Edward Smith, Fort Chipewyan, 31 Dec. 1835, D5/4, p. 148, HBC.

14.   Fort Chipewyan Journal, 1835–1836, B39/a/31, p. 79, HBC.

15.   Ibid., 72.

16.   Simpson Inward, John Rowand, Edmonton House, 31 Dec. 1835, D5/4, p. 143, HBC.

17.   Simpson Inward, Alexander McLeod, Fort Chipewyan, 30 Dec. 1837, D5/4, p. 364, HBC.

18.   Fort Dunvegan Journal, 1838, B56/a/6, p. 4, HBC.

19.   Simpson Inward, McPherson, Fort Simpson, 27 Nov. 1837, D5/4, p. 346, HBC.

20.   Simpson Inward, Nicol Finlayson, Fort Alexander, 1 Dec. 1843, D5/9, p. 313, HBC.

21.   Ile à la Crosse Journal, 1843, B89/a/22, p. 29, HBC.

22.   York Factory Journal, 1845, B239/a/161, p. 47, HBC.

23.   Simpson Inward, James Hargrave, York Factory, 10 Aug. 1845, D5/14, p. 253, HBC.

24.   Simpson Inward, James Hargrave, York Factory, 8 Sep. 1845, D5/15, p. 39, HBC.

25.   Simpson Inward, James Hargrave, York Factory, 10 Aug. 1845, D5/14, p. 253, HBC.

26.   Simpson Inward, Don Ross, Norway House, 10 Dec. 1847, D5/19, p. 629, HBC.

27.   Simpson Inward, William Todd, Fort Pelly, 23 Apr. 1848, D5/22, p. 169, HBC.

28.   Simpson Inward, Don Ross, Norway House, 27 Nov. 1850, D5/25, p. 253, HBC; and Simpson Inward, James Hargrave, York Factory, 1 Dec. 1850, D5/25, p. 298, HBC.

29.   York Factory Journal, 1834–1835, 239/a/148, pp. 60–62, HBC; and Norway House Journal, 1835, B154/2/26, pp. 9–16, HBC.

30.   Simpson Inward, John Rowand, Edmonton House, 31 Dec. 1835, D5/4, p. 143, HBC.

31.   Simpson Inward, Roderick Mackenzie, Ile à la Crosse, 10 Jan. 1836, D5/4, p. 152, HBC.

32.   Fort Chipewyan Journal, 1835–1836, B39/a/31, p. 71, HBC.

33.   Simpson Inward, McPherson, Fort Simpson, 27 Nov. 1837, D5/4, p. 346, HBC; and Fort Dunvegan Journal, 1838, B56/a/6, p. 4, HBC.

34.   Jacques M. May, M.D., *The Ecology of Human Disease* American Geographical Society Studies in Medical Geography no. 1 (New York: MD Publications, 1958), 252.

35.   Simpson Inward, Nicol Finlayson, Fort Alexander, 1 Dec. 1843, D5/9, p. 313, HBC.

36. Ibid.
37. Ibid.
38. May, *Ecology of Human Disease*, 264.
39. Ibid., 264–65.
40. Norway House Journal, 1846, B154/a/46, p. 3, HBC.
41. Ibid., 4.
42. Simpson Inward, Colin Campbell, Cumberland House, 29 July 1846, D5/18, p. 85, HBC.
43. Simpson Inward, Roderick Mackenzie, Ile à la Crosse, 12 Jan. 1847, D5/19, p. 65, HBC.
44. Fort Chipewyan Journal, 1846, B39/a/42, p. 21, HBC.
45. Simpson Inward, James Hargrave, York Factory, 10 Aug. 1846, D5/18, p. 180, HBC.
46. Simpson Inward, Nicol Finlayson, Fort Alexander, 3 Aug. 1846, D5/18, p. 105, HBC.
47. Simpson Inward, James Hargrave, York Factory, 10 Aug. 1846, D5/18, p. 180, HBC.
48. Ibid.
49. May, *Ecology of Human Disease*, 264.
50. Jacques M. May, M.D., ed., *Studies in Disease Ecology*, American Geographical Society Studies in Medical Geography no. 2 (New York: Hafner, 1961), 1–4.
51. Ray, *Indians in the Fur Trade*, 188.
52. Ibid., 190 and 191.
53. Edwin T. Denig, *Five Indian Tribes of the Upper Missouri*, ed. John C. Ewers (Norman, OK: University of Oklahoma, 1961), 71.
54. Arthur J. Ray, "Smallpox: The Epidemic of 1837–38," *The Beaver* (Autumn 1975): 8–13.
55. Ray, *Indians in the Fur Trade*, 188–89.
56. Most of these illnesses were confined to a single district and produced few fatalities. Many cannot be identified because descriptions of symptoms are insufficient. For instance, "sore eyes" were common in the western English District during the autumn and winter of 1844 and in the northern Saskatchewan District in January 1840. In December 1840, many Indians in the Norway District suffered from "putrid fever." Identifiable but localized epidemics included three outbreaks of whooping cough, one in the Nelson River District in 1834, one in the Norway District in 1843, and one in the Ile à la Crosse area in 1845; mumps, in the York District in 1841 and in the Ile à la Crosse region in 1844; and dysentery, in the Norway District in 1845 and 1846.
57. Gerald F. Pyle ,"The Diffusion of Cholera in the United States in the Nineteenth Century,"*Geogr. Analysis* 1 (1969): 59–75.

SECTION 2

IMMIGRATION AND SETTLEMENT

Visiting the Highlands and Western Islands of Scotland in the late eighteenth century, Dr. Samuel Johnson was taken aback by what he described as the "epidemick disease of wandering." Hundreds of Scots were departing their native soil for the wilderness of North America, as indeed were large numbers of English and Irish people, and Johnson and others feared the consequences. By one contemporary account, Western Scotland would soon be left entirely to owls and dragons; by another, even London stood in danger of ruin and decay. Johnson deplored the exodus, and as he struggled to understand what it meant, he compared the dispersion of people from Britain to the divergence of light from a focus. In his sombre vision, it seemed that migrants from the dense, tradition-rich societies of Scotland and elsewhere would be deprived of their familiar, moral, and spiritual supports in the wastes of North America, and that their culture would perish. After relocation, he wrote, "all the rays remain, but the heat is gone." Yet this stern conclusion was not entirely consistent with the evidence. Writing from the Hebrides in 1773, Johnson himself noted that "whole neighbourhoods formed parties for removal," carrying with them "their language, their opinions, their popular songs, and hereditary merriment." More to the point, he recognized that departure was not exile for these migrants, because they changed "nothing but the place of their abode."

Debate has ranged, ever since, over the ground that Johnson somewhat inadvertently defined. So, for example, F.J. Turner and his followers maintained that the American frontier was every bit as effective as Johnson's metaphor of dispersing light implied at stripping migrants of their traditions. A bare handful of phrases drawn from Turner's earliest statement of the frontier thesis effectively convey the gist of the interpretation. European ways entered the continent but were soon modified. The frontier was "the line of most rapid and effective Americanization." There, complex European life was "sharply precipitated by the wilderness into the simplicity of primitive conditions." The United States resembled a huge page in the history of society; read west to east, it revealed the course of social evolution, from Indian and hunter to the city and factory.*

In contrast, Louis Hartz† claimed that limited fragments of old-world political cultures, carried to new territories by their first settlers, flourished and defined the ethos of those places. To again encapsulate a complex idea in a few words, the process begins with "the escape of the fragment from its original European enemy." Transported overseas, it is protected against a whole series of later ideas spawned by the tensions inherent in European society. Unchallenged, its potential is unleashed and it flourishes to a degree impossible in Europe.

Others have argued, as David Grayson Allen has,†† that new American communities took more complex shape than thoroughgoing Turnerian or Hartzian

---

* F.J. Turner, "The Significance of the Frontier in American History," American Historical Association, *Annual Report for 1893* (Washington, 1894), 200–10.
† Louis Hartz, *The Founding of New Societies* (New York: Harcourt, Brace and World, 1964), 3–10.
†† David Grayson Allen, *In English Ways* (Chapel Hill, NC: University of North Carolina Press, 1981), 6–7.

interpretations allow. By focussing on the English backgrounds and American experiences of settlers in five Massachusetts towns, he demonstrates that "even though these men and women were able to reproduce the order of life they knew and thereby to perpetuate the diversity of local England in the New England wilderness, they also developed an unmistakably new society in spite of themselves."

Canadian historical geographers have long been involved, directly and indirectly, in this debate. Much of Andrew Clark's work explored the extent to which old-world backgrounds influenced the settlement patterns and agricultural practices of new-world settlers (see the introduction to this text). Although his analyses failed to advance the discussion decisively, largely because they were coarsegrained and weakly connected to wider interpretive ideas, they identified crucial questions and provided a solid empirical base from which later scholars could move forward. Recent work has paid much closer attention to old-world circumstances than was characteristic of that completed in the 1960s. Current scholarship has moved from a functional/morphological focus on patterns of new-world land use to seek a more rounded understanding of the ways in which migrants responded to their new circumstances. Some of the insights that have come from these new emphases are revealed in the three papers that follow.

Cole Harris is the author of *The Seigneurial System in Early Canada: A Geographical Study* and, with J. Warkentin, of *Canada before Confederation.** In his study of early French settlement in rural Canada, he makes a strong argument for the importance of local context, especially environmental and economic conditions, in shaping new-world societies. Harris recognizes that early Canada was a "clean social slate to which immigrants who settled on the land brought relatively similar backgrounds of poverty," and his comparison of rural circumstances in seventeenth-century France and New France leaves no doubt that early society on the St. Lawrence was by far the more simple and egalitarian. Yet he attributes this rough equality to the weakness of demand for agricultural produce and the relatively low cost of new-world land—conditions that raised the price of labour and allowed ordinary people to achieve independence on their own farms— rather than to the transfer of a narrow fragment of French society across the Atlantic. Indeed, Harris argues that a wide range of customs, values, and ideas typically entered most colonial settings, but that circumstances there allowed some to flourish and caused others to wither. In many parts of the new world, for example, poor markets and cheap land enabled seventeenth- and eighteenth-century Europeans to realize a deep-seated desire for family-centred independence which had long been held in check, in Europe, by the constraints of collective agriculture and the concentration of land title in the hands of a few. Conversely, both the highly skewed distribution of European wealth, largely based on the ownership of land, and the corresponding social hierarchy reflected in honorific titles and patterns of deference, were much diminished in new settings.

---

* Cole Harris, *The Seigneurial System in Early Canada: A Geographical Study* (Madison: University of Wisconsin Press, 1966); Cole Harris and J. Warkentin, *Canada before Confederation* (New York: Oxford University Press, 1974).

Similarly, the richly varied regional cultures of old Europe were never entirely replicated in the new world. The ideas and practices that underlay them were not forgotten on embarkation, but the American and European environments were so different that old habits were often ill-fitted to new circumstances. The new-world mingling of people from different European localities eroded the familiar, unthinking acceptance of traditions long taken for granted in the old country. Thus, by comparison with Europe, remarkably homogeneous and relatively egalitarian societies emerged in these remote new-world settings, forged by the particular terms of the settlers' confrontation with their land.

Many of these themes echo through the second paper in this section, an evocative study of nineteenth-century Scottish settlement in Cape Breton by Stephen Hornsby. Hornsby is a graduate of the universities of St. Andrews and British Columbia who teaches Canadian studies at the University of Maine. By Hornsby's account, life on Cape Breton Island was marked by nuclear families on their own land, a weak institutional framework, extensive farming and, in the earliest years of the century, a fairly egalitarian society. Nonetheless, the nineteenth century was not the seventeenth and Cape Breton was not the St. Lawrence. People flooded into Nova Scotia far more rapidly than they had into early Canada; Cape Breton's tiny pockets of decent agricultural land were filled much more quickly than the more extensive lowlands of New France;* and markets, though hardly large, gave Nova Scotian agriculture a greater commercial side than that of early Canada. In addition, colonial policies restricted access to land.

The results were all too clear. As the availability of land declined, society stratified. By mid-century, the circumstances of settlers on frontland and backland were markedly different. Most of the former found themselves "quite easy"; most of the latter—who found that they had exchanged "landlords and bailiffs for acidic soils and six-month winters," and suffered the ravages of the potato famine to boot—lived hard and precarious lives. Although the differences between wealth and poverty were stark, Hornsby insists that the extremes of European inequality were absent from Cape Breton. If the stratification between frontland and backland settlers mirrored, to some degree, that between crofters and cotters in Scotland, Nova Scotian society was set apart from its old-world antecedents just as decisively as New France differed from Old. Nova Scotians blended or generalized traditions from the old world, and retained at least the memory of the opportunity that new-world land had once provided. For all its poignancy, the story of Scottish settlement in Cape Breton points not to the re-creation of Europe overseas but to the wider pattern of Canadian development. The occupation of a niggardly ecumene has imposed a rhythm of migration, settlement, and repeated migration upon generations of people.

Yet it would be a mistake to conclude that Dr. Johnson's vision of rays dissipating in the wilderness accurately describes the reality of Canadian settlement. "Hereditary merriments," Gaelic, and even elements of Scottish material

---

* Cf. Courville, "Space, Territory and Culture in New France," on p. 165 of this text.

culture such as bannock toasters and the Cas chrom, or foot plough, long survived among the settlers of Cape Breton, just as kinship and common origins structured their emerging communities.

John Lehr's careful geographical analysis of Ukrainian settlement on the Prairie reminds us of how important social ties transferred from the homeland were to people faced with the task of establishing themselves in a new and often forbidding world. Lehr, who teaches at the University of Winnipeg and has written extensively on Ukrainian settlement in the western provinces, recognizes that the horizons of pre-industrial life were far more circumscribed than those of our own day. He begins his investigation with the important insistence that peasant loyalties were to family, village, locality, district or, at most, province, rather than to such abstract, modern conceptions as nation, state, and ethnicity. With analysis of the internal structure of "Ukrainian" block settlements thus adjusted to the appropriate scale, it becomes evident that ties to kin, village, and district were a crucial influence in the migrant's choice of land. Farms were occupied because of their proximity to those of relatives and friends, rather than for the quality of their soils, and noticeably distinct clusters of settlers from various districts of the homeland made the internal geography of the block settlements a microcosm of the western Ukraine. For these migrants to an alien country, departure was closer to exile than Johnson's observations in the Hebrides suggest, but its jarring effects were considerably buffered by a dense web of familiar connections in the new land.

In sum, these three papers, and other related work by historical geographers, point to some general observations about the processes of migration, settlement, and cultural transfer. Broadly, we can affirm the importance of the European encounter with new-world circumstances in shaping settlement societies (a factor that F. J. Turner pointed to without quite grasping analytically). Drastically revised terms of access to land transformed economic and social relations that had rested upon the characteristic European imbalance between people and property. Where this revision was most extreme, as in early Canada, strikingly homogeneous landscapes and societies developed. Modest farmhouses replaced mansions and hovels, and subsistence farms were substituted for vast estates and tiny crofts. Many of the components of these new landscapes were European but in detail they had lost the fine edges of local distinction that differentiated their counterparts in Europe.

Moreover, as J.J. Mannion demonstrated in *Irish Settlements in Eastern Canada*,* there was a good deal of consistency in the patterns of persistence (or otherwise) of traditional beliefs and practices among migrants settling in the new-world countryside. Cultural transfer was most complete with remoteness from the market; adaptation was most rapid and thoroughgoing, and tradition was discarded fastest, in those areas most closely linked to the monetary economy. Thus old ways would continue in areas of subsistence farming but not on the commercial farming frontier; the flails and digging sticks of the Cape Breton

---

* J.J. Mannion, *Irish Settlements in Eastern Canada* (Toronto: University of Toronto, 1974).

backlands would find no place on the productive front farms of Ontario. By the same token, domestic traditions would linger long after farming practice had adapted to new circumstances. Songs and stories, the distinctive design of a hearth, or the forms of wedding celebrations and holy day observances were likely to persist even where there were no differences to be seen in the crops grown and barns built by members of different ethnic groups.

All of this suggests that the nuances of European variety were lost in the new world, that tradition bowed more or less completely and more or less quickly to market forces, and that the imprint of ethnicity on the landscape was ultimately muted. Still, we cannot discount the importance of old-world origins, kinship, and the quest for familiarity, in shaping migration streams and influencing the settler's choice of location in the new world.

THE EXTENSION OF FRANCE INTO RURAL CANADA*

R. COLE HARRIS

The condition of rural life in the middle-latitude New World colonies of Europe in the seventeenth and to some extent in the eighteenth century presented a fundamental geographical contrast with the mother countries that depended less on differences in climate, flora, fauna, or topography than on the availability of land. Indigenous populations, usually hunters and gatherers, could be pushed aside and vast stretches of new territory opened for settlement. If a forest had to be cleared, sod broken, or marshes drained, this racking labour was usually accomplished; farmland became available and, in comparison with European land, it was relatively cheap. Although land was cheap, European markets were far away, and in the seventeenth century European agricultural prices were generally low and falling. Local markets in recently settled colonies were meagre. In these conditions the farmland that Europeans in the seventeenth century slowly won from new middle-latitude settings overseas became less a cog in a commercial economy than a place for ordinary Europeans to live. It was a setting in which European material life and social values would be reproduced but, given the sudden availability of land and the characteristic weakness of the agricultural market, reproduced in drastically simplified and relatively egalitarian societies. In the eighteenth century, the rate of European population growth increased, agricultural prices improved, colonial populations grew, and markets for New World grain and animal products became larger and more lucrative. Agricultural land values rose, agriculture became more centrally commercial, and socio-economic differentiation increased as those in a position to take advantage of rising land prices and improved markets did so. But even in the eighteenth century there were pockets of New World settlement where land was relatively cheap and agricultural markets poor. South Africa beyond the Cape was one such setting, much of the westward fringe of New

* From *European Settlement and Development in North America,* ed. J.R. Gibson (Toronto: University of Toronto Press, 1978), 27–45.

England and the Middle Colonies was perhaps another, and Canada, its tiny population isolated in the interior of a continent and along the climatic margin of wheat cultivation, was a third.

The relationship between society and land in France and in early Canada could hardly have been more different. The France from which a few thousand people emigrated to Canada was densely settled, old, overwhelmingly rural, and profoundly local. There were almost twenty million French people, 90 percent of them rural; the population density averaged almost forty per square kilometre. Although there had been some fairly recent re-clearing of land abandoned during the Hundred Years War, most farmland had been worked for at least four hundred years. Village churches were more likely to be Romanesque than Gothic, and many village houses were also several centuries old. Houses in villages a few miles apart often reflected quite different local styles, each part of a material culture that was the legacy of a long past of a life *in situ*. Whereas intricate networks of cart roads and paths served local areas, ordinary people who did not live close to navigable water were isolated from most outside goods and people by the high cost of overland travel. Life was contained within a web of inherited local custom, some of it codified in *coutumes*, more acquired orally, much transmitted unconsciously by example. Custom differentiated place from place, creating the innumerable *pays* of rural France—those "medals struck in the image of a people," the products of retrospective rural societies each living in a restricted territory for a long, long time.[1]

In this old France land was still the basis of wealth and status. Almost everyone who lived in the countryside, even the artisan and the merchant, worked or controlled a little land. The peasants, the great bulk of the people of France, supported not only themselves and their families but also the small minority of prosperous and wealthy Frenchmen. An oppressive royal tax, the *taille*, that bore particularly on the peasantry, furnished half of the national revenue. Peasants' tithes supported abbeys and priories, while seigneurial charges of many kinds supported an increasingly effete nobility whose high living frequently led them into debt to an urban bourgeoisie—the careful managers and unbending creditors to whom many seigneuries were forfeited. Even this increasingly dynamic and powerful bourgeoisie was characteristically tied to land by the country houses it visited in summer, by its revenue from seigneuries and rotures, or by the many loans to peasants and seigneurs that would be turned eventually into cash or land. In this sharply stratified society, to be landless was to be virtually without position, a beggar, *déclassé*. Day labourers clung to their garden patches. At the other end of the spectrum the king, as the seigneur from whom all seigneuries were held, was the ultimate landholder. This would not be soon an industrial country; the strength of seventeenth-century France lay in the peasant masses who worked a land that was scarce and valuable, avidly sought, and tenaciously held.

For Frenchmen the interminable Canadian land was wilderness—land without social meaning, without boundaries, and valueless except as it was cleared. The shock of the encounter with such land drove many soldiers and *engagés* (indentured servants) back to France when their terms of service expired. Most of those who stayed in a colony where the labour requirements of the fur trade were soon satisfied took up the lifelong work of clearing and farming, as they found French purpose for, and imposed French meaning on, an alien land. There was no reason why they should not think and act in French terms. No radical ideas had propelled them across the Atlantic. Apart from the Indians, with whom few settlers were in regular contact, no new population injected different ways of life. Officials administered Canada as an overseas enclave of France. Yet those who farmed along the lower St. Lawrence would not reproduce the French rural landscape, if only because in Canada land for agricultural expansion would long be available for the ordinary person. The availability of land broke French rural life out of the restrictions inherent in its fixed landed base and created conditions in which one element of a French legacy—the independent nuclear family on its own land—would be accentuated while others would atrophy.

This basic geographical contrast between a Europe where land was scarce and expensive, and a New World colony where it was not, lasted in Canada through several generations, for whom agricultural markets were poor and agricultural prices were low. There was time to establish a European society within these conditions, time for it to acquire a tradition. The human landscape that began to emerge along the St. Lawrence River near Quebec and Montreal in the middle of the seventeenth century was carved out of the fringe of the Canadian Shield in the middle of the nineteenth century. At the heart of this landscape was the farmhouse on a long lot—farm after similar farm in a row along river or road. Each of these farms was the setting for the life of a family, and the circumstances of one family were much like those of another. A setting where land was cheap and markets were poor had provided an admirable base for the expansion of the self-reliant, nuclear household—with very ordinary people establishing families on their own land—and had weakened or eliminated all other elements of the social heritage of French rural life. French rural society had been pared down to a simple remainder, not because a fragment of it had crossed the Atlantic but because conditions in rural Canada had exerted strong selective pressures.

The French Background of Immigrants to Canada

Except in Brittany and in parts of the Auvergne, regions from which almost no settlers came to Canada, the nuclear family was the basic unit of French rural life in the seventeenth century. The ideal of rural life, approached by only a few prosperous farmers, was a family secure in its own house and in control of lands yielding enough to avoid debt—in short, a peasant family able to *vivre de la sienne*.[2] For most peasants, such independence was quite unrealizable. There were too many people on too little land, agricultural technology was too inflexible, and the exactions of royal treasury, seigneury, and church weighed too heavily on them. Inevitably, the ideal was compromised. At worst, the family was driven off the land and scattered in a drifting population of beggars. More commonly, sons and daughters left home at an early age to become day labourers, apprentices, or servants. In much of France, collective constraints on individual agricultural freedom, imposed by the village community, protected the individual family's access to pasture. Access to stubble fields after harvest (*vaine pâture*) and to common pastures and waste lands was closely regulated so that each peasant family might support a cow, perhaps a few sheep. In places, and at times of particular poverty, constraints such as these loomed larger; where life was a little easier the constraints were relaxed, and the family assumed more independence. The primacy of the family could be strikingly expressed on the landscape in the form of the dispersed farmstead, but even where, as in most of France, rural settlement was still agglomerated, the family often closed itself in behind the thick walls of its house, offering a latched door but not a window to the village street and opening out only into its own interior yard. French civil law, too, in all its local variety, built legal walls around the rights and responsibilities of members of the nuclear family.

The essential support of the family was the garden, often tiny, always enclosed, virtually a part of the house to which it was attached. Together with farm buildings it went under a single name: *mazure* in Normandy, *mas* in Languedoc.[3] Apart from cereals, the garden produced the bulk of the household's foodstuffs—its vegetables, fruits and poultry, unless they had to be sold to pay debts. In the garden, flax, hemp, or even a few vines might be grown, their products intended partly for sale. This crucial, heavily manured plot paid no tithe, only the seigneurial *cens*. For most peasants, the garden was more nearly their own land than any other, an enclosed patch where members of the family could plant, harvest, and experiment as they wished. In much of northern France the arable, on the other hand, was worked in a three-course rotation, and individual holdings, scattered unenclosed within large open fields, were subject to the rhythm of the prevailing rotation and were opened to general pasture when the harvest was in. Pastures were few and small, animals scarce, fields under-fertilized, and yields low, seldom more than five or six units of grain for each sown, often much less. Most families depended upon the collective regulation of arable and pasture for their survival, and only a prosperous few managed to enclose their land, thereby removing it from some form of collective control. In western France, pastures were larger and more numerous, and there were more animals. Here, where standards of living were somewhat higher, many peasants worked their own, enclosed fields, but even the owners of enclosed fields usually depended upon commons in marshes, sparse forests, or wastes nearby. Few peasant families were able to extend the independence that they enjoyed in their gardens over the whole of their agricultural activities. The more prosperous were the more independent. The poor accepted the collective constraints that enabled them, without nearly enough land of their own, to exist on the land.

In all areas peasants struggled to acquire enough land to support their families. Usually the peasantry controlled less than half of the village land; the rest was in the hands of noblemen, churchmen, or the bourgeoisie, who let it to the peasants in various forms of leasehold or sharecropping. The land that the peasants did hold was divided very unequally. In most villages only two or three peasant families controlled enough arable to support a team of horses and a heavy plough. These families of *laboureurs*, well under 10 percent of the peasantry, held enough land to live on. Most families had far less than the twenty to twenty-five acres that, in a three-course rotation and after many charges, would supply bread for the subsistence needs of a family. These peasants usually depended upon some form of collective control of arable and pasture, and upon supplementary work or rented land. The poorest became artisans, sharecroppers, or day labourers working for *laboureurs* or for tenant farmers on the large estates. Those who were a little better off rented land to increase their arable, and a handful of tenant farmers became *gros fermiers* (prosperous tenant farmers) on large estates, and they were the most prosperous of all the peasantry. But these arrangements—the sharecropping whereby the landowner supplied seed, stock, and tools and took half of the product, the renting of leaseholds for usually three, six, or nine years for fixed sums that amounted to about a quarter of the produce, and even the day labouring, which was commonly a means of repaying advances of seed or the use of a team and plough—created their own lines of dependence and, often, their debts. When the harvest was good, the year's charges might be paid; when it was not, debts accumulated, and most peasant families lived under a burden of debt that approached the value of their land and threatened the basis of their livelihood.

Other charges pressed in on the peasant family. Royal taxes—the *taille* and the *gabelle* (salt tax)—took 20 percent of its gross product. Tithes varied, a tenth here, a twelfth there, usually about 8 percent and always collected in kind in the field after the harvest. Seigneurial charges varied even more. In Beauvais they were low, about 4 percent;[4] elsewhere they were usually much higher. In many ecclesiastical seigneuries, and in those cleared relatively recently, *censitaires* (*cens payers*) usually paid a *champart*, an exorbitant charge that amounted to a second tithe. Together all of these charges took a third to a half of the peasant's gross product. In addition, rent for leased land had to be paid, and at least 20 percent of the grain had to be kept for seed. Even in good years little enough was left.

Living on the edge of misery, deeply in debt, always faced with the spectre of loss of land, the peasant family could count on little outside support. In principle, the seigneur was the master of the village, and in the seventeenth century there were still seigneurs who interceded at court on behalf of their peasants, who supported peasant revolts against the crown, and who recruited soldiers from among their dependents. In these cases there were still personal bonds, often of considerable affection, between peasant and seigneur. But the seigneur or his appointee was also judge in the seigneurial court, even of cases in which he was also a plaintiff, and he was invariably a creditor. Especially as the bourgeoisie displaced the older seigneurial nobility, the seigneurial system became increasingly a fiscal system, a source of heavy charges for the *censitaire* and of revenue for the seigneur. The *curé* was usually far closer to the peasants than the seigneur. Cultivating a little land, probably the offspring of a *laboureur*, he was virtually a peasant. In a society of believers he could be the much loved leader of his parish flock, a man who sometimes sided with the peasants against seigneur or royal official, but who could do little to lighten their burdens, and who taught of duty, obedience, and humility. The *assemblée des habitants*, usually the principal men of the village, met after Sunday mass to discuss such issues as church maintenance, common or woodcutting regulations and, above all, the collection of royal taxes, for the *assemblée* had to appoint local tax assessors and collectors and furnish an annual lump sum to a royal collector. In some areas this village plutocracy exercised considerable power, even serving as a focus for anti-seigneurial feeling. More often it was dominated by the seigneur or his bailiff, but even when it functioned independently, the *assemblée* could only apportion burdens originating in circumstances far beyond its control. In such circumstances the peasant family had few defences; there could be little upward mobility and always there was some dropping off as the most vulnerable peasant families slipped into the ranks of the perhaps half-million Frenchmen who wandered and begged.

Death or emigration were other escapes. During the peasant revolts in Normandy in the 1830s some of the dying were said to have assured their *curés* that they died in peace knowing that, finally, they would be exempt from the *taille*.[5] Some two hundred thousand French people worked in Spain. Canada was another alternative, but it was so remote and uninviting that few left with the intention of settling there—a few dozen families, and the women from Paris poor houses sent in the 1660s to be brides. In 1634, Robert Giffard had enticed several families from Mortagne in Perche to his Canadian seigneury of Beauport only by offering each of them a thousand arpents (840 acres) of land and part of the harvest from his own farm in Canada.[6] Most men came to Canada under a temporary contract as soldiers or *engagés*. But such contracts were also escapes that drew if not from the beggars at least from the desperately poor in the lowest strata of the peasantry.[7] The majority of immigrants to Canada were people of this sort. When their contract expired or their regiment was recalled many returned to France, but more than half stayed to form the principal male stock of Canada's rural population.[8] There were also bourgeoisie, clerics, and people of noble blood among the immigrants to Canada. Considered overall, the immigrant population included almost all the elements of French society—minus, perhaps, the upper echelons of each stratum—but the people who settled the countryside came overwhelmingly from among the nearly destitute and virtually landless.

They came from western France, principally from the old provinces of Aunis, Saintonge, and Poitou in the hinterland of La Rochelle, and from eastern Normandy. A good many of the women came from Paris. In the early years, when Rouen was the principal port of embarkation for Canada, about a quarter of the emigrants were Norman. In 1663, they and their children, together with people from adjacent Perche, formed a third of the Canadian population.[9] Later, as commercial connections shifted to La Rochelle and as regiments that had been recruited in the southwest were sent to Canada, most immigrants came from south of the Loire.

These western lands had seen some of the bitterest peasant revolts in seventeenth-century France. In 1639, ten thousand Norman peasants, rising against increases in the *taille* that were forcing more of them off the land and into debtors' prisons, conducted a guerilla war against royal officials and soldiers until they were brutally put down by the king's army. This was a revolt of *nu-pieds*—the desperate poor against the fiscal exactions of the crown—and it originated in the type of people who predominated among those who went to Canada. Like most of France, these western lands were overpopulated. In spite of increasingly severe regulations that reflected the interests of crown and towns, the peasants had depleted the forest so much that in many areas scarcely a tree was over twenty years old. Land values had risen sharply, and nobles and bourgeoisie sought to control, and then to subdivide and sell, common marshes and wastes. The bourgeoisie had penetrated the countryside at the expense of both nobles and peasants. In many villages and parishes the great majority of peasants were landless day labourers, tenants, or sharecroppers on the estates of the bourgeoisie. Yet this was also the area where the deep-seated individualism of the French peasant, centred on the nuclear family, had found its fullest expression. Long before the right was codified in revisions of the *coutume de Normandie* in 1579 and 1585, Norman peasants had the right to enclose, which meant that they could use their land as they wished without the collective constraints of a common three-course rotation and of *vaine pâturage*. Many peasants lived in dispersed farmsteads amid their own fields. In parts of eastern Normandy fewer than 30 percent of the farm houses were in villages. Even where poverty was most acute and settlement was largely agglomerated, there were prosperous *laboureurs* who lived away from the village on their own land. Along the lower Seine, source of many of the earliest emigrants to Canada, and here and there on the limestone plains nearby, dispersed farmsteads were aligned along riverbank or road while their land stretched behind in *terroir en arête de poisson*.[10]

Rural Settlement in Canada

Most immigrants to Canada came as individuals. In the early years, there was an acute shortage of women but the crown sent almost a thousand women to Canada in the 1660s, and girls in the colony characteristically married at puberty. Later, women married at an average of twenty or twenty-one, several years under the average age of marriage for their sex in France. These unions created the households of Canada. Even before 1663, when a few seigneurs had brought small groups of immigrants from the same parts of France, only a quarter of Canadian marriages were between people from the same French province.[11] Upsetting the profound localness of French rural life even more than a transatlantic crossing was the mixing from all over western France that took place within the early Canadian household. The effects on accent, tools, diet, clothing, buildings, agricultural methods, and social practices remain to be studied, but there can be no doubt that the overall tendency was towards cultural standardization as the sharp edges of French regional types quickly blurred and merged.[12] And whereas marriage in France took place within sharply defined social categories, the hierarchy of status must have coarsened in Canada because of the initial difficulty of finding any mate, and because of the impossibility among largely destitute people of establishing their precise social fit in a distant society. Men misrepresented themselves to royal officials—calling themselves *laboureurs* when they had been *journaliers* (day labourers) and *journaliers* when they had hardly worked—and they could be equally dissembling when they married.

Most of the *engagés* and demobilized soldiers who married and settled down in Canada became farmers. The fur trade required a small white labour force. Very few people living east of Trois-Rivières ever engaged in it; by 1700 no more than 2 percent of all Canadian men were in the west in any given year, and by 1719 not more than 12 percent of them had spent a season there.[13] The towns employed relatively few artisans and labourers. Yet most of the people who settled in Canada did so voluntarily. They had no niche to return to in France, whereas there was land in Canada and the prospect of a farm. With not nearly enough wage labour in the colony to support its population, labour was always expensive; its price, because any employer had to pay to counteract the alternative of farming, was a measure of the attraction of land. The royal shipyards in Quebec near the end of the French regime paid several times French wages yet had difficulty holding Canadian workers. "As he is Canadian," wrote the intendant Bigot of a worker who wanted to leave a yard, "he prefers his liberty to being subject to a clock."[14]

In the villages of coastal Normandy and along the lower Seine early in the eighteenth century, a *journalier* worked four days to earn a single livre. A thousand livres bought two or three arpents of arable land.[15] In Canada at the same date, a *journalier* earned one and one-half to two livres a day, and a thousand livres would buy an enormous tract of uncleared land—even an unsettled seigneury—or a farm lot with some fifteen cleared arpents, a one-room cabin, barn, and stable, and sixty arpents of forest. To generalize broadly, wages were at least five times higher in Canada than in France, and the price of cleared land in Canada, even after the high labour cost of clearing it, was five to ten times lower. Uncleared land, valuable in France, was almost worthless in Canada. A parcel of arable land that could be earned by a year's work in Canada might not be earned in a lifetime in France. In Canada, almost any man could obtain a forested lot at any time.

Throughout the French regime, seigneurs conceded farm lots without initial charge. Because a forested lot would not produce its first small crop until at least eighteen months after clearing began, a destitute immigrant might begin by renting a partially cleared lot that he would pay for with up to a third or half of its harvest. This was a temporary arrangement. The tenant also obtained a lot *en roture*. If crops on his tenancy were good, he might be able to hire a man to begin clearing his own land; at least he could hope to quit the tenancy with the means to survive the first years of clearing. Permanent tenant farmers were uncommon except near Montreal and Quebec and on some seigneurial domains.[16] Sooner or later most immigrants settled on their own farm lots. Sometimes they were no more than forty to fifty arpents in size, more commonly eighty to 120 arpents of land,[17] which in the first years were cleared at a rate of some two arpents annually and then more slowly as farm work demanded more time. After a lifetime of work a man might have thirty or forty arpents of arable and pasture and hold twice as much forest.

Often he would have acquired additional lots for his sons, one of whom would take over the family farm, gradually paying off his brothers and sisters for their equal shares in the inheritance.

In this way immigrants who left France in poverty eventually lived on their own land. The long, thin lots fronting on the river were introduced by immigrants from eastern Normandy (Pierre Deffontaine's surmise was correct[18]) but the more basic introduction from France was agricultural individualism centred on the nuclear family. After an Atlantic crossing, a period as a soldier or an *engagé*, perhaps a few years as a tenant farmer, and the trauma of clearing the forest, the French peasant's craving for enough land to support a family was satisfied on a farm lot along the St. Lawrence River.

Immigrants who crossed the Atlantic to Canada moved towards land but away from markets. The crop varieties and livestock breeds of northwestern France that were raised in Canada never penetrated the French market in the seventeenth century, when prices were low, and rarely in the eighteenth century, when prices were better. The West Indies were also remote, twice as far away by water from Quebec as from Boston. Louisbourg, the naval base and fortress built on Cape Breton Island in 1718, provided some market for Canadian agricultural produce, and in the 1720s and 1730s there were fairly regular sales in the West Indies, but in the seventeenth and eighteenth centuries Canada was isolated by a severely continental location from sizeable agricultural markets in the North Atlantic world. Many of the quarter of the Canadian population who lived in the towns kept gardens and livestock, and members of religious orders were supplied directly by domainal farms in church seigneuries. There were regular market days in Quebec, Trois-Rivières, and Montreal. In the fall, merchants toured the countryside near Quebec to buy grain. Eventually most habitants sold a little grain and perhaps a calf and some butter every year, but farming developed in Canada within a chronically depressed agricultural market. Wheat prices declined from 1650 to 1720, rising only slowly and irregularly thereafter.[19] Land prices were static and, after a flurry of land trading in the 1660s and early 1670s, there were few sales.[20]

For a time the brutality of the confrontation with the forest obscured both the benefits of cheap land and the constrictions of the market. A Canadian farm of fifteen cleared arpents met the bare subsistence needs of a family.[21] Unless a habitant cleared some of the land while he still lived with his parents, unless he hired labour or bought a partially cleared lot, he and his family would struggle to survive for almost a decade. Such people would fall into debt and would face scurvy each winter. A few might get back to France; many would die. Here, as elsewhere, the initial confrontation of European settlers with the land around the fringe of the Canadian Shield was a devastating experience tempered only somewhat in the early, most bitter years by the availability of fuel, fish, and game. But the habitant was warmer in winter than were most peasants in northwestern France, where wood was so scarce and expensive that bake ovens often burned matted straw. Fish and game, to which French peasants had steadily less legal access and which they poached at greater risk, must have saved many settlers from starvation during their first Canadian winters, and they remained an important part of the Canadian diet long after the stumps had rotted in the first clearings.

If the farm family survived long enough to clear twenty-five or thirty arpents, then certainly by the second farm generation living standards had risen above those of most French peasants. In 1712, the royal engineer Gidéon de Catalogne noted that in Canada everybody ate the wheaten bread afforded by only the most prosperous peasants in France; and if Peter Kalm exaggerated when he wrote in 1749 that meat was the dietary staple of rural Canada, his remark does indicate something of the surprise of an educated European, familiar with the almost meat-free diets of most European peasants, at the amount of meat consumed by ordinary people in Canada. Canadian farms themselves reveal the improvement. A farm worked by the son of its first occupant would have thirty or forty arpents of cleared land. It produced one hundred bushels of wheat and some peas, oats, and barley and carried one or two horses, probably a pair of oxen, five or six cows, three or four pigs, some poultry, and a few sheep. There was a kitchen garden, some apple trees, and a sizeable woodlot, and there was access to the river for fishing and to the forest for hunting.[22] This was unspecialized agriculture, characteristic of subsistence farms, but among the French peasantry only a few *laboureurs* and properous tenant farmers possessed more.

Yet Canadian farms did not grow much larger. In some Norman parishes a very few *laboureurs* held two hundred arpents of arable and pasture and owned as many as ten work horses and a hundred sheep.[23] Such men were considerable employers of agricultural labour; often they were creditors and money lenders, and their relative wealth and power set them apart in the rural community. No Canadian habitants worked such farms during the French regime, partly because of partible inheritance but principally because there was no market for the output of a larger farm. The function of farming in Canada was to provide for the subsistence of a family; when this need was met, there was little other function. Clearing stopped— only a handful of habitant farms in Canada contained a hundred cleared arpents— and much the same family farm passed from generation to generation. These subsistence farms created no wealth, but the standard of living of most Canadian farmers was comparable to the French *laboureur moyen*—well within the top 10 percent of the French peasantry. Probably few French peasants aspired to more; they reached the nobility or the urban bourgeoisie only in their fairy tales. After a generation or two, and after much hardship, Canadians had met this limited aspiration. The independence that most French peasants enjoyed in their gardens and craved for in their farms came far closer to being a reality in a colony where there was land to meet a family's subsistence needs.

Higher living standards depended upon available land rather than upon improved techniques. Livestock were as poorly bred as in France; because of the increased use of the forest for forage and browse, manure was even more rarely spread on the arable; and two-course rotations often replaced three. Some habitants planted fields for several years in succession before relegating them to prolonged pasture or fallow—a form of convertible husbandry used on marginal lands in western France. Average seed/yield ratios were as low in Canada as in France, and would likely have been lower but for the high initial yields of newly cleared land. There had been some drift in Canada towards more extensive agricultural practices as cleared land was substituted for scarce labour, but generally the tools and methods of tradition-bound French peasant agriculture in the seventeenth century, little changed since the late Middle Ages, were transplanted in Canada. Applied to more land than most French peasants controlled, they yielded a higher standard of living.

The Canadian habitant's relative position was further enhanced by the absence of royal taxes. Neither the *gabelle* nor the *taille* was assessed in Canada, and the modest royal demand for road work, a *corvée* of two days a year, was long meaningless in a virtually roadless colony. Royal taxes had been discontinued to encourage settlement, not to alleviate the hardships of the common people, but whether or not royal officials clearly understood the change, their absence reflected the difficulty, common to sparsely settled European colonies overseas, of imposing European charges on inexpensive land amid the fluid conditions of new settlement. In the improbable event that royal taxes had been imposed and collected—to have done so would have made Canada an even less populated colony—the Canadian habitant's standard of living would have remained relatively high, for access to land rather than freedom from taxes was the fundamental change in his situation.

The failure of *gabelle* and *taille* to penetrate the countryside of the lower St. Lawrence reflects the relative autonomy of the nuclear family in rural Canada. However much the French peasant family valued its independence, it lived within the impinging influence of village, parish, seigneury, town, province, and state. The Canadian habitant's rough ease created a large measure of independence as, to some extent, it did for the families of *laboureurs* in France. In Canada, there was another difference. Because there was little market for farm produce there was little commercial pressure on agricultural land. For this reason, the whole institutional infrastructure of French rural life was enormously weakened.

The urban bourgeoisie's massive penetration of the French countryside did not take place in Canada. Even in seigneuries near the towns, habitant families held most of the cleared land,[24] and in remote seigneuries they held virtually all of it. Some merchants had a few farm lots and perhaps a seigneury but most of their energy went into the fur trade, and their impact on rural life was negligible. Faced with chronic agricultural overproduction, capital put into the development of large commercial farms was lost unless, as for the domainal farms on some church seigneuries, there was an assured local market. Land speculations were unprofitable. The few farm purchasers were usually families looking for homes rather than merchants looking for profit. Because of high transportation costs, high wages, and official discouragement of colonial manufacturing, sawmilling, gristmilling, and weaving never developed as export industries. Since the Canadian countryside rewarded neither speculations nor entrepreneurship, the bourgeoisie turned its attention elsewhere.

The seigneurial system faced the same difficulty. Except in a few church seigneuries, there were no large farms on seigneurial domains because there was no market for the production. Seigneurial charges were usually lower than in France—approximately 5 to 10 percent of the habitant's gross income—and many specific charges, including the *champart*, were discontinued. The small population stretched along the St. Lawrence River through almost two hundred different seigneuries, most of which remained unprofitable throughout the French regime. Accounts were poorly kept, and rents went uncollected for years. A few seigneuries, particularly Montreal Island, which had by far the largest population of any Canadian seigneury and was managed fastidiously by the Sulpicians, began to produce considerable revenues well before the end of the French regime. In them, the seigneur or his agents became a considerable presence and the habitants, like their French counterparts, procrastinated as best they could in the payment of rents. More commonly the French seigneurial system, which even in relatively small French seigneuries required a manager, an attorney and an assistant attorney, a clerk, a sergeant, lieutenants, and even a gaoler, hung over Canada during the French regime in a state of suspended animation. Its legal structure remained essentially intact, but the conditions that would make it profitable and give it life were largely absent until growing population pressure on the seigneurial lowlands of Quebec in the nineteenth century gave it some of its intended teeth.[25]

Parishes also developed weakly, although Roman Catholicism had come with most immigrants to Canada as naturally as the French language. Often the habitants were served by itinerant priests through two or three generations until there were enough people in a given local area to support a *curé*. On occasion they resisted the bishop's plan to establish a *curé*, perhaps because of the cost (although the Canadian tithe was only one twenty-sixth of the grain harvest), perhaps because of the priest's moral censures and increasingly alien French background, and perhaps simply because they did not see the need. In some *côtes* (short lines of settlement) a chapel or church had been built and *fabrique* (church vestry) organized to meet intermittently, long before the *curé* arrived. Such organization strengthened with his coming but never gained the power of the *assembleé des habitants* with which the *fabrique* tended to merge in France. Royal taxes did not have to be apportioned and, except where commons had been laid out in riparian marshes, collective agricultural arrangements did not have to be worked out. Villages were virtually absent. A weak rural economy had not brought them into being, and settlers had seized the opportunity to live on their own farms. Men were expected to serve in the militia, but we cannot yet say how often it drilled or what social role, if any, it played in the countryside.[26]

In all of these ways the heavy French burden of institutional constraints and financial exactions on the nuclear family were lightened in Canada. The family stood more nearly on its own within a civil law, a system of government, and a set of customs, institutions, and social values that had come from France but had lost much of their force or had been differently combined and emphasized in a new setting where land was cheap and markets were meagre. As time passed, clusters of surnames began to appear along the *côtes*, adumbrating the intricate consanguineous ties in the rural society of nineteenth-century Quebec. The *côte* itself became a loose rural neighbourhood, but neither kin nor *côte* ever replaced the social primacy of the nuclear family. Unless he took over the family land, a son would eventually move away and—until early in the nineteenth century, when there was no more land and he was forced into the factory towns of New England, the lumber camps of the Shield, or the slums of Montreal, Trois-Rivières, and Quebec—reproduce the family farm and the relative freedom of his parents.

Rural society in Canada quickly became and long remained remarkably egalitarian. The extremes of the French countryside had been pared down to a common, minimal ease. During the entire French regime in Canada there was not a single really prosperous habitant farmer and hardly, after the first years, a rural family without some cleared land. The great majority of rural families held some thirty to fifty arpents of arable and pasture and a considerable woodlot. Rural Canada had been a clean social slate to which immigrants who settled on the land brought relatively similar backgrounds of poverty. Social differentiation had not been stamped on the countryside from the beginning, and the common exigencies of clearing land and establishing a farm undoubtedly elicited a relatively common response in the first generation of farms along a *côte*. Partible inheritance meant that the son who took over the family farm took on a debt to his brothers and sisters that perhaps dampened his initiative. In the longer run, rural society did not become stratified socially or economically because of the availability of land and the weakness of the commercial economy. Larger farms and genteel living were blocked by inadequate markets. Agriculture became primarily subsistent, clearing stopped when family needs were met, and new *côtes* were opened in response to demographic pressure rather than to increases in the price of wheat. Farm families lived in rough sufficiency, their lives dominated by the seasonal rhythm of the land, not by more powerful people who lived in other ways. Rural life in Canada had not developed the complex, interlocking hierarchy of French social relations. Habitant families worked out their friendships and their feuds, habitant society acquired a folklore derived and modified from French traditions, and many old people must have possessed a deep lore about the ways of the land. These were its complexities. Institutionally, Canadian rural society was simple enough: nuclear families spread across the land in small subsistent farms with few and weak institutional constraints on their independence.

Conclusion

The ambition of the ordinary French family to live securely and independently on its own land had found a more common fulfilment in rural Canada than anywhere in France. Farmhouse after small farmhouse lined the St. Lawrence River, each on its own land, each much like its neighbour—a simple landscape created by a simple rural society. In a setting where land was accessible but markets were not, the socio-economic complexity of rural France had been pared away until little more than the ordinary nuclear family remained. As long as cheap land was available, the self-subsistent independence that had become the way of life of the Canadian habitant family could be perpetuated in *côte* after *côte* as settlement spread through the St. Lawrence lowland and into the fringe of the Shield and Appalachian highlands. When land became scarce, as it did early in the nineteenth century, expansion slowed. Land values rose, the young were forced into non-agricultural activities, and society in the older *côtes* became more stratified. In the 1860s, an aged Philippe Aubert de Gaspé could still describe the Canadian habitant as *l' homme le plus indépendant du monde*,[27] but when he wrote this the independence of the habitant family was fast nearing its end. After two centuries of agricultural expansion, the safety valve of cheap land along the lower St. Lawrence was finally plugged, and the basis of the autonomy of the French-Canadian rural family had been undermined.

Were these Canadian developments put in a Hartzian perspective, it would be said that a French fragment, in this case the poorer peasantry, had worked out its own limited aspirations in a remote colony far from the entrammelling whole of French society.[28] While it is true that the great majority of immigrants who settled down to farm in Canada came from relatively common backgrounds of poverty in the lower echelons of the French peasantry, the difficulty with Hartz, I feel, is that he assigns far too passive a role to the particular conditions of environment and economy in New World settings. In Canada, the facts that land was abundant and cheap and that the market for agricultural products was poor meant that, whatever seventeenth-century Frenchmen had tried to farm there, the extremes of wealth and poverty of the French countryside would have tended to diminish rapidly and the nuclear family—the basic unit of all French society—would have asserted itself strongly. A society that was a drastic simplification of rural France had emerged in Canada, but the impetus to simplify had come from Canadian conditions rather than from the fragmentation of French society. Some members of the nobility came to Canada and obtained seigneuries, but then neglected them. The members of the bourgeoisie who controlled the commerce of the Canadian towns had not found it worth their while to extend their hold into the countryside. Had agricultural land in Canada been scarce and valuable, and had there been a regular market for Canadian agricultural products, the very immigrants who came to Canada would have created a strikingly different rural society, undoubtedly more stratified and hierarchical, more representative of the socio-economic variety that characterized all parts of rural France.

The social change that took place in rural Canada in the seventeenth century, and that was sustained in French-Canadian rural society until well into the nineteenth century, would take place wherever northwestern Europeans encountered similar conditions. Cheap land had drastically altered the conditions of European rural life, favouring one element of European society and weakening or eliminating the rest. With the safety valve of such land, an egalitarian, family-centred, rural society would be able to reproduce and extend itself generation after generation. Yet Frederick Jackson Turner neglected the influence of the market and, writing before pre-industrial society in Europe had been rigorously studied, he did not understand that frontier conditions had accentuated and simplified a long process of social evolution in Europe. In medieval society, ties of heredity and name among the nobility and of village community among the poor had tended to obscure the nuclear family. From late in the Middle Ages this compact, diverse society, in which people of different station lived in intimate social interaction and in which the family was often not a private setting for socialization, was slowly giving way to another, in which social life drew back into the nuclear family, supported eventually by a sense of class. By the seventeenth century, the sentiment of the family was widespread and there was a general tendency, where conditions permitted, to push back ties of wider sociability in favour of the intimacy of the family. This massive social reorganization proceeded quite unevenly, more rapidly among the bourgeoisie than among the nobility or the poor, more rapidly in the principal than in the small towns.[29] In the countryside of middle-latitude colonies overseas, Europeans inadvertently found a setting where the ordinary family could find an unusually autonomous existence.

In Canada, where for well over a century a tiny population lived with cheap land and poor markets, conditions particularly favoured the self-sustaining family. The social evolution of plantation colonies was obviously different, and in most middle-latitude colonies cheap land and poor markets were not conditions of settlement for several generations. South African rural society is the closest parallel to the French-Canadian; the stock farm on the veld and the small mixed farm along the lower St. Lawrence were the same socio-economic response in different physical conditions to the long availability of land in a weak market economy.[30] But by its very extremity, rural society in Canada reveals a social tendency inherent in the outreach of Europe to new lands far from European markets where, for a time, land was likely to be much cheaper and markets much poorer than in Europe. In such circumstances the independent, nuclear family would tend to emerge strongly within an egalitarian, family-centred society, a tendency that would be variously checked or modified by any protracted increase in the price of land or improvement in the market.

Notes

1. These and subsequent remarks on seventeenth-century France are drawn principally from the following: Fernand Braudel, ed., *Histoire économique et sociale de la France* (Paris, 1970), 2; Pierre Goubert, *The Ancien Régime: French Society, 1600–1750* (London, 1973); and Fernand Braudel, *Capitalism and Material Life, 1400–1800* (New York, 1975).

2. Pierre Goubert, "Les cadres de la vie rurale," in *Histoire*, ed. Braudel, 88–89.

3. Ibid., 92–93.

4. Pierre Goubert, *Beauvais et le Beauvaisis de 1600 à 1730* (Paris, 1960), 181.

5. Michel Caillard, "La révolte des nu-pieds," in Michel Caillard, Marcel Duval, Philippe Guillot, and Marie Claude Gircourt, *À travers la Normandie des XVIIe et XVIIIe siècles* (Caen, 1963), 102.

6. Caillard notes a contract of 14 Mar. 1634 between Giffard and Jean Guyon and Zacharie Cloutier (ibid., 102n).

7. It can be said, I think, that the very poor but perhaps not quite destitute people whom André Corvisier found to be the principal recruits to the ranks of the French army were also the sort of people who came to Canada. *L'armée française de la fin du XVIIe siècle au ministère de Choiseul* (Paris, 1964), 1: 473–506.

8. On immigration to Canada, see Louise Dechêne, *Habitants et marchands de Montréal au XVIIe siècle* (Paris and Montreal, 1974), chap. 2; R.C. Harris, "The French Background of Immigration to Canada before 1700," *Cahiers de geographie du Québec* 16 (Sept. 1972): 313–24; and Gabriel Debien, "Engagés pour le Canada au XVIIe siècle vus de la Rochelle," *Revue d'histoire de l'Amérique française* 6 (Sept. 1952): 177–233, 374–404.

9. Marcel Trudel, *La population du Canada en 1663* (Montreal, 1973), 49, and *The Beginnings of New France, 1524–1663* (Toronto, 1973), 257ff.

10. The essential reference on evolving society and land use in Normandy is still Jules Sion's brilliant *Les paysans de la Normandie orientale* (Paris, 1909).

11. Trudel, *Beginnings*, 262.

12. Professor Dechêne has gone so far as to suggest that the close juxtaposition in Canada of different folk religions, none of them with many Canadian adherents, favoured the penetration of a purer Christianity (*Habitants et marchands*, 479).

13. Much the best discussion of the habitant's involvement in the fur trade is in ibid., 218–25.

14. Quoted by Jacques Mathieu in *La construction navale royale à Québec, 1739–1759* (Quebec, 1971), 57.

15. For figures on the value of land and labour in Normandy in the early eighteenth century, see Philippe Guillot, "Étude économique et sociale du front de côte entre Orne et Seulles," in Caillard et al., *À travers la Normandie,* 324–31.

16. Dechêne calculates that 20 percent of the farmers on Montreal Island were tenants (*Habitants et marchands*, 279–81).

17. Richard Colebrook Harris, *The Seigneurial System in Early Canada: A Geographical Study* (Madison and Quebec, 1966), 117–19.

18. In Pierre Deffontaine, *Le rang, type de peuplement rural au Canada français* (Quebec, 1953).

19. Dechêne, *Habitants et marchands*, 521.

20. Harris, *Seigneurial System*, 57–62, 140–45; Dechêne, *Habitants et marchands*, 287–94.

21. Harris, *Seigneurial System*, 160.

22. Dechêne, *Habitants et marchands*, chap. 6; Harris, *Seigneurial System*, chap. 8.

23. Guillot, "Étude économique et sociale," 328; also see Marie-Claude Gricourt, "Étude d'histoire démographique, sociale, et religieuse de 5 paroisses de l'archidiacone du petit Caux," in Caillard et al., *À travers la Normandie,* 476–77.

24. See note 16.

25. For a discussion of the seigneurial system in post-conquest Quebec, see R.C. Harris and J. Warkentin, *Canada before Confederation:, A Study in Historical Geography* (Toronto, London, and New York, 1974), chap. 3.

26. W.J. Eccles suggests that the militia extended military values strongly through the Canadian countryside, but until the militia has been thoroughly studied I would hesitate to attach this importance to it. *France in America* (London, 1972), 69–70.

27. In Philippe Aubert de Gaspé, *Mémoires* (Quebec, 1885), 530.

28. Louis Hartz, *The Founding of New Societies* (New York, 1964).

29. See particularly the study by the French demographer Philippe Aries, *L'enfant et la vie familiale sous l'ancien régime* (Paris, 1960).

30. R. Cole Harris and Leonard Guelke, "Land and Society in Early Canada and South Africa," *Journal of Historical Geography* 3 (1977): 135–53.

SCOTTISH EMIGRATION AND SETTLEMENT IN EARLY NINETEENTH CENTURY CAPE BRETON*

STEPHEN J. HORNSBY

In the first half of the nineteenth century almost a million people emigrated from the British Isles to British North America. Many of these emigrants were displaced by the social and economic changes associated with the agricultural and industrial revolutions, and by the economic recession that affected Britain at the end of the Napoleonic Wars. Small tenant farmers and marginal cottars were squeezed off the land by over-population and enclosures, handloom weavers were put out of business by the spread of the factory system, and rural tradesmen suffered from the post-war depression. With few prospects in Britain, most hoped to improve their circumstances in the North American colonies. Although some got no further than the port of entry and others filtered into the fishing and timber industries, many moved inland and occupied agricultural land. Across much of Southern Ontario, along the river valleys of Nova Scotia and New Brunswick, and on Prince Edward Island, lots were settled, forest was cleared, and family farms were created. After years of backbreaking work, thousands of settlers achieved a modest and relatively secure independent living on the land.[1]

Yet as immigration continued and population increased, fertile land in these patches of settlement grew scarce. Land costs rose and the agricultural opportunity for new settlers was severely diminished. Economic stratification and out-migration were the inevitable results. By mid-century, second and third generation settlers were moving away from the family homestead in search of land and

*From *The Island: New Perspectives on Cape Breton History, 1713–1975*, ed. Kenneth Donovan (Fredericton, NB: Acadiensis Press, 1990). The author would like to thank Cole Harris and Graeme Wynn for their comments on an earlier draft of this paper. Much of the paper is based on Stephen J. Hornsby, "An Historical Geography of Cape Breton Island in the Nineteenth Century" (Ph.D. diss., University of British Columbia, 1986), chap. 2 and 3. A shorter version of this paper was published as "Migration and Settlement: The Scots of Cape Breton," in *Geographical Perspectives on the Maritime Provinces*, ed. D. Day (Halifax, Nova Scotia: St. Mary's University, 1988), 15–24.

employment. Many settled along the southern edge of the Canadian Shield and the northern front of the Appalachian Highlands, frequently combining subsistence farming with part-time work in local mines, mills, and lumber camps. Some moved into the growing towns and cities of British North America, while others left for the burgeoning industrial cities and agricultural frontier of the United States.[2]

Among the areas encompassed by this cycle of migration and settlement was Cape Breton Island. At the beginning of the nineteenth century, Cape Breton was thinly settled, extensively forested, and economically underdeveloped. Some 2 500 people lived on the Island, most of them French-speaking Acadians, the rest Loyalists, Irish from Newfoundland, and Scots from mainland Nova Scotia and Prince Edward Island.[3] Virtually all of them were settled around the coast, most engaged in the cod fishery, the leading sector of the economy. The agricultural land that lay in the interior was almost untouched. Then, in 1802, settlers from the Western Highlands and Islands of Scotland began to arrive in Cape Breton. By 1845, approximately 20 000 had done so.[4] Whether voluntary emigrants or victims of the Highland Clearances, they sought land and transformed the Island. At mid-century, Cape Breton's population had increased to almost 55 000; people of Scottish descent outnumbered those of Acadian, Loyalist, and Irish origin by two to one.[5] Much of the coast, and a considerable part of the interior, was settled. Large areas of forest had been cleared, and farming had displaced the fishery as the Island's principal economic activity. By then, the best land had been taken and settlement had spread onto rocky backland. Although some settlers were well established, often much better off than they were in Scotland, many more were struggling to keep a toe-hold on the Island. By mid-century, a growing number were slipping away to the United States.

The Scottish Background

Most Scottish emigrants to Cape Breton in the early nineteenth century were from a triangular wedge of territory that had its eastern point at Fort William in Lochaber, its southwestern at Barra, and its northwestern at Lewis (figure 1). Within this triangle, Lochaber on the mainland, and Skye, Rhum, Harris, and the Uists in the Hebrides were major source areas. Beyond this triangle, Sutherland and the Central Highlands contributed a fraction to the Cape Breton migration.

Towards the end of the eighteenth century, most people in the Western Highlands and Islands of Scotland lived on the large estates of a few clan chiefs.[6] They depended on farming and lived in nucleated villages or clachans dispersed around the coast and along the interior valleys. Each clachan usually consisted of an irregular cluster of stone-and-turf houses set amid a large, arable open-field and surrounding communal grazings which included distant upland pastures or shielings.[7] Among the inhabitants were a few substantial tenant farmers who rented land either from a tacksman (an old clan lieutenant) or direct from the clan chief.

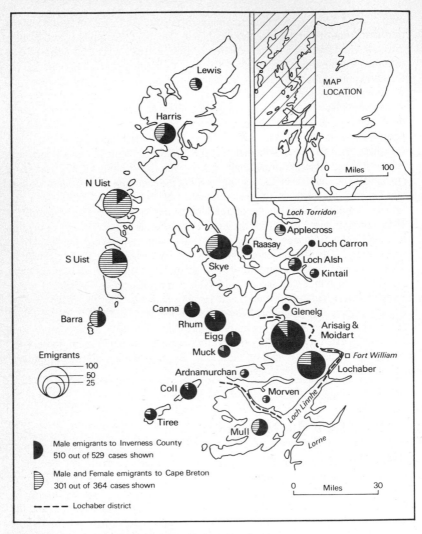

FIGURE 1   Origin of Scottish Emigrants to Cape Breton

SOURCES: Data from J.L. MacDougall, *History of Inverness County* (Truro, Nova Scotia, 1922); and Ferguson Mss., Beaton Institute.

Few of them had written leases, and without leases they could be evicted "at will." Each tenant had shares in the open-field and grazing rights on the commons. These rights were closely protected by a township council. The tenants also sublet scraps of land to cottars, the landless poor who made up much of the population of each village. The tenants drew a living from subsistence crops of oats, potatoes, and barley, and from sales of black cattle to southern drovers—the market connection that paid the rent. The cottars laboured for the tenants. Such an agricultural system, unchanged for generations, was relatively self-sufficient and aimed to accommodate as many clansmen on the land as possible.

In the 1790s and early 1800s all of this was disrupted. Rising prices for wool and meat during the Napoleonic Wars (1793–1815) encouraged clan chiefs to clear many of the agricultural villages in the interior and to lease the land to large, progressive sheep farmers. A French embargo on the export of Spanish barilla (alkali) to Britain also pushed up prices of domestically produced alkali, stimulating the expansion of kelping (the gathering and processing of seaweed to make alkali) along the West Coast and in the Hebrides.[8] As kelping was labour-intensive, landlords converted many clachans into crofting townships to accommodate large kelp workforces.[9] Following the advice of agricultural improvers, who stressed the value of individual holdings, open-fields were consolidated and arable land was divided into separate crofts (of about five or six acres), each of which was allocated to a tenant farmer or crofter (figure 2).[10] These crofts were expected to provide a meagre agricultural subsistence. On the tiny arable strips, the crofter grew oats, barley, and potatoes, with large inputs of labour and fertilizer (seashells, byre manure, old thatch). Beyond the stone dyke or wall that enclosed the crofts were the commons, where crofters grazed black cattle, sheep, and ponies. On average, each crofter in South Uist in 1827 owned three ponies, three cows, and two or three young cattle, usually year olds.[11] The commons also yielded peats for fuel and heather for thatch. Beaches were scoured for shell-fish and driftwood, and cliff-top nests were raided for eggs and seabirds. To ensure that crofters worked in the kelp industry, landlords raised the rent of each croft beyond its agricultural worth. To pay these inflated rents, crofters and their families spent their summers cutting kelp from tidal sounds and rocky islets, drying it on the beaches, and incinerating it to produce an alkaline ash (figure 3), which eventually found a market in the glass and chemical factories of Lowland Scotland and England.[12] Landlords made enormous profits from these sales, almost double their income from land rent.

Together, money from kelp, cattle sales, and the produce of their farms yielded crofters a meagre living. Most of their income went out in rent, although rents were usually less than £5 or £6 a year.[13] In some townships, crofters also had to pay to use the estate mill; anyone found using a hand-quern was fined and the stones dumped into the sea. In good years, crofters made enough to get by. In bad, when the price of kelp or cattle fell, many found themselves in debt, facing loss of their possessions and eviction from their croft. In good times, such spare income as they had was spent on imported meal and salt, but the diet was generally poor: usually some combination of milk, cheese, oatmeal, potatoes, and fish. Red meat was rarely eaten. Living conditions, too, were spartan. Most crofters lived in small, simple "blackhouses" built from drystone walls and roofed with turf or thatch (figure 2). Inside, there was a living-room where the crofter and his family ate and slept; a byre for cattle, sheep, and poultry; and at the rear a barn for storing grain,

FIGURE 2   Crofting Township at Uig Bay, Skye, Late 19th Century

SOURCE: George Washington Wilson Collection, Aberdeen University Library.

potatoes, threshed fodder, and salted food. The few furnishings included stools, (handlines, nets, sheepskin buoys); and wicker creels for carrying peat, kelp, and chests, a cooking-pot, and a spinning-wheel. The crofter also owned some agricultural implements (crooked and straight spades, a sickle, a flail); fishing gear potatoes.[14] Few owned much more than these scanty, utilitarian possessions.

Yet the crofters were relatively well-off compared to the cottars, who had "no means of subsistence but what they derive from the tenants their relatives."[15] In return for a patch of soil, in which to raise potatoes, and the right to pasture a cow on the commons, cottars paid rents to the crofters in money, labour (weeding, ploughing, kelping), or kind (a few fowls, a sheep). They also derived some income from kelping, from harvesting on Lowland farms, and from begging, scavenging, and knitting sweaters for sale. Their diet must have been less nutritious than that of the crofters; scarcely more than milk, potatoes, oatmeal, and shellfish. Their housing, too, was usually much less substantial. With no right to land, they lived in roughly constructed earth-and-stone hovels roofed with driftwood, heather, and turf.[16] Cottars were hardly better off than beggars.

If late nineteenth-century Tiree is any guide, the nuclear family was the most basic unit of crofting society. Most households comprised parents and children; the rest consisted of extended families of parents, newly married children, and grandparents.[17] The "chief earthly anxiety" of many crofters "was to pay their rents, retain their small possessions and keep their families about them."[18] To ensure this

FIGURE 3   Kelp Burning, Orkney, Late 19th Century. Similar scenes occurred along the West Coast and in the Hebrides earlier in the century.

SOURCE: By courtesy of Edinburgh City Libraries.

in densely crowded townships, crofters relied on mutual aid and assistance from kin, and on the rules and regulations governing the collective use of the commons. A township constable was elected to protect crofters' rights, and he rigorously checked the stocking of the grazings and the cutting of peats. Beyond the township, the crofter had few people to rely on. The few tacksmen who remained were poor yet resented by their tenants for the "manerial [i.e., manorial] bondage" that underlay their position.[19] The personal bonds between clan chief and tenants, once so strong, were no longer important. Most chiefs were absentee landlords who were represented on their estates by a factor (manager), often a lowland Scot, who had no intimate connection with the people. Priests and ministers were the only other people of consequence in the lives of the crofters. Many Roman Catholic priests took considerable interest in their pastoral charges and some, in the face of landlord hostility, encouraged their congregations to emigrate.[20] Presbyterian ministers, however, were often on the side of laird and factor, rather than the crofter. They depended upon the landlords for financial support and some, at least in Skye in the 1820s and 1830s, acted as estate factors and ran sheep farms. Many ministers also lacked a working knowledge of Gaelic.[21] The vacuum was filled by evangelicals who preached in many townships, distributed Gaelic Bibles, and tried to provide some moral and spiritual support to a population struggling to eke out a livelihood.

Neither the destruction of the traditional agricultural economy nor its replacement by crofting and kelping were readily accepted by the people. On Lord MacDonald's estate in Skye, the surveyor responsible for laying out the new crofts reported in 1799 that the tenants' "adherence to inveterate opinions and old uncorrected customs operates powerfully against improvements or even alterations."[22] Fearing that they would lose land, rights, and status in the transition, many tenant farmers preferred to emigrate, hoping to re-create overseas something of the life that was being destroyed in Scotland. During the peace between Britain and France in 1802–3, nearly 7 000 Highlanders left for British North America.[23] In August 1802, the first emigrant ship to sail directly to Cape Breton arrived in Sydney, and that year at least 400 new settlers took up land on the Island.[24] Concerned that their estates would be depopulated and that cheap labour for the kelp industry would disappear, Highland landlords joined humanitarians in lobbying for an act to improve conditions on emigrant ships. Stricter regulation of the emigrant trade would, of course, raise the price of a berth and so stem the exodus. Although the Passenger Vessel Act was passed in May 1803, the renewal of hostilities between Britain and France in the same month probably did more to curtail the outflow. The disruption of shipping, army recruiting in the Highlands, and the kelp boom reduced the emigrant flow to a trickle; between 1803 and the American War in 1812, only about 2 500 people left Scotland for British North America.[25] The few hundred people who emigrated to Cape Breton during these years were relatively well-off. In 1802, it cost about £15 for a family of five to cross the Atlantic; after the Passenger Vessel Act was implemented, the price more than doubled.[26] In 1810, a crofter needed to sell at least eight cattle or their equivalent to raise sufficient money to take his wife and three children to Cape Breton.

After 1815, as the British economy slid into post-war depression, cheap foreign alkalis and greater use of salt in chemical manufacturing weakened the market for kelp. Falling cattle prices undermined the other essential foundation of the crofting economy.[27] Faced with shrinking incomes, indebtedness, and the prospect of further agricultural reorganisation, many crofters decided to emigrate. Between 1815 and 1825, at least 9 000 Scottish passengers arrived in Nova Scotia, more than 2 000 of them in Cape Breton (figure 4). Like the earlier emigrants, many of these passengers were relatively well-off, for despite the gradual relaxation of the Passenger Vessel Act after the end of the war, a passage across the Atlantic was still expensive. In 1817, the 382 passengers from Barra who arrived at Sydney on board the *Hope* and the *William Tell* had paid eight guineas for each adult and six guineas for each child under the age of seven.[28] Contemporary observers in Scotland confirmed the pattern, noting that some of the emigrants had "a good deal of money" and reflecting that "the evil of this kind of emigration is that the best and most active tenants go and leave the poor and weak behind."[29] Then, in the late 1820s, the crofting economy fell apart. Abolition of the salt tax in 1825 made that commodity an accessible substitute for kelp; by 1827, only the highest grades of kelp were being produced. With their market destroyed, crofters were unable to meet their inflated rents. With their incomes gone, landlords turned to sheep

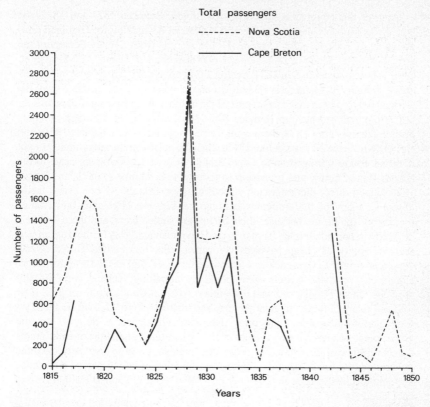

FIGURE 4   Immigration to Nova Scotia and Cape Breton Island from Scottish Ports, 1815–50.

SOURCES: Data from J.S. Martell, *Immigration to and Emigration from Nova Scotia 1815–1838* (Halifax: Public Archives of Nova Scotia, 1942); and R.G. Flewwelling, "Immigration to and Emigration from Nova Scotia 1839–1850," appendix II (Mss. in PANS). These sources are not a complete record of Scottish emigration to Nova Scotia.

farming to maintain the revenue from their estates. In many crofting townships and the few remaining clachans, tenants were evicted, houses demolished, and arable lands turned over to sheep pasture. Although some people were resettled on new crofts laid out on rocky moorland, many took passage overseas.[30] A few landlords were so keen to clear their estates that they helped destitute crofters and cottars to emigrate.[31] More commonly, landlords simply abolished rent arrears, which allowed tenants to scrape together the money for their passage from the sale of livestock and equipment.[32]

Much of this emigration came to Cape Breton. Between 1827 and 1832, the Island was probably the principal North American destination for Highland emigrants. During those years, Customs-House records from Sydney document the arrival of 7 300 Scots; in 1828 alone, 2 600 disembarked (figure 4). Many more came ashore unrecorded; in 1831, customs officers admitted that "several vessels arrive annually and land their passengers on the Western shore of this Island, the Masters neglecting to make any report of the number, in consequence of an officer not being stationed at Ship Harbour [Port Hawkesbury]."[33] Although numbers declined rapidly after 1832, there were further large influxes in the late 1830s and early 1840s. In the 20 years before 1845, when the potato blight and famine brought a virtual end to immigration to Cape Breton, at least 12 000 Scots came to the Island. Ties of family and friendship to those who had come to the Island before 1825 helped direct this migration stream to Cape Breton. As one estate factor observed, many of the emigrants leaving the Western Highlands and Islands preferred Cape Breton because "their friends are settled there, and there will be a difficulty in prevailing upon them to go to Upper Canada."[34] A further reason was the availability of cheap passages on vessels that had carried British North American timber to Greenock and other Scottish ports and needed a return cargo. Conditions on these vessels were generally appalling; vessels were usually crowded, under-provisioned, and unsanitary; small-pox and ship-fever took their toll; and many of those "in great poverty and distress" were "thrown on shore [in Cape Breton] incapable of procuring their own subsistence."[35] So great was the government's expenditure on aid that in 1832 it instituted a head-tax on immigrants to recoup some of its outlay. Ten years later, magistrates in Sydney petitioned the government for funds to build a shelter "for the relief of newly arrived emigrants, and shipwrecked seamen and passengers."[36] Well before, Thomas Haliburton had concluded that the Island was "a refuge for the poor."[37]

Scottish Settlement on Cape Breton Island

Although Cape Breton probably appeared bountiful to crofters cleared from the bogs and rocks of Western Scotland, its agriculture potential is limited.[38] More than half of the Island is rough, glaciated upland, part of the old, worn-down Appalachian mountain region. Only a quarter of the land has any agricultural value; the rest is either too steep, too wet, or covered with thin, acidic soils (figure 5). The best soils are on the alluvial deposits along the river valleys (intervales). In 1800, a dense, coniferous forest of spruce and fir covered much of southern Cape Breton, and a mixed forest dominated by sugar-maple, birch, hemlock, and pine extended around Bras d'Or Lake and over the uplands.[39] Then, as now, the climate was extreme. Long, severe winters follow short cool summers. At Sydney, the average frost-free period is 137 days; at Margaree, ten miles from the coast, it is only 62 days.

The early, relatively well-off Scottish settlers had the most choice of land and quickly occupied the accessible and fertile lands on the coast and along the major

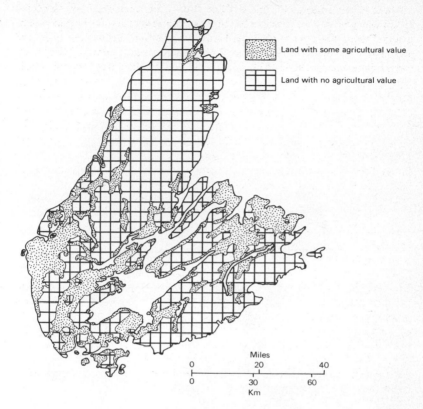

Land with some agricultural value

Land with no agricultural value

Miles

0   20   40

0   30   60

Km

FIGURE 5   Distribution of Agricultural Land on Cape Breton Island

SOURCE: After map in D.B. Cann, J.I. MacDougall, and J.D. Hilchey, *Soil Survey
of Cape Breton Island Nova Scotia* (Truro, Nova Scotia: Nova Scotia
Soil Survey, 1963), 57.

river valleys.[40] By 1820, Scots were settled along much of the northwest coast
between the Acadian settlements at Chéticamp and Inhabitants Bay, and on the east
coast among the Loyalist settlements around Sydney Harbour. A good deal of land
in the Inhabitants, Mabou, Margaree, Baddeck, and Mira river valleys, and at East
Bay and McNab's Cove on Bras d'Or Lake had also been granted (figure 6). In the
next decade, there were further grants to Scottish settlers along the northwest coast
and in the Middle, Mabou, and Margaree river valleys. By 1830, much of the best
land in Cape Breton had been taken. Later settlers were forced onto inhospitable
upland behind the first range of lots. As most of these settlers were squatters, their
holdings are not shown on figure 6. In the south of the Island they occupied such

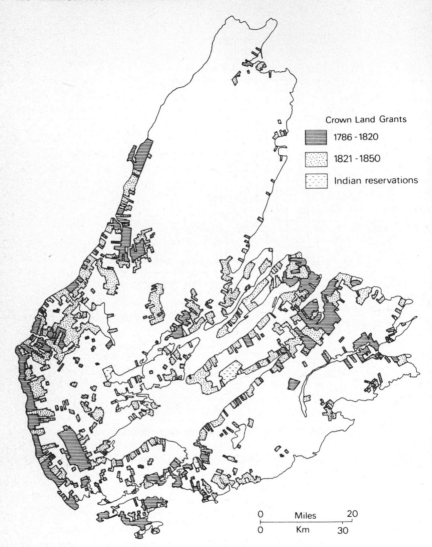

FIGURE 6   Crown Land Grants on Cape Breton Island, 1786–1850

SOURCES: Data from the Records of the Crown Lands Office, 1738 to 1962,
RG 20/A/3, PANS; and the Crown Land Index Sheets 108–12, 114–33,
and 135–40, Nova Scotia Department of Lands and Forests.

lowlands as remained open between Bras d'Or Lake and the Atlantic coast, and
settled the flanks of South Mountain and the Boisdale and Coxheath Hills. In the

north, their farms climbed the Creignish Hills, and fronted on the lands of earlier settlers along Skye Glen, around parts of Lake Ainslie, and at the head of Baddeck River. Much of this "backland" was wretchedly bad, but by mid-century it was home to most of the Island's population.

Before 1817, freehold grants of Crown land in Cape Breton were allowed only to bona fide Loyalists and disbanded soldiers; others were limited to leases.[41] Because Scottish settlers were generally unwilling to become tenants-at-will, many who arrived on the Island moved on to the United States;[42] those who stayed usually squatted illegally on Crown land. Only with increasing social and economic distress in Britain after 1815 did government policy encourage settlement in the colonies.[43] Thus, in 1817, freehold grants in Cape Breton were allowed on generous terms. After paying £3 to £5 to the Crown Lands Office for filing the grant and surveying the lot, a married settler could acquire 200 acres subject to an annual quit-rent of 2s. per 100 acres payable after two years of occupation. The settler also had to erect a house, clear and cultivate three of every fifty acres, and place three neat cattle on the land within three years.[44] Because quit-rents were never collected, a forested 200-acre lot was available for about £5—equivalent to the annual rent of a five-acre croft in Western Scotland. Many of the Scottish settlers already on the Island and a large number of the relatively well-off immigrants who arrived after the end of the war quickly took out grants.[45]

The later, destitute immigrants were much less fortunate. In 1827, just as Highland emigration to Cape Breton was nearing its peak, the Crown land regulations were tightened.[46] In an attempt to standardise the dispersal of Crown land in the British colonies and to encourage settlers with capital, the Colonial Office in London replaced the earlier system of land grants with a system of land sales at public auction. A reserve or upset price of between 2s.3d. and 2s.6d. per acre was set, pushing up the price of a 200-acre lot from about £5 to £25. Payments could be made in four equal instalments, the first at the time of sale and the rest at yearly intervals, but even this inducement was removed in 1837 when the Colonial Office ordered that 10 percent of the purchase money be paid on the day of sale and the balance within 14 days. Drawn up in Whitehall and modelled on regulations devised in New South Wales, the new system of land sales proved almost unworkable in Cape Breton. Most of the settlers were too poor to support themselves, let alone purchase land at the new rate. As a result, H.W. Crawley, the Surveyor General of Cape Breton, turned a blind eye and allowed settlement to proceed under the old regulations. It was not until 1832 that the Colonial Office caught up with the situation on the Island and ordered Crawley to comply with the 1827 directive.[47] Some grants were sold in the mid-1830s, but the number declined rapidly after the payment scheme was changed in 1837 (figure 7). Sales of land only began to recover after 1843 when the purchase price was reduced to 1s.9d. per acre.

Unable to afford land, the overwhelming majority of settlers became squatters. In 1837, Crawley estimated that 20 000 people, more than half the Island's population, occupied Crown land without grants.[48] Seven years later, an army officer granted 500 acres could not find a suitable tract because the country was

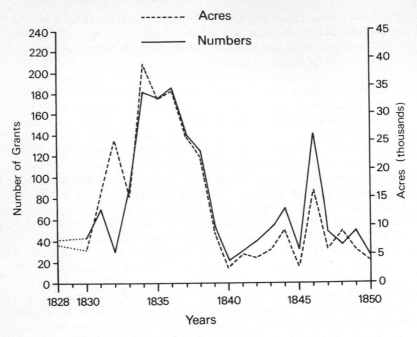

FIGURE 7   Number and Acreage of Crown Land Grants on Cape Breton Island, 1828–50

SOURCES: Data from the Annual Nova Scotia Blue Books, CO 221/43-62; and *Journals of the House of Assembly of Nova Scotia.*

"overspread with persons who ha[d], without permission obtained ... or chosen for themselves all the vacant Crown Lands."[49] There was little the Crown Lands Office could do. The few sales of land hardly covered the salaries of the surveyors and with the government unwilling to provide extra monies, Crown land lay virtually unprotected. The regulations had foundered on the huge expense of policing vast areas of virtually worthless land. As a result, the law was flouted on a massive scale. "*Every* body is against protecting the Crown Lands," Crawley complained in 1844, "all being interested in the plunder." "People learn to look upon the orders of the Govt. as mere matters of form and conclude that they may do as they please, and that the surest way of obtaining land is to take it, without the delay of asking leave, and to plunder at pleasure."[50]

Although many settlers managed to acquire land, markets for the produce of Cape Breton farms were distant and limited. Around the Gulf of St. Lawrence and along the Atlantic shore, there was little demand for the Island's principal crops of oats, potatoes, and hay. Cattle, sheep, salted meat, and butter were sold in Halifax and they also accounted for over 90 percent of the agricultural products shipped beyond Nova Scotia from Cape Breton.[51] Much of this external trade was to St. Pierre and Miquelon, and to St. John's, Newfoundland. On average, between 1842 and 1848, almost 1 500 cattle and nearly 1 400 sheep were shipped to St. John's each year; the city also took a considerable quantity of salted meat.[52] Even if these amounts are doubled (a generous estimate) to include exports to Halifax, trade beyond the Island was trifling: about one animal from each farm.[53] Within Cape Breton, the most important markets for agricultural produce were probably the fishing villages. In 1842, the Richmond County Agricultural Society reported that the demand was "more than our farmers can furnish, so that a comparatively large amount of flour, pork, etc is annually imported by our merchants—also many cargoes of potatoes etc from Prince E[dward] Island are sold every season in Arichat and the adjacent fishing stations."[54] There was also some demand from the approximately 1 000 inhabitants of Sydney, North Sydney, and Baddeck, the principal towns in Cape Breton, and from the many backland farmers who often needed to purchase extra supplies of hay, potatoes, oats, and livestock.[55]

By mid-century, two relatively distinct farming communities had emerged in Cape Breton (figure 8). Along the frontlands—the intervales, lakeshores, and parts of the coast—the early Scottish immigrants were settled on dispersed farms, each about a quarter of a mile apart and occupying a rectangular lot (usually with a ratio of width to length of 1:5). Virtually all the approximately 1 500 frontland farmers operated mixed farms that provided sustenance for their families and small commercial surpluses for sale in local and regional markets. On the backlands—the interior uplands and lowlands—the later Scottish settlers occupied irregular, dispersed holdings. Many of the approximately 4 500 backland farmers scratched a living from "scrub" farms and supplementary employment.[56] While frontland farmers sold their surplus crops and livestock, backland settlers sold their labour.

By 1850, a generation of backbreaking labour had yielded substantial improvements on many a frontland farm (figure 9). In the Mabou, East and West Lake Ainslie, Broad Cove, and Margaree districts in Inverness County, for example, improvements along the intervales and lakeshores were probably at least 40 acres in extent.[57] Similar-sized improvements most likely existed on intervales elsewhere on the Island. Some two-thirds of the cleared land on frontland farms would have been in pasture and grass, the rest in arable and orchard. A woodlot at the back of the farm provided extra forage for cattle and pigs, as well as timber for building and fuel. The principal cash items on frontland farms were livestock and livestock products. Farmers on the intervale land of Inverness County in 1851 almost certainly had more than the 8 cattle and 10 sheep that were average for their districts.[58] Indeed, as early as 1811, a handful of Scottish farmers in River Inhabitants, Richmond County, had 40 to 50 cattle and 20 to 30 sheep each.[59] Most of the livestock on frontland farms were "scrub" animals, usually underweight and of mixed breed. Only in the 1840s, when the government provided subsidies, were improved breeds imported and crossed with local livestock but even these initiatives failed to produce a rapid and substantial increase in the quality of stock.[60] Milk, butter, cheese, hides, wool, tallow, and meat were used for domestic

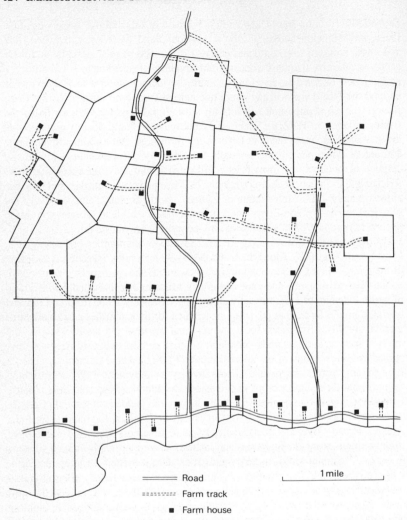

FIGURE 8 Hypothetical Pattern of Frontland and Backland Settlement on Cape Breton Island

consumption and for sale. Hay was the most important crop grown on frontland farms, often determining the number of animals that could be supported through the Island's six-month winter. Oats were the main grain crop, but many farmers grew barley and wheat. Turnips and potatoes supplemented hay fodder during long winters. Farmers also kept kitchen gardens (cultivating a greater range of vegetables than had been grown in Scotland), planted apple trees, picked berries, and tapped sugar-maple trees.

FIGURE 9   Frontland Settlement, Christmas Island, Bras d'Or Lake, Late 19th
Century

SOURCE: National Archives of Canada/PA-21554.

Although the crops and livestock raised on frontland farms were mostly the same
as those raised in the Western Highlands and Islands of Scotland, the agricultural
system was radically different. As farmers in Cape Breton had a relative abundance
of land and relied heavily upon family labour, the intensive use of land, labour, and
fertilizer that characterised crofting agriculture was quickly abandoned. Farming
became much more individualistic and extensive. Instead of a communal system
of grazing, farmers pastured livestock on their own farms. Initially, arable land was
cropped year after year until yields declined, and then new clearances were
planted.[61] On some frontland farms, manure was probably not collected and
ploughed in, while lime, needed to counteract the natural acidity of the soil, was
rarely applied. In 1822, the Agricultural Society at Sydney offered a prize of
£2.10s. to encourage the use of lime, but discontinued it two years later "principally
because [it] had excited little or no competition...."[62] A prize for summer fallow
was also withdrawn. Yet by the 1840s, more intensive practices began to be
introduced. According to Hiram Blanchard, Secretary of the Port Hood Agricultural Society, farmers had noted the "advantages to be derived from a judicious
rotation of crops, particularly the now frequent ploughing of grass lands, which
were formerly mowed as long as any hay could be obtained from them, frequently
for 14 or 15 years successively." The rotation of grains, grasses, and pasture

became more common; lime began to be applied; and some intervale farmers drained wetland to provide "fertile fields yielding best of crops and hay...."[63] Similar advances marked the use of agricultural implements. In the early years of settlement, agricultural tools were rudimentary. Locally made spades, forks, hoes, sickles, scythes, and flails were ubiquitous. After the stumps had been cleared, wooden ploughs with iron-plated mouldboards, such as Small's Plough, were probably also used. But as farmers accumulated capital and the use of improved agricultural implements became widespread in other parts of Nova Scotia, new tools were introduced. During the 1840s, forks and scythes were imported from Pictou, and more sophisticated implements, such as cast-iron, double mouldboard ploughs, winnowing machines, and harrows, were shipped in from Boston.[64] Few crofters in Scotland owned such improved implements.

Many frontland settlers enjoyed a far higher standard of living than they had known in Scotland. The great majority had acquired freehold ownership of at least 100 acres, and created farms that provided a comfortable subsistence. Although potatoes and oatmeal remained important elements of the settlers' diet, vegetables were more varied, and fruit was more accessible. Red meat was less a luxury and game, no longer watched over by a keeper, was freely available. The sale of surplus produce and timber allowed the purchase of other essential foodstuffs. The principal expense was imported American flour; settlers also purchased salt, sugar, molasses, rum, tea, and tobacco. Living conditions were also superior. Secure ownership of land and the ready availability of wood encouraged frontland settlers to build farmhouses that were considerably more substantial and comfortable than the crofter's blackhouse (figure 9). The houses were usually of one-and-a-half storeys, built from either squared logs or battens covered with clapboard, and had a central chimney or chimneys on the gable walls. A central stairway gave access to an attic, usually lit by dormer windows.[65] Such houses had 4 to 6 small rooms that allowed much more privacy for the family than the single room of the blackhouse. More importantly for the comfort of the family, livestock, hay, and agricultural implements were housed in a separate building, commonly a two-bay or "English" barn.

Although Gaelic songs composed on the Island frequently lamented the break with Scotland, successful frontland farmers were well aware of their improved standard of living in Cape Breton. "I did not envy *even* your larger *possessions* at home" wrote one Captain McNeil to his brother in North Uist, "as my property was improving apace, all my own, and to pass to my kin and successors for ever; such was my consolation, with a living, in comfort, tho' no in luxury." No longer bound by the rents and obligations of the Scottish feudal system, frontland settlers enjoyed considerable independence. "Thank God I am well pleased for coming to this country," wrote one settler in 1830 to a relative in Lewis, "as I find myself quite easy, having occupied land called my own free from all burdens whatsoever. I go out and in [my house] at my pleasure, no soul living forces me to do a turn against my will, no laird, no factor, having no rent, nor any toilsome work but what I do myself." When the Nova Scotia Government attempted to collect quit-rents in the

1820s, the Lieutenant-Governor reported that "the people are so *unaccustomed to pay rents of any kind or even the most-trifling taxes*, that ... the collection of the Quit Rents will occasion endless litigation and a great irritation...."[66]

Although the nuclear family living on its own land was the primary social institution of frontland settlements, kith and kin usually lived close by. Many related families had left Scotland together and settled side by side where land was available in Cape Breton. In 1817 John Mathewson, Farquhar Mathewson, William Corbet, David Corbet, and Robert McCoy petitioned for 300 acres each along Grand River so "that Petitioners having left Scotland together and wishing to settle near one another would be tempted to endeavour to make a good settlement in said place...."[67] Settlers sent letters back to Scotland to encourage relatives to join them. Donald Campbell, a settler on the north side of Bras d'Or Lake, regretted that his brother-in-law had not sailed with him "as you would have lands near me but now occupied by others," and offered part of his own lot as an inducement to emigrate: "If you come I will give you a house and part of what I have till you find a place to your wish or should you stop upon my land for ever you are quite welcome."[68] Where related families settled together, highly distinctive clusterings emerged. In the late 1820s, the settlement along the Southwest Margaree of Gillises, MacLellans, and MacDonalds, all Roman Catholics from Morar and Moidart, produced a series of related kin groups (figure 10).[69]

Initially, at least, there were few social institutions in frontland communities. Scottish institutions—the township constable and estate structure—had been left behind, while institutions in Cape Breton—local government and the church— were either very weak or entirely absent. One missionary, sent to Cape Breton in 1837 by the Glasgow Colonial Society, reported meeting "many persons grown up to be men and women who never saw the face of a clergyman before. Multitudes even of adults were unbaptized, and thousands to whom the sacred rite had been administered sunk in the most deplorable state."[70] With few formal institutions to turn to, settlers formed their own compensating groups. Farmers got together at a work "bee" or "frolic" to help one another clear land or put up buildings. One missionary observed that "when a house was erected, trees to fell and burn, the neighbours collected to assist, and would have a frolic before parting...dancing and drinking rum being the entertainment."[71] There were also "spinning" and "tucking" frolics where women met to spin wool, beat cloth, and swap gossip; and informal "house churches" where settlers congregated to worship, sing psalms, and read scripture.[72]

The formal organizations that developed reflected the social and economic order of the frontland settlements. With no gentry to support the established church, the Church of Scotland had little sway in Cape Breton. Instead, churches that had scarcely any recognition from Scottish landlords but were the spiritual support of many crofters, flourished. Roman Catholicism was successfully transferred to Cape Breton; so, too, was evangelical Presbyterianism. Some settlers had experienced the evangelical revivals in the Western Highlands and Islands in the 1820s and 1830s, while others, after the material hardships of pioneering, were

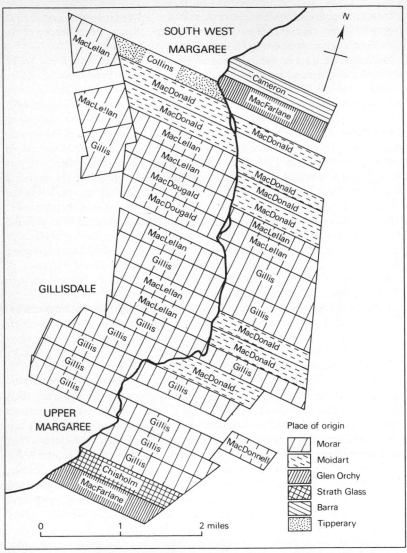

FIGURE 10   Settlement along the Southwest Margaree River, Inverness County,
Showing Land Granted, 1831–36, and the Name and Place of Origin in
Scotland of the Settlers

SOURCES: Data from the Records of the Crown Lands Office, 1738–1962,
RG 20/A/3, PANS; Crown Land Index Sheets 114–15, Nova Scotia
Department of Lands and Forests; and J.L. MacDougall, *History of
Inverness County* (Truro, Nova Scotia, 1922), 385–420.

perhaps attracted by the asceticism of Calvinism. Certainly, the evangelical church took hold. By the late 1830s and early 1840s, open-air services were attracting thousands of people and in 1843, when the split between the Church of Scotland and evangelicals occurred, most Presbyterians in Cape Breton joined the Free Church.[73] Agricultural societies emerged in response to initiatives and grants from the Nova Scotia Board of Agriculture.[74] In the 1820s, small groups of frontland farmers in Sydney, Arichat, Judique, Port Hood, and Mabou clubbed together to form societies. Although they collapsed in 1825, when government support was withdrawn, many re-formed in the 1840s when the Board of Agriculture was revived. By 1850, there were societies at Gut of Canso, Port Hood, Broad Cove, Margaree, Middle River, and Baddeck. To qualify for the government grant, each society had to put up £10, usually collected from membership subscriptions. Such charges could be afforded by only the more "influential farmers" and the societies, which quickly became the preserve of the affluent, were probably the first institutions in Cape Breton that reflected the growing differentiation in wealth between frontland and backland farmers.[75]

On the backlands most of the farmers in Cape Breton eked out livings from small, subsistence farms (figure 11). According to the 1851 census, many backland settlers had cleared 10 to 20 acres, enough to pasture a few livestock and grow essential crops. They owned perhaps one or two milch cows, two or three horned cattle, and six to eight sheep—virtually all of them undernourished "scrub" stock.[76] On the uplands only oats could be grown with much success. Potatoes were a dietary staple and the most important root crop—"the only article," according to farmers from the uplands behind Little Narrows, "which a poor man and his family have to live upon for years on new backland farms in the Island of Cape Breton."[77] Backland farmers subsisted on essentially the same crops as those grown in Western Scotland. Their agricultural techniques and technology were unsophisticated. Like many frontland farmers, they practised extensive farming, cultivating the same patch of land until yields declined and then planting a new clearing. But improved agricultural techniques were not introduced until late in the century, and there were few, if any, improved implements. "Such a thing as a good harrow, plough, cart, etc .... is not to be seen," explained a Crown surveyor at St. Patrick's Channel, Victoria County, "whilst a drill machine, horse hoe, double moulded plough, and the implements of the most obvious utility, are not even known by name."[78] Backland farmers made do with a digging stick, a hoe, a flail, and other simple tools..

Such subsistence farming rarely produced a marketable surplus, and to purchase land, essential supplies, and implements, many backland farmers had to look for additional employment. In large part, they were able to find it locally. Many settlers needed help clearing land and establishing farms, and frontland farmers frequently hired men at harvest to help bring in the hay crop. Labour was usually exchanged for foodstuffs and goods, rather than for cash.[79] There were also a few jobs available in the fishery, particularly on American vessels fishing in the Gulf, and in the coal mines at Sydney Mines, where at least 100 labourers were hired

FIGURE 11   Backland Settlement, Tarbot, near St. Anns, Late 19th Century

SOURCE: J.M. Gow, *Cape Breton Illustrated* (Toronto: W. Briggs, 1893).

each summer in the late 1830s.[80] Backland settlers also earned money from selling timber—stripped off unprotected Crown land—to local merchants for shipment to Britain.[81] A few men were hired by merchants to process fish, fence land, and plough fields.[82] In many respects, backland farms were homes for seasonal labourers.

Although travellers to Cape Breton chastised settlers for their "mixed employment of agriculture, fishing, and lumbering,"[83] the need for additional work was a measure of the economic insecurity of many backland farmers. Even with extra employment, the annual income of many families must have been paltry; most probably saw no cash from one year to the next. Debt was widespread, and many were almost destitute. At mid-century most backland settlers still lived in small log shanties of one or two rooms, and subsisted on a frugal diet. At best, families ate oatmeal, potatoes, fish, game, and some red meat; often, they had much less. In 1834, a missionary at West Bay reported that he had lived on nothing but gaspereaux and potatoes for a week, but considered himself fortunate for a week earlier the family he was staying with "could have offered me only milk."[84] There were few social institutions that backland settlers could fall back on. Formal institutions such as the church were largely absent, although missionaries visited the backlands. Few, if any, backland farmers could afford to join an agricultural society. Informal networks were probably more useful. Some backland settlers had relatives living nearby and may have relied on them to help clear land, erect buildings, and provide food in the early, lean years of settlement.[85] Yet compared to frontland farmers, backland settlers lived an isolated life, detached from much community activity by terrain, distance, and poverty.

Arriving from Scotland with no capital and settling some of the worst agricultural land in Maritime Canada, backland farmers were extremely vulnerable. Within a few years of settlement, crop failure had reduced many families to starvation. In 1829, a group of emigrants arrived "destitute of money and clothing... from Scotland" and settled in a "remote place" about four miles from St. George's Channel on Bras d'Or Lake. After "many things to encounter in supporting [themselves]," they managed to raise a few crops only to see them wither in the fall of 1833, leaving at least twenty families "poor and indigent without means of subsistence."[86] Relief supplies and money were distributed by the government to some parts of Cape Breton that year.[87] In July 1836, a severe frost almost completely destroyed the potato and grain crops in many backland areas, reducing settlers to just a few supplies for the coming winter. By the following spring, distress was widespread; James Fraser, a missionary who had spent time in some of the most congested crofting townships, reckoned that he had "never witnessed such destitution in any part of Scotland."[88]

Yet these intermittent crop failures paled in comparison with the potato blight that struck the Island a few years later. First observed in North America in 1843, the potato blight (*phytophthora infestans*) reached Cape Breton two years later and soon spread across the Atlantic to Europe. Between 1845 and 1849, the disease decimated Cape Breton's potato crop, reducing thousands of backland settlers to starvation. After the blight struck in 1845, many backland farmers sold the few animals they owned in order to purchase meal and seed potatoes. When the blight reappeared the following year, they were left with no food, no livestock to sell, and often no land title to pledge as security for further supplies from local merchants. With famine threatening, the government was forced to intervene. Between 1846 and 1849, the government sent large amounts of flour, meal, and seed potatoes to the Island for distribution to the needy. Although the aid ensured that few died from the effects of privation, many backland settlers lost virtually everything but their lives. Hundreds had sold their livestock, mortgaged their land, and fallen deeply in debt. Ten to twenty years of effort had been wiped away. For those cleared from the land in Scotland, it was another crushing blow. As the Commissioners organising relief in Inverness County reflected in June 1847: "The prospects of emigrants [from Scotland] were that at last they should triumph and rest even in a foreign grave, thereafter their successors to reflect of the vast field held before them for industry and cultivation—Alas they are now nearly discouraged—Times have failed."[89]

For a growing number of backland settlers and for second and subsequent sons of frontland farmers who were unlikely to inherit the family farm, there was little alternative but emigration. In the early 1840s, a few Scots and Irish moved from the Broad Cove–Margaree area to settle the closest vacant agricultural land, the Codroy Valley in Southwestern Newfoundland.[90] During the potato blight, young men left Cape Breton in search of employment, often working in Boston for the summer and returning to the Island in the fall.[91] Those who were too poor to leave the Island asked the government for aid. In 1849, 16 families at St. Anns petitioned the Lieutenant-Governor of Nova Scotia for assistance in moving to Canada, explaining:

> That your petitioners are British subjects natives of Sutherland and Rosshire in the North of Scotland, that some of your petitioners are younger branches of families that emigrated to this Island about twenty years ago and who could not get land fit for supporting them after becoming of years, and others...have only emigrated from the Highlands in later years when all the good lots were also occupied, this keeping your petitioners in a constant state of dependence.

> That the chief part of your petitioners have large families, and owing to the failure of crops for years past found it difficult to get means of subsistence, and from the experience of the past, dread the future....[92]

A few years later, several hundred people left the same district for the farthest corners of the globe. After receiving favourable accounts of Australia from his son, the Reverend Norman McLeod, preacher and community leader at St. Anns, organised a mass emigration; between 1851 and 1859 six ships left Cape Breton for Victoria and New Zealand carrying 876 people, mostly from the St. Anns, Boularderie, Baddeck, and Middle River areas.[93] A "great number of persons" from other parts of Cape Breton were also reported to have left for the United States and the Canadas in 1853, and "a still greater exodus of [the] population" was expected to leave the following year.[94] By the early 1850s, the great emigration from Cape Breton that was to run into the twentieth century had begun.

In the early nineteenth century the frontlands of Cape Breton provided a meagre agricultural niche for several hundred, relatively well-off settlers from Scotland, who were able, with time, to create farms that produced comfortable livings for families through sales of livestock. Compared to the tenant farmers and crofters in the Western Highlands and Islands of Scotland, these frontland farmers enjoyed a relatively untrammelled, independent living on the land. Yet within a generation this agricultural niche had been occupied, and later, destitute settlers were forced onto rocky backland. Although these settlers often squatted illegally on Crown land and at least enjoyed a prospect of improvement, the realities of farming such marginal land quickly became apparent. Backland settlers found that they had exchanged landlords and bailiffs for acidic soils and six-month winters. Few could support themselves by farming alone and many turned to whatever additional employment was available. Some worked in the Island's staple industries, others laboured on frontland farms. To some extent, the economic stratification between frontland and backland settlers in Cape Breton replicated that between crofters and cottars in Scotland. Yet even with extra employment, many backland settlers were unable to purchase land, and in some years, when the harvest failed, subsistence quickly turned to starvation. For the majority of these Highland emigrants, a trans-Atlantic migration had scarcely improved their situation; they still faced rural poverty, part-time work, and emigration.

In Southern Ontario, the Saint John River Valley of New Brunswick, the Annapolis Valley of Nova Scotia, and on Prince Edward Island, agricultural opportunities for immigrants from the British Isles were much greater than they were on Cape Breton Island. In general, farms in these areas were considerably more prosperous than those on the Island. Yet everywhere the influx and natural increase of population were so great and the limits of good agricultural land so finite that opportunities to acquire land were soon restricted. Within a generation, there was a growing landless population and a stream of people moving onto marginal agricultural land or emigrating to the United States. In Cape Breton during the early nineteenth century this cycle of immigration, settlement, and emigration, so common a part of the pattern of Canadian settlement, was particularly stark.

Notes

Abbreviations
BI   Beaton Institute, Sydney, Cape Breton
CO   Colonial Office Papers in NAC
NAC   National Archives of Canada
PANS Public Archives of Nova Scotia
SRO   Scottish Record Office

1. H.I. Cowan, *British Emigration to British North America* (Toronto: University of Toronto Press, 1961); and R.C. Harris and J. Warkentin, *Canada before Confederation* (New York: Oxford University Press, 1974).

2. Part of this cycle has been examined in T.W. Acheson, "A Study in the Historical Demography of a Loyalist County," *Histoire sociale/Social History* 1 (1968): 53–64; B. Craig, "Immigrants in a Frontier Community: Madawaska 1785–1850," *Histoire sociale/Social History* 19 (1986): 277–97; and "Agriculture and the Lumberman's Frontier in the Upper St. John Valley, 1800–70," *Journal of Forest History* 32 (1988): 125–37; D. Gagan, "Land, Population, and Social Change: The 'Critical Years' in Rural Canada West," *Canadian Historical Review* 59 (1978): 293–318; C. Harris, "Of Poverty and Helplessness in Petite-Nation," *Canadian Historical Review* 52 (1971): 23–50; L.A. Johnson, "Land Policy, Population Growth and Social Structure in the Home District, 1793–1851," *Ontario History* 63 (1971): 41–60; and G. Wynn, "Notes on Society and Environment in Old Ontario," *Journal of Social History* 13 (1979): 49–65; and "A Share of the Necessaries of Life: Remarks on Migration, Development, and Dependency in Atlantic Canada," in *Beyond Anger and Longing: Community and Development in Atlantic Canada*, ed. B. Fleming (Fredericton, New Brunswick: Acadiensis Press, 1988), 17–52.

3. The population return is enclosed in General Despard to Lord Hobart, 24 Dec. 1801, CO/CB/A 22.

4. Because of the paucity of passenger records, it is impossible to know exactly how many Highlanders arrived in Cape Breton, but given the rapid rise of population during the early nineteenth century the estimate of 20 000 immigrants in D.C. Harvey, "Scottish Immigration to Cape Breton," *Dalhousie Review* 21 (1941): 313–24, seems reasonable.

5. Census of 1851, RG1/453, PANS. The ethnic composition is based on the *Census of Canada 1870–1871*. It is unlikely that the ethnic balance was very different at mid-century.

6. M. Gray, *The Highland Economy 1750–1850* (Edinburgh: Oliver and Boyd, 1957).

7. R.A. Gailey, "The Evolution of Highland Settlement with Particular Reference to Argyllshire," *Scottish Studies* 6 (1962): 155–77.

8. Gray, *Highland Economy*; A.J. Youngson, *After the Forty-Five: The Economic Impact on the Scottish Highlands* (Edinburgh: Edinburgh University Press, 1973).

9. The standard account of the development of the crofting economy and society is J. Hunter, *The Making of the Crofting Community* (Edinburgh: John Donald Publishers, 1976). The economic and social changes are also considered in E. Richards, *A History of the Highland Clearances: Agrarian Transformation and the Evictions 1746–1886*, vol. 1 (London: Croom Helm, 1982).

10. An excellent geographical account of the laying out of the crofting townships in the Uists is in J.B. Caird, "Land Use in the Uists since 1800," *Proceedings of the Royal Society of Edinburgh* 77B (1979): 505–26.

11. D. Shaw to A. Hunter, 25 Feb. 1827, GD 201/4/97, SRO.

12. L. Gittins, "Soapmaking in Britain, 1824–1851: A Study in Industrial Location," *Journal of Historical Geography* 8 (1982): 29–40.

13. Gray, *Highland Economy*, 197–98.

14. A. Fenton, *The Island Blackhouse* (Edinburgh: Her Majesty's Stationery Office, 1978); D. Macdonald, *Lewis: A History of the Island* (Edinburgh: Gordon Wright Publishing, 1978), 57–62.

15. Shaw to Hunter, 25 Feb. 1827, GD 201/4/97, SRO.

16. J.L. Buchanan, *Travels in the Western Hebrides: From 1782 to 1790* (London, 1793), 198.

17. Personal communication to the author from Dr. Margaret A. Mackay, School of Scottish Studies, University of Edinburgh. Dr. Mackay is undertaking important work on the demography of the island community of Tiree in the late nineteenth and twentieth centuries.

18. *New Statistical Account* (Edinburgh: William Blackwood and Sons, 1843), 14: 173.

19. Buchanan, *Western Hebrides*, 52–53.

20. J.M. Bumsted, "Highland Emigration to the Island of St. John and the Scottish Catholic Church, 1769–1774," *Dalhousie Review* 58 (1978): 511–27.

21. J. Hunter, "The Emergence of the Crofting Community: The Religious Contribution 1798–1843," *Scottish Studies* 18 (1974): 95–116.

22. Quoted in Hunter, *Crofting Community*, 20.

23. J.M. Bumsted, *The People's Clearance: Highland Emigration to North America 1770–1815* (Edinburgh: Edinburgh University Press, 1982), appendix A, table II. Highland emigration is also considered in E. Richards, *A History of the Highland Clearances: Emigration, Protest, Reasons*, vol. 2 (London: Croom Helm, 1985).

24. General Despard to J. Sullivan, 10 Sept. 1802, CO/CB/A/23/127.

25. Bumsted, *People's Clearance*, appendix A, table II.

26. Select Committee on Emigration from the United Kingdom, *British Parliamentary Papers*, vol. 4, 1826, 38.

27. Factor's Report, 21 Apr. 1823, GD 201/1/352, SRO; Gray, *Highland Economy*, 182.

28. "A Statement relative to the treatment received by the Passengers in the Ship William Tell and Brig Hope from Greenock to the Island," enclosed in General Ainslie to Lord Bathurst, 1 Oct. 1817, CO 217/135.

29. Select Committee on Emigration from the United Kingdom, *British Parliamentary Papers*, vol. 5, 1827, 288; J. Adam to Lord Seaforth, 31 Mar. 1827, GD 46/17/72, SRO.

30. For the laying out of new crofts, see J.B. Caird, "The Isle of Harris," *Scottish Geographical Magazine* 67 (1951): 85–100; and Caird, "Land Use in the Uists." Crofters could have migrated to Britain's growing industrial cities, but few did so according to T.M. Devine, "Highland Migration to Lowland Scotland, 1760–1860," *Scottish Historical Review* 62 (1983): 137–49.

31. See, for example, Factor's Report on the Clan Ranald Estate, 19 Nov. 1827, GD 201/1/354, SRO.

32. Hunter, *Crofting Community*, 46; and R. Brown to A. Swinton, 16 Feb. 1827, GD 201/5/1228/3, SRO.

33. "A Return of Emigrants arrived in the Island of Cape Breton for the years 1821 to the present time," enclosed in Sir Peregrine Maitland to Viscount Goderich, 24 June 1831, CO 217/152. Scottish emigration to Cape Breton is also considered in D. Campbell and R.A. MacLean, *Beyond the Atlantic Roar: A Study of the Nova Scotian Scots* (Toronto: McClelland and Stewart, 1974); Harvey, "Scottish Immigration"; and B.A. Kincaid, "Scottish Immigration to Cape Breton, 1758 –1838" (M.A. thesis, Dalhousie University, 1964).

34. Select Committee on Emigration from the United Kingdom, *British Parliamentary Papers*, vol. 5, 1827, 289.

35. J.S. Martell, *Immigration to and Emigration from Nova Scotia 1815–1838* (Halifax: Public Archives of Nova Scotia, 1942); and R.G. Flewwelling, "Immigration to and Emigration from Nova Scotia 1839–1851," *Nova Scotia Historical Society Collections* 28 (1949): 75–105. Sir Colin Campbell to Lord Glenelg, 18 July 1836, CO 217/161; and Report of Commissioners of H.M. Council, enclosed in Sir James Kempt to W. Huskisson, 25 Nov. 1827, CO 217/154. For the timber trade, see G. Wynn, *Timber Colony: A Historical Geography of Early Nineteenth Century New Brunswick* (Toronto: University of Toronto Press, 1981); and B. Greenhill and A. Giffard, *Westcountrymen in Prince Edward's Isle* (Toronto: University of Toronto Press, 1975). For the Scottish emigrant trade, see J.M. Cameron, "The Role of Shipping from Scottish Ports in Emigration to the Canadas, 1815–1855," in *Canadian Papers in Rural History*, ed. D.H. Akenson (Gananoque, Ontario: Langdale Press, 1980), 2: 135–54.

36. *Journals of the House of Assembly of Nova Scotia*, 1843, 395.

37. T.C. Haliburton, *An Historical and Statistical Account of Nova Scotia* (Halifax: Joseph Howe, 1829), 260.

38. D.B. Cann, J.I. MacDougall, and J.D. Hilchey, *Soil Survey of Cape Breton Island Nova Scotia* (Truro, Nova Scotia: Nova Scotia Soil Survey, 1963).

39. O.L. Loucks, "A Forest Classification for the Maritime Provinces," *Proceedings of the Nova Scotia Institute of Science* 25 (1962): 85–167.

40. Other accounts of the Scottish settlement in Cape Breton are contained in K.R. Bittermann, "Middle River: The Social Structure of Agriculture in a Nineteenth Century Cape Breton Community" (M.A. thesis, University of New Brunswick, 1987); Campbell and MacLean, *Beyond the Atlantic Roar*; C.W. Dunn, *Highland Settler: A Portrait of the Scottish Gael in Nova Scotia* (Toronto: University of Toronto Press, 1953); Harvey, "Scottish Immigration"; and Kincaid, "Scottish Immigration." As the first micro-study of Scottish settlement in one area of Cape Breton, Bittermann's thesis

is particularly useful and insightful. A summary of its central argument is in "The Hierarchy of the Soil: Land and Labour in a 19th Century Cape Breton Community," *Acadiensis* 18 (1988): 33–55.

41.   Extracts from H.M. General Instructions to the Governors of Nova Scotia, 1789, CO/CB/A/35/5.

42.   General Ainslie to Lord Bathurst, 25 Nov. 1816, CO/CB/A/37/15–18.

43.   H.J.M. Johnson, *British Emigration Policy 1815–1830* (Oxford: Oxford University Press, 1972).

44.   Instructions for Captain Crawley, Surveyor General of Cape Breton,1820, CO 217/138.

45.   In 1827, a factor reported that recent emigrants to Cape Breton had "got land; a number of them had a little money with them… and those who had money got grants of land" (*British Parliamentary Papers*, vol. 5, 1827, 289).

46.   R.G. Riddell, "A Study in the Land Policy of the Colonial Office, 1763–1855," *Canadian Historical Review* 18 (1937): 385–405.

47.   Sir Peregrine Maitland to Viscount Goderich, 12 Aug. 1831, CO 217/152.

48.   H.W. Crawley to Sir Rupert George, 5 Apr. 1837, RG20/C/54, PANS.

49.   H.W. Crawley to Sir Rupert George, 8 May 1844, RG20/C/54, PANS.

50.   H.W. Crawley to Crown Lands Office, 17 Feb. 1844; and Crawley to Sir Rupert George, 22 Jan. 1844, RG20/C/56, PANS.

51.   Annual Nova Scotia Blue Book, 1843, CO 221/57.

52.   See the annual reports of the agricultural societies in the *Journals of the House of Assembly of Nova Scotia*, 1846, appendix 77; 1847, appendix 39; 1848, appendix 39; 1849, appendix 100; and 1850, appendix 39.

53.   The Census of 1851 records 5 884 farmers in Cape Breton.

54.   Annual Report of the Richmond Agricultural Society, 31 Dec. 1842, RG8/13/22, PANS.

55.   See the Farm Accounts of John B. Moore, Documents, 1848–99, MG1/Biography, PANS. The importance of the local market provided by farmers has been stressed by B.H. Pruitt, "Self-Sufficiency and the Agricultural Economy of Eighteenth-Century Massachusetts," *William and Mary Quarterly* 3rd series, 41 (1984): 333–64.

56.   The number of frontland and backland farmers was estimated from the Crown Land Index Sheets, PANS. For an overview of agriculture in Nova Scotia at mid-century, see R. MacKinnon and G. Wynn, "Nova Scotian Agriculture in the 'Golden Age': A New Look," in *Geographical Perspectives*, ed. Day, 47–60.

57.   The only available data on frontland improvements at mid-century are average figures for census subdistricts that include both front and backland.

58.   Census of 1851.

59.   Nominal census of Cape Breton Island, 1811, printed in *Holland's Description of Cape Breton Island*, ed. D.C. Harvey (PANS Publication 2), appendix B, 138.

60.   J.S. Martell, "The Achievements of Agricola and the Agricultural Societies, 1818–1825," and "From Central Board to Secretary of Agriculture, 1826–1885," *Bulletin of the Public Archives of Nova Scotia* 2 and 3 (1940). For an important reappraisal of the agricultural improver movement in Nova Scotia, see G. Wynn, "Exciting a Spirit of Emulation among the 'Plodholes': Agricultural Reform in Pre-Confederation Nova Scotia," *Acadiensis* (forthcoming).

61.   *Journals of the House of Assembly of Nova Scotia*, 1844, appendix 72.

62.   Scheme of Agricultural Prizes for the year 1822 selected by the Agricultural Society of Sydney, Cape Breton, RG8/7/136, PANS; and H.W. Crawley to J. Young, 24 Apr. 1824, RG8/7/158, PANS.

63. H. Blanchard to T. Smith, 15 Jan. 1845, RG8/13/22, PANS; Annual Report of the Broad Cove Agricultural Society, 17 Feb. 1845, RG8/13/22, PANS.

64. "An account of Implements, Stock, Seeds, etc. Imported and Sold by the Inverness Agricultural Society in the Year 1842," RG8/13/22, PANS; Annual Report of the Margaree Agricultural Society, 1846, RG8/13/22, PANS; Martell, "From Central Board"; and Wynn, "Agricultural Reform."

65. P. Ennals and D. Holdsworth, "Vernacular Architecture and the Cultural Landscape of the Maritime Provinces—A Reconnaisance," *Acadiensis* 10, 2 (1981): 86–105. Reprinted in this volume, section 3.

66. For the Gaelic songs composed by settlers in Cape Breton, see M. MacDonnell, *The Emigrant Experience: Songs of Highland Emigrants in North America* (Toronto: University of Toronto Press, 1982); D. McNeil to W. McNeil, 25 June 1849, GD 403/27/2, SRO; D. Campbell to H. McKay, 7 Oct. 1830, reprinted in the *Stornoway Gazette*, 30 Sept. 1972, also filed in MG100/115/33, PANS; Sir James Kempt to W. Huskisson, 2 May 1828, CO 217/148.

67. Petition of John Mathewson et al., RG20/B/1774, PANS.

68. Campbell to McKay, 7 Oct. 1830, MG100/115/33, PANS.

69. See also R.E. Ommer, "Highland Scots Migration to Southwestern Newfoundland: A Study of Kinship," in *The Peopling of Newfoundland*, ed. J.J. Mannion (St. John's, Newfoundland: Institute of Social and Economic Research, Memorial University of Newfoundland, 1977), 212–33; and "Primitive Accumulation and the Scottish Clan in the Old World and the New," *Journal of Historical Geography* 12 (1985): 121–41. During his travels through the Hebrides in 1773, Dr. Johnson observed the early emigrations to North America and noted that "whole neighbourhoods formed parties for removal; so that departure from their native country is no longer exile. He that goes thus accompanied, carries with him all that makes life pleasant. He sits down in a better climate, surrounded by his kindred and his friends: they carry with them their language, their opinions, their popular songs, and hereditary merriment: they change nothing but the place of their abode; and of that change they perceive the benefit" (*Johnson's Journey to the Western Islands of Scotland and Boswell's Journal of a Tour to the Hebrides with Samuel Johnson, L.L.D.*, ed. R.W. Chapman (Oxford: Oxford University Press, 1970), 86–87). Nearly fifty years later, the same process took place in the settlement of the frontlands of Cape Breton.

70. Quoted in L.M. Toward, "The Influence of the Scottish Clergy on Early Education in Cape Breton," *Collections of the Nova Scotia Historical Society* 29 (1951): 158.

71. Quoted in L. Stanley, *The Well-Watered Garden: The Presbyterian Church in Cape Breton, 1798–1860* (Sydney, Cape Breton: University College of Cape Breton Press, 1983), 35.

72. Stanley, *Well-Watered Garden*, 59.

73. A.A. Johnston, *A History of the Catholic Church in Eastern Nova Scotia*, vols. 1–2 (Antigonish, Nova Scotia: St. Francis Xavier University Press, 1960–71); and Stanley, *Well-Watered Garden*.

74. Martell, "Achievements of Agricola," and "From Central Board"; Wynn, "Agricultural Reform."

75. Annual Report of the Richmond Agricultural Society, 31 Dec. 1841, RG 8/13/22, PANS.

76. These are average figures calculated for backland areas in the Census of 1851.

77. Petition, 12 Feb. 1847, RG5/P/83/109, PANS. A similar petition from settlers on the front and rear of St. Patrick's Channel, Little Narrows, also spoke of the "well known fact that the inland settlements about the Bras d'Or Lake are no grain country;

the potatoes are almost all they have to live upon throughout the year'' (25 Jan. 1847, RG5/P/83/67, PANS).

78. D.B. McNab to T. Smith, 16 Apr. 1844, RG8/13/22, PANS.

79. See Farm Accounts of John B. Moore; Bittermann, "Middle River"; and L.D. McCann, "'Living a Double Life': Town and Country in the Industrialization of the Maritimes," in *Geographical Perspectives*, ed. Day, 93–113.

80. The American mackerel fishery in the Gulf of St. Lawrence expanded rapidly in the early 1830s and often employed labour from Nova Scotia; see H.A. Innis, *The Cod Fisheries*, rev. ed. (Toronto: University of Toronto Press, 1954), 323–28. In 1839, Richard Brown, the General Mining Association's agent at Sydney Mines, reported that "about 100 men" were hired during the summer shipping season (Lord Durham's Commission, *British Parliamentary Papers*, Canada, vol. 2, 1839).

81. H.W. Crawley to Sir Rupert George, 28 Feb. 1837, RG20/C/54, PANS.

82. See the Ledger of John McKay & Co., which records the employment of backland settlers, MG 3/8, PANS.

83. A. Gesner, *The Industrial Resources of Nova Scotia* (Halifax: A.W. Mackinlay, 1849), 310.

84. Extract of a letter written by Revd. John Stewart, quoted in a "Memorial Regarding the Religious State of the Island of Cape Breton, respectfully addressed by the Glasgow North American Colonial Society, to the Right Honorable the Secretary of State for the British Colonies," 1835, CO 217/159.

85. Some insight into the life of backland settlers can be gleaned from Petition of Samuel Campbell to Sir Colin Campbell, 4 June 1837, RG5/GP/1/85, PANS.

86. Petition, 26 Jan. 1833, RG5/P/80/67, PANS.

87. *Journals of the House of Assembly of Nova Scotia*, 1834–35, 715.

88. Petition, 5 Dec. 1836, RG 5/P/18/23, PANS; and Stanley, Well-Watered Garden, 100.

89. Petition of the Commissioners for the distribution of provisions for the helpless and needy, County of Inverness, 8 June 1847, RG5/P/83/51, PANS. See also Hornsby, "Cape Breton Island," chap. 5; and R.J. Morgan, "'Poverty, Wretchedness, and Misery': The Great Famine in Cape Breton, 1845–1851," *Nova Scotia Historical Review* 6 (1986): 88–104.

90. Ommer, "Highland Scots Migration."

91. *Journals of the House of Assembly of Nova Scotia*, 1857, appendix 71.

92. Petition of Murdoch Kerr et al., 6 Feb. 1849, RG5/GP/6/24, PANS.

93. N.R. McKenzie, *The Gael Fares Forth* (Wellington, New Zealand: Whitcombe and Tombs, 1942), appendix II.

94. *Cape Breton News*, 27 May 1854. For the late nineteenth-century emigration, see A.A. Brookes, "Out-Migration from the Maritime Provinces, 1860–1900: Some Preliminary Considerations," *Acadiensis* 5 (1976): 26–55; and *"The Provincials* by Albert Kennedy," *Acadiensis* 4 (1975): 85–101; Hornsby, "Cape Breton Island," chap. 8; and P.A. Thornton, "The Problem of Out-Migration from Atlantic Canada, 1871–1921: A New Look," *Acadiensis* 15 (1985): 3–34.

KINSHIP AND SOCIETY IN THE UKRAINIAN PIONEER SETTLEMENT OF THE CANADIAN WEST*

JOHN C. LEHR

In the European colonization of the frontierlands of the New World, various nationalities have tended to seek the company of their fellows in settlement. At the time of the agricultural settlement of the Canadian prairies, this was acknowledged as a natural inclination by the Dominion Government when it set aside special areas for the settlement of such groups as Doukhobors and Mennonites.[1] By locating with their fellows, new settlers could in some measure secure a familiar social, religious, and linguistic environment which, in the opinion of the Department of the Interior, did much to promote successful agricultural settlement.

The drive to seek out familiar milieux is common to all peoples. In-group preference is so nearly universal that it competes with physiological drives for food or sex for recognition as a basic human trait.[2] Yet while group settlement has been noted as a feature of the agricultural settlement of western Canada, the contributions of kinship and society to that area's distinctive social geography have been largely neglected. As an initial step toward correcting this situation, this essay presents an examination of the spatial form and internal structure of the block settlements of one of the most significant groups to settle independently in western Canada, the Ukrainians. It identifies the nature and role of social ties and divisions within this immigrant community. It argues that intra-group relationships were strongly expressed in both the micro- and macro-geography of Ukrainian settlement, and that they were in large measure responsible for the occupation of sub-marginal homestead land by Ukrainians in parts of the Canadian west.

* *The Canadian Geographer /Le Géographe canadien* 29, 3 (1985): 207–19.

Group Settlement

English-speaking settlers of the western Canadian agricultural frontier were fortunate to be settling a territory that, in many important respects, maintained the basic societal framework of their points of origin. They encountered familiar elements of law and administration; the creed of the ruling majority was Protestant; and English was the de jure, if not the de facto, language of all in the newly settled west. Nonetheless, ties of blood and custom were still sufficient to cause many English-speaking immigrants to cluster together in settlement.[3] Even independently minded American settlers, when surrounded by "foreigners," lost little time in seeking new homesteads within an area of English-speaking settlement.[4]

For the "foreign" settlers the social experience of settlement was far different. British laws, Anglo-Saxon customs, the Protestant creed, the English language, often the Latin script, were unfamiliar, even incomprehensible. Only settlement among their fellows offered some amelioration of the alien British ambiance. Among their country- and kin-folk, foreign settlers could hope to retain some elements of their homeland society and culture. Group settlement allowed them to practise their own religion, gave spiritual comfort, and ministered to their psychological well-being.

Several ethnic or religious groups settling in the west sought the social security of group settlement, but few extended their quest as far as the Ukrainians. Many were seemingly content to achieve a general sense of "at homeness," and were comforted by a few transposed common elements of their national culture. There was little perpetuation of "old-country" regional groupings within the larger ethnic group settlement, and little, if any, homogeneity was displayed at the micro-scale. This was the situation, for example, with the three areas of Irish settlement in eastern Canada examined by Mannion.[5] It was no less true of the Mormon settlement in southern Alberta.[6] In both instances the circumstances of emigration caused unifying factors to predominate, and divisive forces within the group were submerged by common religious and cultural elements.

Group settlement was by no means universal in the international migration of Europeans, but it has been remarked that most group settlements "have a decided 'locality flavour' about them," in that "the majority of the group derive from one particular area of Europe."[7] Contributing to a study of cultural integration among immigrants some thirty years ago, C.A. Price defined four levels of group settlement: village, district, regional, and national. He cautioned, however, that what "at first sight appear to be concentrations of this or that nationality very often turn out to be simply numbers of migrants from one particular village or district."

For the most part, geographers have concentrated on explaining the creation of the macro-geography of group settlement in the New World. Bohland, Brunger, and Ostergren are among the few to have extended the level of geographical inquiry to the consideration of familial and old-country village ties in settlement.[8] In his pioneering study of the social role of the pioneering process, Dawson dealt with social ties in a general fashion, and a number of Canadian geographers have since commented on the tendency of territorially defined sub-groups to concentrate in different parts of a common settlement area.[9] Apart from Richtik's examination of kinship linkages among Ontario British settlers in Manitoba, however, analyses of the macro-geography of ethnic settlement in the Canadian west have stopped short of examining the role of kin linkages in settlement.[10]

Ukrainian Settlement

Ukrainian immigrants from the Austrian-administered provinces of Halychyna (Galicia) and Bukovyna (Bukowina) began to settle in western Canada in 1892. Until 1896, they all located near Star, in east-central Alberta, but with the trickle of Ukrainian immigrants turning into a flood in that year, a number of other Ukrainian settlements were established throughout the parkland belt, in an arc from Edmonton in the west to Winnipeg in the east.

When the outbreak of the First World War terminated their emigration, there were an estimated 170 000 Ukrainians in Canada.[11] The majority had sought homestead land in western Canada, and almost all of them had come from western Ukraine, an area governed until 1919 by Hapsburg monarchs of the Austro-Hungarian Empire. Halychyna and Bukovyna were economically depressed and politically oppressed agricultural backwaters of Austrian dominion.[12] The Ukrainian population of these provinces was almost entirely peasant, identified little with Austria, and was ruled by an alien, or alienated, aristocracy. The peasantry possessed little affection for the multinational Austria of which it was a part, and it did not possess a strong sense of ethnicity in the national sense. Most loyalties were bounded by the restricted horizons drawn by the limited mobility of peasant life in eastern Europe in the nineteenth century. The family, the village, the church, and, to a lesser extent, the province were the foci of peasant emotion and loyalty.

As Ukrainians arrived in western Canada they established a well-defined pattern of behaviour, sufficiently different from the norm to elicit comment from the colonization officers of the Department of the Interior who settled thousands of immigrants of all nationalities on the homestead lands. The Ukrainians were marked as "peculiar people" by Immigration Commissioner William F. McCreary, who wondered at their refusal of prime wheat-growing prairie land in favour of the less fertile woodlands on the northern fringes of the parkland belt. Their determination to settle together was soon found to be a major problem in the administration of western settlement.[13] It also became a major factor in the development of the basic geographical pattern of Ukrainian settlement in western Canada (figure 1). In the early years, group or block settlement was favoured by the Department of the Interior, since it simplified the tasks of the colonization officers and reduced the chances of failure in settlement.[14] Once begun, however, the process acquired an almost uncontrollable momentum of its own, as Commissioner McCreary reported to the deputy minister in 1898: "They are apparently an obstreperous, obstinate, rebellious lot. I am just about sick of these people. They are worse than cattle to handle. You cannot get them, by persuasion or argument, to go to a new colony except by force. They all want to go where the others have gone."[15] This single-minded determination created a distinctive geography of block settlements across the west. The macro-geography of these blocks reflects the Ukrainians' desire for woodlands, but their internal structure— their micro-geography— reflects the intensity with which the benefits of a familiar milieu were pursued.

Settlement Structure

There are many incidental references to the internal morphology of Ukrainian block settlements in western Canada, and many authors have commented on the tendency of Ukrainian pioneers to settle on an old-country village basis.[16] More substantial comment has been provided by Goresky, Lazarenko, and Royick, who have identified specific village groupings in the Star-Vegreville block settlement of Alberta.[17] Pohorecky and Royick have identified linguistic differences among the Ukrainians in Alberta, which they hold to reflect the perpetuation of old-country dialects in the New World.[18] Since dialect survival is dependent on the grouping of dialect speakers in settlement, the implication is that such groupings were perpetuated in Ukrainian settlements in Alberta, a contention that is supported by evidence from Goresky and Byrne.[19]

Old-country villages were commemorated in the landscape of the prairie provinces in toponyms transferred by the settlers from Ukraine. The villages of Ispas, Stry, Luzan, and Shepenge (or Szpenitz, but properly Shypyntsi) in Alberta, and Jaroslav, Senkiw, Melnice, Zbarazh, and Komarno in Manitoba, are but a few examples.[20] However, since the Ukrainians were seldom in a position to name places—that was the preserve of the railway companies and the English-speaking surveyors and administrators—the strongest record of Ukrainian occupance and of old-country village ties survives in the names of their rural schools and school districts, where examples abound.

That the Ukrainians perpetuated their old-country village groups in western Canada is not as significant as the frequency with which they did so. This trait was sufficient to impart to the Ukrainian block settlement an internal structure that varied little. Since it is impractical to examine all Ukrainian block settlements in western Canada, data from three areas will be drawn upon in a discussion of the various hierarchical linkages found within such settlements. Those selected are the Star-Vegreville block of central Alberta, the first established and ultimately the largest Ukrainian settlement; the Manitoba Interlake (Pleasant Home) block; and the Stuartburn block in southeastern Manitoba (figure 1).

Kinship and Village Ties

In most peasant societies, families are generally large and non-nuclear. Indeed, it is not unusual for peasants to be related to the majority of their fellow villagers by ties of blood or marriage. Nor is it unusual to find that the

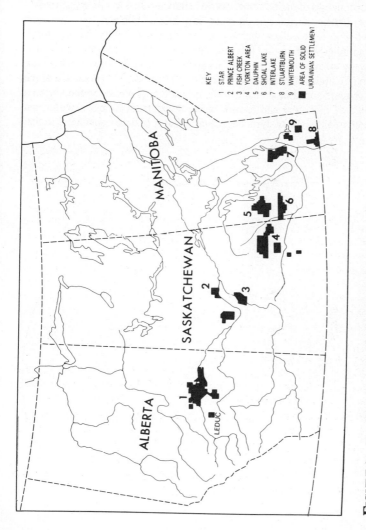

FIGURE 1 Ukrainian Settlements in Western Canada, 1914

SOURCES: Public Archives of Canada, RG76; and Records of Homestead Entry, Alberta, Saskatchewan and Manitoba.

concepts of village and kin are virtually synonymous. Ties to kinfolk are strong, and they are kept strong by economic and social interdependence, heightened by the restricted horizons of village life. To the peasant in nineteenth-century Ukraine, loyalties were to family, village, locality, district, and province rather than to the more abstract concepts of nation, state, or even ethnicity. Just as villagers grouped together in settlement when they emigrated, so groups of villagers from the same region tended to group together, thereby perpetuating old-country district groupings. Although village groups are here considered in isolation, in both social and spatial terms the village was a *holon*; it functioned as a unit in its own right, but it was also part of a higher group within a hierarchy (figure 2).[21] To conceive of the village as a discrete social or spatial unit is misleading. It was only one unit in a closely integrated hierarchy and cannot be separated from its place within the district or region, although analysis necessitates that it first be considered in that way here.

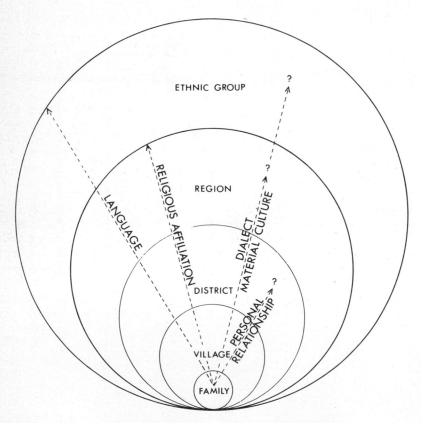

FIGURE 2 Social Structure and Interrelationships in Western Ukraine

Contemporary observers of Ukrainian settlement made frequent comment on its cohesiveness, as evidenced by the immigrants seeking out their fellows and kin.[22] Records of homestead cancellation are equally revealing. In those areas of Alberta settled by Ukrainians, homestead entries were frequently cancelled, even after improvements had been made, when settlers sought to relocate near more recently arrived relatives.[23] Social reasons were cited on the declarations of abandonment almost as frequently as environmental ones. A terse scrawl, "My brother has moved and I wish to homestead beside him" or "I wish to locate near friends," barely conveys the strength of the magnetism that family and friends exerted on the socially isolated settler.[24] Interviews with surviving settlers and their families in Alberta and Manitoba confirmed that the vast majority of immigrants chose their locations because they "wanted to be with friends—to help out in hard times and stick together."[25] Todor Kutzak, a pioneer of Sirko, Manitoba, was more blunt: "When I arrived in Canada in 1905 I headed for Gardenton where I had an uncle who would feed us when we [Kutzak and friend] arrived."[26] The great majority of over 250 Ukrainian settlers who were interviewed in a research project in 1971, and who gave reasons for settlement in a specific area, mentioned the presence of friends, relatives, or fellow villagers as a major factor in their decisions.[27] Several also commented that they subsequently changed their location so as to secure an even tighter family settlement.

The spatial impact of the close agglomeration of settlers on the basis of family groups can be illustrated by the Stuartburn area of Manitoba (figure 3). This area was first settled in 1896, and already by 1900 the Ukrainian settlement had extended over five townships, and a number of distinct old-country village and district agglomerations were apparent. In Township 1, Range 6 East, 12 families from the village of Bridok, Zastavna District, Bukovyna, had settled in a well-defined cluster, although there was a certain amount of mixing with 13 families from the village of Onuth, also of Zastavna District (figure 4). Villagers from Lukivci, Chernivci District, Bukovyna, had settled alongside them, but they remained almost totally separate, even after five years of settlement. In the northern area of the Stuartburn block, 45 families from Senkiw (Synkiv), Zalishchyky District, Halychyna, were less tightly grouped. They formed two closely linked clusters centred on Township 2, Range 6 East, which together contained 33 of the Senkiw families. A similar pattern was evident with the settlement of families from the village of Postolivka of Huisatyn District, Halychyna. The first Postolivka settlers took land in 1897, on Section 36, Township 1, Range 5 East, and subsequent arrivals settled on adjoining sections. In 1898, a second nucleus of Postolivka settlers was established some twelve miles east, in the centre of Township 2, Range 7 East. The reason is difficult to determine, for at the time of the establishment of the second group there was no shortage of vacant homestead lands surrounding the initial settlers from Postolivka. Since the second group also clustered in its settlement, kinship was probably a factor, for all but one of the second group held the surname Podolsky, and travelled to Canada on the SS *Christiana*, arriving at Halifax on 12 July 1898.[28] As far as can be ascertained, no members of this family settled outside this group of settlers.

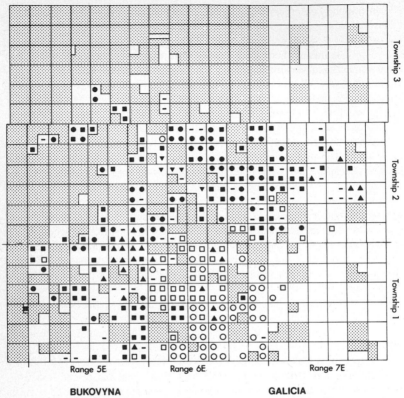

BUKOVYNA
O Chernivci District
□ Zastavna District
△ Kitsman District

GALICIA
■ Borshchiv District
▲ Husiatyn District
● Zalishchyky District
▼ Kolomya District

— Ukrainian: origin not determined

Not open for homestead settlement 1895–1901

  Section divided in quarters

FIGURE 3 District of Origin of Ukrainian Settlers at Stuartburn, Manitoba, 1901

SOURCES: V.J. Kaye, *Dictionary of Ukrainian Pioneer Biography* (Toronto: Ukrainian Canadian Research Foundation, 1975); Township General Registers, Department of Lands, Government of Manitoba; and field research in southeastern Manitoba. Reprinted from J.C. Lehr, "The Peculiar People: Ukrainian Settlement of the Stuartburn District of S.E. Manitoba," in *Building Beyond the Homestead,* ed. David C. Jones and Ian MacPherson (Calgary: University of Calgary Press, 1985).

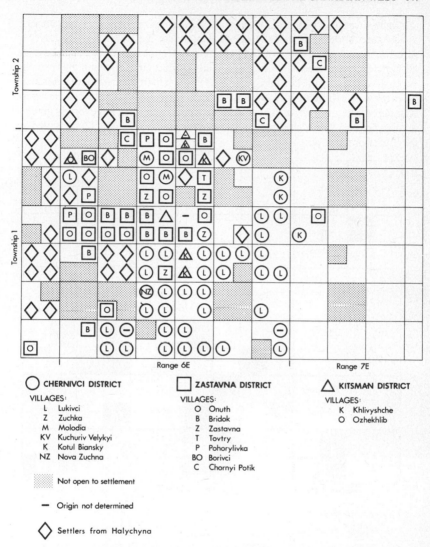

FIGURE 4   Villages of Origin of Bukovynan Settlers at Stuartburn, Manitoba, 1901

SOURCES: Kaye, *Dictionary;* and Township Registers. Reprinted from J.C. Lehr, "The Peculiar People: Ukrainian Settlement of the Stuartburn District of S.E. Manitoba," in *Building Beyond the Homestead,* ed. David C. Jones and Ian MacPherson (Calgary: University of Calgary Press, 1985).

Kinship was undoubtedly a major factor in the perpetuation of old-country village ties. Thirteen of the 32 families comprising the Lukivci group had the surname Kossowan, four Zyha, and three Shypot (figure 5). While this in itself is not conclusive evidence of kinship, it certainly points in that direction. It is usually impossible to determine kin linkages created through marriage, yet marital ties may have been as effective as blood relationships in maintaining closely clustered patterns of settlement.[29] At all events, what appear to be three large family groups account for over half of the immigrants from the village of Lukivci who settled in the Stuartburn district.

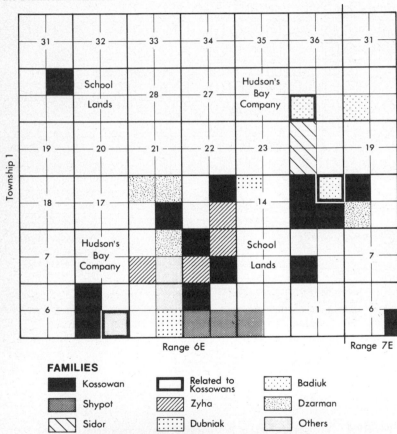

FIGURE 5 Family Groups of Settlers from the Village of Lukivci, Bukovyna, at Stuartburn, Manitoba

SOURCES: Kaye, *Dictionary*; and Township Registers. Reprinted from J.C. Lehr, "The Peculiar People: Ukrainian Settlement of the Stuartburn District of S.E. Manitoba," in *Building Beyond the Homestead*, ed. David C. Jones and Ian MacPherson (Calgary: University of Calgary Press, 1985).

The general pattern of old-country village agglomeration was replicated in the Ukrainian settlement of the Manitoba Interlake region. Settlers from the village of Bereziv Vyzhnyi, Kolomya District, Halychyna, settled together in Township 17, Range 2 East (figure 6). Members of another small group from the village of Luka, Buchach District, Halychyna, were apparently all related and formed a close settlement occupying seven quarters on two adjoining sections. Villagers from Melnycia, Borshchiv District, Halychyna, also formed a small, loosely clustered settlement in Township 17, Range 3 East.

In summary, agglomeration of settlers on a basis of old-country village origins was common within Ukrainian block settlements throughout the Canadian west. Furthermore, kinship was a factor of considerable significance in perpetuating what were, in effect, European social organisms on the Canadian settlement frontier.

District and Provincial Segregation

Agglomeration in settlement by district and province of origin was another marked feature of the Ukrainian block settlements, perhaps even more marked than agglomeration by village. Most notably of all, at the highest level in the hierarchy, there was an almost total separation between settlers from Halychyna and Bukovyna.

Contiguity of settlement by district of origin is clearly evident in the Stuartburn block (figure 3). This settlement contained immigrants from seven districts in the western Ukraine: Borshchiv, Husiatyn, Zalishchyky, and Kolomya in Halychyna, and Chernivci, Kitsman, and Zastavna in Bukovyna.

In the case of Zalischyky District, the majority of settlers came from Senkiw, yet others from villages within Zalischyky District settled beside them. Notably, immigrants from Kolodribka village, although settling on adjacent quarter-sections, also chose sites within an area of Zalishchyky District settlement. Similarly, immigrants from four villages in Husiatyn District—Postolivka, Zelena, Khorostkiv, and Tovstenko—all settled together. Those from Postolivka, who formed the majority, also constituted the geographical hub of the Husiatyn settlement.

Settlers from Bukovyna came from three districts: Chernivci, Kitsman, and Zastavna. The few settlers from Kitsman District did not locate together, but those from Chernivci and Zastavna settled as two distinct groups within the same area (figure 4). Eighty-two percent of the settlers from Chernivci were from the village of Lukivci, so in that case district settlement was virtually synonymous with village settlement. Among those from Zastavna District, however, there were villagers from Bridok (13 families), Chornyi Potik (3 families), Tovtry (1 family), Pohorylivka (3 families), and Zastavna town (2 families). All settled together (see figure 4).

A similar pattern was manifested in the Interlake area of Manitoba, where a number of groups tended to cluster according to district of origin (figure 6). Considering the unorganized and loosely administered process of land selection and settlement, the social cohesion shown by these settlers was remarkable.

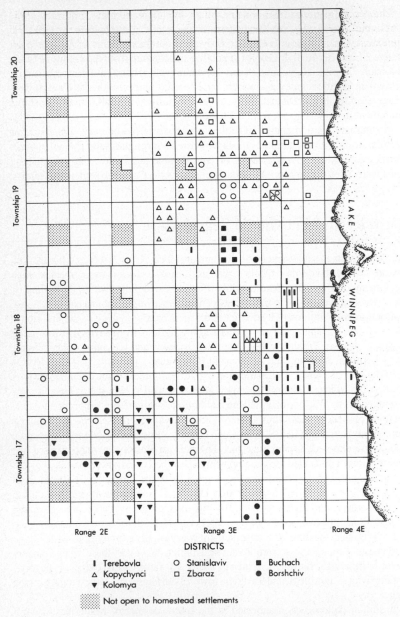

FIGURE 6   Ukrainian Settlers in the Manitoba Interlake District

SOURCES: Kaye, *Dictionary;* and M. Ewanchuk, *Spruce, Swamp and Stone* (Winnipeg: Published by the author, 1977).

Social cohesion was also manifested in the separation of settlers by their province of origin, although this pattern was obscured by the fact that some block settlements contained immigrants from only one province. The Interlake block, for example, was settled initially by immigrants from Halychyna, and those from Bukovyna entered only in small numbers and toward the end of the settlement period. In contrast, the Stuartburn district in Manitoba and the Star-Vegreville district of Alberta were settled almost from the beginning by immigrants from both provinces. A clear separation developed between the two groups, replicating old-country social and spatial groupings on the settlement frontier of western Canada.

In the Alberta case, Bukovynian settlers expanded north and east from the initial point of Ukrainian settlement near Star, while those from Halychyna confined themselves to areas west and south of the Bukovynan territory (figure 7).[30] Mixing was unusual and was generally confined to those areas that were last to be settled: the sub-marginal lands of the boreal forest north of Smoky Lake and the eastern-most district of Ukrainian settlement beyond Myrnam. These areas were mainly settled after 1905 by re-migration from the area around Wostok, Andrew, and St. Michael. Most settlers were the sons of pioneers seeking homestead land of their own. Otherwise, there was little mixing between the two groups; the contact zone remained shallow and easily defined.[31]

A similar pattern was evident in the Stuartburn district, where Bukovynan immigrants formed a solid contiguous block of settlement in the townships along the American border (figure 3). As in the Star-Vegreville case, their separation from the Halychyni began to break down only in the areas last to be settled. Similar circumstances prevailed in the final phase of settlement in both areas: a scramble for a rapidly diminishing area of homestead land in the general area of Ukrainian settlement, and a good deal of re-migration by the sons of the earlier Ukrainian settlers.

The separation of the two groups was voluntary. It was not due to any deliberate action by government agents, although there is considerable evidence of connivance by the Department of the Interior: "I found I had to put the Bukowinians and Galicians in two separate groups as they were not friendly with each other ...There was some religious difference between them which appeared to cause friction. Probably there was some obscure racial trouble as well, tracing back to the past history of these people."[32] In fact, the division of the Ukrainian block settlement on the basis of old-country provincial origin is explainable in terms of Catholic–Orthodox rivalries and conflicts that were heightened by the provincialism of the Ukrainian peasant.

It is difficult for outsiders to appreciate the intensity of feeling that was associated with the religious differences between the Orthodox Bukovynans and the Uniate (Greek Catholic) of Halychyna.[33] To many of the Ukrainian peasants, religion was the cornerstone of life. Religious affiliation meant more than adherence to a style of worship; it carried strong national and political overtones. The Greek Catholics feared Russophile sympathies by the Orthodox who, for their part,

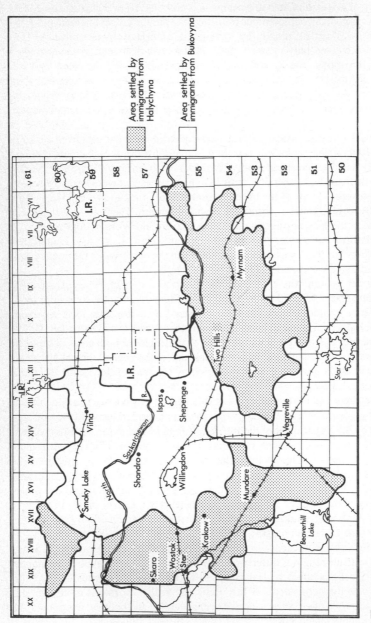

FIGURE 7   Ukrainian Settlement in the Star-Vegreville Block of East-Central Alberta to 1914

SOURCE: Data from Records of Homestead Entry, Alberta.

were equally suspicious of Roman Catholic and Polish dominance of the Uniate Church. This rift was exacerbated by differences in folk culture between Halychyna and Bukovyna, and by the mental images each group had of the other.[34] To many Bukovynans, people from Halychyna were stereotyped as miserly and without compassion; to the latter, Bukovynans were unsophisticated, bucolic "hayseeds."[35]

The intensity of their mutual antipathy was early remarked upon by many officials of the Department of the Interior who worked with the two groups. In 1897, Commissioner William McCreary noted that the Bukovynans "do not affiliate, and, in fact are detested by the Galicians."[36] Considerable trouble was experienced when officials disregarded such animosities and treated the Ukrainians as a homogeneous group. Colonization Agent C.W. Speers reported one such instance: "After a little trouble which arose, the Galicians, not wishing to go with the Bukowinians—verily the Jews not wishing to deal with the Samaritans—I assured them they were all Canadians now under free institutions and they were well satisfied as we agreed to colonize them in different parts of the Township."[37] The Department of the Interior rapidly learned to accommodate itself to these prejudices. Indeed, it soon became the practice to segregate the Bukovynans from the Halychnyi even while in transit and during their stay in the Winnipeg immigration sheds.[38]

It is more difficult to account for the perpetuation of a clear pattern of settlement by district of origin. Religious allegiance along old-country provincial lines played an important role in maintaining segregation at the macro-level; family ties clearly account for segregation at the micro-level, at the scale of the old-country village. Yet strong district loyalties operated between these extremes, as well.

Two explanations can be advanced: regional consciousness and chain migration. There is little doubt that the limited horizons of the peasant world heightened local loyalties. In some cases, peasants' horizons scarcely extend beyond their own villages, but in the densely settled environments of western Ukraine, social contacts and kinship linkages often extended over a number of villages, all of which fell within a relatively restricted geographic area. This seems to have been the case in the Stanislaviv District settlement of the Manitoba Interlake, where many families came from the village of Mariampol and its immediate environs. Unfortunately, paucity of data makes it impossible to determine the extent to which district settlement was actually "locality settlement." It is also unwise to ascribe too little physical mobility to the Ukrainian peasant at the turn of the century. Marital ties, for example, spanned the Prut River between Halychyna and Bukovyna and were directly responsible for the initial close settlement of immigrants from Halychyna and Bukovyna in the Stuartburn area. The relationship between the Storeschuk and Zahara families, from Halychyna and Bukovyna respectively, was a major factor in securing the presence of both groups in Stuartburn, although subsequent settlement saw them segregate.[39]

The second possible explanation for segregation at the district level is chain migration. According to Price, this mechanism, whereby knowledge of immigration opportunity is diffused through personal contacts between the old and new lands, accounts for most old-country groupings in New World settlement.[40] He suggests that chain migration was largely responsible for the growth of the Ukrainian population in Canada, and there can be little doubt that it was a factor of primary importance. The effect of immigration propaganda should not be overlooked, however. Dr. Josef Oleskow, an influential advocate of Ukrainian emigration to western Canada, advised Ukrainian emigrants to try to settle near to, or alongside, other Ukrainians or other minority groups from the ethnically Ukrainian areas of eastern Europe. The consensus of those Ukrainians who wrote on the subject was that in settlement abroad the peasant should follow the advice of the Ukrainian aphorism: "svyi do Svoho—Let each keep to his own."[41]

Culture and Mobility

The internal morphology of the Ukrainian block settlement may be interpreted as the spatial manifestation of the strong cohesive social forces found within a traditional peasant society. These were sufficiently strong to have a considerable effect on the decision making process in homestead selection. Ukrainian immigrants were apparently prepared to rank social factors above environmental factors in their decision-making in settlement, and traded off economic prosperity against the opportunity for social and cultural satisfaction.

When Ukrainian settlers first entered into sub-marginal sandy and stony lands in the Stuartburn and Interlake districts, they were probably unaware that the lands were "left overs" and "totally unfit for grain growing or other types of farming."[42] Marunchak, a historian of the Ukrainians in Canada, attributes this to poor judgement of new conditions, compounded by lack of time for experimentation,[43] and these were certainly factors. Yet they do not explain why Ukrainians continued to homestead in notoriously poor areas, even after they were warned against doing so.[44] They may not have fully understood the limitations of the sites they chose, but to assume that most peasant farmers were totally naive in such matters strains the bounds of credulity.[45] Rather, the Ukrainians evaluated land according to criteria quite different from those employed by non-Slavic, market-oriented pioneers.[46] Above all, they were apparently prepared to overlook deficiencies in aspects of land quality if, by so doing, they could remain within, or in contact with, a chosen cultural and social environment. Indeed, they sometimes took as homesteads land abandoned as unfit for settlement by earlier Ukrainian settlers, as in the Sniatyn area of Alberta. The reasons given for abandonment, such as "mostly covered by water," "all sand and bush and not fit for farming," "too much water and too many stones," or "land flooded for past two years," reflected conditions usually evident to the most casual observer![47] It is difficult to believe that settlers who were obliged to wade waist-deep to their homesteads, as some did in the Interlake and Stuartburn districts, did not have doubts about the quality of the land in the area.[48] Yet Ukrainian immigrants persisted in going into such areas, despite the efforts of Crown Agents to persuade them otherwise. By 1900, government interpreter Cyril Genik was advising Ukrainian immigrants to go to Alberta where good land was still available, and to avoid Stuartburn and the Interlake.[49] His advice went unheeded by those with connections in these areas, and sub-marginal land continued to be homesteaded.

Conclusion

The *initial* decision of the first Ukrainian pioneers to locate within a specific area was influenced by such factors as a desire for timber, the quest for a wide resource base, a fear of the prairie, poor evaluation of land quality, lack of mobility, and ignorance of alternative areas open to homesteading. The *perpetuation* and *expansion* of settlement, in contrast, was largely dependent upon the willingness of subsequent Ukrainian settlers to rank social-cultural factors above economic or environmental ones. Such decisions were essentially individual, but uniformity of choice created a pattern of group behaviour in which the tide of settlement thrust many into sub-marginal areas. This argument does not imply that the Ukrainians were immobile either as individuals or as a group. Nor is it meant to suggest that this behavioural pattern in settlement was confined to the Ukrainians. An incident at Fish Creek, Saskatchewan, where Ukrainian immigrants defied the efforts of the Crown to dictate their point of settlement in the west, was a dramatic refutation of the former, and Richtik has argued that settlers from Ontario displayed a similar pattern of behaviour in their settlement of southwestern Manitoba.[50] Faced with the choice of locating on a less desirable site or settling away from their friends, Ontario settlers, like the Ukrainians, often chose the former. Less desirable *sites* were chosen because of their more desirable *locations*.

The crucial difference between the Ontario and Ukrainian settlers lay in the extent to which each group was prepared to pursue social advantages. Ontario settlers soon reached the point at which they were not prepared to accept a further decline in land quality. In moving away from their fellows to secure better land they demonstrated that their kinship ties were neither as strong nor as meaningful as those of the Ukrainians. A few Ukrainian settlers also moved away from the block settlements in attempts to secure better land, but usually after they had been in the country for some time. Often they were the children of early immigrants, and when relocating to new areas they frequently did so in groups. One such group moved from the Manitoba Interlake to Prelate, Saskatchewan;[51] another from Stuartburn moved to Rycroft in the Peace River district.[52]

There is scattered evidence to suggest that although the initial decisions in settlement were those of the man, much of the subsequent inertia was due to the reluctance of the woman to break her social ties. Confined to the farm and less exposed to assimilative pressures, the woman most needed the social ties transferred from the homeland. In the absence of the daily intercourse of village life the pioneer woman became more reliant on the presence of neighbours and friends. To move away, even for economic benefit, was intolerable.[53]

Social ties, it is clear, explain many of the paradoxes of Ukrainian settlement.[54] The initial occupation of much of the poorer sub-marginal land by Ukrainian settlers is explainable only in such terms, and their continued occupation is easily understood in the light of those ties of which Edmund Burke spoke in 1775: "Close affection. . . grows from common names, from similar privileges, and equal protection. These are ties which, though light as air, are as strong as links of iron."[55]

Notes

1. H. Schlichtmann, "Ethnic Themes in Geographical Research on Western Canada," *Canadian Ethnic Studies* 9, 2 (1977): 9–41.

2. D.R. Taft and R. Robbins, *International Migrations: The Immigrant in the Modern World* (New York: Ronald Press, 1955), 111.

3. J.M. Richtik, "Manitoba Settlement, 1870–1886" (Ph.D. diss., University of Minnesota, 1971), 558–62.

4. *Winnipeg Telegram*, 26 June 1889.

5. J.J. Mannion, *Irish Settlements in Eastern Canada: A Study of Transfer and Adaptation* (Toronto: University of Toronto Press, Department of Geography Research Publications, 1974), 13.

6. J.C. Lehr, "Mormon Settlement Morphology in Southern Alberta," *Albertan Geographer* 8 (1972): 11–12.

7. C.A. Price, "Immigration and Group Settlement," in *The Cultural Integration of Immigrants*, ed. W. D. Borrie (Paris: UNESCO, 1959), 273–74.

8. J. Bohland, "The Influence of Kinship Ties on the Settlement Pattern of Northeast Georgia," *Professional Geographer* 22 (1970): 267–69; A. Brunger, "A Spatial Analysis of Individual Settlement in Southern London District, Upper Canada, 1800–1836" (Ph.D. diss., University of Western Ontario, 1973), 104–7; and R.C. Ostergren, "Prairie Bound: Migration Patterns to a Swedish Settlement on the Dakota Frontier," *Ethnicity on the Great Plains*, ed. F.C. Luebke (Lincoln, NB: University of Nebraska Press, 1980), 54–72.

9. C.A. Dawson, *Group Settlement, Ethnic Communities in Western Canada*, Canadian Frontiers of Settlement Series 7 (Toronto: Macmillan, 1936), 278–79.

10. Richtik, "Manitoba Settlement," 558–62.

11. W. Darcovich, ed., *A Statistical Compendium of the Ukrainians in Canada 1891–1976* (Ottawa: University of Ottawa Press, 1980), 500–2.

12. See P.F. Sugar, "The Nature of the non-Germanic Societies under Habsburg Rule," *Slavic Review* 22 (1963): 17; I.L. Rudnytsky, "The Ukrainians in Galicia under Austrian Rule," *Austrian History Yearbook* 3 (1967): 394–429; E.G. Balch, "Slav Emigration at its Source," *Charities and the Commons* 16 (1906): 171–83; J.P. Himka, "The Background to Emigration: Ukrainians of Galicia and Bukovyna, 1848–1914," in *A Heritage in Transition*, ed. M.R. Lupel (Toronto: McClelland and Stewart, 1982), 11–31; and A.M. Shepakov, *Ukrains' ka Trudova Emigratsiya v S.Sh.A. i Kanadi*

[*Ukrainian Workers' Emigration to the U.S.A. and Canada*] (Kiev: Akademiya Nauk Ukrains'kaya, R.S.R., 1960), 13–45.

13. W.F. McCreary, Commissioner of Immigration, Winnipeg, to J.A. Smart, Deputy Minister of the Interior, Ottawa, 14 May 1897, RG76, vol. 144, file 34214, pt. 1, Public Archives of Canada (hereinafter PAC). This file contains an extensive correspondence between McCreary and Smart covering the period 1897–1900, in which may be found numerous references by McCreary to the Ukrainians' determination to stay together.

14. Ibid., 13 May 1897.

15. Ibid., 20 May 1898.

16. P. Yuzyk, *The Ukrainians in Manitoba: A Social History* (Toronto: University of Toronto Press, 1953), 42; V.J. Kaye, *Early Ukrainian Settlements in Canada 1895–1900* (Toronto: University of Toronto Press for the Ukrainian Canadian Research Foundation, 1964), 142; V.J. Kaye, *Canadians of Recent European Origin: Survey* (Ottawa: Department of National War Services, Citizenship Division, 1945), 46; J.G. MacGregor, *Vilni Zemli: Free Lands* (Toronto: McClelland and Stewart, 1969), 157; C.H. Young, *The Ukrainian Canadians* (Toronto: Thomas Nelson and Sons, 1931), 75; J. Stechishin, *Istoriya Poselen'nya Ukraintsiv u Kanadi* [*History of Ukrainian Settlement in Canada*] (Edmonton: Ukrainian Self-Reliance League, 1975) 242–47; M. Ewanchuk, *Istoriya Ukrains'koho Poselen'nya v Okolytsi Gimli* [*A History of the Ukrainian Settlements in the Gimli Area*] (Winnipeg: Trident Press, 1975), 24–28; and P. Zvarych [Svarych], "Do Pytan'nya Rozvytku y Postupu v Materiyal'niy Kul'turi Ukrains'kykh Poselentsiv u Kanadi" ["On the Problem of Development and Progress in the Material Culture of Ukrainian Settlers in Canada"], in *Zbirnyk na Poshanu Zenona Kuzeli* (Paris: Shevshenko Scientific Society, 1962), 151.

17. I. Goresky, "Early Ukrainian Settlement in Alberta" in *Ukrainians in Alberta*, Ukrainian Pioneers' Association (Edmonton: Ukrainian Pioneers' Association of Alberta, 1975), 17–38; J.M. Lazarneko "Rusiw Pioneers in Alberta," in *Ukrainians in Alberta*, 38–41; and A. Royick, "Ukrainian Settlements in Alberta," *Canadian Slavonic Papers* 10 (1968): 278–97.

18. Z.S. Phorecky and A. Royick, "Anglicization of Ukrainian in Canada between 1895 and 1970; A Case Study in Crystallization," *Canadian Ethnic Studies* 1 (1970): 150.

19. Goresky, "Early Ukrainian" and "Minutes of the Founding of One of the First Ukrainian Greek Catholic Churches in Alberta, March 1900," *Canadian Ethnic Studies* 6 (1974): 67–69; also T.C. Byrne, "The Ukrainian Community in North Central Alberta" (M.A. thesis, University of Alberta, 1931), 31.

20. See E.G. Mardon, *Community Names of Alberta* (Lethbridge: University of Lethbridge, 1973); J.B. Rudnyc'kyj, *Manitoba Mosaic of Place Names* (Winnipeg: Canadian Institute of Onomastic Sciences, 1970); and J.B. Rudnyc'kyj, *Canadian Place Names of Ukrainian Origin* (Winnipeg: n.p., 1951). Rudnyc'kyj disputes Komarno as a transferred toponym; he claims that it is derived from the Ukrainian "komar," or mosquito, and means "full of mosquitoes."

21. A. Koestler, *The Ghost in the Machine* (London: Pan Books, 1970), 65.

22. For example, *The Russell Banner*, 22 Oct. 1903.

23. See, for example, the pioneer biographies in *Ukrainians in Alberta*, 263–556.

24. Declarations of Abandonment, N.W. 20, Township 55, Range 16 West, 4, and N.W. 20, Township 55, Range 15 West, 4, Homestead Files, Provincial Museum and Archives of Alberta.

25. Interview with John Gregorchuk, Arbakka, Manitoba, 8 Oct. 1975. See also interviews with George Alexiuk, Sundown, Manitoba, 15 July 1975; Mrs. M. Sportak, Vita, Manitoba, 3 July 1975; Mrs. Wasylyna Koshelanyk, Caliento, Manitoba, 3 July

1975; N. Chornopysky, Vita, Manitoba, 8 Oct. 1975; George Penteliuk, Arbakka, Manitoba, 10 Oct. 1975; Andrew Lamash, St. Michael, Alberta, 15 June 1972; Andrew Basisty, Andrew, Alberta, 6 June 1972; and Mrs. W. Melynyk, Delph, Alberta, 30 May 1972. Immigrants from the same village gravitated together even in the emerging ethnic enclaves in western Canadian cities: see M. Vinohradova, "Recollections of a Pioneer Woman," *The Ukrainian-Canadian* (March 1972): 22–24.

26. Interview with Todor Kutzak, Sirko, Manitoba, 10 Oct. 1975.

27. Project SUCH (Save Ukrainian Canadians' Heritage), under the Opportunities for Youth Programme, was undertaken during the summer of 1971. It aimed at interviewing Ukrainian settlers, or their immediate families, to compile a collection of oral history and folklore. The data collected, comprising 251 General Information Questionnaires, 58 Detailed Informant Sheets, and some 200 hours of tape-recorded interviews, are now held in the Ukrainian Arts and Crafts Museum, 1240 Temperance St., Saskatoon.

28. V.J. Kaye, *Dictionary of Ukrainian Canadian Pioneer Biography: Pioneer Settlement in Manitoba* (Toronto: Ukrainian Canadian Research Foundation, 1975), 165–66.

29. In the case of the settlers from Lukivci, the Badiuk family was linked by marriage to the Kossowan family, and at least one of the four families that appeared to be unrelated to any others in the area was, in fact, related to the Kossowans by marriage. In one account of Ukrainian settlement in the Interlake district, it is indicated that a good many village groups were bound together by marital ties (M. Ewanchuk, *Spruce, Swamp and Stone: A History of the Pioneer Ukrainian Settlements in the Gimli Area* (Winnipeg: Published by the author, 1977), 19–23).

30. The Ukrainian settlement at Star was established by immigrants from the Kalush district of Halychyna. The first Bukovynan settlers did not arrive in Canada until 1896.

31. Data abstracted from the Homestead General Registers and Records of Homestead Entry, Provincial Museum and Archives of Alberta. Supplementary data were derived from *Ukrainians in Alberta*, 263–556, and from field research in east-central Alberta.

32. T. McNutt, "Galicians and Bukowinians" in *The Story of Saskatchewan and Its People*, ed. J. Hawkes (Chicago-Regina: S.J. Clarke, 1924), 731–32.

33. A good indication of the intensity of feeling that accompanied religious affiliation in the pioneer environment is given by MacGregor, *Vilni Zemli*, 164–82, in his discussion of the religious conflicts between Orthodox and Uniate pioneers in Alberta.

34. On differences in the material culture of the two groups, see J.C. Lehr, "Ukrainian Houses in Alberta," *Alberta Historical Review* 21, 4 (1973): 9–15.

35. Interviews within the Ukrainian community of east-central Alberta, 1971–75. See J.C. Lehr, "The Process and Pattern of Ukrainian Rural Settlement in Western Canada, 1891–1914" (Ph.D. diss., University of Manitoba, 1978) 318–19.

36. McCreary to Smart, 15 May 1897, RG76, vol. 144, file 34214, PAC.

37. C.W. Speers to McCreary, 9 July 1897, RG76, vol. 144, file 34214, PAC.

38. Handwritten diary of Anton Keyz.

39. Interview with Stephan Storeschuk, Gardenton, Manitoba, 21 July 1975.

40. Price, "Immigration," 270.

41. J. Oloskow, *O Emigratsii [On Emigration]* (L'viv: Michael Kachkowskyi Society, 1895), 39. The first Ukrainians to settle in western Canada chose to locate in east-central Alberta, to be close to a small group of *Völksdeutsche* (ethnic Germans) from the western Ukraine. The *Völksdeutsche* were conversant with Ukrainian, and the newcomers had close relations with them in their early years. The proximity of *Völksdeutsche* was also a major determinant in the selection of lands by the first Ukrainians to settle in the Stuartburn district, at Grenfell, and at other points in the west.

In addition, Poles, Romanians, and, on occasion, on an individual basis, Jews were closely associated with Ukrainian settlement. Poles, usually from western Halychyna, settled alongside Ukrainians from that province in the Skaro area of Alberta and at Cook's Creek in Manitoba. Romanians from Bukovyna settled at Marea Boian, Alberta, replicating a previously close geographical relationship between Romanian and Ukrainian villages in Bukovyna. Similarities of religion, a common understanding of languages, and a shared peasant *Weltanschaaung* explain these associations. Ukrainians from Halychyna probably had comprehension, even fluency, in Polish, and were of the Greek Catholic (Uniate) church; some were even of the Roman Catholic church. The Romanians shared with the Bukovynans a common adherence to Orthodoxy, mutual comprehension of language, and certain folkways and attitudes.

42. M.H. Marunchak, *The Ukrainian Canadians: A History* (Winnipeg: Ukrainian Free Academy of Sciences, 1970), 86.

43. Ibid., 43.

44. A.B. Woywitka, "Homesteader's Woman," *Alberta History* 24 (1976): 20; and M. Ewanchuk, *Pioneer Profiles: Ukrainian Settlers in Manitoba* (Winnipeg: Published by the author, 1981), 128–29.

45. Most Ukrainian immigrants were from an agricultural background. Few of the emerging Ukrainian industrial proletariat were involved in agricultural settlement in Canada. Although some of the better educated, non-farm elements of Ukrainian society migrated to Canada before 1914, few did so before 1905, and they seldom went on to the land. In 1901, it was estimated that only 2 percent of Ukrainian settlers in the Dauphin region were literate. This may be an unduly low estimate, but an examination of signatures on applications for homestead entry in Alberta between 1892 and 1914 suggested that less than 20 percent of all Ukrainian applicants were literate. On literacy rates, see *Winnipeg Telegram*, 2 Jan. 1901; and Canada, *Sessional Papers*, 1897, "Department of the Interior," 120.

46. J.C. Lehr, "The Rural Settlement Behaviour of Ukrainian Pioneers in Western Canada, 1891–1914" in *Western Canadian Research in Geography: The Lethbridge Papers*, ed. B. M. Barr, B.C. Geographical Series 21 (Vancouver: Tantalus Research Ltd., 1975), 51–66; and interview with Stefan Yendik, Frazerwood, Manitoba, 12 Nov. 1974.

47. Declarations of Abandonment, Records of Homestead Entry, S.E. 18, Township 57, Range 18 West, 4; N.E. 10, Township 59, Range 17 West, 4; S.E. 22, Township 59, Range 17 West, 4; and N.W. 30, Township 57, Range 16 West, 4, Homestead Files, Provincial Museum and Archives of Alberta.

48. Ewanchuk, *Pioneer Profiles*, 128.

49. Ibid., 66; Woywitka, "Homesteader's Woman," 20; and Wasyl Mihaychuk, "Mihaychuk Family Tree" (unpublished typescript, n.d.), 2 pp.

50. Richtik, "Manitoba Settlement," 558–62. For details of the confrontation between officials of the Department of the Interior and Ukrainian immigrants at Fish Creek, Saskatchewan, see Kaye, *Early Ukrainian Settlements*, 300–8; and John C. Lehr, "Government Coercion in the Settlement of Ukrainian Immigrants in Western Canada," *Prairie Forum* 8 (1983): 179–94.

51. *Ukrainians in Alberta*, 357.

52. Woywitka, "Homesteader's Woman," 21–22; and *Ukrainians in Alberta*, 286–87.

53. E. Shlanka, "Krydor Community No 13, Interviews of Pioneers" (April 1944, typewritten ms), 5; J.S. Woodsworth "Ukrainians in Rural Communities: Report of Investigation by the Bureau of Social Research, Governments of Manitoba, Saskatchewan and Alberta" (Winnipeg, 25 Jan. 1917, typewritten ms), 130; and Ewanchuk, *Spruce, Swamp and Stone,* 22–23.

54. Merrill explains the density of Ukrainian settlement in the Riding Mountain area

of Manitoba as a reflection of the immigrants' desire to maintain close family ties; see
L. Merrill, "Population Distribution in the Riding Mountains and Adjacent Plains of
Manitoba and Saskatchewan, 1870–1946" (M.A. thesis, McGill University, 1953),
64–91; also MacGregor, *Vilni Zemli*, 184–85.

55.   Edmund Burke, Second Speech on Conciliation with America, 22 Mar. 1775,
House of Commons.

SECTION 3
THE DEVELOPING COUNTRYSIDE

Historical geographers have given a good deal of effort to understanding the developing Canadian countryside. They have investigated everything from the decorative tastes of ethnic groups to the spatial organization of rural society, and taken together their studies provide often vivid accounts of evolving rural landscapes in a country whose population was overwhelmingly rural into the twentieth century. In some respects, of course, the division between studies treating the developing countryside and those included in other parts of this volume is an artificial one. Native peoples created new geographies, as we saw in section 1. Settlement, the subject of section 2, changed the look of the land as well as economic and social relationships among people. Studies of particular places, seen in section 5, also reveal the settings of everyday existence.

The four papers that follow, however, are distinctive in their collective emphasis upon the processes by which landscapes were shaped. Here we encounter people *making* places. Although they generally remain anonymous, we find them shaping their surroundings by experiment and adjustment, chance and design, intuition and decree, while variously leaning on tradition, responding to current need or fashion, and looking to the future. We are thus brought to recognize that the landscape is not simply a collection of tangible objects on the surface of the earth, as early suppositions about the cultural landscape sometimes implied. It is instead a complex repository of artifacts, aspirations, ideas, achievements, failures, and unintended consequences which can be interpreted both literally and symbolically, as well as for what it contains and what it does not.

The first of the four articles in this section is by Serge Courville of the Department of Geography and CELAT in Laval University. It is a lyrical essay on the roots of Quebec's distinctive landscape and culture. Courville combines the results of his own research on settlement in the St. Lawrence lowland with the recent work of Quebec historians and the insights of Claude Raffestin into the geography of power,* to produce a fresh, thought-provoking synthesis. The substance of his interpretation is readily summarized. The countryside of New France was organized on two levels: officialdom imposed its structured design on the landscape in the form of seigneuries, long lots, and parishes; and settlers created their own domestic spaces to meet their familial needs. The bounds of the family tracts often bore little relationship to official lines on the land. Behind these two imprints lay different logics, one reflecting metropolitan purposes, the other a grass-roots response to the particular challenges and opportunities of settlement along the St. Lawrence. Together, they gave distinctive shape to land and life in the colony. Offering a compelling view of the dynamic that drove settlement into the thin soils and short summers of the Canadian Shield, and of the attachment of people to land and family, Courville's essay reaches well beyond its nominal termination date (1760) to bear on our understanding of Quebec into the twentieth century.

This article is also important methodologically, for the questions it asks and the connections it makes. It reflects the influence of recent French scholarship in the

---

* Claude Raffestin, *Pour une géographie du pouvoir* (Paris: Librairies techniques, 1980).

social sciences and, more than any other essay in this volume, engages the concerns of social theory that have come to the fore in recent English-language literature in human geography. Its picture of a countryside woven from institutional ambition and people establishing themselves on the land is therefore, in formal terms, an account of the dialectic of structure and agency. Its emphasis on the colonizer's inability to impose official patterns on the lives of the colonized is a commentary on the limits of the power of the state in New France. Although Courville hardly makes these connections explicit, his paper provides a timely example of the way in which our understanding of the past can be brought into sharper focus by appropriate reference to the conceptual frameworks and analytical concerns of social theory.

Common houses have long attracted the attention of geographers because they mark migration paths, mirror cultural origins, and reflect adaptation to new environments. When Peter Ennals, of Mount Allison University, and Deryck Holdsworth, of Pennsylvania State University, began their investigations of the cultural landscape of the Maritime provinces, however, they brought a new perspective to regional studies in that area of the country. The authors treat a complex region in which time, population movements, and changing technologies have created richly textured landscapes. They describe their paper as a reconnaissance but it remains both the most complete treatment of vernacular architecture in the Maritimes and an important Canadian example of work in this venerable tradition of geographical inquiry.

As in so many geographical studies, the initial task facing Ennals and Holdsworth was to establish what was where. The first section of their paper is therefore given to identifying and classifying housing types and to mapping their locations in order to establish patterns of distribution. Here, generalization was essential. The dimensions and façades of Maritime houses are almost endlessly varied in detail, and there are examples of almost every type of structure in most parts of the region. Nevertheless, careful attention to floor plans as well as façades, and to the relative frequency with which different styles were used, revealed six basic house types and clear regional concentrations of some styles. Only with these patterns identified could Ennals and Holdsworth broach the vital task of interpretation, and the remainder of their paper ranges widely to explain the social meaning of Maritime housing. Many influences are seen to have affected the architectural fabric of the Maritimes: the transfer of culture with migration; the diffusion of designs through books and newspapers; the way that taste was shaped by people and events remote from the region; local adaptations; changes in construction techniques and the availability of materials; economic considerations; and changing social attitudes. More generally, these factors underlie the complex cloth of landscapes east and west across the developing country.

The difficulties of overland travel in British North America were notorious. Railroad promoters made much of the ability of the new technology to break winter's icy grip, and books and pamphlets describing travels and prospects in the early nineteenth-century colonies offered colourful stories of rutted tracks, bruised bones, broken axles, and painful progress through mud and driving sleet. Yet settlers spread inland rapidly and, far from retreating into isolation and self-sufficiency, they generally depended upon some market connection. In his article on rural roads, Thomas F. McIlwraith, of the University of Toronto, recognizes the disjunction between published descriptions of the problems of movement and the behaviour of ordinary colonists (a disjunction that bears comparison with Courville's distinction between an official world and unofficial reality). He sets out to determine the adequacy of rural roads to the needs of those who used them most, and his analysis is a model of its kind. It addresses a large question through a case study, pursues answers through the skilful use of records collected for purposes other than the one at hand, uses maps to make sense of disparate data, and respects the capacity of those who settled British North American land to make judicious choices. Through McIlwraith's discussion, we are led to appreciate the challenges and constraints faced by settlers and to understand better how and why the countryside developed as it did.

However judicious decisions may seem in their time, unforeseen consequences can call their wisdom into question in the longer term. Kenneth Kelly, of the University of Guelph, has written extensively on agricultural settlement in Upper Canada; in the final paper of this section, he discusses the unintended results of settlers' agricultural decisions. Anxious to turn their uncleared acres into productive farms, settlers stripped the land of its tree cover. Elsewhere, lumberers took the best trees to market from the seemingly endless forest, but left slash and debris behind as fuel for devastating fires. Through the pre-Confederation years, the march of commerce and improvement went almost unquestioned. Then the ecological consequences were recognized. The effects of human disturbance were widespread—soil erosion, wide fluctuations in run-off, floods, and parched fields.

Yet new ideas were at least as important as this physical evidence in shaping the response that Kelly documents in his paper. In 1864, George Perkins Marsh, a widely travelled native of the Vermont hill country, published *Man and Nature*.* The book asked whether the Earth's resources are given to us for exploitation or "for usufruct alone," and quickly began to change the way that people looked at their environment. Indeed, it is scant exaggeration to claim that the late nineteenth-century drive to reforest large parts of Ontario grew out of Marsh's book. Whatever the details of its pedigree, however, the image of a new, planned, and efficient landscape that emerged in reaction to the damage of decades had an enormous influence upon the countryside of modern Ontario. Furthermore, this account of its origins and its contentious and piecemeal realization usefully reminds us of the power of modern human societies to transform their environments and of their continuing capacity to adapt to new ideas and changing circumstances.

---

* George Perkins Marsh, *Man and Nature* (New York: Charles Scribner, 1864).

SPACE, TERRITORY, AND CULTURE IN NEW FRANCE: A GEOGRAPHICAL PERSPECTIVE*

SERGE COURVILLE

The countryside of Quebec in the seventeenth and eighteenth centuries is often considered only in terms of the structures put in place by France as it established its Laurentian colony. This short essay aims to reveal another type of territorial organization and, in so doing, to point towards a fuller understanding of Quebec's landscape and culture. Based on recent research in history and geography, it addresses old questions about the relationships between people and place, colonizers and the colonized, official worlds and lived realities. It intends to show that the development of Quebec during the French regime and later can be read at many levels.

In effect, the human geography of the lower St. Lawrence Valley before 1760 comprised at least two territorial frameworks. Their co-existence reflected the distance that separated New France from Old. Along an axis from the heights of Quebec City to the Island of Montreal, with higher population densities in the oldest settled areas, there existed a thin strip of settlements embedded in a geometric landscape. This was structured space, the result of careful planning

* Translated by Patricia Kealy with the assistance of Cole Harris, from ''Espace, territoire et culture en Nouvelle-France: une vision géographique,'' *Revue d'histoire de l'Amérique française* 37, 3 (1983): 417–29. A preliminary version of this text was submitted to Jean-Claude Robert (Department of History, Université du Québec à Montréal) and Normand Seguin (Department of History, Université du Québec à Trois-Rivières). The author wishes to thank them for their comments. He also wishes to thank all those who contributed observations and suggestions, particularly Marcel Bélanger (Department of Geography, Laval University), Jacques Mathieu (Department of History, Laval University), and Heather Parker, who helped with an early translation of this paper.

uncommon in North America at that time. But this space was also locally organized. Beyond the administrative divisions of the land into seigneuries, parishes, and *censives* (long lots) was another reality, a multitude of domestic spaces created out of the close relationship between habitants and their physical and human environments.

Divided between the political will of the colonizer to subordinate the development of the colony to metropolitan needs and the immigrants' desire to take advantage of new-world opportunities, the St. Lawrence Valley expressed two logics: *urbanité,[1]* of French origin and the source of macro-forms and macro-structures; and *territorialité,[2]* originating in the intimate local places shaped by habitants out of the structured space that the French state imposed. From these logics emerged a cultural space, or cultural region, that would survive the British conquest of 1760 and leave its mark on all subsequent development of this area.

A Structured Space

For France in the seventeenth and eighteenth centuries, the first step towards the conquest of the new world was control of the St. Lawrence Valley, the principal access to the wealth of the vast hinterland of North America.[3] The idea of colonization for exploitation took hold early, and as soon as the limits of a coastal establishment became evident, the French state began to move inland.[4] Although its early settlement efforts were hesitant and produced only mediocre results, its power remained extraordinarily effective. In less than half a century, the colonial world was structured by institutions that would govern economic and social relationships, and by a system of land division (developed in the 1630s) that formed the framework for rural settlement.[5] The territory was divided into seigneuries and *censives* perpendicular to the St. Lawrence River (figure 1), and an early network of towns was created, each, even then, with administrative, military, and commercial facilities.

This intense colonizing effort followed from a single, integrating rationality. The seigneury, the *côte* (a discrete line of farmhouses along the river), and the *Coutume de Paris* (the code of French civil law that prevailed in Canada) represented more than a simple juxtaposition of familiar institutions that might be expected to contribute to colonial development. They were part of a common enterprise, which helps to explain why they were transplanted to the new world in the first place and why they spread throughout the colony.[6] In the St. Lawrence Valley, France sought complete territorial control through the establishment of a stable rural society capable of reproducing itself. To achieve this, officials chose a combination of structures that would lead not only to the effective settlement of colonists around the seigneur, defined as the state's partner in the colonization effort, but also to their collective adherence to values appropriate to the ideal of a land-owning society under the old regime.[7]

FIGURE 1 The Laurentian Colony. Tracts 1, 2, 3, 4, and 5 represent the areas monopolized by the founding families. They include their land holdings, meeting places, and places where they fished, hunted, and gathered.

Although mitigated for a time by the initial difficulties of colonization, this ambition strengthened under royal government after 1663, as administrative reforms established the state's power in all areas of economic and social life. Land ownership, the distribution of settlers, demographic behaviour, religion, civil law, and trade were only some of the areas that, henceforth, would be controlled by the administration. Through the years, the regulatory apparatus was fortified as new regulations were added relating to fishing, hunting, farming, settlement, statute labour, payment of seigneurial dues, and the fur trade. At the same time that officials were attempting to concentrate the population in villages and to restrict the size of seigneuries (which grew considerably in number between 1663 and 1760), a settlement policy was established. Bonuses were paid for early marriages and large families, bachelors and their parents were fined, aid was provided to soldiers who had been sent to pacify the country and who decided to settle there, and young women known as *filles du roi* were sent to be quickly married off to pioneers.[8]

Despite the creation of a parish system at the beginning of the eighteenth century, officials paid scant attention to the local setting. An entire colony, after all, had to be settled and developed. The development of individual seigneuries was left to the initiative of the seigneurs, subject to the regulatory control of the state. A metropolitan logic gave the colony its initial shape and framed its subsequent development. This logic was rooted in medieval tradition, but steeped in the rationalist thought of the Renaissance and touched by the new economic theories that were taking hold throughout Europe. It gave rise to structures and standards intended to ensure the success, and to define the form and function of, colonization. According to the precepts of French mercantilism, the Laurentian colony would never be more than a planned offshoot, a satellite region, of France.[9] Shaped in a mould intended to ensure a solid foundation for continental development, the colony appeared "prefabricated," closed to change.[10] Yet change would come, not as a result of government decisions but of the actual conditions of life in New France.

As soon as it was established, colonial society escaped the regulatory control of the state and deviated from imposed models. Deviance began with the seigneurs, who did not wholly share the state's goals, preferring the city and the fur trade to the development of their seigneuries.[11] The habitants, for their part, managed to come to terms with the demands of seigneurs and priests, seeking not so much to remove themselves from established spatial structures and the role reserved for them, as to take advantage of those structures and to live according to their own priorities. This transformation was rapid and resulted in the emergence, alongside the world of the towns, of a parallel system that evolved at its own pace.[12] One world was dominated by the colonial elite and structured by trans-Atlantic trade and culture; the other was dominated by the habitants themselves, who lived in a much closer relationship with the land. There was no clear dividing line between the two, but there were enough points of contrast to allow one to speak of different actors, of different social groups, methods of production, and trade.[13] Thus, quite early, a new type of spatial organization, the product of people establishing themselves in space, became interwoven with the institutional structure imposed from above.

A Mosaic of Domestic Spaces

Retarded at first by Iroquois raids and the small number of settlers, rural settlement was soon accelerated by overproduction of furs at the end of the seventeenth century, the resulting reduced demand for labour in the fur trade, and a rapid increase in population from under 10 000 in 1681 to nearly 52 000 in 1739. By the latter date, less than a quarter of the population lived in towns and within a few decades, the empty spaces between Quebec City and Montreal were largely occupied. New territories such as Charlevoix and the lower valleys of the Chaudière and Richelieu rivers were settled, as populations spilled beyond the borders of earlier settlements and people migrated well away from their native regions.

The influence of seigneurs may have accounted for the choice of some new settlement locations, but in most cases the decision was taken by individuals and families and had nothing to do with seigneurial boundaries. When settlers colonized an area near the one from which they had come, they usually settled on land their parents had acquired and reserved for the purpose. Settlement in such areas was more rapid, and it was facilitated by the presence of neighbours from the same region, many of whom were kin. In the case of migrations to more distant places, people settled on newly acquired land that was divided among different groups coming from different regions. Settlement in these areas was more difficult, depending as it did on neighbourhood relationships established among the newcomers. It appears, in fact, that for individuals who shared no common background with other settlers, the first two years were crucial. Either they managed to make a fortunate marriage, thus becoming integrated into the community, or they remained outsiders, in which case they would probably have to leave, the fate most often of bachelors and isolated couples. On the other hand, members of established families would settle permanently on adjacent lots.[14]

Although initially open to arrivals from outside, these settled areas had a tendency, once organized, to close in upon themselves and to rely on a locally defined system of relationships (see figure 1). Without ever being completely broken, connections with the original settlements became weaker and were soon limited to family ties. And while new communities (*solidarités*) were taking shape, formed through combinations of marriages among the founding families,[15] fewer newcomers arrived. They were discouraged both by the scarcity of land and by already established settlers' more or less overt distrust of anyone who might represent a threat to their land holdings. Land represented wealth to the settlers, of course, but it was equally important as the principal mediator of social relationships: ties with neighbours were forged both through the land and for it.

Although they were somewhat hampered by the obligation to live on their own concessions (*tenir feu et lieu*) and by the speculative practices of certain seigneurs, the settlers' greatest efforts during the settlement phase were directed towards acquiring land by buying or trading wooded or abandoned lots, by combining inheritances, and by requesting further concessions intended to provide for their children's future. The majority of pioneer families engaged in such land acquisition, prizing land not for its exchange but for its use value,[16] and the practice soon spread throughout the territory and even beyond, thus creating permanent settlements from what had been nothing more than formal spatial structures imposed by the state. Within these settlements, people developed a strong sense of belonging to place. Felt most strongly in relation to land holdings and, secondarily, where social cohesion was strongest,[17] this attachment was long expressed locally by place names that were heavily charged with spatial and social meaning (the "Rang du Bord de l'Eau" and the "Rang des Caron," for example). Parishes—which like the seigneuries were the result of the state's political goals, but appeared only after settlement was established and land holdings assured—introduced a new level of spatial order and identity. Yet they never completely superseded the earlier, locally expressed sense of belonging felt by habitant families.

With time and population growth, all of the land in these family tracts or domestic spaces would be taken up. Sons of habitants descended from pioneer families would no longer be able to settle locally unless they took up a trade or became tenant farmers or sharecroppers on the farm of a neighbour or of the seigneur himself. They found themselves excluded from their native territory and were forced, as their families had been, to migrate to the back country of their seigneury or to some frontier seigneury in order to find land. This type of migration usually took place at the time of marriage; it was often to a familiar area where the husband had already cleared and built a house on a lot obtained from his parents. Sometimes the young couple would live temporarily with one of their families before moving, in order to put aside enough to establish themselves permanently or to acquire a new tract of land that they would then have to develop. Sometimes, too, groups would migrate together; these were composed not only of young people but of entire families of three, four, or even five siblings who for various economic and social reasons decided to join the movement in hopes of building a new life for themselves. Only the heir would stay behind, or return later, to settle on the family homestead, in exchange for which he would help support his parents and help his brothers and sisters become established. In this way, balance was restored to the home parishes as family members moved away from overcrowded family farms, forming new territories and extending the boundaries of organized space.[18]

This process, which established newly settled areas with each generation, can be explained not only by the close ties that formed between families and their land, but also by the kind of farming practised by habitants. Benefiting from a person–land ratio more favourable than in France, Canadian settlers tended to adopt extensive methods of cultivation, using land to replace the techniques of intensive cultivation that, in Canada, were restricted to the kitchen garden. Thus colonists sought land, not necessarily to increase their crop area (although there are not enough case studies to permit a conclusion about this) but to avoid land divisions that undermined the viability of a farm.

As soon as the pioneering stage was over, a double system of production appeared. On the one hand, farmers practised extensive single-crop cultivation based on wheat, the only truly commercial crop at the time, but including peas, a field crop in New France. On the other hand, they devoted a small area to mixed vegetable farming, which was carried out near the house and accompanied by the raising of a few animals, used for ploughing and domestic needs. Grown both for domestic consumption and for sale, wheat soon made up three-quarters of the harvest, a measure of the commercialization of agriculture. Should a crisis occur, production could shift quickly to less immediately threatened crops. The crisis over, it would return to the production of crops for which there was a reliable demand. Thus, by the beginning of the eighteenth century, farming had become a viable activity that could, in and of itself, meet family needs and define social status.

Few colonial administrators recognized this evolution. One possible exception was Intendant Antoine-Denis Raudot, who wrote early in the eighteenth century that "the fur trade must henceforth be regarded as of secondary importance"[19] compared to the export potential of agriculture. Official indifference towards the rural world, combined with the administration's practice of doing almost nothing except during periods when food was scarce (and even then usually resorting to official rather than concrete remedies), moved farming towards an individual and familial space-time setting. Farmers therefore remained sensitive to the importance of profit yet suspicious of outside interference, even if its purpose was to increase productivity. In 1742, when Intendant Hocquart fixed the price of wheat to prevent an excessive increase in the price of bread, farmers responded by refusing to take their grain to town.[20] By the same token, when he imported cylindrical winnowing screens from France to improve the quality of exported flour, he made a point of informing the Minister that he had to be very forceful to get the screens into general use.[21] Thus Laurentian agriculture long remained the product of a distinctive relationship between family and land, contributing to the development of a type of culture that would shape life in the colony long after 1760.

A Dense Cultural Area

By the time of the English conquest, the territory of Canada was structured by a rational division of land into seigneuries and censives, but organized by the geography of its domestic spaces (see figure 1). The territory was settled by people who were relatively homogeneous in place of origin, language, and religion, and composed of a multitude of family holdings established within the structures introduced by the colonizer. It thus became the place where a culture was forged,[22] and patterns of collective behaviour defined—patterns that would be spread by rural expansion in the late eighteenth and nineteenth centuries.[23]

Originally encouraged by state initiatives, settlement in the seigneurial lowlands quickly became autonomous, stimulated by local social and environmental circumstances and increasingly cut off from the type of contacts generated by the fur trade. The result has sometimes been seen as a rather introverted world, insensitive to trade and closed to innovation. Population was sparse, and a coherent urban network that might have encouraged trade had not developed. Only a few small centres appeared; aside from the two major commercial towns of Quebec City and Montreal, the urban framework of the Laurentian colony consisted of nothing more than a skeletal network of small port villages.[24]

Closer analysis reveals, however, that this world was surprisingly dynamic. It was hostile to outside intrusion, which was seen as a potential source of constraint, but much more open to external contacts than is generally recognized—provided such contacts coincided with domestic goals. While not denying their origins, Canadian habitants took advantage of the opportunities offered by the new world to assert the differences between themselves and French peasants,[25] rejecting the norms of the metropolis in favour of a North American way of life. (This process of social change was also exemplified in the English colonies to the south.) Because land was abundant, habitants were able to develop an economy based on extensive agriculture that was productive enough to provide a fairly comfortable living. Nevertheless, its maintenance depended upon the movement of children away from the family farm when they married.[26] Resulting from the need to maintain the balance between family and farm and the availability of new lands, migration engendered a form of agricultural development that, while sensitive to profit, was essentially the product of the migrants' experience, resourcefulness, and ability to fend for themselves. The argument advanced by some as evidence of the backwardness of New France, that when iron tools became scarce they were replaced by wooden ones, only illustrates this. Though it reveals the limited means of the population and the colony's difficulty in ironworking, it also says much for the ability of farmers to meet their own technological needs.[27]

Seen from this point of view, the history of the St. Lawrence colony appears to have been, above all, that of group adhesion to territory. Relationships among people, relationships with nature, and the intensity of these relationships within the local setting were all significant or determining factors in the colony's development.[28] Of course, there were obstacles. One can cite, for example, France's policy of requiring settlers to clear and work the land they owned, or the fact that many settlers abandoned their land. The attachment of people to place does imply, however, that territoriality was based on domestic priorities, which reinforced family strategies to the detriment of official needs and subordinated external stimuli to local requirements. It also goes a long way to explain the hold that some family groups had on the territory, shown clearly by certain place names, and the impact that the expansion of trade between New France and the Antilles in the 1730s had on the development of local agriculture.[29]

The Laurentian colony was created as the land was cleared, and set within the framework of a seigneurial system that eventually monetarized property relationships. Within this realm, domestic and commercial spheres tended to coincide. The farm, the farm house, the neighbourhood, and the *rang* were aspects of a single environment, or habitat. The assemblage of people and houses had a social significance that outweighed its economic functions. When economic activity extended beyond this local space it was always to satisfy domestic needs, even in the face of official disapproval. In the seventeenth and eighteenth centuries, this outreach turned to the fur trade and in the early nineteenth century to the timber trade to support the family farm. The process eventually generated seasonal migrations to the forests of Maine and Ontario and permanent migrations to the towns and cities of Quebec and the United States.

Such mobility did not reflect a simple desire to move[30]—other things being equal, new places were usually more threatening than old. It had its origin in a method of colonization based on exclusion and the constant forced migration of a certain part of the population to new territory. For some, forced migration became permanent; for others it was a temporary adventure that would eventually enable them to establish themselves on their own land. It is necessary, in this context, to distinguish between the real voyageurs, for whom the fur trade was a career, and the more numerous participants in the fur trade who sought to accumulate a small nest egg in order to establish a farm. After 1700, however, few farmers' sons found employment in this essentially urban-based activity.[31] Because the St. Lawrence Valley was far from the territory of the fur trade, rural settlement tended to become increasingly removed from it, and was materially and morally supported by strong family ties that favoured the re-creation of farms similar to those the settlers had just left. Because relations between habitants and seigneurs seem generally to have been distant and characterized by distrust, if not contempt, these pioneer settlements not only became economically autonomous but were also cut off socially from everyone who was not directly involved with the concerns of the group.

By 1760, the colonial period had lasted long enough to establish attitudes and forms of behaviour that would be passed on to future generations.[32] The seigneurial space in the St. Lawrence Valley, a generally artificial entity superimposed on a dense network of local spaces, was no longer an abstract formulation, but a place where a human tradition and a physical environment converged, an intensely lived-in space that expressed the colonizer's logic much less than it did the habitants' life. It was a setting for a human society based on new relationships among people and things, and these new relationships defined a type of civilization that is better understood in terms of individual and familial spaces and times than of official institutions.

Conclusion

New France was structured by France but organized by the people who lived there. It was shaped by two logics, which were expressed not only by the evolution of forms in space but also by the distance that, very early, separated habitants from everyone connected with European culture and trans-Atlantic trade. Already firmly entrenched by the end of the French regime, the distinctive way of life that emerged from these circumstances did not really come into its own until the century following the conquest. By then a new francophone middle class (*moyenne bourgeoisie*) had appeared, supported by seigneurial property, government positions, and parliamentary office. Thus cut off from a new elite that was soon to prove as distant as the previous one, country people closed themselves off and found their own way to adapt to change and to life on the periphery of an urban world they rejected. (They had nevertheless to come to terms with it, occasionally at the risk of endorsing its values.) Contacts with the outside world increased, and there were new migrations that took habitants and their way of life to new places, but local domestic space in the St. Lawrence Valley remained apart, still incorporated within the traditional framework of familial experience. From all this grew a truly local culture that reflected the originality of settlement in the St. Lawrence Valley much better than did the culture of the elite. This local culture would also favour the development of a fairly rigid set of beliefs, values, and standards that political leaders would later exploit in promoting their own ideas of collective development.

Notes

1. The concept of *urbanité* refers to characteristics of civilization as expressed in the areas of law, the arts, science, and religion. See M. Bélanger, "L'urbanité de Québec," *Cahiers de géographie du Québec* 25, 4 (1981): 11–16. In the specific process of colonization, *urbanité* denotes the transplantation both of institutions intended to govern colonial development and, more generally, of everything deriving from the nature of the state itself. By extension, it means a way of being, acting, and feeling that is different from that associated with *territorialité*.

2. The concept of *territorialité* refers to the actual content of civilizations, to their own specific nature, and to their internal equilibrium. Claude Raffestin and others have defined it as the sum of relationships that arise within a given three-dimensional system (society–space–time) in order for civilizations to achieve the greatest possible autonomy within the limits of that system's resources. It reflects the multidimensional nature of a group's territorial reality, the way in which human societies satisfy their material and spiritual needs at a given time, in a given place, with a given population and a given set of tools. In this context, relationship is seen as a process of exchange and communication. Space itself is not important; what is important here is the use that people make and the knowledge they have of the reality that we call space.

Territorialities, not territoriality, thus arise from the sum of the variety of relationships that people have with their social and physical environment, whether they are seigneurs, habitants, merchants, solicitors, or craftspeople. This sum is not mathematical; it is bio-social. It refers to the totality of interconnecting relationships or, more precisely, to the dynamic totality of those relationships, since the components can vary in time. The territory in which these relationships are expressed is in fact the product of the interconnection among actors, starting from a primary reality—

space—which is perceived as a support, a resource, a reward, and a mediator in human exchange.

The concept of territoriality thus points the way to a true geography of difference, but invites us to consider it not solely with respect to concrete forms of landscape and culture, but in that richer light of "constituent fields" of language, power, economy, and territorial organization. These fields are interwoven, have their own durations, and together define areas in which a group's originality is expressed (see figure 1 of this article). For a more complete analysis, see C. Raffestin, *Pour une géographie du pouvoir* (Paris: Librairies techniques, 1980); and R.D. Sack, *Human Territoriality, Its Theory and History* (Cambridge: Cambridge University Press, 1986).

3. See S. Courville, "Contribution à l'étude de l'origine du rang au Québec: la politique spatiale des Cent-Associés," *Cahiers de géographie du Québec* 25, 65 (1981): 197–236.

4. J. Hamelin, ed., *Histoire du Québec* (Sainte-Hyacinthe: Edisem, Privat, 1976).

5. This theme has already been treated by several authors, including R.C. Harris, *The Seigneurial System in Early Canada* (Quebec City, Madison, Milwaukee, and London: Les Presses de l'Université Laval, University of Wisconsin Press, 1968); and M. Trudel, *Les débuts du régime seigneurial au Canada* (Montreal: Fides, 1974).

6. S. Courville, "Contribution à l'étude de l'origine du rang au Québec," 198–99.

7. See F. Ouellet, "La formation d'une société dans la vallée du Saint-Laurent: d'une société sans classes à une société de classes," *Canadian Historical Review* 62, 4 (1981): 407–50.

8. See G. Paquet and J.-P. Wallot, "Sur quelques discontinuités dans l'expérience socio-économique du Québec: une hypothèse," *Revue d'histoire de l'Amérique française* 35, 4 (March 1982): 483–521.

9. See L. Dechêne, *Habitants et marchands de Montréal au XVIIe siècle* (Montreal: Plon, 1974).

10. See S. Diamond, "Le Canada français au XVIIIe: une société préfabriquée," *Annales* 16, 2 (1961): 317–53.

11. This topic has been treated most thoroughly by C. Nish in *Les bourgeois-gentilshommes de la Nouvelle-France 1729–1748* (Montreal: Fides, 1968); and by R.C. Harris, *The Seigneurial System.*

12. L. Dechêne, *Habitants et marchands,* 482.

13. G. Paquet and J.-P. Wallot, "Sur quelques discontinuités," 497.

14. See J. Mathieau, François Béland, Michèle Jean, Jeannette Larouche, and Rénald Lessard, "Peuplement colonisateur au XVIIIe siècle dans le gouvernement du Québec," in *L'homme et la nature. Actes de la société canadienne d'étude du dix-huitième siècle,* ed. R.L. Emerson, W. Kinsley, and W. Moser (Montreal: Société canadienne d'étude du dix-huitième siècle, 1984), 2: 127–38.

15. See L. Lavallée, "La famille et les stratégies matrimoniales dans le gouvernement de Montréal au XVIIIe siècle," in *Société rurale dans la France de l'Ouest et au Québec (XVIIe-XXe siècles),* Actes des colloques de 1979 et 1980 (Montreal: Université de Montréal, École des Hautes Études en sciences sociales, 1980), 141–47; see also J. Mathieu, C. Cyr, G. Dinel, J. Pozzo, and J. St-Pierre, "Les alliances matrimoniales exogames dans le gouvernement du Québec 1700–1760," *Revue d'histoire de l'Amérique française* 35, 1 (1981): 3–32.

16. Land was valued as a means of providing farms and a future for sons and daughters, rather than as a commodity for the realization of profit. We lack meticulous studies of this particular subject, but on the general point see L. Dechêne, *Habitants et marchands,* 296.

17. J. Mathieu et al., "Les alliances matrimoniales," 26.

18. Ibid., 34–35.

19. J. Hamelin, ed., *Histoire du Québec*, 198.

20. See J. Mathieu, "Les relations ville-campagne: Québec et sa région au XVIIIe," in *Société rurale de la France de l'Ouest et au Québec (XVIIe-XXe siècles)*, Actes des colloques de 1979 et 1980, 190–206.

21. Ibid., 203.

22. See M. Bélanger, "Le Québec rural," in *Études sur la géographie du Canada*, 22nd Congrés international de géographie (Montreal: University of Toronto Press, 1972), 31–46.

23. See G. Bouchard, "Les systèmes de transmission des patrimoines et le cycle de la société rurale au Québec, du 17e au 20e siècle" (Paper given at the University of Ottawa, June 1982).

24. Research in progress on the development of villages in Quebec in the eighteenth and nineteenth centuries indicates that by 1760 only about twenty such establishments existed, most of them located on the edge of a seigneury.

25. The difference between the French peasant and the Canadian habitant is one of territoriality. The French peasant's territoriality is entirely saturated by information coming from his or her own territory, where he or she has always lived, whereas the habitant's territoriality has also absorbed new information originating from territory that she or he has settled. The attitude and behaviour of the two groups may appear to be similar and part of a continuity, but may in fact be seen to be different in that they have different underlying contexts and systems of relationships.

26. J. Mathieu et al., "Les alliances matrimoniales," 34–35.

27. This hypothesis was principally developed by R.L. Séguin in *La civilisation traditionnelle de l'habitant aux 17e et 18e siècles* (Montreal and Paris: Fides, 1967).

28. M. Bélanger, "Le Québec rural," 32ff.

29. See J. Mathieu, *Le commerce entre la Nouvelle-France et les Antilles au XVIIIe siècle* (Montreal: Fides, 1981).

30. See C. Morissonneau's theory on this subject in "Mobilité et identité québécoise," *Cahiers de géographie du Québec* 28 (1979): 29–38.

31. L. Dechêne, *Habitants et marchands*, 386–487.

32. M. Bélanger, "Le Québec rural," 33.

VERNACULAR ARCHITECTURE AND THE CULTURAL LANDSCAPE OF THE MARITIME PROVINCES: A RECONNAISSANCE*

PETER ENNALS AND DERYCK HOLDSWORTH

By contemporary Canadian standards, the Maritimes remains a highly traditional region, its cultural landscape little altered by the post-war building boom, its rich folk traditions less atrophied than those in other parts of the country. But while the settlement landscape of the Maritimes has an individuality all of its own, there are no simple landscape metaphors that apply to the entire region in the way that an ordered cadastre and the remains of a strong agrarian heritage mark the rural landscape of Quebec and Southern Ontario. Diversity is the mark of Maritime Canada. This might well be expected, given the separate colonial histories of the three provinces, and given an economic base variously oriented to fishing, lumbering, farming, mining and factories. Recent attention to migration and settlement histories and to the rapidly changing economic condition of eighteenth- and nineteenth-century society have begun to unravel some of the diverse strands of the region, but surprisingly little attention has been paid to domestic architecture.[1]

This paper attempts to describe the houses of the majority of the rural population of the Maritime region, particularly those houses built before 1900, and emphasizes the more widespread and more prosaic "folk" or "vernacular" architecture—the array of buildings constructed by and for common people.[2] Initially, the builders of these houses relied on ideas and designs passed from one generation to another informally. But increasingly in the nineteenth-century, builders were also reacting, in one way or another, to changing architectural fashions which penetrated the region through a variety of more formal published sources, and some

* *Acadiensis* 10, 2 (1981): 86–105. The financial assistance of Mount Allison University and Erindale College, University of Toronto, is gratefully acknowledged. The authors also wish to thank Graeme Wynn, John Mannion, John Warkentin, and Clarence LeBreton, who offered helpful comments on an earlier version of this paper.

of these ideas were adapted to older traditional designs. In either case, few of the houses can be precisely dated through extant records. Our concern here is not with precise chronological description, but rather with the broad patterns of life and livelihood revealed through field inspection of house form and house appearance.[3]

An examination of the surviving housing stock illuminates the regional variety of the Maritimes.[4] Housing reveals much of past patterns of living, of cultural antecedents, social aspirations, economic circumstances and adaptation to new environmental settings.[5] This is particularly true in Maritime Canada, where pre-industrial ways of building, often connecting individual ways of living to long-standing regional traditions, persisted well into the nineteenth century. Though affected by stylistic fads, the house remains a durable indicator of economy and society. Consequently, the house can illuminate questions of regional variety, highlight the intensity of external influences (such as aesthetic fashions and encroaching industrialism as a way of life), and cogently point up cultural orientations and persistences. Subsequent research will adopt more rigorous sampling procedures: the descriptions presented here are generalizations arising from field inspection and measurement of houses scattered widely throughout the region.[6] This field reconnaissance is integrated into a synthesis of the limited existing work on Maritime housing, setting the stage for a discussion of the social meaning of the house.[7]

Six distinct house types can be found in Maritime Canada. None is exclusive to a particular part of the region, but regional concentrations of some styles are evident (figure 1). Each of the house types is classified on the basis of floor plan, nature of construction, roof design, and exterior detail, and their temporal and regional distributions are noted.

The simplest house identified is a version of the hall and parlour house found throughout eastern North America.[8] Houses of this type are small, single-storey, rectangular structures with a gable roof and loft (Type I, figure 2). Originally, most comprised only two or three rooms: a large kitchen (hall) occupying up to two-thirds of the floor space, and one or two bedrooms at one end of the house. Entry doors—not necessarily located symmetrically in the façade or opposite each other—occurred on both long sides of the house; in some cases the door was on the end wall. Single chimneys within the walls of the house were set in locations ranging from the centre of the house to the end wall of the kitchen. Generally of timber frame construction, these houses were finished in the simplest of materials.[9] Shingles and clapboard were prominent in early examples; more recently tar paper and insulbrick have been used. In some cases, the wall cavity between the timbers and sheathing may have been packed with mud and clay, wood and mortar, sawdust, seaweed, straw, birch bark, or stone rubble.[10] Almost ubiquitous in the region, the hall and parlour house is most common in Acadian New Brunswick, in areas of Irish settlement (the Miramichi and parts of the New Brunswick interior), and in Cape Breton and the counties of Pictou and Antigonish, where it is associated with Scottish settlement. Type I houses are among the most difficult to date even roughly for they appear to have been built from the late eighteenth

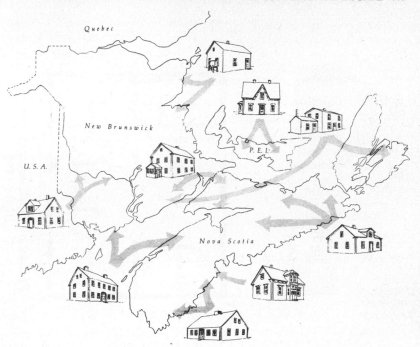

FIGURE 1   Regional Distribution of Vernacular Housing Types in the Maritimes

century until the present. Most surviving examples, however, appear to have been constructed during the second half of the nineteenth century.

The Cape Cod cottage forms a second common house type.[11] This is a more formal and rigidly symmetrical dwelling than the hall and parlour house; of one and a half storeys it usually has a central chimney and a large, steeply pitched gable roof whose eaves almost meet the tops of the first-floor windows (Type II, figure 3). The Cape Cod cottage is approximately square in plan. Two large front rooms flank the central front entrance; that to the south and/or west formed the "winter parlour," while the other, a more formal parlour, was unused in winter. In the rear of the house there were three or more small rooms; one was a kitchen, the others generally served as bedrooms. The front door opened onto a small vestibule from which a tight box staircase led to two or four upper-floor rooms. Most examples included a fully excavated cellar accessible from above by stairs or trap door. Later additions—typical features of all Maritime house types—frequently added one or more rooms to side or rear. Timber framed upon a field stone foundation, these buildings are generally shingle clad; clapboard is an infrequent alternative. Original windows are small; six over six, or six over nine light combinations are common. The simple decoration of main doorways included a four-light transom and a "Christian door" (a panelled door in which the proportions of the upper four

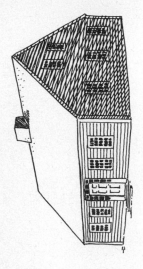

FIGURE 3   Type II, the Cape Cod House (1770 to 1850)

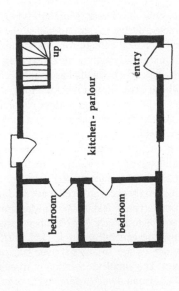

FIGURE 2   Type I, the Hall and Parlour House (1750? to 1950)

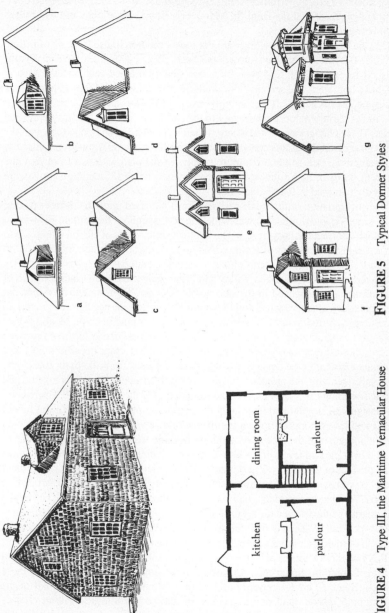

FIGURE 5   Typical Dormer Styles

FIGURE 4   Type III, the Maritime Vernacular House (1800 to 1900)

panels depict a cross).[12] Houses of this type are found along the Nova Scotia coast west and south of Halifax from St. Margaret's Bay to Yarmouth and most were built between 1770 and 1840.

One and a half storey dwellings are the most common house form of Maritime Canada. By the 1840s, they formed the basis of a regional vernacular. Distinguished from the Cape Cod type by a less steeply pitched roof and the greater height of both first- and second-floor walls, houses of this third type (figure 4) are also set apart from Type II by the replacement of the large central chimney stack by smaller chimneys located half way to the end walls, or later, just inside the end walls. These changes permitted a central hall or passage to be opened through the house, increased the usable space on the second floor, especially with the addition of a central dormer, and led to a more rigidly formal plan with two front parlours flanking the hall, and a dining room and kitchen behind. Sleeping rooms were generally confined to the second floor.

Stylistic variation of this basic regional form focussed upon the dormer (figure 5). A simple gable dormer (a) was widely used throughout the region. Five-sided "Scottish" dormers (b) occurred in the Scottish settlements of Pictou County, and in the fishing coves south of Halifax.[13] A large triangular dormer, integrated into the roof line and reminiscent of the classical pediment (c), was particularly characteristic of the Annapolis Valley and Prince Edward Island. Later the pitch of the dormer was steepened in the neo-gothic fashion (d) promoted by American designers such as Andrew Jackson Downing.[14] A simple vernacular interpretation, sometimes referred to as "Fisherman's gothic" (e), occurs in some localities as a triangular capped window; these often appeared in a sequence of three dormers. During the last quarter of the nineteenth century the dormer became a far more complex element in the design, and was thrust forward from the main line of the roof. In Lunenburg, the projecting dormer (g) took on an elaborately bracketed and tiered "wedding cake" appearance and extended over the front door.[15] Elsewhere, the design was simpler and invariably the projecting plane extended through both upper and lower floors (f) so that the main entrance was also thrust forward. As a final elaboration of the type, bay windows became widely used; they too came to extend over the two levels of the house, thus producing a style that appears to have been distinct to the region. But whatever these changes, the interior arrangement of space remained largely unaltered, except that the upper room or projecting dormers frequently served as a bathroom, a use absent from houses built before the last quarter of the nineteenth century.[16] Type III houses were built from the early 1800s to about 1900; it is difficult to precisely date appearance and duration of specific dormer styles, but generally the sequence is that shown in figure 5.

Full two-storey houses of Type IV closely resemble Type III houses in plan and design. Larger in dimensions and often more pretentious in decoration, these houses (figure 6) have a central hall and two chimneys, each serving half of the house, both upstairs and down. Symmetry and proportion are striking characteristics of these two-storey houses. Windows in the upper level are set directly above the openings below, giving all bedrooms one or more windows on the front or rear of the house. There are two typical roof forms: hipped, which like the stone houses of Chignecto reflect British models, and the more common simple gable. Entrances are formal, opening onto a spacious hall and staircase. Main doorways are frequently of neo-classical design with elliptical transoms and sidelights, although some are obscured by a small enclosed porch. By the 1830s and 40s, these houses were finished with wide pilasters on the corners, with matching cornice boards and return eaves.

A fifth common house type has its main entrance on the shorter gable side of the house and as a consequence, its plan is radically different from previous examples. Generally, the main door, near one corner of the house, opens onto a spacious vestibule and a staircase leading to the second floor. Rooms open off a hallway running the length of the house along one long wall (Type V, figure 7). The first room off the hall is the parlour; the second room most often serves as a dining room, although it too may have been a parlour in the past. A third room beside the dining room at the end of the hall passage was usually the kitchen. This small kitchen is often extended by an appended wing; originally a summer kitchen, this was

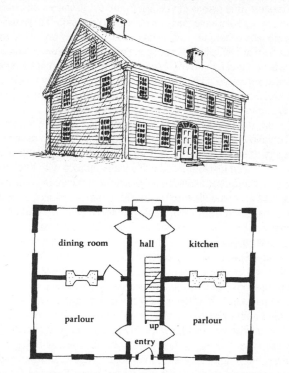

FIGURE 6   Type IV, the Full Two-Storey House, popularly referred to as the "Loyalist," or the Georgian Style (1770 to 1850)

frequently upgraded later and integrated into the main kitchen. The upper floor was given exclusively to bed chambers, usually matching the room arrangement of the ground floor with the addition of a small bedroom over the entrance hall. In some examples, the kitchen extension is also two storeys and provides additional sleeping space accessible by a staircase from the kitchen, and may also be connected to the upper landing of the main house.[17] The earliest of these houses, which probably made their appearance in the region during the late 1830s, were finished in clapboard and were similar to later Type III houses in their vernacular interpretation of neo-classical trim. Houses with the same plan were built during the second half of the nineteenth century, but these later examples were smaller in their dimensions and plain and unadorned, except perhaps for a gothic dormer added to the roof line, or a bay window placed on the front or side (figure 8). Whereas the earlier houses are particularly evident in an area between Sussex and Truro, the more common later form occurs widely in the towns and farms of the region.

A sixth house type is distinguished by its extremely low pitched, almost flat, roof and the simplicity of exterior trim. The house is a full two-storey rectangular dwelling of modest dimensions (Type VI, figure 9). It has a symmetrical façade, although a few exceptions have the front door set to one side. The exterior cladding is usually clapboard or tongue-and-groove siding. Corner boards, cornices, window and door trim are invariably very spare, giving the house a plain appearance. These houses have a greater variability of floor plan than most other regional types. Many examples resemble Type IV, with two rooms on either side of a central passage. In cases where the door is offset, the plan follows that of Type V; in others the kitchen occupies half of the house, a parlour and dining room the remainder. Frequently, a one-storey kitchen wing with a separate entrance built onto one end of the dwelling allowed one or more ground-floor rooms to be used as bedrooms. In all examples, there were three or four bedrooms and a bathroom upstairs. Chimneys were located inside the end gable walls; houses with kitchen wings had another prominent chimney, extended to the height of the main gable ridge to carry smoke and sparks aloft and clear of the dwelling. Unlike most earlier types, these houses were constructed from sawn lumber rather than heavy timber.

From our broad survey a number of observations can be made about the extent of persistence and innovation in Maritime folk architecture. The evidence suggests that settlers in the region were extremely slow to initiate or absorb new forms of building. The first house for most immigrants was a mere shack, with minimal space and little aesthetic pretension; the succeeding permanent dwelling, generally on the hall and parlour plan, reflected a continuity of traditional ways of creating shelter, modified both by materials at hand and current economic conditions. Only when a modest subsistence had been established might it be replaced by a more elaborate house type. Indeed, it took about two decades of living at Chignecto before the Yorkshire migrants of the 1770s began to build in stone and brick.[18] A similar time was required before the more prosperous Scots of Pictou began to replicate the cut stone houses of their homeland, and throughout the region one senses a strongly persistent conservative strain in many house types.

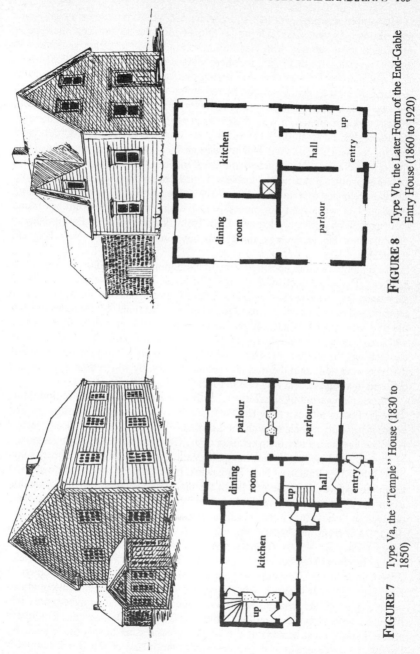

FIGURE 8   Type Vb, the Later Form of the End-Gable Entry House (1860 to 1920)

FIGURE 7   Type Va, the "Temple" House (1830 to 1850)

The simple, asymmetrical hall and parlour folk house represents a significant and surprisingly persistent building tradition within the region. That the type is associated most strongly with Acadian areas and those of Celtic settlement is hardly surprising, for these groups appear to have had a greater internal cohesiveness and consequently less cultural fusion than many of their neighbours from England, or New England. It might be too that groups like the Irish and the Scots were self-consciously trying to preserve in the Miramichi or, in rural Antigonish, Pictou, or Cape Breton, a way of life snatched from them in their homeland. Re-established on small plots of marginal land, they continued to use traditional farming techniques. The small hall and parlour house was but one example of this conservative ethos.[19] Nevertheless, the small folk house represented by Type I did undergo significant adaptation to New World conditions. Few emigrants from Highland Scotland or from Ireland would have been familiar with wooden building techniques of whatever form, and the adaptation of the plan to timber frame construction was probably learned from New England settlers. Post-expulsion Acadian building technology must also have come from this New England source.[20]

The majority of other housing forms in the region probably derived from New England. The antecedents of the Cape Cod house are clear. Settlers from Massachusetts who came to southwest Nova Scotia after 1760 knew the form; similar climatic and economic conditions required no modifications.[21] It is interesting that the type was apparently adopted by Lunenburgers and later arrivals from Britain whose own building traditions apparently were not as immediately adaptable to the new setting. The majority of extant examples were built before 1830 but houses of the type were built until the mid-nineteenth century, by which time the type had diffused in a very modest way to other locations in the region.[22]

Other American immigrants introduced different house types to the region. Most Type IV houses reflect a New England root and in the minds of Maritimers, this house is typically associated with the Loyalists.[23] In this case, the house reflects a New England vernacular interpretation of the Georgian form, and is characteristic of the farms and villages of the Annapolis Valley, as well as the Kennebecasis and Saint John River Valleys of New Brunswick. It is a house that was built with little alteration in form up to the middle of the nineteenth century, providing another example of a very persistent and perhaps conservative ideal that resisted the changes in fashion that were occurring elsewhere in North America during the period. American influences continued to dominate throughout the nineteenth century. For example, the strongly neo-classical look of Type V(a) is a clue not only to its chronology but also to its origins. During the two decades after 1820, American architectural fashion was dominated by the Greek Revival movement.[24] Emerging from this was not only the high-style house complete with columned portico, of which the southern plantation manor is a vivid and popular expression, but also a more vernacular "temple" style that is found widely across the northern states. Type V must be seen as the Maritime expression of this movement. By turning the gable end into the main façade, the image of the Greek temple is

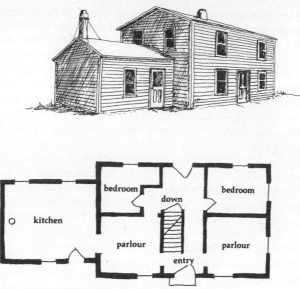

FIGURE 9   Type VI, the Hatch-Roofed House (1890 to 1920)

recalled. The image is incomplete without the portico but the pilasters and other minor elements of trim reinforce the style, albeit in a modest way. The later variant of this house, Type V(b), was probably also introduced from the United States, but it seems likely that it arose out of the need to provide cheap working-class housing particularly suited to narrow urban lots. This house with its end to the street satisfied these requirements and it was probably diffused across the continent during the latter part of the century.

Connections with the United States, particularly New England, were strong. People moved back and forth in considerable numbers and New England journals circulated in the Maritimes. The two regions also shared traditions of building in wood, and in the decorative arts, whereas the use of stone and brick in Britain, and in other parts of North America, demanded different skills. Even when European craft building traditions were implemented, by Scottish stone masons in Pictou and Yorkshire masons in Chignecto, they quickly gave way to the less costly and less specialized wooden technique. But the borrowing of New England technology and style was both selective and conservative. Maritime Canada did not become an extension of the New England cultural region, parroting every stylistic change as it came along. While the Cape Cod house was transferred to Nova Scotia, the Connecticut salt box house was not.[25] Nor was the more ebullient neo-classical or late nineteenth-century ornamentation as widely used. Maritime houses all display an economy of materials and a plainness of decoration that is in striking contrast to American houses and one notices the differences as soon as one crosses the border. Is this difference a reflection of poorer people, or were the craftspeople not available to produce the embellishments? It may be that the differences point to a more fundamental cultural distinction: Maritimers were less expansive, less given to displaying their wealth through their houses than their American cousins. Moreover, much of the American neo-classical architectural movement was tied through its images and ideals to the emerging American ideology, and for this reason Maritimers, and for that matter Ontarians, may have been reluctant to adopt the style. Thus, while the American temple style neo-classical house appears in the Maritimes as Type V, it is a pale reflection of its high-style antecedent, and in the hands of Maritime builders it was very much a vernacular relative that never became widespread.

It is true that a Maritime vernacular architecture does emerge out of the transplanted New England forms. The Cape Cod cottage and the temple style house had by mid-century begun to develop a distinctive appearance. The application of dormers in the centre of the façade roof line transformed the appearance of the earlier house and served also to open the landing or upstairs hall to more light and headroom. By the end of the century, a radically different roof line was applied to the early designs. The influence of neo-gothic stylings on dormers, windows and roof pitch, again via New England sources but again with conservative Maritime translations, contributed to this later nineteenth-century Maritime vernacular.

By the end of the century, a distinctly Atlantic house type emerged in the region. The origins of these Type VI houses are not readily evident. Their most distinctive feature is the unusual roof line,[26] often associated with Newfoundland. Yet houses of this type, which probably date to the period after 1890, are found widely in the Maritimes, from the industrial towns of Cape Breton, to much of early twentieth-century Halifax, and to the small outports of South Shore Nova Scotia and the Fundy Coast. One tantalizing hypothesis for the sudden appearance of this roof line links shipbuilding and housebuilding. The roof line bears a striking similarity to the form and construction technique of hatch covers and the cabin roof of nineteenth-century wooden sailing vessels. A low pitched roof would shed water but create little wind resistance or obstruction to the activities on deck. It is not unreasonable that ship carpenters might have adapted the form to housing, and the frequent occurrence of this house type in shipbuilding centres on the Fundy shore (Port Greville, Harvey Bank and St. Martins) supports the connection. The unorthodox, truncated roof line would not have been unusual to the nautical eye. Moreover, there is a striking correspondence in timing between the expansion of industrial Cape Breton and Halifax and the period when shipbuilding was declining and it may be that shipbuilders turned to housebuilding. Of course, by the end of the century house-building technique was changing. The advance of "balloon framing," which used a large number of lighter pieces of wood in place of a heavy rigid box frame, represented a major break from earlier building technique.[27] Not only did construction become less costly but the building trades became less specialized and much of the rough carpentry could be done by almost anyone, including the prospective home owner. In this sense, these buildings are truly modern—they used mass-produced materials and no longer demanded the services of a master craftsman. Such buildings provided an ideal solution to the need for cheap, mass housing in the cities of the region. But whatever the reason, and the two hypotheses need not be mutually exclusive, the modification of form and technique seems to have produced a house type distinctive to Atlantic Canada, and it is likely that its appearance in Newfoundland represents a diffusion from the mainland.[28]

The persistence of these forms and plans varied within sub-regions, and might well be understood within the context of the different pace of social and economic change occurring within the Maritimes, rather than that of the migration and diffusion histories of the various settler groups. To date we know little of domestic life within the region. Family size probably varied markedly but most couples could expect at least five or six children to reach adulthood. The addition of other relatives (aged parents, orphaned nieces and nephews), live-in domestics, labourers, or lodgers added to household size.[29] Seasonal labour migration to the woods or to the sea may have reduced numbers temporarily, but many houses were crowded by modern standards. Not surprisingly, many houses expanded over time to meet the needs of a growing household. Expansion took many forms: a larger house incorporating the earlier dwelling as an appendage, the addition of a new wing of one to two storeys, or the addition of a second storey on an existing structure. Kitchen wings were common to many early Maritime houses and frequently the space above the kitchen was set aside as the sleeping area for the domestics, or the seasonal workers. These sleeping areas were usually more crudely finished, and may not have been connected to the upper floor of the main dwelling. In this way the separation of the family and workers could be maintained.

In general, most Maritime houses reveal a tendency to develop a highly compartmentalized space. The four or more bedrooms within most houses allowed the separation of adults from children, boys from girls, family from domestics. Technological change facilitated some of these developments. With the advent of heating and cooking stoves during the 1860s, life no longer had to revolve around the fireplace. Stoves could be located almost anywhere and connected by stove pipes to the chimney. Many late nineteenth-century houses had a maze of pipes linking rooms, joining upper and lower floors and distributing heat about the house. Yet many Maritime households closed off certain rooms during the winter. Families slept communally on upstairs landings warmed by stove pipes, landings designed sufficiently large to accommodate the entire family. In this way the rhythms of the season punctuated life within the house, and while the house itself was becoming modern, the imperatives of climate forced the society into living patterns that were pre-modern.

Changes in social attitudes generally, and towards the use of space particularly, were manifest in other ways. The desire for greater personal privacy paralleled the assertion of a more individualistic world. This new emphasis was also expressed in the weakening of community bonds and by a retreat into the private world of the family. Henry Glassie argues that these changes led to the more rigidly formal houseplan. Rather than the door opening into the multipurposed hearth, it only revealed the impersonal entrance hall, which served as a social screen protecting the householder from intrusions into the series of private spaces within the house.[30] Moreover, the whole façade, with its symmetry and classically dictated rules of design, served to highlight the more scientific and less organic world that accompanied the Industrial Revolution.[31] Ironically, in many Maritime houses the formal front door was rarely used although it was incorporated into the house. Like the formal Victorian parlour that also became a commonplace during the latter part of the century, the front door served a largely ceremonial function being used only for visits from distinguished guests such as the clergyman. By custom, most familiar visitors entered by the back door into the kitchen complex. Such practices highlight again the persistence of older folk patterns of life within the dwelling and suggest that for many rural families there was an ambivalence toward many aspects of the modern house form. Thus while many Maritime houses may have offered outward displays of modernity in their fashionable neo-classical façades, life within them was attuned to traditional rhythms.

The transition of social ideology and its attendant house forms proceeded haltingly. There was no continuous line of evolution, and old ways persisted alongside the new order. Even within the industrial world of Douglastown, Glace Bay, and Stellarton, a distinctive type of housing developed in the hands of corporate planners. What is striking about these house forms is the extent to which the older folk tradition as represented by Type I is joined with the emerging regional vernacular as represented by Type III. The result is a semi-detached dwelling that was contemporary in external appearance but maintained the multi-purpose hall and parlour form inside. For the people recruited from rural Cape Breton or elsewhere to work in the collieries or mills, the living space provided by the company must have been familiar indeed. Perhaps only in the brick company houses of Marysville or the three-decker tenements of Saint John were there emphatically new industrial house types.[32]

Maritime Canada is no single cultural or economic region but a complex layering of landscapes, each reflecting the specific origins of its inhabitants, economic orientations, and chronology. It is a region that developed from geographically separate remnants of an earlier Acadian population, colonies of Swiss and German "foreign Protestants," New Englanders, and Yorkshiremen, displaced Highland Scots, Loyalists from as far away as the Carolinas, and early nineteenth-century British and Irish emigrants. These groups tended to create a cellular structure within the region and sub-regional distinctions could for a time be established and reinforced. Thus the Yorkshire settlers could transfer to Chignecto, in the first generations at least, the brick house types they had known in the Vale of York, and Scots could maintain the Gaelic language through several generations after migration. But all experienced cultural adaptations and change. Some groups such as the Lunenburgers turned to harvesting the sea after a heritage on the land in Europe and initially in Nova Scotia. Generally, connections to and participation in the Maritime economy of the North Atlantic as seamen and traders, and the almost continuous to-ing and fro-ing by Maritimers with the "Boston States" after 1850, had a modifying effect on all transplanted cultures.

On the basis of housing evidence alone, it is hardly possible or proper to draw firm cultural boundaries within the region. It may be that a more microscopic analysis of areas such as Pictou, the Annapolis Valley, or Prince Edward Island, or of specific elements such as structural technique, will provide a sharper delineation of both sub-types and sub-regions. Nevertheless, given the complex geographic intermixing of economies in the nineteenth century, it seems likely that building forms and other cultural features may be more strongly reflective of particular economic orientations than they are of local and ethnic origins. The result is that many landscapes contain a mix of housing styles. It is not uncommon to find a small hall and parlour cottage alongside the more pretentious high-style Queen Anne house of a local merchant or sea captain. The latter, because of his greater wealth, his travels to cities outside the region, and his willingness to act as an arbiter of taste, became the agent for bringing new styles and new ideas to many a community. Diffusion of American styles also occurred by means of a variety of published sources, particularly the agricultural journals published in Albany, New York.[33] Through these publications, the ideas and designs of Andrew Jackson Downing and others gained wide expression in eastern North America. Pattern books aided local carpenters to interpret the designs, and by the 1870s if not earlier, a measure of standardization was becoming apparent across the North American continent. This standardizing trend became the enemy of the folk and regional vernacular traditions, and the Maritimes did not escape. For this reason, we have deliberately avoided incorporating many of the later nineteenth-century styles into our classification, but recognition of their presence is essential. Indeed, the Victorian exuberance of many streetscapes in Amherst or Moncton or New Glasgow is testimony to the wealth generated in the first flowering of Maritime industrialization. Much more needs to be learned about the extent to which Halifax, Saint John, and other urban centres served as gateways for innovation and diffusion of architectural ideas for a wider hinterland.

On top of the eighteenth- and nineteenth-century landscape are the accretions of the twentieth century, all of which enhance the sense of complexity. The modern observer is likely to be struck by two contrasting images. On the one hand, there are lines of settlement that seem isolated from any strong economic base and that lead one to wonder how people survive. Testament to past population expansion and to once vigorous local economies, they are now poignant reminders of the tenacity and sense of place that many Maritimers have. That many of these older houses display a fresh coat of paint and are carefully maintained reinforces the impression. On the other hand, there are landscapes of squalid mobile homes, abandoned cars, and venerable houses transformed beyond recognition by modern sash, vinyl siding, and artificial stone. Only when one recognizes that the new vernacular that asserts itself around every corner is part of the ongoing, long-continued process of adaptation and change does one gain perspective, if grudgingly, on the modern scene.

Notes

1. Several people have written on the exceptional houses of the region, the houses of the wealthy and powerful, those who could afford grand designs as a statement of their social eminence and taste. See, for example, Arthur W. Wallace, *An Album of Drawings on Early Buildings in Nova Scotia* (Halifax, 1976); Alan Gowans, *Building Canada: An Architectural History of Canadian Life* (Toronto, 1966); Thomas Ritchie, *Canada Builds, 1876–1976* (Toronto, 1967); W.W. Alward, "Architecture in New Brunswick," in *The Arts in New Brunswick*, ed. R.A. Tweedie, F. Cogswell, and W.S. MacNutt (Fredericton, 1967); Stuart Smith, "Architecture in New Brunswick," *Canadian Collector*, 10, 3 (1975): 37–42.

2. For good examples of the study of folk architecture, see R.W. Brunskill, *Illustrated Handbook of Vernacular Architecture* (London, 1971); Henry Glassie, *Pattern in the Material Folk Culture of the Eastern United States* (Philadelphia, 1968); Peter Ennals, "Nineteenth Century Barns in Southern Ontario," *Canadian Geographer* 16 (1972): 257–70; Michael Lessard and Gilles Vilandre, *La maison traditionelle au Québec* (Montreal, 1974).

3. The assigning of precise dates to particular houses or house types presents problems. Rarely was the building of a house recorded except incidentally and there are no systematic records one can use for this purpose on a broad regional scale. Even the assignment of very rough time periods does not prevent the later appearance of a specific type. Unlike "high-style" houses of the nineteenth century, whose appearance and fashionable appeal tended to be chronologically discrete, folk or vernacular housing forms were more enduring, and in some instances the conservative yearnings of individuals or groups such as the Loyalists, led to the construction of house types a generation or more after the form had been superseded elsewhere. Recognizing these problems we have assigned very broad dating parameters to suggest a general chronological sequence.

4. The use of surviving housing stock also presents problems. Large numbers of earlier structures have long since disappeared—the victims of fire, neglect or replacement—and many others have been significantly altered. It is very difficult to know how representative is the array of surviving buildings. Nevertheless, in the absence of alternative sources for studying building form, the surviving buildings represent the best and only record for examination, albeit one that must be judged with appropriate prudence.

5. Within geography, this perspective is exemplified by Fred Kniffen, "Folk Housing: Key to Diffusion," *Annals, Association of American Geographers* 53 (1963): 549–77; Pierce Lewis, "Common Houses, Cultural Spoor," *Landscape* 19 (1975): 1–22; David B. Mills, "The Development of Folk Architecture in Trinity Bay, Newfoundland," in *The Peopling of Newfoundland*, ed. J.J. Mannion (St. John's, 1977), 77–101; John Lehr, *Ukrainian Vernacular Architecture in Alberta* (Edmonton, 1976); Deryck Holdsworth, "House and Home in Vancouver: Images of West Coast Urbanism, 1886–1929," in *The Canadian City: Essays in Urban History*, ed. G.A. Stelter and A.F.J. Artibise (Toronto, 1977), 186–211. Also see Henry Glassie, *Folk Housing in Middle Virginia* (Knoxville, 1975).

6. Extensive traverses were carried out by the authors over a two-year period. In addition to the superficial inspection of hundreds of houses encountered along the way, detailed interior and exterior measurements were taken of some forty houses.

7. The visual record and most detailed description of individual houses in Nova Scotia are provided in the volumes published by the Heritage Trust of Nova Scotia:

Founded Upon a Rock (Halifax, 1971); *Seasoned Timbers*, vol. 1 (Halifax, 1972); and *South Shore: Seasoned Timbers*, vol. 2 (Halifax, 1974). Also see Sharon Reilly, *Selected Buildings in Yarmouth, Nova Scotia* (Ottawa, 1977); Ronald McDonald, *Report on Selected Buildings in Mahone Bay, Nova Scotia* (Ottawa, 1977); and Gordon B. Kinsman, *Colchester County Century Farms* (Truro, 1979). For Prince Edward Island, see Irene L. Rogers, "An Approach to Island Architecture," in *Exploring Island History*, ed. Harry Baglole (Belfast, P.E.I., 1977); and Irene L. Rogers, "Island Homes," *The Island Magazine* no. 1 (1976). For New Brunswick, see Smith, "Architecture in New Brunswick," in J.R. Bourque, *Social and Architectural Aspects of Acadians in New Brunswick* (Fredericton, 1971).

8. See Lewis, "Common Houses," Glassie, *Pattern in the Material Folk Culture*, and Glassie, *Folk Housing*. The use of the term "hall and parlour" in reference to early Maritime houses may gloss over subtle and important cultural distinctions. European folk housing scholars have distinguished several regional variants of the simple one- and two-room house which is found throughout Britain and France. We have not yet attempted to differentiate between houses built by Maritime Scots, Irish, Acadian, or others. Nevertheless, in a personal communication, Professor John Mannion argues that the Irish on the Miramichi only adopted our Type I house form during the second half of the nineteenth century, having earlier built a cruder "cabin"—a more self-consciously Irish version of the traditional peasant cottage. Also see John J. Mannion, *Irish Settlements in Eastern Canada: A Study in Cultural Transfer and Adaptation* (Toronto, 1974), chap. 7.

9. In the past, log building techniques were used in some parts of the region, and many of the log buildings probably were of this type. A striking feature of the landscape sketches made by John Woolford are the number of simple hall and parlour houses, crudely built, often with logs and interior end chimney. See his "Sketches in Nova Scotia in 1817," Nova Scotia Museum, and the "Woolford Sketches" in the William Inglis Morse Collection, Dalhousie University Library. For a detailed study of one Acadian example, see Ronald Poirier and Bernard LeBlanc, *Maison Célestin Bourque* (Moncton, 1976). For the Irish houses of the Miramichi, see Mannion, *Irish Settlements*, 138–64. Good examples of this house type which are accessible to the public are the Mazerolle House, a log building at the Village Historique Acadienne, and the Lint House at King's Landing Historical Settlement.

10. The practice of filling the wall cavity with various insulating materials was probably common in all early Maritime houses. Even now, many rural people continue to pack the outside foundation wall with spruce boughs, sawdust or seaweed as a way of creating a dead air space to help prevent heat loss in winter.

11. Ernest Allen Connolly, "The Cape Cod House: An Introductory Study," *Journal of the Society of Architectural Historians* 19 (1960): 47–56; Doris Doane, *A Book of Cape Cod Houses* (New York, 1970).

12. Robert Cunningham and John B. Prince, *Tamped Clay and Salt Marsh Hay* (Fredericton, 1976), 85; Eric Sloane, *A Reverence for Wood* (New York, 1965).

13. The five-sided dormer is a striking element of Scottish vernacular housing. It has been suggested that the masons working on the Shubenacadie Canal in 1832 were responsible for introducing this dormer, but it may easily have been a solution used by other Nova Scotia Scots for whom it may have been the way to add a dormer. See *Founded Upon a Rock*, 76.

14. Andrew Jackson Downing, *Cottage Residences* (New York, 1842).

15. This type of dormer is so strongly evident in Lunenberg that it is popularly termed the "Lunenberg dormer." It is also found in many fishing settlements further around the coast, particularly Clark's Harbour, Yarmouth and Digby, suggesting that there are diffusion links to be explored within the fishing economy.

16. The technology for water closets had existed in the eighteenth century but they only began to appear in the houses of the Canadian elite after the middle of the nineteenth century. After 1875, patented water closet design improved the technology, and they became more widely accepted. Anthony Adamson and Marion MacRae, *The Ancestral Roof* (Toronto, 1963), 249.

17. In other cases, this auxiliary attic sleeping space was kept quite separate from the family's bedrooms, indicating perhaps a conscious desire to maintain a social distance between family and hired help.

18. Cunningham and Prince, *Tamped Clay*, 50–52.

19. For an analysis of Scottish houses, see I.F. Grant, *Highland Folkways* (London, 1961), 141–97. Some sense of the continuity of old ways of living, including the presence of some animals in the house, emerges from a reading of C.H. Farnham, "Cape Breton Folk" (1886), reprinted in *Acadiensis* 9 (Spring 1979): 90–104. For rural Ireland, see E. Estyn Evans, *Irish Folk Ways* (London, 1959); and Caoimhin O. Danachair, *Ireland's Vernacular Architecture* (Cork, 1975).

20. Cunningham and Prince offer a conjectural pre-clearance Acadian house form for the Tantramar area, but both the Maison Célestin Bourque and the Vielle Maison Meteghan suggest clear New England origins. Cunningham and Prince, *Tamped Clay*, 12–14; Poirier and LeBlanc, *Maison Célestin*. See also *La maison Hélène et Roma Bourgeois* (Moncton, 1977); C. Chevrier, *Les défricheurs d'eau* (Ottawa, 1978); Jacques Boucher, *Les éléments du village historique Acadien* (Bathurst, 1978). For Nova Scotian Acadian examples, see *Seasoned Timbers*, 1:130–31. The tradition of owner-built houses seems very strong among Acadians. Whether it is a function of culture or of poverty is uncertain. For evidence of the persistence of Type I houses, one need only look at large sections of Dieppe, a suburb of Moncton.

21. *South Shore: Seasoned Timbers*, vol. 2, passim.

22. Examples can be found in Colchester County. See Kinsman, *Colchester County Century Farms*.

23. Smith, "Architecture in New Brunswick." The linking of Loyalists and this house type is evident in the interpretation of buildings at King's Landing, the outdoor museum created by the New Brunswick government near Prince William, N.B. It is important to recognize that a few examples of this type owe their origin to British immigrants, such as the Yorkshire settlers of Chignecto and the timber merchants in Pictou and in the Miramichi.

24. For a discussion of Greek Revival architecture, see Marcus Whiffen, *American Architecture since 1780, A Guide to the Styles* (Cambridge, MA, 1969); Henry L. Williams and Ottalie K. Williams, *A Guide to Old American Houses 1700–1900* (New York, 1962), chap. 3.

25. Woolford's 1817 volume records the existence of five salt box houses. An early example (1736) built at Annapolis Royal still stands. If salt boxes are an organic stage of a house reflecting additions to an earlier smaller structure, then it is unlikely that the form would be built as an initial house by new immigrants. By the time additions were required, summer kitchens and other lightly constructed sheds were added in train-like fashion. In parts of Newfoundland where several generations occupied a house site, salt box silhouettes typify one stage of the organic evolution. See David Mills, "The Development of Folk Architecture," 88.

26. The roof is extremely simple to construct. The rafters are tied to a ridge pole and to a heavier (2" x 6" or 2" x 8") joist, which also supports the ridge pole. The whole unit then forms a shallow truss which rests on the top plate of the walls. Because it rarely spanned a width of more than about five metres the structure was both strong and cheaply constructed.

27. For a discussion of balloon framing, see John I. Rempel, *Building in Wood* (Toronto, 1967), 114–17; John A. Kouwenhoven, *The Arts in Modern American Civilization* (New York, 1967), 49–53, 62–67.

28. David Mills, "The Development of Folk Architecture"; Michael Staveley, "Population Dynamics in Newfoundland: The Regional Patterns," in *The Peopling of Newfoundland* , ed. Mannion, 69. Newfoundlanders were apparently involved in the construction of company housing in Sydney and built houses for themselves nearby; see C.W. Vernon, *Cape Breton Canada at the Beginning of the Twentieth Century* (Toronto, 1903), 277.

29. A cursory analysis of the manuscript censuses of the region provides ample evidence of the size and composition of Maritime households after 1851. A sampling of completed families from the 1851 Census of Kings County, N.B. reveals that the average size of family was 8.2 while the average household consisted of 8.7 persons. There is evidence to suggest that similar figures were typical for an earlier period. Debra A. McNabb, "The Historical Demography of Horton Township—The First Sixty Years" (Historical Atlas of Canada Project, Toronto, June 1980, unpublished research report).

30. Henry Glassie, "Folk Architecture and the Social Revolution" (Address to a symposium on folk housing held at the University of Maine, Orono, 23 February 1978). Also see Glassie, *Folk Housing in Middle Virginia*, 188–89.

31. David P. Handlin, "The Detached House in the Age of the Object and Beyond," in *Environmental Design-Resources and Practice*, ed. J.W. Mitchell (Los Angeles, 1972), 721–28.

32. The architecture and layout of Marysville, New Brunswick, is similar to the New England milltowns of Lowell or Lawrencetown, Massachusetts; equally, it might be argued, the morphology of Marysville is reminiscent of English milltowns such as Saltaire, Yorkshire. Clearly there is considerable scope for work on the region's industrial housing landscapes as well as those of earlier and rural ways. Indeed, there may well be considerable continuity of rural building types and floor plans in early industrial housing. See, for example, the continuity of rural building types and floor plans for industrial housing which has been documented by J.B. Lowe, *Welsh Industrial Workers Housing, 1775–1875* (Cardiff, 1977).

33. Journals such as *The Agriculturalist* and *The Cultivator* carried a regular feature on "rural architecture." While it is difficult to know how widely these journals circulated among the rural population, it is also true that these features were frequently "lifted" for presentation in local and more widely read newspapers.

THE ADEQUACY OF RURAL ROADS IN THE ERA BEFORE RAILWAYS: AN ILLUSTRATION FROM UPPER CANADA*

THOMAS F. MCILWRAITH

Transportation history is a story of the continuing effort to facilitate access and movement and to reduce the proportion of the final cost of a good consumed in its transport. This is the theme of Glazebrook's *History of Transportation in Canada*,[1] and it is epitomized in the title of George Rogers Taylor's outstanding study, *The Transportation Revolution*, covering the years of great change from 1815 to 1860.[2] Taylor's monograph opens with a discussion of American roads in the early nineteenth century and notes the slowness, the discomfort, and the high price of overland travel, conditions that were true on both public roads and privately operated turnpikes. Similarly disparaging assessments were common among those contemporaries who wrote of travel in early nineteenth-century Upper Canada; travellers' accounts, directories, and pamphlets all decried the prevailing conditions.[3] One observer tells of an occasion when it took three days to haul a wagonload of goods 50 miles, and of another when stumps and mud limited his progress to eight miles in a day.[4] For the author of a book for the information of prospective emigrants in the 1820s, the noteworthy point about spring was that the roads "became so bad, that it is hardly possible to go out of doors."[5] This was an extreme evaluation, but its tone matched that of most commentators. It is hardly surprising that local histories, popular accounts of pioneering, and scholarly works have taken up the theme.[6] Indeed, bad roads have become symbols of the hardships of pioneer life, their wretchedness a lowly datum against which the notable conquests of the transportation revolution appear all the more impressive.

* *The Canadian Geographer/Le Géographe canadien* 14, 4 (1970): 344–60. The author extends thanks to Professor R.C. Harris, for his comments on an earlier draft of this paper. The maps were drawn in the Cartographic Office of the University of Toronto under the direction of Geoffrey Matthews. Erindale Campus, University of Toronto, gave financial assistance for the production of the maps.

Yet this is only one side of the story. Criticisms of early nineteenth-century Canadian roads come from a tiny fraction of those who used them, and they were road users with very special interests. One reads of bad roads from the accounts of English travellers, from the pens of literate, progressive town dwellers, and from the authors of road-making treatises that indicated just how good roads could be.[7] Almost never has the viewpoint of farmers been considered, although they far outnumbered travellers and professional traders as users of roads.[8] Furthermore, the comments of travellers and traders were usually confined to roads connecting larger towns. Having rated these "main" roads so poorly, they could easily imagine the byways to be many times worse, and deliberately avoid them. But the speed, comfort, and continuous reliability valued by these travellers were not necessarily critical to the agricultural population. Roads and their users each fell into more than one category, and no test of adequacy is satisfactory if it presumes that the observations of a few persons using "main" roads summarized the views of the great majority who used, in addition, the thousands of miles of unnamed local roads.[9]

This paper argues that published contemporary observations have created a misleading picture of early roads in eastern North America.[10] By drawing evidence from municipal and provincial committee reports, statutes, land and survey records, assessment rolls and directories, and offering a case study of roads and rural development in a few townships in Upper Canada (Ontario) from 1790 to the 1850s, this essay provides a more balanced account of the assets and drawbacks of roads, as indicated by the behaviour of individuals in the agricultural population. Answers are sought for two basic questions. First, were roads necessary to the selecting and taking up of land in Upper Canada and, if so, were those that were built sufficient to meet the demands put upon them for this process? The second question relates to the subsequent development of land. Again, were roads necessary and, if this was the case, what degree of improvement was required? The York County area, as the study region may be called, is barely 1 000 square miles in extent (see figure 1), but the conclusions should be valid over the large portion of the northern United States and southern Canada settled before the construction of railroads.[11]

Roads and Land Occupance

Throughout Upper Canada, road allowances were part of the original land survey, a provision which today hampers efforts to reconstruct the development of the road system. The word "road" was frequently used as a casual substitute for "road allowance," although the latter might have been nothing more than a line of surveyors' stakes through the forests. When the publishers of maps failed to differentiate between the terms, the results could be ludicrous. For instance, an 1860 map shows the Holland River swamp (Holland Marsh today) laced with

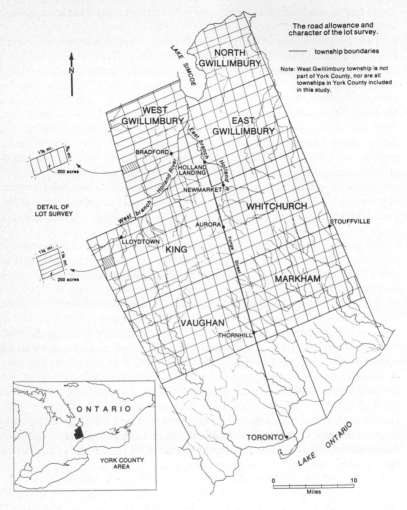

FIGURE 1   The York County Area

roads at a time when it is known that no development past the survey had been attempted there.[12] In many reports a distinction is made between roads "open" and "not open," which is a slight improvement in terminology, but at least one land official wrote in his field book "road not open but passable."[13] Obviously, to the man on horseback most roads were "open" as soon as the chain gangs had staked them out. On the other hand, the visiting gentleman from England in the 1840s may have wondered if there were any open roads in Canada. Stagecoach operators found a few open roads, and farmers many more; the number fluctuated with the seasons.

Here an "open road" is defined as a right-of-way along which trees have been felled leaving stumps short enough to be cleared by the axle of a wagon, to a width sufficient for a team to draw the wagon through. On such a road a sleigh could also pass. This definition is deliberately simple. It assumes that a road once open did not cease to exist. This conforms with the evidence, except in the case of routes opened for convenience across farm lots. As settlers moved in, they frequently forced the closure of such segments, diverting traffic onto the proper right-of-way. The definition is not qualified by consideration of seasonal variations in road quality. Nor is there any attempt to specify stages of improvement, although it took no more than the removal of logs and rotting of stumps to improve openness. Such refinement would require more data than are available, but it is possible to determine with fair certainty the spread of "open roads" as defined above. The definition specifies a state of improvement of road allowances that was believed, rightly or wrongly, to have been important for the process of settlement. In essence, it reiterates the roadwork instructions given to each person acquiring land, and to be fulfilled before that person could receive title.[14] The fact that loopholes permitted thousands of acres to be patented before this roadwork was done is not pertinent to the questions at hand, except to warn that land patent records cannot be used to determine whether a road was opened.[15]

Few roads in Upper Canada were opened prior to settlement. One of the exceptions was Yonge Street, cut through from York (later Toronto) to Holland Landing in 1795. From this point, Lake Simcoe could be reached by way of the Holland River (see figure 1). Yonge Street was no more than a fairly straight swath of chopped trees, left to decay on the right-of-way where they fell. Nonetheless, it replaced the southern part of the river and portage route that had linked Lake Ontario and Georgian Bay for well over a century, and was considered by Governor Simcoe to be of strategic significance to the new province. He anticipated that it would draw settlers inland from Lake Ontario, and visualized a ribbon of continuous occupancy along either side of the road. Simply by living on their roadside lots, settlers would keep the road in usable condition, and would make it the axis from which further settlement would spread east and west.[16]

A report upon the condition of Yonge Street lots in 1801 shows a situation far different from Simcoe's expectations (see table 1).[17] Although all lots along the road had fallen into private hands, and in spite of special stipulations intended to ensure the rapid development of the properties, only 21 of the lots, or 15 percent, measured up to the minimum standards. These conditions, set down in 1794 and reaffirmed in 1798, called for the removal of brush and logs on half of the allowance in front of each lot, the clearing and fencing of at least five acres of land, and the erection of a house, all within one year of assuming these obligations.[18] It is questionable whether the 21 satisfactory lots had been improved within the given time, but even waiving that proviso, the record of attainment is poor. Assuming that there were token improvements on those properties represented as "partly

TABLE 1   *Summary of Report of 140 Lots, of 200 Acres Each, along Yonge Street from Thornhill to Holland Landing, 1801*

| | Road duty | | | |
Land duty	Done	Partly done	Not done	Total
Done	21	42	16	79
Partly done	5	5	7	17
Not done	2	1	41	44
Total	28	48	64	140

SOURCE: See note 17.

done," nearly one-third of the lots still remained untouched. Twenty-one of these were in a contiguous block south of Aurora. According to John Stegmann, the compiler of the report, the road was overgrown and impassable at most times of the year, especially in front of undeveloped lots. Yonge Street was a far cry from the "great trunk road" described by some historians.[19]

Although several families had been drawn to land along Yonge Street, Stegmann's inspection suggests that an opened road was not enough to ensure settlement. This impression is confirmed by the adjacent township of Markham, densely settled and without prior roads. It is the most uniformly and extensively fertile township in the study area, and its land capability was undoubtedly attractive. Most of the settlers who came before about 1815 were experienced in farm-making in western New York state or in the German areas of Pennsylvania, and they brought with them expertise in the identification of good land. Soil with recognized productive capabilities and water for drinking and generating power were judged to be indispensable. Thus, the well-watered clay or till plains of Markham, southeastern Vaughan, and East Gwillimbury townships were occupied first, while the tumbled and poorly watered interlobate moraine and the Holland River marsh stood vacant (see figure 2).[20] Revealingly, a group of French Huguenots, inexperienced in North American pioneering, chose lots on Yonge Street in the moraine, and abandoned them within three years.[21] Apparently, they considered accessibility a greater asset than productive capability. These lots were not reoccupied until the 1830s, long after lands with no special accessibility advantages were supporting prosperous farms.

It is debatable whether non-resident land speculation was a factor in the selection of lots to be occupied and cultivated. The normal North American settlement experience was to choose the land nearest to areas already occupied, consistent with other criteria of selection. But this pattern could become deranged by speculation, forcing bona fide settlers to more distant lands beyond the holdings of the absentee owners. Settlement was displaced to remote areas because the top priority of the speculator was land likely to grow rapidly in value and permit a quick return

trend in spread of settling

N

SWAMP

SWAMP

MARSH

SHARON

NEWMARKET

MORAINE

HOLLAND

Yonge

INTERLOBATE

MARKHAM VILLAGE

Street

UNIONVILLE Rouge R.

Humber

THORNHILL GERMAN MILLS

River

EDGELEY

0   10
Miles

Physiography after L. J. Chapman and D. F. Putnam,
physiography of Southern Ontario (Toronto, 1951).

FIGURE 2   Settlements before 1805

SOURCES: See note 20.

by rapid resale—that is, lands closest to, or most accessible to, existing settlement. Quite possibly a speculator not interested in farming would place a roadside location at the top of his list of desirable features, just as the Yonge Street Huguenots did, whereas a settler would choose a roadside lot only if it looked good for farming. It is arguable that Yonge Street may have been of real importance in the selection of farm lots, but that its role became obscured because of the land held inactive by non-residents.

The counter-argument, that speculation had little effect on the selection of lots by settlers, appears to be the stronger one. For one thing, church and state were the principal speculators in the York County area. They controlled two-sevenths of the land, but held lots in a uniformly dispersed pattern dictated by the survey rather than by the agricultural potential of the land.[22] Individuals may have speculated in Yonge Street lots when they were first made available, but within three years many were occupied and the inclination to select land according to its agricultural value was clear. Immigration to Markham township was sufficiently heavy that before 1805, 60 percent of the clergy reserves were under private lease.[23] Land speculation was so general a characteristic of early Ontario that the pattern of alienation reflected little more than the sequence of surveys and placing of land on the market. Yonge Street lots were the first made available in the study area and they were the first to go. But it is occupancy, and not alienation, that is being considered here. No directories are available before 1837, so a rigorous test beyond Yonge Street is not possible, but all indications (such as the location of mills) imply that people settled on good farm lands. This was true of the 8 percent of lots touching Yonge Street and of the 92 percent that were not. Since occupancy reflected the primary criteria of farmers, and the interests of non-resident speculators only as regards distance from Lake Ontario, it is very probable that speculation interfered little with the selection of land by settlers.

Yonge Street was not particularly important in providing access to desirable lots. Certainly, the settlers that Stegmann found on the good lots along Yonge Street probably used it as a colonization road. But many others made their way to their lots elsewhere without ever setting foot on it. Those at Edgeley ascended the Humber River and Black Creek, and the Markham village area was reached via the Rouge River (see figure 2). It is believed that the Quakers settling in East Gwillimbury came by way of a sister settlement to the east (at Uxbridge) and an old trail along the moraine. Within the study area, there was no limit to the distance settlers would go without a road. Even in parts of the York County area that were more than 40 miles from Lake Ontario and 15 from Yonge Street, land quality held sway over access. The importance placed upon colonization roads built into the Muskoka and Haliburton regions later in the century indicates that disregard for roads could not apply inland indefinitely, but settlers certainly were prepared to go more than 15 miles without roads in quest of desirable land.

Yonge Street was the only road in the York County area opened prior to settlement, yet roads were developed through the district as land was taken up. Whether they were opened in the process of getting to the lots selected, or opened immediately thereafter to get back out to market, is a moot point. The relationship between roads and occupancy cannot be set down in black and white terms, but for settlers intent on creating farms in the bush the priorities were fairly consistent. An opened road was not necessary to the selection of an inland lot. Nor was its absence a barrier to reaching that land. Invariably, however, roads were opened as land was occupied.

Roads and Land Development

Figure 3 shows the roads believed to have been open in 1800, 1813, 1827, 1841, and 1851.[24] Because there may be no information about a specific road for years after its opening, these are minimum estimates of the road system for each date.[25] In figures 4 and 5, two indicators of land development are presented for a single township, superimposed over the road system as it existed in the mid-1830s. The

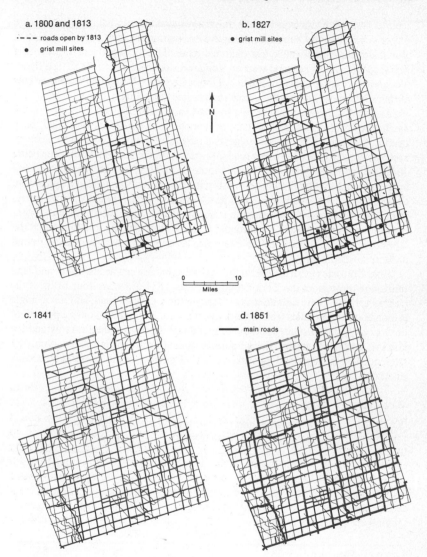

a. 1800 and 1813
- - - - roads open by 1813
• grist mill sites

b. 1827
• grist mill sites

N

0   10
Miles

c. 1841

d. 1851
—— main roads

FIGURE 3   Open Roads in the York County Area, Shown by Heavy Lines

SOURCES: See note 24.

former is the cruder of the two, giving only the number of householders per lot of 200 acres, in 1837.[26] There is no indication of where in the lot these persons lived or, in particular, upon which road allowance their houses faced. But it is clear that their lots tended to touch open roads. It is known that the original lots along Yonge Street were generally subdivided lengthwise, permitting later occupants also to abut that route. Significantly, less than one-tenth of the surveyed length of the first line road allowances east and west of Yonge was opened prior to 1850 (see figure 3(c) and (d)). People in the second tier of lots were served instead by short segments of many later east–west roads, visible in the same illustrations. The 1827 road map (figure 3(b)) shows that farther east in Markham Township the lines were alternately opened and closed. This pattern demonstrates the ability of a road, once opened, to retain traffic. It also suggests a rational response of settlers to a survey system which provided too many road allowances for the size of holding then being developed and the resources at hand. Figure 5, which shows acreage cleared and open roads in East Gwillimbury township in 1834, reveals that cleared lands were adjacent to known roads and that less desirable areas (swamps, principally) remained untouched.[27] Topographic maps show that farm wood lots today generally lie midway between open roads. It is not unreasonable to assume that the cleared areas of uniformly desirable lots also lay closest to open roads in the period of farm development.

Table 2 presents evidence about the relationship between accessibility and land utilization throughout the York County area for 1834.[28] Nearly four-fifths of the cleared acreage in the sample was on lots abutting an open road, and not a single lot more than three miles from a road was touched. It is true that only 2 percent of the lots lay at this distance, and the real contrast is between the first row and the last four grouped together. The 42 percent of the lots off roads contained only 21 percent of the cleared land, and nearly half of the lots in this group were totally uncleared.[29]

TABLE 2   *Land Clearance and Distance to Nearest Open Road, 5 Percent Sample of 200-Acre Lots, York County Area, 1834*

Distance groups (from closest corner)	Percentage of lots in sample	Percentage of cleared area in sample	Percentage of lots in group that were totally uncleared	Maximum area cleared (acres, average of top 10% of lots)
Lots on an open road	58	79	14	84
1/4 to 1 mile	22	13	27	62
1 1/4 to 2 miles	11	6	46	35
2 1/4 to 3 miles	7	2	75	15
3 1/4 to 4 miles	2	0	100	0
	100	100		

SOURCE: See note 28.

The changes of values are remarkably orderly, and one might say that the figures expressed the fact that land was poorly developed because it was inaccessible. Yet considering earlier conclusions about the initial occupancy of the richest land, it could also be argued that land remote from roads was undeveloped because it was of poor quality, and unable to command the immediate attention of the road builders. The true state of affairs lies somewhere between: occupancy created roads, roads permitted development, and further development led to more roads.

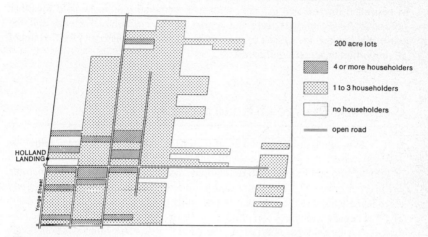

FIGURE 4   East Gwillimbury Township, Householders, 1837

SOURCE: See note 26.

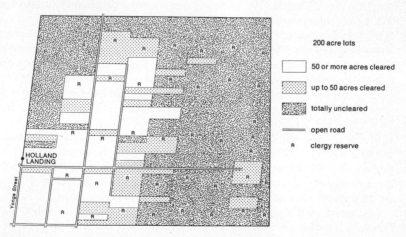

FIGURE 5   East Gwillimbury Township, Land Improvement, 1834

SOURCE: See note 27.

This process was constantly working from more to less desirable land, and the access afforded by open roads was itself one of the factors determining desirability, if only a small one.

The conclusion is clear. The agricultural way of life established in the York County area before 1850 depended upon open roads along which wagons could travel. It may have been possible to do some clearing and to build a house with only footpath access, but by the end of the first full growing season there was grain to be milled for personal use and, with luck, some surplus to be sold for other necessities. Pack-animals were not a part of the commercial scene, and the proverbial pioneer with a sack of grain over one shoulder has been glorified out of all proportion to actual significance.

Requisite Degree of Road Access

Table 1 shows that, in 1801, upon 86 of the 140 lots along Yonge Street, either the land requirements or the road requirements, or both, had been met. Excluding the 21 settlers who had heeded both regulations, recipients of 58 of the 65 remaining lots had performed the land duties and left the road in an incomplete state. Only seven had attended to the road first. At the other end of the scale, 23 of 26 holders who had neglected entirely one or other of the responsibilities had disregarded the road. Again the evidence is strikingly clear. For those establishing farms on Yonge Street, the condition of the thoroughfare as originally opened was sufficient for their purposes. Not only did farmers work on clearing the land first, but they continued beyond levels required for acquiring title. Several farms of 25 or 30 acres lay along Yonge Street in 1797, including ones for which Stegmann found the road in front still substandard four years later.

It might be expected that at some stage in farm development the crude opened road would become a barrier to further expansion. Amounts of land cleared or under crops are possible indicators but grouping these values into distance categories, as in table 2, is not very satisfactory because of the variety of ages of farms. In the process of settlement, 200-acre lots were subdivided into farms of 100 or 50 acres when later immigration pressed upon the available land. A single lot might have had as many as four farms ranging in age from a generation down to a few weeks. In any year before the 1850s for which figures exist, a very large number of farms had 30 to 40 acres of land cleared, regardless of the total size of the property. Possibly better roads were needed, but the nature of the farm products, the assurance of markets, or the availability of investment capital, land, or labour are all alternative considerations in fixing limits for the size of farms.

One means of testing the adequacy of an opened road is to see whether an "improved" road was more useful. Efforts at improving roads went on continually throughout the period York County was being settled. Yonge Street was gradually macadamized in the 1830s and 1840s, a half dozen private companies were organized to build plank roads on public rights-of-way in the later 1840s, and townships began to allocate funds for bridges and major grading projects in the same decade.[30] All these were much more elaborate undertakings than were the initial settlement road duties and subsequent annual statute labour each settler was obliged to perform.[31] Indications are that statute labour did little more than maintain or restore previous conditions. Open roads may have been better cleared but it is unlikely that they were upgraded sufficiently over time to justify defining an intermediate category.

A grouping called "improved" roads does seem appropriate, however, in consideration of the amount of attention given to them in public affairs of the period and subsequently in settlement literature. Potentially excellent thoroughfares, they had their drawbacks too. Because tolls were assessed, it is said that people avoided Yonge Street in favour of a parallel road farther east.[32] Macadamized roads broke up in frost, and plank roads needed constant repair without which they rapidly deteriorated and became dangerous. Indeed, heavy traffic was extremely hard on roads, and the best ones in name may have been among the worst in fact.

Tabulations similar to those in table 2 were prepared for 1834, 1846, and 1851, measuring distances to the nearest improved road. In 1834, the southern part of Yonge Street was the only road in that category. There were more by 1846, including those upon which heavy expenditure had been made from about 1840 onward, and figure 3(d) shows a substantial network of improved roads in 1851. Yet there was no discernible trend toward the concentration of cleared acreages around improved roads. One might argue that there were too few improved roads to meet requirements, and therefore settlers were resigned to making do with what they had. More likely, however, simple opened roads of the stump-and-rut variety were just as useful as the improved ones.

Prior to the 1850s, none of the various forms of road improvement were dramatic enough to make improved roads a significant factor in farm development. Had barely opened roads been inadequate for farming, we should expect to have found cleared areas adjacent to improved roads and rarely at any distance from them. However, at no time during the settling period did this situation exist. Nor was there any noticeable decline in the proportion of cleared land per lot with increasing distance from an improved road, a reasonable expectation had minor roads severely restricted the maximum area cleared per farm.

Road improvements were not among the many grievances for which correction was sought in the politically restless years of the 1820s and 1830s. Robert Gourlay, the champion of the rural populace, conducted a survey among settlers in 1817.[33] In answer to a specific question on the condition of roads, he found mild praise for their serviceability. Only three of 97 replies placed the need for roads or improvements first in the list of complaints, and many townships described their roads as "tolerably good."[34] These observations are all the more momentous if one considers that this account came closer to being an objective statement of rural views than any in the early decades of the century.

A recent inspection of documents reveals practically no complaint that lands held in reserve by the clergy were detrimental to the opening of roads.[35] The allowance might have been opened by the neighbour across the way; if not, and if the situation was acute, statute labour could have made the deficient segment at least as good as any other parts of the road. Roads were not directly mentioned in the famous Seventh Report of Grievances, laid before the provincial executive by William Lyon Mackenzie in 1834.[36] The characteristic open road emerged under circumstances in which settlement road duties were seldom performed on lands of non-resident owners, and the statute labour force was weakened by absentees. But these were administrative problems, and the roads themselves were not under fire. Had better roads been needed, the statute labour of the residents could have contributed much more to the general state of repair than was the case. The same washout was ineffectively patched, year after year, by a reluctant gang of farmers, when one, more concerted effort might have solved the problem.[37] Statute labour may have been repugnant because it bore the marks of a tithe to the ruling oligarchy, but this argument carries little weight if work that could have been performed was all that stood in the way of larger personal returns.

The principal reason for acceptance of unimproved roads lies in the annual opportunity for relatively unrestricted movement each winter. A submission to Gourlay's *Statistical Account* stated: "What contributes to the neglect of the roads is that the business is mostly contrived to be done by sleighing."[38] At times over a period of seven or eight weeks the crudest cart-track matched the newest plank road, and this release came at a time that meshed well with the annual cycle of agricultural activity. With runners placed under wagon-boxes laden with grain, a farmer could — and did — wait for the proper snow conditions and then leave his chopping or other postponable activity and drive to the mill or lakeshore storage point, perhaps 40 miles away. Traffic jams were common, but the delay was at a season when time was relatively expendable.[39]

An analysis of wheat deliveries at Yonge Mills, near Brockville, in the 1830s shows that well over half of the wheat delivered there each year arrived in the winter, in a very irregular fashion from day to day, no doubt tied to changeable sleighing conditions.[40] Much of the remainder came to this large mill by water during the navigation season. The engineer Thomas Keefer was so impressed by the facility with which goods could be moved in winter that he wrote, in 1850: "The operations of agriculture and commerce do not necessarily require perennial communication with a market."[41] Yet a substantial amount of wheat did come to the mills from inland points in September and October, immediately after harvest. The neighbourhood farmer had many incentives to go to market at this time. Recent settlers were anxious for purchasing power to lay in supplies for the winter; others would have to build granaries if they retained their produce until snow came. Cash circulated at harvest time, and there was the chance of high prices for the person early to market with the first offerings of the new crop. Better roads would have reduced the effort necessary to travel at this time, provided they really were an improvement in the way that railroads were in the 1850s. But even in the absence of such opportunities, farmers retained the assurance of being able to take their production to market at least as often as there was a harvest. The removal of standing trees, making a clear right-of-way, was a necessary condition for commerce, and also a sufficient one.

Conclusion

Perhaps somewhere beyond the study area, in regions remote from lakes or navigable rivers, even the best local roads were not reliable enough to promote commercial agriculture. Canals and railroads are known to have enhanced land values close at hand and to have generated agricultural diversification or other signs of commercial progress. Certain improved roads in areas far from these facilities may have assumed a similar role. Improvements in main thoroughfares, or in the overall standards of the road system, must also have been considerations in areas where sleighing could not be relied upon as a marketing technique. Somewhere not very far south of New York state and Lake Erie this annual salvation did not occur, and, on the basis of the argument of this paper, a somewhat different quality of road system must have been developed. Nor could an agricultural system involving either a large local retail market or perishable products have been carried on with such infrequent business contacts. It is of considerable interest that Ontario's first system of all-weather roads developed at the same time that the export wheat economy was superseded by a mixed farming system with emphasis upon perishable dairy products.

None of these contingencies was relevant to the York County area before Confederation. The rural population there showed little regard for roads as a factor in occupying land, and thereafter could get along quite well with the rudimentary ones available. This is only sensible, for, had opened roads not sufficed, either better ones would have materialized or there would have been no settlers. But there would have been little comfort in these conclusions for merchants, carters, and stagecoach operators, working under different priorities. Non-agricultural commerce could not conveniently wait for winter. The spring and fall cycle of deliveries of manufactured items from Britain put heavy pressure on the roads leading inland from ports at seasons when roads were in their worst condition. Travellers most often visited in summer when it may have been dry but roads were rutty and rough. These are the people whose imprecations have been used as a basis for the condemnation of roads in Upper Canada. In fact, it appears that for the majority of users roads were considerably more tolerable than has been believed.

Notes

1. G.P. de T. Glazebrook, *A History of Transportation in Canada* (New Haven, 1938; republished in 2 vols., Toronto, 1964).
2. George R. Taylor, *The Transportation Revolution* (New York, 1951).
3. See the examples in Gerald M. Craig, *Early Travellers in the Canadas, 1791–1867* (Toronto, 1955). In W.H. Smith, *Gazetteer of Canada for 1846* (Toronto, 1846), the descriptive passage for the area around Toronto applauds its agricultural potential, but apologetically informs the reader that most roads each spring are "in such

a state that no farmer having any regard for his horses would allow them to travel on [them]" (p. 81). James J. Talman, "Travel in Ontario before the Coming of the Railway," *Ontario Historical Society Papers and Records* 29 (1933): 85–102, draws together many of these ideas regarding roads. Period paintings and quotations may be found in Thomas F. McIlwraith,"Way to Go," *Horizon Canada* 95 (1987): 2264–69.

4. Samuel Strickland, *Twenty-Seven Years in Canada West*, 2 vols. (London, 1853), 1:92, 2:194.

5. John Howison, *Sketches of Upper Canada* (London, 1821), 230.

6. Among many examples may be included Edwin C. Guillet, *The Story of Canadian Roads* (Toronto, 1966); Glazebrook, *A History of Transportation*; and Michael S. Cross, "The Stormy History of the York Roads, 1833–1865," *Ontario History* 54 (1962): 1–23.

7. See, for example, William M. Gillespie, *A Manual on the Principles of Road-Making* (New York, 1847). Most transportation histories indirectly glorify roads upon which improvements have been effected by describing the recognizable stages of improvement. These included the felling of trees, clearing, grubbing (the removal of stumps), corduroying (the application of transverse cedar poles, especially in wet places), turnpiking (a term for making a central crown and ditches at the sides), and finally macadamizing (the application of crushed rock), planking, or gravelling. The many roads not passing through all these stages early in their existence have "looked" bad ever since.

8. The 1851 census by occupations lists 377 carters and stagecoach drivers in Upper Canada, compared with 86 224 farmers, or 228 times as many of the latter (*Census of Canada 1851–2*, 2 vols. (Quebec, 1853, 1855), vol. 1). Allowing carters and coachmen to work more than 300 days a year, an absurdly low figure of two days of wagoning annually per farmer would put the latter ahead in trips and probably in miles. Twelve to fifteen trips per year is probably a more realistic number, each wagonload representing about two acres of wheat. See Thomas F. McIlwraith, "Transportation in the Landscape of Early Upper Canada," in *Perspectives on Landscape and Settlement in Nineteenth Century Ontario*, ed. J.D. Wood (Toronto, 1975), 51–63.

9. Failure to acknowledge any differences among roads and users is apparent in such statements as this one by Cross: "The condition of the roads in Upper Canada by 1833 was truly deplorable" ("The Stormy History," 1).

10. Indeed Taylor, *The Transportation Revolution*, 16, notes that "bad" roads continued to exist and suggests that this was the case because they were not entirely out of keeping with needs.

11. The first railroad in the York County area ran north from Toronto to Newmarket and Barrie, and was opened in 1853.

12. George Tremaine, Map of York County, 1860, Provincial Archives of Ontario (hereinafter PAO).

13. Notebook of surveyor John Goessman, 1827, Crown Lands Papers, RG1, A–V, box 6, PAO.

14. These requirements did not include the building of bridges or other substantial projects. They were not consistently enforced on the lands taken by the United Empire Loyalists; see Lillian F. Gates, *Land Policies of Upper Canada* (Toronto, 1968), 131.

15. A fuller discussion of terminology is given in Thomas McIlwraith, "Accessibility and Rural Land Utilization in the Yonge Street area of Upper Canada" (MA thesis, University of Toronto, 1966), chap. 2.

16. E.A. Cruikshank, ed., *The Correspondence of Lt. Governor John Graves Simcoe...*, 5 vols. (Toronto, 1924), 2:90–91, 3:192, 226–27.

17. John Stegmann, inspection of Yonge Street, summer of 1801, Ontario Department of Lands and Forests, Surveys Branch, *Surveyors' Letters*, Stegmann,

243–62. An inset showing the lot survey appears on figure 1.

18. The time limit was shorter than for elsewhere; see G.C. Paterson, "Land Settlement in Upper Canada, 1783–1840," *Sixteenth Report of the Department of Archives for the Province of Ontario* (Toronto, 1921), 56; and Cruikshank, ed., *The Correspondence*, 3:333.

19. Harold A. Innis and Arthur R.M. Lower, *Select Documents in Canadian Economic History, 1783–1885* (Toronto, 1933), 54.

20. Many sources were used to piece together the evidence in this paragraph and in figure 2. Note particularly Paterson, "Land Settlement," 184, passim; William Chewett, "Map of the Western Part of Upper Canada" (1813); Ontario Department of Planning and Development, *The Humber Valley Report* (Toronto, 1947), and *Upper Holland Conservation Report* (Toronto, 1953).

21. Stegmann's inspection.

22. This pattern is illustrated in Gates, *Land Policies*, 53, and in part in figure 5.

23. Schedule of Leases Granted for Clergy Reserves, 1802–1821, Crown Lands Papers, RG1, C-II-3, vol. 5, PAO.

24. These maps are based upon the following sources, most of which are in Crown Lands Papers, and Municipal Records Collection, PAO: province, district (the predecessor of county), and township reports by standing committees on roads and bridges; provincial grants to specific roads, listed in statute books; district bylaws; records of the Court of Quarter Session, which heard petitions regarding roads; clergy reserve inspections; precise statements by travellers; and surveyors' notebooks. Published maps were frequently unreliable at the local level, and for this reason were avoided. See McIlwraith, "Accessibility and Rural Land Utilization," 45–52, for a fuller discussion.

25. It would have been circuitous to have used population or land improvement statistics to make inferences about the presence of roads. Some sources did indeed describe both roads and development—the clergy reserve inspection reports, for example—but the information was used only if road and land facts were set down independently. Sometimes there were expressions, such as "road in front of lot 31," which called for interpretation. In this example there was no indication how far the road extended in either direction or even, in this instance of a lot at the corner of intersecting road allowances, whether the reference was to the north–south allowance or "line" (the usual case in York County) or to the cross-road at right angles. In another case, money spent on several bridges along a single right-of-way strongly suggested a road there, despite the absence of any specific reference to it (King Township council minutes, 1845–49, Municipal Records Collection, RG21, PAO).

26. Data taken from George Walton, *Home District Commercial Directory and Register, 1837* (Toronto, 1837).

27. Data taken from tax roll, Municipal Records Collection, RG21, PAO.

28. Table 2 is based upon an inspection of clergy reserve lots throughout the York County area; records in Crown Lands Papers, RG1, A-VI-9, vol. 7, PAO. This is not a truly random selection of lots, but they occur uniformly throughout the study area and all were subject to the same regulations regarding their disposal. Most reserves were already under lease by this time and not perceptibly behind the development of surrounding lots, as shown in figure 5.

29. Acreage cleared is a less precise indicator than are land values, land actually under improvement (which may not have been all the land "cleared"), or acreage put to different uses. But these latter measures either do not exist or are beset with problems created by other factors.

30. See Cross, "The Stormy History," regarding macadamization of Yonge Street. Charters for plank road companies proliferate in the Statutes of the Province of Canada,

beginning about 1846. Markham and King township council records of the late 1840s show the increased activity at this level.

31. Statute labour was road work to be performed annually by adult males, in proportion to the amount of property held, and under the supervision of township officials (Upper Canada Statutes, 33 Geo. III, chap. 4).

32. W.H. Smith, *Canada: Past, Present, and Future* (Toronto, 1851), 1:289.

33. Robert Gourlay, *Statistical Account of Upper Canada*, 2 vols. (London, 1822), vol. 1.

34. Ibid., 1:624, passim.

35. G. Alan Wilson, "The Clergy Reserves: 'Economical Mischiefs' or Sectarian Issue?" *Canadian Historical Review* 42 (1961): 281–99.

36. Appendix 21, *Journal of the Legislative Assembly of Upper Canada*, 1835.

37. See McIlwraith, "Accessibility and Rural Land Utilization," 37–39, for an illustration of the apparent ineffectiveness of many repairs near water-courses, required each year as the spring freshet washed away the previous year's effort. Innis and Lower describe the events of statute labour days as "a kind of picnic" in which little was accomplished (*Select Documents*, 54).

38. Gourlay, *Statistical Account*, 1:478.

39. "[A]t each of the lake ports during the winter, a daily string of sleighs perhaps a mile long could be seen waiting to unload" (*British American Cultivator* (May 1842): 65).

40. Figure compiled from day books in Private Manuscripts Section, Yonge Mills Records, PAO. No such record for the York County area has been found, and this eastern Ontario example is taken as representative since it was also part of the wheat region and had a climate that favoured sleighing.

41. Henry Y. Hind, Thomas C. Keefer, and M.H. Perley, *Eighty Years' Progress in British North America* (Toronto, 1868), 117.

DAMAGED AND EFFICIENT LANDSCAPES IN RURAL SOUTHERN ONTARIO, 1880–1900*

KENNETH KELLY

During the last quarter of the nineteenth century, protest movements such as the Patrons of Industry reflected the tremendous sense of unrest in rural Ontario. Not only were small cottage industries being dislocated, but there was also a growing movement from the countryside into the cities. Politicians such as Sir Oliver Mowat recognized the need to re-orient their parties to take account of the rural protest and equally to win new strength in the cities. The Methodist Church became aware of the migration to the cities and of the need for the church to cope with new urban problems, not the least of which was unemployment. Few observers, however, sought to isolate the economic and social problems of those who remained on the land, although there was growing awareness that the deforestation of agricultural districts led directly to devastated and unproductive landscapes. Furthermore, as lumbering expanded into the Canadian shield, government agencies and lumbering interests recognized that the existing techniques and controls for timber exploitation were no longer satisfactory. Plans were proposed for protecting and planting trees and those which were implemented have imparted a distinctive character to sections of southern Ontario. This paper will attempt to assess those problems threatening the prosperity of rural southern Ontario which were believed to have resulted from deforestation and then to examine briefly the changes proposed between 1880 and 1900.

The Damaged Landscapes

Most of the damage evident in the cultural landscape of southern Ontario in the late nineteenth century had been caused by the removal of the forest. By 1880, a very substantial area running along the front of Lake Ontario and penetrating deeply into

* *Ontario History* 66 (March 1974): 1–14.

peninsular Ontario had been stripped of from 75 to 80 percent of its forest cover (figure 1). Eastern Ontario was not cleared to the same extent, but much of the merchantable timber had been cut. One result of over-clearance in the west and south and of selective felling in the east was that by 1880, the major commercial lumbering area of southern Ontario lay on the Canadian Shield. The exploitation of the forests of the shield not only occasioned an enormous destruction and wastage of timber but also caused serious problems of flooding and deposition in the agricultural lands on its periphery. In terms of actual and potential damage to the resource base and of the character of the landscape, two major regions can be established: agricultural southern Ontario, and the lumber region of the Centre-Shield. It is also necessary, however, to recognize a number of sub-regions within the agricultural area whose characteristics were clearly recognizable by 1880, but became accentuated and were grasped in more detail during the remainder of the nineteenth century

Agricultural Southern Ontario

Although most of the land in agricultural southern Ontario was considered reasonably good for agriculture, within the region there were two major land types, occupying large areas, which simply should not have been cleared. These were the pockets of sandy or rocky land unfit for agriculture (I(a) on figure 2) and the two major heights of land in the region, the Garafraxa Swamps and the Oak Ridges moraine–southern Niagara Escarpment (I(b) on figure 2). The larger pockets of land unfit for agriculture had been cleared for the most part by lumbermen. Waste lands developed on them which posed problems of erosion and deposition, threatening adjacent farmlands. Only the larger waste areas are shown on figure 2, and most of these are well described by Zavitz.[1] However, there were smaller pockets of such land scattered throughout agricultural southern Ontario. In Simcoe County, for example, there were—in addition to the 50 000 acres of sandy waste shown on the map—5 000 acres of sandy waste around Midhurst; 2 000 to 3 000 acres of the same around Craighurst and Orr Lake; a large stretch of sandy and rocky land north of Penetanguishene; and a still larger stretch of rocky, broken land between Orillia and Midland.[2] The clearing of the two major heights of land had repercussions over a wider area of countryside, disrupting river regimes and changing the run-off: percolation ratio. Although the forestry report for 1883 had seen forests on these heights of land primarily as attracting or increasing spring and summer rainfall,[3] by 1886 it viewed them, correctly, as regulators of run-off and as protectors of the sources of rivers.[4] Writing one year later in the *Farmer's Advocate*, Thomas Beall outlined some of the consequences for the surrounding area of the clearing of the Oak Ridges moraines. He reported the decline of water-powered industries, summer drought, the drying up of springs and creeks, wind damage to crops, highways blocked by snow drifts, and soil erosion.[5]

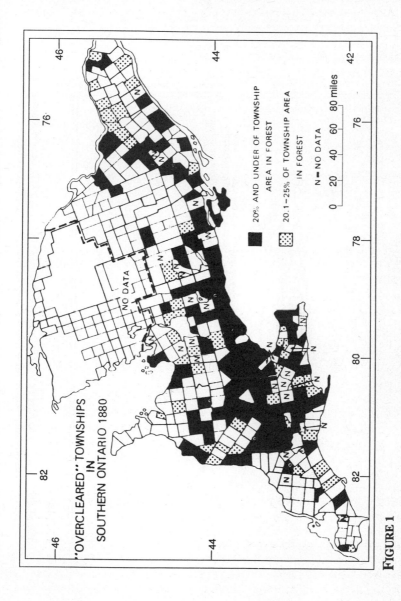

FIGURE 1

SOURCE: Ontario Agricultural Commission, *Report of the Commissioners* (1881), II, appendix B.

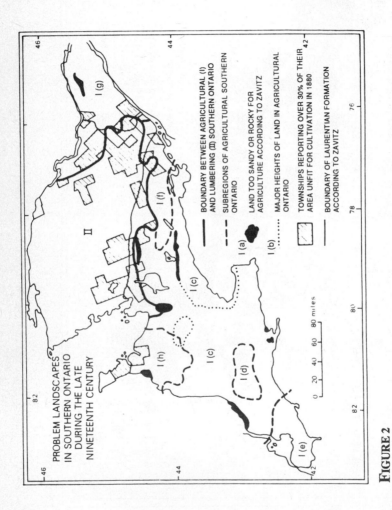

FIGURE 2

SOURCES: E.J. Zavitz, *Fifty Years of Reforestation in Ontario* (Toronto, 1908); Ontario Agricultural Commission, *Report of the Commissioners*; *Ontario Forestry Reports*, 1883–1901.

These same problems were experienced at different scales throughout agricultural southern Ontario as the lesser heights of land were cleared and as farmers discovered that parts of their land were virtually useless even as third-rate pasture. By 1891, the greater part of agricultural southern Ontario (I(c) on figure 2) suffered from a broad range of adverse effects of the destruction of the forest. Deforestation had caused changes in the runoff:percolation ratio, giving rise to accelerated soil erosion. Springs and creeks had failed and stream and river levels fluctuated widely. The lack of shelter accentuated summer drought and in winter allowed the protective snow cover to be blown from the fields into drifts across the highways, and exposed man and beast to increased cold. Furthermore, if not yet widely felt, shortages of fuelwood and building and fencing timber threatened. Most of the region, then, experienced seasonal water deficiencies, local flooding, the large-scale failure of the fall wheat crop through winter kill, decreased yields from grasslands and orchards because of the lack of shelter, and increased difficulty in winter transportation. It faced either the collapse of much of its water-powered rural industry or greater costs occasioned by conversion to steam power. The costs of livestock raising were increasing because the greater winter cold in the barns necessitated increased feeding. Finally, a rise in the cost of living seemed imminent with the prospect of the need to import fuel and building materials.

Still, in 1891 there were sub-regions within the agricultural south which did not experience the entire range of difficulties outlined above. Middlesex and Oxford counties (I(d) on figure 2) reported that no problems resulting from deforestation affected agriculture. Serious flooding occurred, especially along the Thames, but this was attributed to drainage schemes and not to overclearing. Essex and Kent counties (I(e) on figure 2) saw their basic agricultural problem as a lack of shelter during winter. Here few difficulties were experienced with river and stream regimes because of the flatness and wetness of much of the area, combined with the relatively high percentage of forest remaining. The periphery of the Centre-Shield (I(f) on figure 2) reported flooding as the major problem, although this sub-region also suffered from the drying up of creeks and springs in summer and from the lack of shelter. The east (I(g) on figure 2) experienced a lack of shelter in winter, but did not find this much of a problem because little fall wheat was grown there. Furthermore, the preservation of forest, especially in the form of sugar bush, was already common in the east. Here, to a greater extent than anywhere else in agricultural southern Ontario, the woodlot had become a significant component of the landscape. As a result, problems of drought were not felt as acutely as elsewhere. By 1891, however, the Bruce-Grey sub-region (I(h) on figure 2) was beginning to feel the range of problems experienced in the core of the agricultural region.

The Centre-Shield

By 1880, this region had become the major lumbering area of southern Ontario.[6] Not all of the area was exploited for lumber at this date but in the west, lumbering occurred at least as far north as Humphrey township in the Parry Sound District, and in the east, as far north as the northern part of Renfrew County. The northern limit of exploitation in 1880 apparently dipped southward between these two points. The forests in western Renfrew County were relatively untouched and the northernmost tier of townships in Hastings County were uncut.[7] During the next decade, however, lumbering spread throughout the Centre-Shield of southern Ontario.

Within the exploited area of the Centre-Shield a great deal of timber was wasted and destroyed in the course of lumbering as well as by forest fires. At the same time, it was recognized that much of the land laid bare could not, and should not, be taken up by agricultural settlers. The forest was underlain in many areas by lands too stony, rocky, or hilly for cultivation (see figure 2). There were also large areas of swamp. The danger existed, then, that forest exploitation and destruction would run rapidly through the region leaving in its wake vast areas of useless and unproductive land.

The forestry report for 1886 describes the common practices of the lumberman who had leased timber limits on Crown land, and gives some indication of the various degrees of damage done the landscape. During the 1880s and early 1890s, the rights to limits were practically always renewed so that the lumberman could work in a relatively leisurely fashion. First, he cut the merchantable timber from those parts of his limits that were closest to settlement and that were therefore believed to be in the greatest danger from fire. Often he accomplished this task in two or three cuttings made in successive years. The lumberman then allowed a smaller firm or jobber to glean through the cut-over area, while he turned to the more remote areas on his limits, cutting over them only once or at long intervals.[8] The most thoroughgoing modification was to the areas adjacent to settlements, the same areas that were also liable to the highest degree of modification from fires and the effects of livestock browsing. Felling was selective, and mature specimens of merchantable species were rapidly eradicated. For example, pine was the chief timber culled from the Muskoka forests in 1880; by 1891 it had largely disappeared and a beginning was being made on the removal of the hemlock.[9] Much of the wood of the merchantable species was wasted; most of the pine was squared in the forest, and the hemlock was used only for its bark (which was used in the tanning industry). The tops and branches of merchantable trees were left to rot unused on the ground. Furthermore, in the course of lumbering operations young trees were broken and many mature but non-commercial species were felled to ease the extraction of, say, the pine.

Such waste and destruction spelled vast amounts of debris, posing great risk of spreading fires. During the 1870s, a series of fires had swept through the margins of the Centre-Shield, in parts of Renfrew, Leeds, Frontenac, Hastings, Peterborough, and Victoria counties.[10] During the early 1880s, fires continued to do enormous damage. Serious fires occurred in northern Hastings, Peterborough, and Victoria counties and in the Muskoka and Parry Sound districts.[11] The blame for such fires was laid at the door of settlers, hunters, miners, campers, berry pickers, and wild hay gatherers as well as lumbermen. Where fires were relatively infrequent, a second growth, commonly of poplar and white birch, developed (for example, in parts of Hastings and Peterborough counties).[12] Over large areas, however, repeated burning had left only bare rock.

The major concerns expressed in connection with the Centre-Shield were the waste or destruction of timber and the reduction of the long-term lumber-producing capacity of the region. But two other problems were observed and helped shape the image of the new landscape. The first of these problems was that the flow of water out of the region was disrupted, causing (as well as difficulties in rafting out cut timber) floods and deposition on its periphery. The second problem lay in the occurrence of pockets of low-income farming in the region. In many cases, settlers had been lured into the Centre-Shield by the market offered for farm produce in the lumber camps and by the opportunities for winter work there,[13] as well as by a spirit of optimism which took no account of the transportation costs to southern markets, or of soil characteristics. As lumbering moved out of their area, many settlers accepted a reduced level of living rather than the loss of the entire sum they had invested in developing the farm. Deprived of markets they were unable to support even such rudimentary social services as schools or churches. In the words of Zavitz, the province could not afford "to allow citizens to live and develop under the enforced conditions existing in many of these waste areas."[14]

An Image of the New Landscapes

The growing awareness of the problems of the rural landscapes of southern Ontario precipitated the development of general principles of land use as well as specific solutions to particular problems. The general principles and specific solutions, both of which embodied reforestation on a significant scale, can be combined to produce a picture of the rather vaguely conceived new and more efficient landscapes.

Three major principles of land use emerged in southern Ontario during the latter part of the nineteenth century. The first, which was based largely on the experience of the Centre-Shield, was that land which could be used profitably only for the production of timber should be permanently devoted to sustained yield forestry. Such land should not be allowed "to lose its distinctively forest character, which can only be recovered by slow degrees."[15] The second principle was that all heights of land, regardless of their location or soil condition, should be put and kept under forest. The final principle was that, as a general rule of thumb, 20 to 25 percent of each agricultural township should be in forest. To quote the forestry report for 1901, "The proportion of the total areas of a district which should be covered with timber in order to secure favourable climatic conditions and regulate the water supply is usually fixed by authorities on forestry at about 25 percent." Twenty percent could be viewed as the lowest proportion in forest possible "without seriously endangering agricultural interests."[16]

Agricultural Southern Ontario

All three of these principles were integral to the image of the new landscape for agricultural southern Ontario. The feeling developed, and by the end of the century was very clearly expressed, that areas of land too sandy or rocky for cultivation should be put under a permanent forest cover. The idea was repeatedly expressed that all heights of land should be reforested. Finally it was suggested that substantial areas in each township be put under trees to protect against erosion, to provide shelter, and to ensure an adequate supply of fuel and building timber. However, the ideas current on the redesign of the landscape of agricultural areas were implemented only in a piecemeal fashion. The private ownership of most of the land made it difficult for the provincial government to play a direct role in the development of the new landscape; by and large the government role during the nineteenth century in agricultural southern Ontario was limited to exhortation and the offering of subsidies for tree planting.

The larger areas of cleared land unfit for cultivation were untypical of agricultural southern Ontario in that parts of them were in the hands of municipalities (through abandonment and tax delinquency), while other sections could be purchased at low prices. Concern over the future of these areas was expressed as early as the 1870s,[17] but the classical diagnosis of, and prescription for, the problems of these sites was made by Zavitz in 1908.[18] Despite the recognition of the desirability and necessity of reforestation on these lands, little large-scale planting was undertaken on them before the turn of the century. Ultimately, however, several of these areas became the sites of county forests.

A similar inaction prevailed where large-scale reforestation of the more significant heights of land was suggested. The forestry reports urged the establishment of large areas of woodland on such sites, but the concrete plan of action suggested was appropriate only to areas in the early stages of settlement. The reports urged that the heights of land be withheld from settlement or that the retention of hill tops in forest be made a condition for the issue of a patent. However, they could offer no device for the reforestation of large tracts on heights of land already in private ownership. Consequently, despite calls for the development of blocks of forest of up to twenty or thirty square miles, which would regulate water availability, provide fuel and fencing materials, shelter wildlife, and serve as summer resorts, these did not appear on the land during the nineteenth century.[19]

The ideas discussed above were on a broad scale, calling for the reforestation of substantial areas of land in order to solve problems affecting large sections of agricultural southern Ontario. These were not implemented because government bodies were unwilling or unable to purchase or assemble the necessary large blocks of land. But the provincial government also urged farmers to reforest parts of their land, and at the individual farm level some of the smaller components of the envisaged new landscape became visible during the latter part of the nineteenth century. A relatively small proportion of farmers were engaged in serious reforestation—the forestry report of 1901 noted that the forested area in very many townships had declined since 1896—but on some farms the new and more efficient landscape was developed.

The forestry reports recommended that farmers plant and protect large woodlots. The woodlot could be located on the summit or steeper slopes of a hill, where it would check erosion and regulate run-off as well as provide shelter and timber, or on land that was of low quality even as pasture.[20] The report for 1886 observed that some such land occurred on almost every farm so that the development of a woodlot normally would entail no loss of agricultural productivity. However, it urged that even in those cases where the farm was composed entirely of good land the farmer should still have a woodlot, presenting the maxim that the better the land the better the timber it would produce.[21] The image offered was of a ten-acre woodlot for each hundred acres of land owned. In 1882, the clerk of forestry suggested that properly managed woodlots be exempt from taxation, but such exemption never materialized.[22] The only assistance provided by government for the establishment of woodlots was advice on the species to plant, on management techniques, and repeated warnings to keep cattle—and indeed all livestock—out.[23]

The provincial government also encouraged the planting of lines or rows of trees to provide shade and shelter. In 1871, the Ontario legislature had passed "An Act to encourage the planting of trees upon the highways in this Province...," which defined the ownership of road-side trees, provided for the protection of the trees, and permitted municipal councils themselves to spend money on the planting of shade and ornamental trees or to make grants to individuals or associations for the same purpose.[24] No data are available on township responses to the last provision. This Act was superseded by the Ontario Tree Planting Act of 1883 which, among other things, committed the provincial government to pay farmers a premium of up to 12.5 cents for every shade tree (of an approved species) planted along highways or farm boundaries and which survived for three years.[25] From 1883 to 1894, 42 townships (and six towns or villages) participated in the programme and some 75 000 trees were planted under its stipulations.[26] However, the government did not feel that this Act functioned satisfactorily. By the end of 1894, the fund initially set aside for the payment of premiums had not been exhausted, and many townships were encouraging planting without recourse to the Act. A questionnaire circulated among townships that had not drawn on the bonus fund established by the Act revealed that in 152 of them, planting "on or near highways, on farm boundaries, and in other situations than immediately around farm buildings" had been undertaken to a fair or considerable extent. Planting to a small extent had taken place in 73 other townships.[27] As a result, the 1896 Tree Planting Act abolished the provincial bonus, while allowing townships to pay farmers 25 cents for each tree planted along highways and farm boundaries.[28]

An image of a reforested agricultural southern Ontario was formulated during the last two decades of the nineteenth century. Large blocks of forest were envisioned, located on the larger areas of land too sandy or rocky for cultivation and on the major heights of land. The highways were to be lined with shade trees. Several farm woodlots together would clothe the summits and steeper slopes of hills. Every farm would have at least a ten-acre woodlot and a grid of field-side plantings would shelter the crops. Small groves would shelter the farm houses and be scattered through the permanent pastures, and thickets would snake across the countryside, marking and protecting the banks of water courses.

The Lumbering Area of the Centre-Shield

The need to reduce the incidence of fires was essential to the redesign of the landscape of the Centre-Shield; without this, the spontaneous regrowth of the forest would be set at nought, and regardless of any other actions, the preservation of a timber cover and the development of sustained yield forestry would be impossible. Consequently, fire control received first attention. In 1878, the Ontario legislative assembly passed an Act to preserve the forests from destruction by fire. The Act empowered the Lieutenant-Governor to declare any part of Ontario a fire district. The southern boundary of Fire District No. 1, which was announced in 1878 and which embraced much of the Centre-Shield of southern Ontario, is shown on figure 3. Within the fire districts (all except No. 1 lay entirely within northern Ontario), fires were permitted between April 1 and November 1 only for the purposes of "clearing land, cooking, obtaining warmth, or for some industrial purpose." The Act specified a series of precautions to be taken with fires and a set of penalties for negligence.[29] Despite the passage of this Act, serious fires continued. As a result, in 1885, the Commissioner of Crown Lands sent a circular to all limit holders inviting them to hire fire rangers to enforce the 1878 Act. The provincial government offered to pay half of the rangers' salaries. The fire ranger system found immediate acceptance (as can be seen from the following data),[30] effectively preventing serious fire damage in the patrolled areas:

1885	37 rangers
1886	45 rangers
1887	55 rangers
1891	98 rangers
1896	160 rangers
1897	191 rangers
1898	206 rangers

With a beginning made in fire control during the late 1870s, two broad images of a new and efficient landscape were offered in the forestry reports. In 1883, the clerk of forestry suggested a landscape largely of permanent forest but with the forest dissected by grassed fire lanes and dotted with manufacturing villages and towns. His concept of a more efficient landscape allowed, as well as for fire control and sustained yield forestry, for a continuation of the free grant system of disposing of Crown land and for a substantial non-lumbering population. He took the notion of fire lanes from forestry practice in India, but based his idea of fattening cattle on them from his analysis of the agricultural potential of the shield. He suggested "giving out" the fire lane/cattle runs (which would be fenced to prevent the cattle

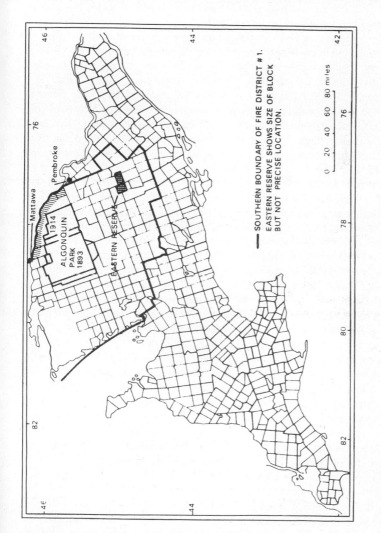

FIGURE 3

SOURCE: *Ontario Forestry Reports, 1890–1901.*

from damaging the forest) to graziers who had sufficient capital to develop them and to induce a grass and clover cover. He saw the disposal of Crown lands as free grants also as a device to maintain a forest cover. In his scheme, free land grants would be made to persons who would undertake to keep the land under forest. The manufacturing activity his idea called for was to be based on textile production, utilizing the lime-free waters of the region.[31]

The forestry report for 1884 introduced an entirely different conception of the efficient landscape. It envisioned the area under a permanent cover of forest and with a very small non-lumbering population. Thus the multiple resource-use proposal of 1883 was succeeded by a virtually single resource-use "plan." The image presented in 1884 was based in part on the observed damage to forest in areas open to settlement and on the destruction wrought in the woods by livestock, but also on concern over the consequences of the deforestation of the Lake Nipissing–Kingston height of land. The forestry report for 1884 noted that there still remained from twenty to thirty townships in the Nipissing District that contained few or no settlers. It urged that this area be closed to settlement and be kept in forest.[32] As the idea of such a block of permanently forested land was discussed over the next decade, its supporters developed the argument that as well as protecting the sources of such important rivers as the Muskoka, the Madawaska, and the Petawawa, the area would provide the setting for experiments to devise economical and yet effective ways of disposing of pine refuse and to develop techniques of timber extraction which would reduce the damage to the forest.[33] They also believed that the area would offer recreational amenities, for camping, hunting, and fishing. It would "confer on the country the inestimable benefit of retaining a forest within some reasonable distance of the cities of Ontario."[34] After almost a decade of discussion, Algonquin Park was established in the Nipissing District in 1893 with an initial area of 1 109 383 acres (see figure 3).

One year before the establishment of Algonquin Park, the Ontario government introduced a new regulation regarding felling on leased timber limits. Whereas licences issued before 1892 had conferred rights to cut all species of timber, henceforth they would permit the cutting of red and white pine only. The government, anticipating a rise in the value of other species such as birch and spruce, sought to protect this timber and to keep it in its own hands.[35] This regulation, which originally was to pertain to new licences, was applied retroactively in 1893 to limits leased in Algonquin Park.[36] However, this legislation was laxly enforced in the park, for in 1898 the government found it necessary to restate its position that only pine was to be taken. It was becoming concerned about the danger posed by lumbering to the park as both a timber and game reserve.[37]

It was not until 1898 that it was decided which image of the new landscape should be pursued and implemented on the Centre-Shield. In that year, both the lessons learned from the operation of Algonquin Park and the findings of the Forestry Commission of 1897 led the government to aim for continued Crown ownership of land and the exclusion of settlers, coupled with more stringent felling and fire-control regulations, as the major means to maintain a permanent forest cover in the lumbering areas of the province. The forestry report for 1896, noting the success of the Algonquin Park venture, suggested that further areas be set aside purely as forestry reserves. It urged "the expansion of the policy inaugurated by the setting apart of Algonquin Park, having for its object the preservation of large areas of land permanently in timber, and treating the forest as a continually productive source of wealth."[38] The Forestry Commission of 1897 agreed; its major recommendation was that the government should withdraw from sale, and set aside as permanent Crown forest reserves, such areas of territory as were generally unsuitable for settlement and yet of value for growing timber. In 1898, the provincial government passed an Act to Establish Forest Reserves (the Forest Reserves Act). The Act empowered the Lieutenant-Governor in Council to set aside permanent Crown forest reserves. When a reserve had been proclaimed, no lands within its boundaries were to be sold, leased for settlement, or otherwise disposed of; no person was to locate or settle upon any of the land; and no one was to hunt, fish, shoot, trap, spear, or use firearms or explosives within or upon the reserve.[39] The first area set aside under this Act consisted of 80 000 acres in the northern parts of Frontenac and Addington counties; this was the Eastern Reserve established in 1899 [40] (see figure 3). At the same time, other reserves were proclaimed in northern Ontario, and by 1900 active consideration was being given to the setting aside of a second reserve within southern Ontario to run on both sides of the C.P.R. tracks between Pembroke and Mattawa (see figure 3).

By the end of the nineteenth century, then, an image had been developed of a more efficient landscape for the Centre-Shield and a beginning had been made to implement it. The landscape was to be dominated by forest with a few pockets of cultivation confined to the very best of soils. The nuclei of the new landscape were Algonquin Park and the Eastern Reserve. The forest lands around the nuclei—comprising part of Fire District No. 1 under the Act of 1878—were to be protected by an increasingly effective fire ranging system and by more rigid regulations governing the cutting of timber. It was confidently felt at the turn of the century that the problems of the Centre-Shield had been solved and that a new era in forestry had begun.[41]

Conclusions

This paper has outlined the nature of the problems threatening continued productivity in agriculture and lumbering which were recognized during the late nineteenth century. It was realized that the modifications to the physical setting that were made in the course of both agricultural settlement and lumbering had produced or threatened to produce inefficient and damaged landscapes. The response was an attempt to impose a new series of planned modifications and land-use controls in order to rebuild the landscape. The paper has sketched a composite image of the new landscapes for southern Ontario envisaged by the provincial government. The image became manifest on the land more readily in the Centre-Shield largely because the Crown owned most of the land and the persons leasing rights to cut timber were more amenable to government legislation. The new landscape was less easily and less completely translated into reality in agricultural southern Ontario. The government did not buy up blocks of land for the larger scale reforestation projects, legislation was permissive rather than regulatory, and most farmers were unconvinced that reforestation would repay their effort in their lifetime. Nevertheless, vestiges of the late nineteenth-century concern over the rebuilding of the landscape are still visible on the land today on scales ranging from Algonquin Park to tree-lined highways, and there is much evidence to connect the late nineteenth-century images of a more efficient landscape with the reforestation projects carried on in the present day.

Notes

1. E.J. Zavitz, *Fifty Years of Reforestation in Ontario* (Toronto, 1908), 10–14.
2. A picture of the smaller areas of waste land can be obtained only with great difficulty, largely from scattered references in the Annual Report of the Commissioner of Agriculture and Arts and in the reports of the judges of the Ontario prize farm competitions.
3. "Forestry Report for 1883," *Ontario Forestry Reports, 1882–1886*, 122–23.
4. "Forestry Report for 1886," *Ontario Sessional Papers*, 1887, 69.
5. T. Beall, "Personal Observations on the Effects of the Removal of our Forests," *Farmer's Advocate* 22 (1887): 37.
6. Lumbering is defined for the purpose of this paper as the production of timber for use outside the area of extraction. Lumbering areas produced more than fuel, fencing, and building materials for purely local use.
7. Ontario Agricultural Commission, *Report of the Commissioners* (Toronto, 1881), II, appendix B, statistical reports by township.
8. "Forestry Reports for 1886," 36.
9. "Forestry Report for 1891," *Ontario Sessional Papers*, 1892, 12.
10. Ontario Agricultural Commission, *Report*.
11. "Forestry Report for 1891," 8–9.
12. Ibid., 8, 16.
13. "Forestry Report for 1901," *Ontario Sessional Papers*, 1902, 4.
14. Zavitz, *Fifty Years of Reforestation*, 24.
15. "Forestry Report for 1901," 6–7.
16. Ibid., 22–23.
17. See, for example, the feelings of the editor of the Orillia newspaper, the *Packet*, about the future of the area between Orillia and Midland, in *The Orillia Packet*, 14 Mar. 1872.
18. This diagnosis is scattered through the whole of Zavitz's *Fifty Years of Reforestation*.
19. See, for example, "Forestry Report for 1886," 105 and "Forestry Report for 1889–90," *Ontario Forestry Reports, 1887–1898*, 9.
20. See, for example, "Forestry Report for 1886," 69.
21. Ibid., 103.
22. "Forestry Report for 1882," *Ontario Forestry Reports, 1882–1886*, 139.

23. See, for example, "Forestry Report for 1884," *Ontario Forestry Reports, 1882–1886*, 7.

24. Ontario Department of Lands and Forests, *A History of Crown Timber Regulations from the Date of the French Occupation to the Year 1889* (Toronto, 1957), 297.

25. Townships electing to participate under the Act paid a similar sum.

26. "Forestry Report for 1896," *Ontario Forestry Reports, 1887–1898*, 43.

27. Ibid., 49. The townships are not named in this report.

28. The text of this Act is reprinted in Ontario, *A History of Crown Timber Regulations*, 280–82.

29, For the 1878 Act see ibid., 270–73.

30. Ibid., 278–79.

31. "Forestry Report for 1883," 124–27.

32. "Forestry Report for 1884," 16.

33. "Forestry Report for 1886," 70–71.

34. Ibid.

35. Ontario, *A History of Crown Timber Regulations*, 266–67.

36. Ibid., 283.

37. Ibid., 267.

38. "Forestry Report for 1896," 5.

39. The Act is reprinted in Ontario, *A History of Crown Timber Regulations*, 284.

40. "Forestry Report for 1901," 6.

41. See, for example, "Forestry Report for 1898," *Ontario Forestry Reports, 1887–1898*, 8, reprinted from the *Canada Lumberman*; and "Forestry Report for 1901," 3.

SECTION 4
URBAN GROWTH AND FORM

From their seventeenth- and eighteenth-century beginnings as tiny European outposts to their twentieth-century pre-eminence as national and provincial centres of population, power, wealth, and culture, towns and cities have held a pivotal place in the development of Canada. Despite their small size (Quebec, by far the largest urban centre north of Boston in the mid-eighteenth century, had approximately five thousand residents), Canada's earliest urban places were important commercial and military centres. In the eyes of the colonial powers, they were also key administrative centres, although the difficulties of inland communication severely limited the penetration of authority into their hinterlands.

Although contemporaries occasionally likened them to second-rank provincial towns in France or Britain, early Canadian towns were set apart from those European places by their newness, their appearance, and the mix of people within them. Still, in common with most towns of their day, they were strikingly heterogeneous. Docks and warehouses, government buildings, churches, substantial houses, and humble shacks stood cheek by jowl, and wealthy merchants, colonial officials, servants, sailors, soldiers, artisans, labourers, and paupers mingled on the streets. Although these towns were distinct from the countryside that surrounded them, they formed points of attachment between British North America and Europe. They were well located for water-borne commerce and as the population and trade of the colonies expanded in the late eighteenth and early nineteenth centuries, each town grew to command its own section of the back country.

In broad terms, these developing urban centres exhibited many similarities in form and in their combination of functions. Goods and people moved upon wagons, carriages, horses, or foot in these so-called "pedestrian cities." Thus, they remained compact places, within which earlier patterns of mixed land use were intensified. Into the third quarter of the nineteenth century, stores, banks, offices, warehouses, residences, artisanal shops, and small factories stood in close proximity in most districts of British North America's cities. Yet these cities remained markedly isolated from one another. Their most important connections, shaped by staple trades and the imperial relationship, were across the Atlantic, with Britain and to a lesser degree with the West Indies and the American states. Even commercial information travelled relatively slowly and sparsely from the cities of Nova Scotia and New Brunswick to those of the St. Lawrence Valley. Although each of the major port cities had close links with smaller places in its hinterland, these small networks were poorly integrated with each other. In the 1850s, there was no British North American urban system.

Fifty years or so later, both the shape of Canadian cities and the links between them were radically different. Together, Confederation, the National Policy, industrialization, revolutionary improvements in transportation and communication, and technological innovations in building construction recast Canada's urban fabric. It is with this dramatic set of changes that the three essays that follow are concerned.

A highly original analysis by L.D. McCann, a geographer who teaches Canadian studies at Mount Allison University, illuminates the way in which the Canadian urban system was forged. The creation of a nation state with Ottawa as its centre in 1867 was a fundamental step in the political integration of the provinces, not least by the creation of new channels of patronage. It is the Macdonald government's National Policy of 1879, however, that has generally been seen as the major influence upon patterns of urban growth and interconnection in the country. Certainly it was enormously influential. The Policy envisioned a trans-continental nation and imposed a tariff structure on imports in order to promote industrial growth in Canada. Railroads linked central Canada to territories east and west; with improved access to markets, producers were able to specialize and to reap the benefits of economies of scale. Large new sugar refineries and cotton factories in Nova Scotian towns changed the face of those places and the nature of life within them, and tied their fortunes, to some degree, to developments in distant parts of the country. Conversely, producers of flour and meat products in central Canada benefited from their sales in the eastern provinces.

As McCann demonstrates, all of this occurred in the context of other changes—from the passage of the Bank Act in 1871 to the rise of managerialism and the emergence of large, integrated enterprises combining mass production and mass marketing. These developments extended the dominance of metropolitan interests over peripheral areas of the country, first from Montreal and then from Toronto. As the "natural protection" afforded early nineteenth-century cities by the costs of movement was broken down, many communities found opportunities in the new order. On the other hand, improved technologies and the rationalization that followed in their wake often swept away the foothold that these places had gained. Firms at the centre extended their reach, authority, and market share; local enterprise on the periphery fell under external sway. So, in a sense, dependence followed interdependence, and some of the foundations of the modern, heartland–hinterland structure of the country were laid down.

Yet this is not simply an account of how the country came to be. Profoundly geographical questions of scale lie at the heart of McCann's analysis, and readers of his article might be provoked to reflect on the future shape of the Canadian, continental, and global economies. Consider that pedestrian cities provided a wide range of services for their inhabitants. Most of the services were small in scale and duplicated in the cities' hinterlands and in other, similar cities. With improvements in production and transportation many services, such as shoemaking, fell into decline as needs were met by mass producers elsewhere. In the towns and cities of the late nineteenth-century Maritimes, at least, new industrial, commercial, and financial enterprises developed to cater to local, regional, and even eastern Canadian needs. For a time, they were appropriate to the technological, managerial, and fiscal circumstances of their settings, but technological innovations, the settlement of the West, and the development of a truly national economy rendered most of them increasingly marginal. Today, some scholars assert that national economies are no longer competitive; multinational blocks and global trade are the appropriate scales for industry and enterprise in the twenty-first century. There will again be adjustments, and we might well ponder whether the pattern of the past indicates what the future will hold.

Many of those who lived in Canada's largest cities in the first decades of the twentieth century surely doubted that the past had much relevance to their present, except as a measure of how dramatically their settings had been transformed. Montreal, a city of 100 000 at Confederation, exceeded 750 000 in the 1920s; Toronto grew almost tenfold in fifty years from its 1871 total of 56 000; and Ottawa, Hamilton, Winnipeg, and Vancouver all topped 100 000 before the end of the century's second decade. In these places and in their slightly smaller counter-parts across the country, the specialization of land use and the differentiation of urban space created a new, fragmented, urban fabric. Wholesale, retail, and financial activities claimed separate parts of the downtown core. Industry concentrated where it had access to the waterfront, canals, or railroads. Residential areas spread on the periphery and were increasingly set apart by the socio-economic status of their inhabitants.

Most simply, these changes can be attributed to the development of mass transportation. New modes of movement broke the tight bounds of the pedestrian city, allowed urban populations to increase without insufferable crowding, and helped to sort out people and land uses. In this view, the streetcar was a potent instrument that drove the bounds of the city outward, as suburb after suburb spread over cheap land on the periphery, and pushed the core of the city upwards, as stores and offices grew to serve and employ the thousands of commuters who streamed downtown each morning. This is only part of the story, however, and the papers by Gad and Holdsworth, and McCririck and Wynn, add important nuances to it while providing neatly complementary perspectives on the processes that transformed central city and suburb in early twentieth-century Canada.

Gunter Gad teaches urban geography at the University of Toronto, and Deryck Holdsworth is an editor of volume 3 of the *Historical Atlas of Canada** and a member of the Geography Department at Pennsylvania State University. Their detailed study of developing downtown Toronto stems from a long-standing interest among geographers in the built form, or morphology, of cities. They recognize that the central city was shaped by many forces. Technological advances were crucial. In construction, advances made tall buildings feasible; in the development of elevators, they allowed people easy access to the upper floors of tall buildings; in transportation, they brought workers to the new towers. Political-institutional factors, such as city height limitations, also affected the cityscape. So did the symbolic importance attached to large corporate structures.

Yet Gad and Holdsworth insist that the changing built environment was, and is, the complex product of broad economic and social changes. More specifically, they argue that the changing space requirements of firms using downtown office buildings were instrumental in shaping the high-rise streetscape of the city core. Their study accounts for the timing, extent and character of high-rise building in

*D. Kerr and D. Holdsworth, eds., *Addressing the Twentieth Century*, vol. 3 of *Historical Atlas of Canada* (Toronto: University of Toronto Press, forthcoming).

Toronto by reference to, among other things, the distinctive structure of the Canadian economy, the interrelated functions of the many small firms who together occupied the first large buildings, and the new gender mix in office employment. In doing so, the work succeeds in revealing a good deal about the development of a crucial node of the Canadian urban system and in refining our understanding of the processes that created the modern downtown silhouette.

Donna McCririck, whose M.A. thesis in geography at the University of British Columbia forms the basis for the final essay in this section, was led into an investigation of land accessibility and the growth of blue-collar suburbs in early Vancouver by the challenge of viewing the process of city building "from the standpoint of its carpenters instead of its architects." No mean task in the best of circumstances, this proved especially difficult in Vancouver. Many of the detailed records that are essential to analysis "from the bottom up," such as assessment rolls and nominal census returns, have either been destroyed or are not yet available to the researcher.

Piecing together a picture of rapidly rising land prices and a volatile employment market from fragmentary data, McCririck argued that many newly arrived wage earners found it difficult to acquire their own dwellings in "the city of homes," especially in the boom years between 1909 and 1913. Those fortunate enough to do so might well have found themselves in either of the two blue-collar suburbs whose development is considered in the selection that follows. Hillcrest and Grandview were in many respects representative of the new suburbs that were springing up around many Canadian cities at the time. They made handsome profits for those "architects" of real estate development who had capital and an understanding of where to invest it, and provided modest dwellings in rough, unevenly developed, and initially poorly serviced surroundings for those "carpenters" who made their homes there. Yet in the end, these and other suburbs— relatively homogeneous communities removed from the growing problems of the core and its immediate perimeter—helped to change perceptions of urban space. They gave substance to a new, persistent, urban order in which detached houses and private yards became the assumed residential norm.

METROPOLITANISM AND BRANCH BUSINESSES IN THE MARITIMES, 1881–1931*

L.D. MCCANN

Metropolitanism is an old theme in the historiography of the Maritimes, and the sting of the metropolis is felt throughout the region, from the smallest village to the largest city.[1] In the 19th century, the locus of metropolitan dominance was based across the Atlantic in Britain. Now it rests in central Canada. Despite our awareness of the metropolis and its impact on the Maritime economy, surprisingly little is known about the *unfolding* of metropolitan dominance across the Maritime region in the years between Confederation and the Great Depression.[2] New evidence on the process of metropolitanism in the Maritimes suggests answers for several basic yet unresolved questions. First, which metropolis dominated the region in the post-Confederation period? Second, which sectors of the regional economy were linked most strongly to the metropolis? And third, what was the geographical sphere of influence of the metropolis?

One of the inherent features of metropolitanism is the extension into the hinterland of economic activities headquartered in the metropolis. Branch businesses may be regarded as the emissaries, so to speak, of the metropolis, advancing its economic interests and consolidating its empire throughout the hinterland. Among other activities, branch businesses engage in manufacturing, facilitate the distribution of goods, channel capital flows, and sell and service the products of the metropolis. Drawing chiefly upon Dun and Bradstreet records, it is possible to build a

* *Acadiensis* 13, 1 (1983): 112–25. Research on branch businesses in Canada has been funded by the Social Sciences and Humanities Research Council of Canada in conjunction with the Historical Atlas of Canada Project. Able research and computer assistance was provided by Janice Milton, Virginia Lieter, and Libby Napper. A more extended version of this paper was read in 1983 before the annual meetings of the Canadian Historical Association (Vancouver) and the Social Science History Association (Washington, D.C.), and the helpful remarks of Graeme Wynn and Gil Stelter, commentators at these meetings, are gratefully acknowledged.

comprehensive picture of branch businesses operating in the Maritimes in the post-Confederation period. Information on all branch businesses, as well as a 10 percent sample of the composite business structure of the Maritimes, was collected from the *Mercantile Agency Reference Books* of Dun, Wiman and Company and its successor, R.G. Dun and Company, at ten-year intervals from 1881 to 1931. This yielded a computerized data base of more than 11 000 businesses.[3] Analysis of the emergence of different types of metropolitan branch businesses offers an opportunity to measure not only urban dominance and control over different economic sectors, but also the actual process of integrating metropolis and hinterland. Moreover, the geographical patterns of branch businesses in the hinterland identify spheres of metropolitan influence.

The rise of branch businesses gained considerable momentum after Confederation. Overall, as figure 1 shows, their numbers increased fourfold, with the most noticeable advance between 1901 and 1921, when they more than doubled from 416 to 950. During this period of branch development, the composite make-up of the region's business structure remained remarkably stable. Manufacturing fell back gradually, its losses absorbed by the retail trades, but the relative share of the other sectors deviated little over the fifty-year period. When the economy of the Maritimes went into serious decline in the 1920s, forcing a net loss of about 1 100 businesses, branch businesses managed to hold firm, and in so doing gained a greater share of all business activities. From the first, branch businesses were prominent in the resource, manufacturing, retailing, and banking sectors, but over time the most appreciable advance occurred in wholesaling and distribution, where Maritime businessmen were steadily eased aside.

This gathering momentum of branch enterprise can also be measured in another way. Most branch businesses are parented by companies of considerable financial strength. In 1931, for example, more than 90 percent of the branch businesses headquartered outside of the Maritimes were backed by companies holding assets of more than $1 000 000. At the same date, less than 2 percent of regional firms, including those managing branch businesses, were similarly financed.

As figure 2 shows, branch businesses based beyond the Maritimes became increasingly prominent over time, commanding a share of less than 10 percent in 1881 and more than 55 percent in 1931. Measured by companies holding assets of more than $1 000 000, the external share increased even more dramatically, from 22 to 79 percent. At the end of the 1920s, nearly half of all branches in the Maritimes traced their chain of command to either Montreal or Toronto; the balance was distributed among more than 400 communities. This was essentially a reversal of the metropolitan pattern that had existed shortly after Confederation, when Saint John and Halifax spawned the majority of the region's branches. In fact, in 1881 Toronto maintained not one branch in the Maritimes, and Montreal only 13. Expanding only slowly throughout the late 19th century, Montreal's presence was more commonplace by the First World War. Many towns and cities established branch businesses in nearby communities at this time, but none could compare to the prominence of this expanding Canadian metropolis. Through a

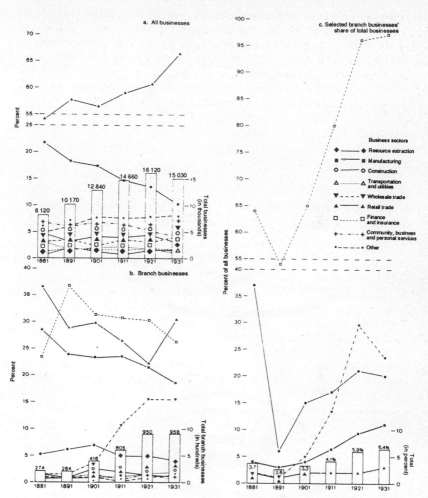

FIGURE 1 Changes in the Business Structure of the Maritimes, 1881–1931

flurry of merger and takeover activity, particularly in the 1890s and early 1900s, Montreal replaced Halifax and Saint John as the dominating metropolitan influence in the Maritimes. But this leadership was soon challenged by Toronto during the 1910s and 1920s. In 1901, Toronto firms had located only nine branches in the region; by 1931, the total was 228, just one less than Montreal. No other urban centres were nearly as competitive, not even American or British cities, and Halifax and Saint John by this time offered only limited competition.

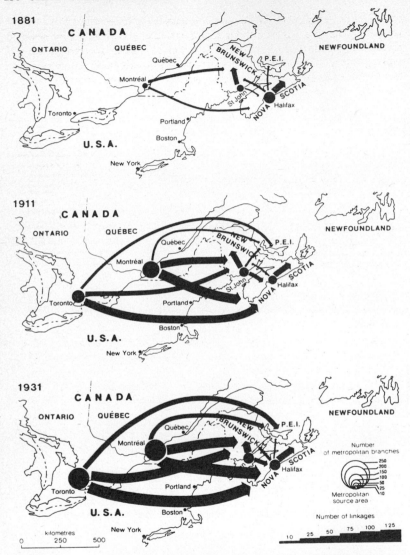

FIGURE 2 Changing Spatial Patterns of Metropolitan Branch Businesses in the Maritimes, 1881–1931

The metropolitan outreach was facilitated by a number of factors, such as the construction of the national railways across the region during the 1870s (Intercolonial) and the 1890s (CPR), but these advances only partially explain the rise of branch businesses in the Maritimes. Metropolitan interests expanded their operations by responding to more specific factors that affected individual business activities.[4] The spread of branch banks, for example, was directly attributable to government policies, including the Bank Act of 1871, that favoured this type of banking system.[5] The metropolitan domination of this sector, in turn, rested with the growth of central Canadian banks on their own terms, and the eventual centralization of Maritime banks either in Montreal or in Toronto.[6] Metropolitan dominance in banking became strongest in the 1910s, when Toronto's banks doubled their branches in the Maritimes (from 63 to 125), challenging strongly the previous and almost complete control of Montreal (figure 3).

Seeking explanations for the metropolitan involvement in the manufacturing industries of the Maritimes is much more complex, but several basic patterns do prevail. First, metropolitan involvement has been restricted to a limited number of industries. Second, unlike the spillover of American industry into southern Ontario and the construction there of branch plants, branch manufacturing in the Maritimes usually grew when central Canadian firms bought out earlier, community-established companies. Typical of hinterland areas, the Maritime industrial base has always been narrowly focused, emphasizing the primary manufacturing of forest, fish, and iron and steel products.[7] Significant shares of these industries fell under metropolitan control after Confederation, either through takeover and merger activity (in fish processing and iron and steel),[8] or by some new plant construction (in pulp and paper).[9] The force of the metropolis in manufacturing was exerted most dramatically in the 1890s and early 1900s through the takeovers and subsequent dismantling of key manufacturing industries, including cotton textiles, rope and cordage, sugar, glass, and paint—almost all by corporations headquartered in Montreal.[10]

Toronto's failure to participate directly in the de-industrialization of the Maritimes might at first seem surprising, especially considering its national prominence in manufacturing, but this is not to say that Toronto failed to influence manufacturing across the region. It did, and in a way that coincided with the rise of the large industrial enterprise that integrated mass production with mass distribution, and with associated changes in managerial organization.[11] Appearing first in the United States during the 1880s, the integrated industrial enterprise made little headway in Canada until after the turn of the century. When it did, however, it was tied inextricably to the American model, and frequently to an American parent company maintaining a Canadian head office in Toronto.

Many Toronto-based enterprises entered the Maritime market not by building manufacturing plants, but by establishing a regional distribution network for their products. This included such industries as food processing (Swift Canadian, Harris Abattoir, and Maple Leaf Milling); agricultural implements (Massey-Harris); business machines (National Cash Register, International Business Machines, and United Typewriter); rubber products (Goodyear and Dunlop); and heavy machinery (Canadian General Electric, Canadian Westinghouse, and Otis Elevator). They appeared mostly in the region's major towns and cities, and accounted for Toronto's rapid surge and dominance in the branch wholesaling sector after 1911

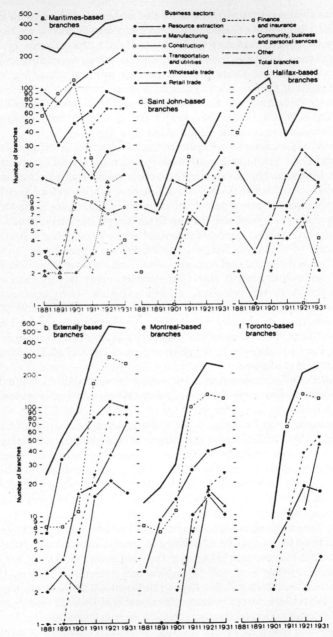

FIGURE 3   Changes in the Types of Metropolitan Branch Businesses in the Maritimes, 1881–1931

(figure 3). Such industries, of course, mirrored the capital-intensive and diversified industrial structure of the Ontario metropolis. By contrast, Montreal's wholesaling advance was more limited, emphasizing its national prominence in labour-intensive manufacturing such as tobacco (Imperial Tobacco) and drugs (National Drug), as well as its traditional import–export function in metals, dry goods, and specialized food products.

The visible hand of management also made its mark on retailing, and the growth of branches in this sector also accelerated Toronto's metropolitan outreach. Small retail shops—grocery and general stores, produce and meat markets—were the most numerous activities in the region's composite business structure. Many faced stiff competition from branches originating within the Maritimes, but external competition was limited until after the First World War. Although Maritimers could order catalogue items from the T. Eaton Company of Toronto by the 1890s, it was not until the 1920s that they were forced to make conscious decisions about shopping in a metropolitan-based store. More favourable freight rates for shipping goods into the region, a growing consumer demand for nationally advertised brands, and the growth of national retail chains, all affected the timing of this metropolitan outreach. As a result, the residents of Halifax, Truro, Sydney, New Glasgow, Moncton, or Saint John could, if they so chose, buy groceries at Dominion, shop for novelty items at a Woolworth or Metropolitan store, look for clothes at Tip Top Tailors, try on shoes at Agnew Surpass, or order all of these items from an outlet of T. Eaton and Company. All of these Canadian and American retail chains were based in Ontario, and except for Agnew Surpass and Metropolitan Stores, all were managed from Toronto head offices. It is difficult to gauge the full impact of these chains, but it is clear that the indigenous retail sector remained largely intact through the 1920s; indeed, there was modest growth in the actual number of local retail businesses (see figure 1). The fullest impact on retailing would not be felt until after the Second World War, when suburban shopping centres actively sought the national chains as their major clientele. This pattern would also coincide with branch expansion in highly specialized service industries such as national advertising agencies, financial counselling companies, and engineering firms.

To ascertain the spheres of influence of the dominant metropolitan centres throughout the Maritimes, the numbers of Halifax, Saint John, Montreal, and Toronto branch businesses located in the region's counties and large urban places were first tallied. Dominant status was then assigned to the metropolitan centre controlling the greatest number of branches in each county or place. If no clear majority existed, where two or more centres shared the same number of branches, the sphere of influence was recorded as overlapping between two or more centres (see figure 4). The results of these analyses for 1881, 1911, and 1931 reveal, rather dramatically, the changing geographical relationships between the Maritimes and central Canada.

Confederation is purported to have seriously undermined the economic development of the Maritimes, but even if this was so, the impact was not seriously felt

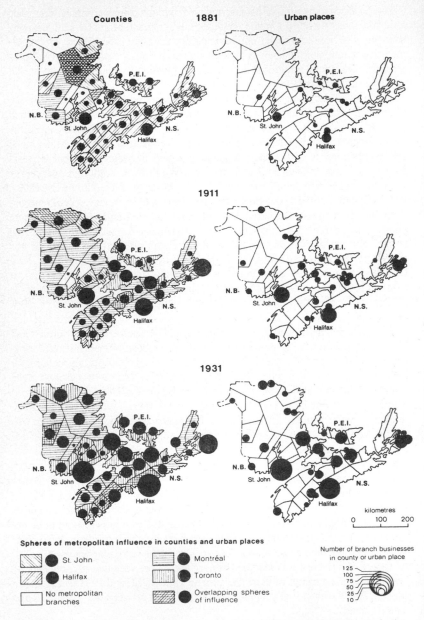

FIGURE 4   Metropolitan Dominance and Spheres of Geographical Influence in the Maritimes, 1881–1931

until early in the 20th century. In 1881, regional autonomy still largely prevailed. The region managed its own banks and its merchants had recently rallied to finance a burst of industrial activity.[12] Halifax dominated all of the Nova Scotia counties, those of Prince Edward Island, and even some in New Brunswick. Most large urban places across the region were linked to the Nova Scotia capital. Montreal shared influence in the New Brunswick countryside with Saint John, whose business people took an active interest in the forest industry. By 1911, however, Montreal had taken over leadership throughout most of Nova Scotia and New Brunswick, largely because of its control of banking, takeovers in manufacturing, and the quest for industrial materials such as Cape Breton coal. Its bankers and industrialists managed a variety of branches in Halifax, Saint John, Fredericton, and lesser places, while its coal companies were the principal employers in Springhill, Westville, Stellarton, Inverness, and Glace Bay. In "Busy Amherst," the 20th ranking industrial town in the country, Montreal companies had gained control of many industries, including the Canadian Car and Foundry Company, one of the largest of its kind in Canada.[13] On the eve of the First World War, therefore, the Maritimes was unmistakably a hinterland to Montreal.

Montreal's dominance is acknowledged by most scholars who have written about the economic development of the Maritimes, but less recognized is the build-up of Toronto's influence over the region.[14] As figure 4 reveals, Toronto in 1931 held complete sway over Prince Edward Island and the important belt of urban and industrial counties in southern New Brunswick and central Nova Scotia, as well as industrial Cape Breton. In fact, Toronto could claim dominance over Montreal and other competing cities in a majority of the region's counties and large urban places. During the 1910s and 1920s, Toronto had beaten out Montreal's leadership in about one-third of these counties and places. Toronto's dominance was based on banking, its considerable interests in wholesale distribution and retail trade, and some manufacturing. In this reshuffling, Montreal continued to hold onto northern New Brunswick, the Annapolis Valley of Nova Scotia, and the coal mining counties outside of industrial Cape Breton. In Montreal's drive for regional hegemony, it had remained largely aloof from the American influence so common in Toronto, but with the development of pulp and paper in northern New Brunswick during the 1920s, Montreal finally also became more active as an intermediary for American corporate enterprise.[15]

Between the post-Confederation period and the Great Depression, the pattern of metropolitanism in the Maritimes was substantially revised at least three times. This reorientation, from a Halifax-centred region, to Montreal's sting, and then to the challenging force of Toronto, coincided with the mercantile–industrial, rural–urban transformation of the region. As the Maritimes shifted away from the Atlantic economy, based on staple trades, and slowly integrated with the emerging continental market, focused on the new industrialism, new alliances took form. These alliances were essentially urban in character; they reveal a changing structure of geographical interdependencies or linkages that is important for interpreting urban dominance and economic growth in the region (figure 5).

Until late in the 19th century, the economy of Maritime towns and cities grew largely by success in the staple trades. Most communities went about these trades independently of each other. When local merchants required extra supplies or capital, they were usually serviced directly from Halifax or Saint John, or through the branch houses of these centres. The new industrialism in time brought increasing interdependence among cities, forging new and deeper links with central Canada. As Montreal gained ascendancy, the numbers of metropolitan branches in urban places became more prominent, and the population growth of these industrial towns became more dependent on externally made decisions. The structure of interdependencies in 1931, however, measures new and stronger alliances focused on Toronto. Indeed, Toronto's remarkable hegemony over all but one of the region's 16 largest urban places in 1931, based largely on tertiary economic activities, forces us to reconsider the basis of urban growth in many places across the region during the 1910s and 1920s.[16]

Many towns and cities lost population during the 1920s—Amherst, Trenton, Westville, Sydney Mines, to cite only a few. But some of those that actually gained population—Moncton, Glace Bay, and Truro, for example—grew, it appears, largely because of changes in the tertiary sector of their economies. Indeed, increased urban employment was frequently the result of newly established branch businesses engaged in the wholesale or retail trades. A case in point is Moncton, which grew from just over 11 000 in 1911, to about 17 500 in 1921, and then to some 20 000 in 1931. In the mid-19th century, Moncton prospered briefly as a shipbuilding centre, only to decline shortly after Confederation.[17] However, with the arrival of the Intercolonial Railway's headquarters, repair shops, and marshalling yards after 1872, and a revitalized economic climate, new industries soon appeared (a sugar refinery, a cotton factory, and a woollen mill). Many of these industries went into decline after 1900, but Moncton's potential as a distribution centre soon attracted another round of growth, this time based on branch businesses in the tertiary sector, chiefly in transportation, wholesaling, financial and insurance activity, and retailing. Massey-Harris made Moncton its Maritimes distribution centre in 1907, and in 1920, the T. Eaton Company opened its mail order house for the Maritime provinces there, employing more than 750 people.[18] Between 1911 and 1931, Moncton's population doubled and its total number of businesses climbed from 248 to 370, but its branch businesses, which now included many of the city's largest employers, increased fourfold, from 11 to 41. Such expansion, nevertheless, did little to lessen the growing interdependence between Maritime centres and the metropolis; on the contrary, urban dominance and interdependence had increased appreciably.

The presence of a metropolitan branch business in a community is evidence of the economic interdependence between metropolis and hinterland. There are other forms of interdependencies, of course, including cultural and political ties, which are implicit in the concept of metropolitanism. But examination of branch businesses, set within the context of the composite business structure of a region, provides a meaningful indication of the interplay between metropolis and

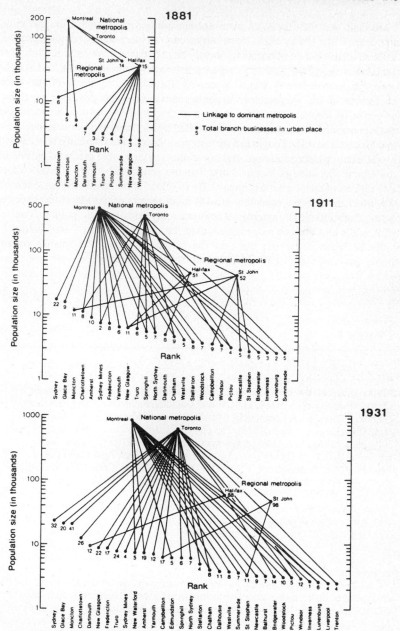

FIGURE 5   Metropolis and Hinterland: Changes in the Structure of Urban Relationships, 1881–1931

hinterland. As the forces of metropolitanism unfolded after Confederation, Maritimers, like all Canadians, were subjected to an increasingly complex array of changes in the sphere of business. Shortly after Confederation, it was likely that Maritimers deposited their accounts in a regionally controlled bank and bought groceries from a locally owned store. At the same time, many of the basic necessities of life—vegetables, furniture, carriages—were produced by themselves or by local craftsmen. By the eve of the Great Depression, however, the savings in their bank accounts were controlled by Montreal and Toronto financiers and groceries could be bought in a metropolitan-based chain store; the new canned foods, mass produced furniture, and horseless carriages, were produced outside of the region. The sting of Montreal and Toronto penetrated deeply into all sectors and regions of the Maritime economy. By the close of the 1920s, the basic stimuli for urban and regional economic growth in all sectors of the Maritime economy were greatly affected by external forces emanating from the metropolis. Of course, Montreal's and Toronto's dominance over the region was also shared indirectly with American enterprise; this was the particular nature of Canadian metropolitanism after the First World War, and it has remained so.[19]

Notes

1. See, for example, J.B. Brebner, *New England's Outpost: Acadia before the British Conquest of Canada* (New York, 1927); J.M.S. Careless, "Aspects of Metropolitanism in Atlantic Canada," in *Regionalism in the Canadian Community*, ed. Mason Wade (Toronto, 1969), 117–29; and David A. Sutherland, "The Merchants of Halifax, 1815–1850: A Commercial Class in Pursuit of Metropolitan Status" (Ph.D. diss., University of Toronto, 1975). The classic Canadian statement on metropolitanism is Careless, "Frontierism, Metropolitanism, and Canadian History," *Canadian Historical Review* 35 (1954): 1–21; but see also N.S.B. Gras, *An Introduction to Economic History* (New York, 1922), 186–240; and L.D. McCann, "The Myth of the Metropolis: The Role of the City in Canadian Regionalism," *Urban History Review* 9 (1981): 52–58.

2. For a recent interpretation of the regional development of the Maritimes, set within the context of metropolis and hinterland, see Graeme Wynn, "The Maritimes: The Geography of Fragmentation and Underdevelopment," in *Heartland and Hinterland: A Geography of Canada*, ed. L.D. McCann (Toronto, 1982), 156–213. Despite his framework of inquiry, Wynn does not focus specifically on the theme of metropolitan dominance.

3. For each business, the following information was recorded: (1) name of company; (2) type of business, coded according to Statistics Canada's *Standard Industrial Classification Manual* (1970); (3) settlement location, including large urban place ($\geq 2\,500$ people), county and province; (4) pecuniary strength; (5) if branch business, location of the headquarters of the company; and (6) product lines, if listed. This information was subjected to various statistical analyses to provide the data reported in the text and used in the maps and diagrams. This paper emphasizes the aggregate changes in the business structure of the Maritimes, focusing attention on the theme of

metropolitan dominance. Data on all branch businesses for all of Canada between 1881 and 1931 have also been collected; they will be the subject of other papers.

4. Branch business development, of course, is one particular strategy related to the growth of the firm. For reviews of this theme which are relevant to an interpretation of the metropolitan outreach, see Alfred Chandler, *Strategy and Structure: The History of the American Industrial Enterprise* (Cambridge, MA, 1962); Lars Hakanson, "Towards a Theory of Location and Corporate Growth," in *Spatial Analysis, Industry, and the Industrial Environment*, ed. F.E. Ian Hamilton and G.J.R. Linge (New York, 1979), 1:115–38; and H.D. Watts, *The Large Industrial Enterprise* (London, 1980).

5. E.P. Neufeld, *The Financial System of Canada* (Toronto, 1972), 81–89, 97–102.

6. The centralization process took place between 1900 and 1920, and was highlighted by the movement of the Bank of Nova Scotia to Toronto (1900) and the Merchants' Bank of Halifax (later the Royal Bank of Canada) to Montreal (1904). Of further significance, the Halifax Banking Company was absorbed by Toronto's Bank of Commerce (1903), The People's Bank of Halifax by the Bank of Montreal (1905), and the Union Bank of Halifax by the Royal (1910); *Annual Financial Review* (1923), 111, 126. See also James Frost, "The 'Nationalization' of the Bank of Nova Scotia, 1880–1910," *Acadiensis* 12, 1 (Autumn 1982): 29–30.

7. R.E. Caves and R. Holton, *The Canadian Economy: Prospect and Retrospect* (Cambridge, MA, 1959), 140–94.

8. Fish processing remained controlled largely from within the region, particularly at Halifax, although the Portland Packing Company of Maine held an important share of the industry before World War I.

9. Donald W. Emmerson, "Pulp and Paper Manufacturing in the Maritimes," *Pulp and Paper Magazine of Canada* (Dec. 1947), 129–55.

10. T.W. Acheson, "The National Policy and the Industrialization of the Maritimes, 1880–1910," *Acadiensis* 1, 2 (Spring 1972): 3–29.

11. Alfred Chandler has written persuasively of a managerial revolution in American business, whereby "The visible hand of managerial direction… replaced the invisible hand of market mechanisms… in coordinating flows and allocating resources in major modern industries." Typical were mass producers of low-priced, semi-perishable, packaged products (e.g., flour and cereals); processors of perishable products for national markets (e.g., meatpacking); manufacturers of new mass-produced machines that required specialized marketing services if they were to be sold in volume (e.g., agricultural implements and business machines); and the makers of high-volume producer goods that were technologically complex but standardized (e.g., electrical equipment). Alfred Chandler, "The United States: Seedbed of Managerial Capitalism," in *Managerial Hierarchies: Comparative Perspectives on the Rise of the Modern Industrial Enterprise*, ed. Chandler and Herman Daems (Cambridge, MA, 1980), 9, 23. See also Chandler, *The Visible Hand* (Cambridge, MA, 1978).

12. The mercantile–industrial transition is treated in L.D. McCann, "Staples and the New Industrialism in the Growth of Post-Confederation Halifax," *Acadiensis* 7, 2 (Spring 1979): 47–79, and "The Mercantile–Industrial Transition in the Metals Towns of Pictou County, 1857–1931," *Acadiensis* 10, 2 (Spring 1981): 29–64.

13. Nolan Reilly, "The General Strike in Amherst, Nova Scotia, 1919," *Acadiensis* 9, 2 (Spring 1980): 56–77.

14. See, for example, T.W. Acheson, "The Maritimes and 'Empire Canada,' " in *Canada and the Burden of Unity*, ed. David Bercuson (Toronto, 1979), 87–114.

15. The development of the pulp and paper industry was led by regional entrepreneurs before the First World War, by American interests in the interwar period, and by a combination of local, American, European, and British Columbian companies after 1960 (Emmerson, "Pulp and Paper").

16. We lack studies of urban growth in the Maritimes during this period, but for one attempt which details data on the population growth of all urban places in Nova Scotia between 1871 and 1931, see McCann, "The Mercantile–Industrial Transition."

17. James Appleton, "The Town of Moncton: A Metropolitan Approach, 1880–1889" (B.A. thesis, Mount Allison University, 1975); and Sheva Medjuck, "Wooden Ships and Iron People: The Lives of the People of Moncton, New Brunswick, 1851–1871" (Ph.D. diss., York University, 1978).

18. Lloyd A. Machum, *A History of Moncton: Town and City, 1885–1965* (Moncton, 1965), 207–281.

19. R. Keith Semple and W. Randy Smith, "Metropolitan Dominance and Foreign Ownership in the Canadian Urban System," *The Canadian Geographer* 25 (1981): 4–26.

CORPORATE CAPITALISM AND THE EMERGENCE OF THE HIGH-RISE OFFICE BUILDING*

GUNTER GAD AND DERYCK HOLDSWORTH

The two most dramatic and distinctive morphological changes in the North American city over the last century have been the horizontal spread of suburbia and the vertical expansion of downtown. Technological explanations have been invoked for both—streetcars, automobiles and freeways for suburbia, and the elevator and the steel frame for the skyscraper—but suburbia has been seen, increasingly, as a product of complex social and economic forces. Assessments of the downtown silhouette have generally been less sophisticated. Strongly influenced by the architectural historian's preoccupation with the exceptional—the most outstanding or tallest buildings of a particular era or a particular place[1]—or by the rather difficult concept of symbolism,[2] they have tended toward particularity. Other explanations have focused on the economics of real estate[3] or agglomeration forces.[4] Gottman answered the question "Why the skyscraper?" by pointing to the ease of communication between many related firms in one place. Although Gottman's argument is brief and lacks evidence that is specific to the time of skyscraper genesis, it addresses an important dimension: the work that is carried out in a building. Similarly, in an essay that is one of the few attempts to synthesize arguments related to symbolism, land values, construction costs, and land availability, Francis Duffy emphasized the changing organization of office work as one of the key determinants of built form (or more broadly of morphology).[5] Most morphological analysis of the inner city's built environment has occurred in a European context,[6] where the problem of how to deal with height has rarely been addressed. In North America, the researcher assessing the changing built form of the downtown area has to confront issues involving the height of buildings. Here we argue that it is sensible to avoid viewing the tall office building

*Urban Geography 8, 3 (1987): 212–31.

simply as a distinct cultural artifact, and to see it as firmly embedded in the specific network of conditions surrounding its first appearance and subsequent development. Perhaps the most important—and so far neglected—set of conditions influencing skyscraper development is based on the specific requirements of firms using office space either as owner-occupiers or renters. So this paper seeks to understand both the broad context of a growing demand for space, and the relationship between that demand and built form.

High-rise buildings (defined as structures with six or more floors) appeared in many North American cities from the end of the 19th century onward. Their early appearance coincided with the initial stages of corporate capitalism and they became larger and more dominant in the urban landscape as corporate capitalism developed fully in the 1920s. Directly or indirectly, several authors have linked the appearance of the skyscraper to the requirements of corporate capitalism,[7] the corporate economy,[8] giant combines,[9] or the concentration of capital.[10] As with other statements on economic development and built form,[11] the precise connection between the two—in the case here, corporate capitalism and the high-rise office building—is not detailed. Most authors just equate big buildings with big corporations. This simple equation neither satisfies our curiosity nor does it accord with our earlier research into the evolution of early twentieth-century central business districts and their office buildings.[12] We need to know which characteristics of corporate capitalism might have affected the nature of office work and thus of space demand and built form.

Factors of Corporate Capitalism Relevant to Built Form

The term "corporate capitalism"—and its variants, the corporate economy,[13] managerial capitalism,[14] or monopoly capitalism[15]—summarizes the emergence of fewer and much larger economic units in some of the older branches of economic activity. These very large firms were often vertically and horizontally integrated, and usually spread across multiple locations. Even if little or no vertical integration was present, as in the case of banking and insurance, large markets resulted in a geographically far-flung organization. The large scale of operation required a high degree of rationalization, the planning of production, and research in order to increase market share. These activities in turn required enormous information flows between the central control unit and other units of the firm, and between the central control unit and the economic and social "environment."

Associated with large-scale operations was the gradual separation of ownership and management. Professional management not only directed day-to-day affairs, but was also increasingly involved in setting the long-term agenda for the firm.[16] The head office became organized into specialized departments, each so large that it became subject to scientific management. The result was the introduction of semi-skilled and cheap labour into the head office—indicated particularly by the sharp relative decline of clerical salaries and the increasing numbers of female clerks.[17]

Generally overlooked is the parallel emergence of a whole set of new small firms, especially so-called business services. Accounting and auditing firms and also advertising agencies could be regarded, as direct results of joint-stock, large-scale corporations.[18] Similarly, the appearance of different kinds of engineering and design consultants may have been associated with the rationalization or planning process.[19] Existing small-scale service firms, such as law firms, credit reporting agencies, and various agencies involved in transportation, may have received a sharp boost due to the new requirements of the corporate economy.

These major features of corporate capitalist organization had several implications for built form. First, one would expect a demand for increasingly large office buildings concordant with the growth of the head offices of big corporations. One could also expect a demand for considerable amounts of space on each floor, given the differentiation of the head office into distinct departments and the task of directing and supervising many interdependent clerical workers within each department. The large scale of operations within the head office and the execution of many tasks by cheap labour also imply concentrated urban form, since the many clerical workers required easy access to these large workplaces. Considerable pressure on key locations in a city may have resulted. Finally, the continued and regenerated presence of many small firms required the supply of many office units with moderate amounts of floor space. These, one can assume, would have had to be in close spatial proximity to facilitate the interdependence of many small, and of small and large, firms. Thus even the presence of small firms may have contributed to intensive land development in a very restricted area of the city.

The Toronto Case Study

Between 1861 and 1891, the population of the City of Toronto grew from 45 000 to over 180 000, and the expansion of its mid-nineteenth-century regional trading facilities and financial services led to the formation of a central business district to the west of the Market and north of the wharfs and railway facilities.[20] During these years, and even more so from the turn of the century to the 1950s, Toronto shared pre-eminence with Montreal as the focus of financial and managerial activity in Canada,[21] and competed with it for national markets and international investment funds. As the city's population tripled in the decades up to the Depression and as its position as a national financial and industrial centre solidified, skyscraper clusters emerged primarily west of the small, nineteenth-century office district (figure 1). The main axis of growth was King Street, the address of nine Canadian bank head offices by 1914.

One measure of the changing morphology of Toronto's "old" business or downtown district[22] is the number of tall and large office buildings erected over

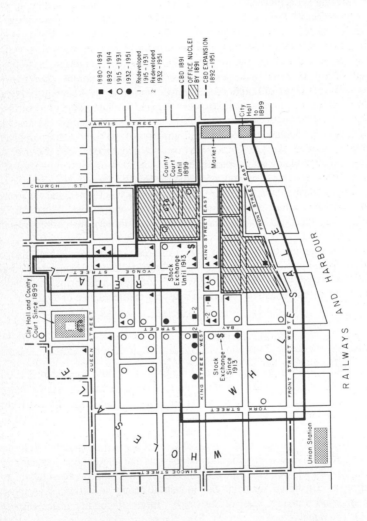

FIGURE 1   Toronto's Downtown District and the Location of Office Buildings with Six or More Floors, 1880–1951

half a century (see tables 1 and 2). In 1891, Toronto's downtown district had four buildings with 6 or more storeys; this increased to 28 by 1914. Between 1914 and 1931, with expansion especially concentrated in the 1920s, the total rose to 49. By 1951, two large office buildings planned in the late 1920s had replaced earlier large office buildings and four additional high-rise structures had brought the number of such buildings to 53. Maps of their distributions show them clustered on King and Yonge streets in 1914. King Street remained the city's most important business address, but by 1930 there was a second, north–south axis of tall buildings along Bay Street. Through this period there was a dramatic increase in the floor space available in large buildings. Buildings were no larger than 75 000 sq. ft. in 1891 and 200 000 sq. ft. in 1914. At the end of the 1920s, the largest building incorporated 450 000 sq. ft. and by 1951 the maximum was 513 000 sq. ft. Yet not all of this expansion was achieved by vertical growth. The largest building of 1951 was 6 storeys lower than that which had the maximum amount of floor space in 1931.

Changes in building height and width affected streetscapes, as continental fads in architecture changed the emphasis first from the horizontal to the vertical[23] and then streamlined and tapered designs in the 1920s.[24] Far more important for understanding the downtown silhouette, however, is the changing use to which these buildings were put.[25]

The Predominance of Small Offices until 1914

Until the First World War, occupancy of large buildings can be portrayed as a finely grained mosaic, composed of many small establishments. The three early large buildings completed by 1890 housed 15, 35, and 51 establishments a year later. Corporate names for the office buildings, such as "Canada Life" and "Canadian Bank of Commerce," had no equivalence in large-scale occupancy by these major companies. Instead, the occupancy mix was dominated by many small establishments, including firms from a wide range of economic sectors; especially numerous were brokers, agents, and branch offices.

A very similar occupancy pattern was present in 1914, even after several buildings with more than 10 floors came into existence (figure 2). Thus the 15-storey Traders Bank Building of 1906 housed 98 establishments by 1914, the Canadian Pacific Railway Building, also with 15 floors, accommodated 53 establishments, and the just-completed Dominion Bank Building (10 floors) was occupied by 37 establishments. Generally, a range of 30 to 100 tenants was typical for the large (about 10–20 floors, 100–200 000 sq. ft.) buildings.

An analysis of the 1914 occupancy mix of the Traders Bank Building shows again the presence of a wide range of firms. There are indications of some functional clusters: groupings of interrelated firms such as mining companies, stock brokers associated with mining companies, mining engineers and geologists, mining contractors, mining machinery suppliers, northern railway companies, and lumber companies with operations on the Canadian Shield. Several other functional clusters in this and further buildings can be identified.

TABLE 1 *Number and Size of Office Buildings With Six or More Floors in the Downtown District of Toronto**

Year	No. of buildings	Max. no. of floors	Max. amount of floorspace
1891	4	7	75 000
1914	28	20	200 000
1931	49	32	450 000
1951	53	32	513 000

*Area bounded by Front, Church, Queen (Albert), and York Streets.

TABLE 2 *Characteristics of the Three Largest Office Buildings Completed in Four Periods of Construction, Downtown District of Toronto*

Period	Name of building	Date of construction	No. of floors	Amount of floorspace (in sq. ft.)
1880–1891	Canada Life	1889–90	7	75 000
	Board of Trade	1889–90	7	50 000
	Canadian Bank of Commerce I	1889–90	7	53 000
1892–1914	Traders Bank	1905–06	15	130 000
	Dominion Bank	1913–14	10	160 000
	Royal Bank	1913–14	20	200 000
1915–1931	Toronto Star	1927–29	22	160 000
	Canada Permanent	1929–31	18	240 000
	Canadian Bank of Commerce II	1929–30	32	450 000
1932–1951	Imperial Bank	1935	7	70 000
	Bank of Montreal	1938–48	17	215 000
	Bank of Nova Scotia	1946–51	26	513 000

Although it is not unproblematic to infer functional linkages, especially face-to-face contacts, from the observation of spatial proximity, the clustering of scores of small establishments around key facilities — such as law firms and mortgage loan companies around courts and registry offices, transportation companies and agencies around the customs house, or stockbrokers around the stock exchange—as well as the close spatial association of the mining-related businesses mentioned above or the appearance in a small set of office buildings of grain, coal, and other bulk commodity dealers near offices of railway companies, all suggest the existence of functional relationships. This inference is strengthened when one observes the rapid spatial shift of the majority of these firms in the wake of the relocation of a key institution or associated businesses.

FIGURE 2   Skyscraper Cluster in Toronto's Downtown District, 1914. Buildings at King and Yonge Streets from left to right: Royal Bank, Canadian Pacific Railway, Traders Bank (partially obscured), and Dominion Bank.

SOURCE: Board of Trade of the City of Toronto, *Year Book* (Toronto: Board of Trade, 1915), 66.

Interlocking directorships are another element of the linkage network. Most directors were local residents and, although involved in the leadership of large firms, they were usually owners of or partners in small firms located in the downtown district. Further evidence is anecdotal. Robert Haig, for instance, quotes a New York businessman who claimed: "The skyscraper facilitates personal contacts in a way never possible before. From my window on the 28th floor of a building in the Times Square district, I can get to practically every person of importance in the architectural and business world in fifteen minutes' time."[26] The eventual move of some businesses away from the spatially narrow cluster to new locations when spatial proximity became redundant (as was the case with the insurance companies discussed later on) is indirect evidence of the importance of face-to-face and other functional linkages.

A striking feature in the occupancy pattern in 1914 is the virtual absence of establishments occupying one or more floors. In each of the dozen largest office buildings, there was only one establishment occupying a whole floor. These were generally banks and insurance companies, with about half a dozen transportation or utility companies forming exceptions. Where then were the corporations or "combines" that corporate capitalism is supposed to have spawned? Especially, where were the large manufacturers? They were present in the Canadian economy, since important conglomerates had been formed in the Canadian merger movement,[27] and there were the first signs of an encroachment by international firms such as Westinghouse, Siemens, and Rolls Royce. In terms of office floor space, however, they were pitifully small, rarely occupying more than half a floor. Most of these had no more than 10 employees, while a few probably had 25 to 50 in downtown Toronto office buildings. Until the mid-1890s, these employees were usually men (see figure 3), but by the early 1910s female clerical workers had started to appear (see figure 4a).

The users of large amounts of office floor space in 1914 were the banks and the insurance companies; the biggest of these, Canada's second largest bank, had an estimated 200 to 300 employees in the combined head-office/Toronto main-branch complex. The other large banks and insurance companies, including Canada's second largest insurance company, had about 100 head-office/main-branch employees. Although the employment record is sketchy, it can be concluded that in Toronto there were maybe two or three office establishments with 150 to 300 employees and perhaps a dozen with 80 to 150 in 1914.

The general lack of large-scale offices is due to a number of factors, including some related to the characteristics of the Canadian economy. First, manufacturers could and did have their head offices at the main plant. Second, Canadian manufacturing was dominated by American and British firms, and there was (and still is) a significant absence of important head-office functions in Canada.[28] Third, Toronto shared high-level business functions with Montreal, and Montreal was the head-office location of important transportation concerns (Canadian Pacific Railway, and later Canadian National Railways), utilities (Bell Canada), and manufacturing companies. Head offices in these sectors were generally lacking or underrepresented in Toronto. Given these circumstances, the leaders in demand for space on a large scale were the Toronto-based banks and insurance companies. Other large occupiers of space emerged in the 1920s, but the banks and insurance companies were spearheading demand for large blocks of office space from before the 1890s and into the post-World War II years. The rapid growth in head-office employment from one or two dozen people in the early 1890s to several hundred by World War II, was accompanied by the formation of distinct departments and the swift increase in the number of female clerical workers. Figure 4, especially when compared to figure 3, illustrates the new gender mix in the office as well as the large scale of individual departments.

The Emergence of Large Space-Users

An investigation of the relationship between corporate growth and corporate space acquisition programs necessitates a dense web of time-series data. Therefore, a case-study approach focusing on two banks and two insurance companies was

FIGURE 3   The Office of the 1890s. Employees of the Union Loan and Savings
Company, Toronto, 1895

SOURCE: Metropolitan Toronto Reference Library, T10493.

chosen. Among the more prominent Toronto-based head offices that had a dynamic history of building development were the Canadian Bank of Commerce, the
Bank of Nova Scotia, Canada Life Assurance, and Manufacturers Life Insurance.
All built large new office buildings during the years we are concerned with here:
the Canadian Bank of Commerce and Canada Life Assurance in 1929–1931, the
Bank of Nova Scotia between 1946 and 1951, and Manufacturers Life Insurance
in 1924–1925. The latter erected a smaller building on a large lot and in a mid-town
location rather than in the downtown district; Canada Life also built outside the
downtown district. In all cases, the picture is one of rapid growth and growing
space needs.

   The Canadian Bank of Commerce grew quickly from a regional to a national
company (table 3). Its 7-storey building of 1890 (figure 5) was filled by 1912 (the
15 tenants of the 1890s had to be displaced). Even then, there was considerable
overspill, necessitating the purchase of adjoining properties and the establishment
of a separate archives building some 5 miles to the west of the downtown
head-office location, in an industrial district.[29] The weekly flow of reports from
branch managers—documenting crop conditions, new settlers, and general
economic indicators, not to mention requests for approvals of loans—meant a large

FIGURE 4A The Feminization of Clerical Work. The Bank of Nova Scotia, Toronto, staff at desks ca. 1950.

SOURCE: The Bank of Nova Scotia Archives.

FIGURE 4B The Large Department. Manufacturers Life Insurance Company, Toronto, Claims Department, 1930s.

SOURCE: Manufacturers Life Insurance Company Archives.

and increasing flow of information into and out of the Toronto head office. Plans for a new head-office building for this expanding operation were being discussed by 1912 and various complaints about crowding are on record. According to the bank's historian, both World War I and high construction costs delayed a new building.[30] Eventually it was constructed between 1929 and 1931 (figure 5). This new 32-storey edifice was not only Toronto's tallest and largest building in terms of floor space but also "the tallest in the British Empire." The bank occupied a massive floor space area—all nine floors of the building's base—and claimed that the rest would be absorbed over the next 50 years by the bank itself.[31] In the meantime, the Canadian Bank of Commerce attracted a number of prestigious tenants, several of which rented a floor each and in the process adjusted their own space requirements, from cramped offices in earlier buildings. Gradually the Bank percolated upwards to satisfy its need for space, while several upper-floor tenants (especially legal and resource extraction firms) organized their growing office labour force in clusters of adjacent floors. By 1972, the Bank had overflowed its 1931 building and erected a 57-storey tower on an adjacent site. (Further space problems were solved by a massive back office decentralization in the early 1980s.)

The Bank of Nova Scotia completed its first office building in Toronto in 1904 (figure 6), after moving its important decision-making staff from Halifax to Toronto in 1900. It was a small 3-storey building, dominated by a showy banking hall. A 6-storey addition at the rear was soon needed when the Bank of Nova Scotia also expanded from a regional to a national financial institution (table 3). The staff at the head office (without the main branch) grew from 27 in 1910 to 43 in 1913 and 175 in 1924.[32] While the head-office personnel were divided into only five small groups in 1910 (general office, accountants, inspectors, adjustment, and staff offices), an organization with some 11 departments, including those concerned with investments, "statistical" information (economic intelligence), new

TABLE 3 *The Development of National Banking Systems: Regional Branch Distribution of Two Toronto-Based Companies*

	Western Canada	Ontario	Quebec	Maritimes	Total
The Canadian Bank of Commerce					
1891	—	41	1	—	43
1916	175	89	81	23	368
1931	284	317	70	32	803
The Bank of Nova Scotia					
1891	—	—	1	27	28
1916	14	64	10	70	158
1931	50	134	23	84	291

SOURCES: N.S. Garland, ed., *Garland's Banks, Bankers and Banking in Canada* (Ottawa: Mortimer, 1890), 22, 23; Canada, *Canada Year Book 1916–17* (Ottawa: Government of Canada, 1917), 555; and Canada, *Canada Year Book, 1932* (Ottawa: Government of Canada, 1932), 776.

FIGURE 5   The Canadian Bank of Commerce Head Office Buildings, Toronto, King Street West. Left, building of 1890; right, building completed 1931.

SOURCE: Canadian Imperial Bank of Commerce Archives.

business development, and foreign banking, had emerged by 1931.[33] By 1911, the stationery and printing departments were formed and "decentralized" to a factory area one mile from the head office. There were complaints about space by the early 1920s.[34] A plan and drawings for a new building were ready by 1929, but the Depression and World War II delayed its construction. In 1951, the new 26-storey building was completed (figure 6) with the bank at first taking only 8 floors.[35] By the late 1970s, the bank filled the structure; several departments were in other downtown office buildings and large suburban data centres complemented the downtown facilities.

In the case of the Canada Life Assurance Company, the 1890s building (7 floors, 75 000 sq. ft.) was gradually filled by the firm's head office, and other tenants were displaced. By the early 1920s, Canada Life occupied almost the whole structure and the head office had spilled over into four other buildings. The response to the accommodation problem was an 11-storey structure incorporating 300 000 sq. ft. of floor space. In comparison to the majority of buildings erected in the 1920–1931 period, the Canada Life Building was low and squat. It was also located six blocks or a half mile away from its old head office in the downtown district. With a new

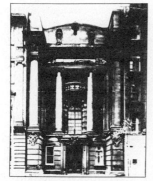

FIGURE 6   The Bank of Nova Scotia Head Office Buildings, Toronto, King Street West. Left, building completed 1904; right, building completed 1951.

SOURCE: The Bank of Nova Scotia Archives.

location outside the downtown district, in an area still dominated by wooden buildings, factory chimneys, and some mansions set in spacious grounds, the company also adopted a setting in a large "landscaped" lot. Departmental organization had developed strongly from the 1910s onward, reflected to some extent in the city directories through the full-floor occupancy by the "stenographers" department and partial floors occupied by several other departments. The new building better reflected this departmental organization with large floors for rows and rows of clerical stations. At the time of the relocation in 1931, the Canada Life head office consisted of 626 people,[36] who occupied about half of the space in the new building. Gradually, it filled with Canada Life head-office employees, who accounted for two-thirds of the building's 1 400 workers by 1961,[37] and in 1972 a rear extension of nine floors was necessary to accommodate further head-office growth.

The Manufacturers Life Insurance Company, the fourth example, seems to have had continuous severe space problems, reflected in five moves from one rented quarter to another, all within the downtown district. Employment grew from 43 in 1901 to 105 in 1916,[38] when the head office occupied one and a half floors in the recently completed 10-storey Dominion Bank Building (right in figure 2). Further employment growth to 200 by 1921[39] was met by the leasing of more rooms on two other floors in the Dominion Bank Building and by overspill into other buildings.[40] Eventually, a new building was planned in the early 1920s. Rather than a tall edifice in the downtown district or very close to it, Manufacturers Life built a 6-storey structure in large grounds in Toronto's mid-town area, nearly 2 miles from its previous head-office location (figure 7); this relocation signaled the beginning of "mid-town" office development[41] or "proto-suburbanization." The size of the head-office staff continued to grow rapidly after the move. By the end of the 1920s, the building (used solely by Manufacturers Life) housed 445 people, and eventually there were three major lateral expansions on the company's large site, one in 1953, another one in 1967, and the latest in 1984 (see figure 7).

The examples of these four rapidly growing head offices indicate that two responses to the space dilemma were possible: either to hoard space in a towering structure downtown or to hoard land in a less expensive location outside of the intensively developed downtown district. The possibility of taking advantage of

FIGURE 7 Buildings of Manufacturers Life Insurance, Toronto, Bloor Street East, ca. 1970. Foreground: first phase, 1925; left rear: addition of 1953; right: addition of 1967.

SOURCE: Manufacturers Life Insurance Company Archives.

these cheaper sites depended presumably on the changing operating characteristics of life insurance companies. The growth in business led to the development of life insurance policies as standardized mass products. In turn, the old linkage system of the downtown district fell apart, primarily due to the removal of directors and even top managers from the day-to-day conduct of business. Many linkages were now conducted over channels suitable for the transmission of high-volume and yet low-quality information (mail, messengers, telephone). At the same time, standardization of the product and rationalization of the production process allowed the adoption of low-wage labour. Large departments on single floors are one expression of this new form of production. A location outside of the high land-value core yet close to it in order to be accessible to the labour force is another aspect.

Speculative Towers and Other Large Buildings

Throughout the study period, other tall office buildings were constructed in the downtown district. Sometimes they were built for the head-office purposes of major companies, but initially these corporations only occupied a very small proportion of the total space. Presumably these companies knew it would be only in the very distant future that they would occupy a substantial part of their buildings. However, they gained important visibility and imageability, in addition to generating revenues by leasing space. Good examples include the Canada Permanent Mortgage Company in its move to an 18-storey tower in 1931, even though it only occupied one floor for several decades,[42] and the Excelsior Life Insurance Company, which made four moves between smaller office blocks before building an 11-storey structure in 1916—in which it consumed but one floor by 1922. Yet the building gave the impression that Excelsior Life was as important as Canada Life, a company that had more than 10 times the assets of Excelsior.

Another set of tall buildings, particularly those of the 1920s generation, were "purely speculative" office buildings that were mostly occupied by a myriad of small and medium-sized establishments. On Bay Street, the "development frontier" at the western edge of the Central Business District (CBD) during the 1920s, 10 buildings of 10 storeys or more were built or begun by 1929, not one of which had a large corporation dominating its occupancy profiles. Nevertheless, these too are a facet of urban development under corporate capitalism: continuation of demand by small firms or small offices of big firms. Proximity to stock exchanges and the law courts were probably important considerations, given the predominance of legal and brokerage firms on many floors.

A third group of buildings can be categorized as public-sector office buildings. In Toronto, three noticeable consumers of custom-built office space were the Hydro-Electric Power Commission of Ontario (with a 6-storey building of 1914 and an adjacent building of 17 floors constructed in two phases during the 1930s and 40s); Toronto Hydro (9 storeys); and the Government of Ontario. By the late 1920s, a significant increase in the provincial government civil service had led to the construction of the East Block of the Provincial Legislative Building, in the form of a large 7-storey base, topped by an additional 10-floor tower, the whole comprising some 250 000 sq. ft. Like the two insurance companies discussed in detail, all three buildings occupied sites peripheral to the downtown district. The distinct public mandates of the organizations they accommodated meant that they needed neither to attract short-term tenants for speculative revenue nor to take advantage of the close proximity sought by the firms staying in the spatially confined downtown or "old" business district.

Conclusions

Looking inside tall office buildings in Toronto suggests that there were two periods of distinctive occupancy characteristics. First, these buildings were occupied by many small establishments up to 1914, and, then, from the 1920s onwards, continual demand by many small establishments was accompanied by rapidly growing, very large space-users. There would appear to be two major demand reasons for the development of large office buildings. Until the period of the First World War, the impetus for large buildings did not stem from the demands of large head offices but rather from the requirements of many small to medium-size offices, most probably relying on close spatial proximity due to their highly interrelated functions. While demand by many small establishments continued, since the late 1910s a second demand component made itself felt. The rapidly growing major corporations, in the case of Toronto mostly banks and insurance companies, required large amounts of floor space—and in addition to their immediate requirements, they planned space for future expansion. If, for reasons of business linkages and accessibility to labour these head offices required downtown locations, only tall structures may have been possible on expensive land. If, however, an intricate business linkage network was absent and when labour inputs became increasingly standardized, medium-rise head-office buildings in locations peripheral to the downtown district became possible.

It can safely be expected that further studies focusing on the occupancy of large buildings in other cities will reveal similar patterns. A detailed scrutiny of city directories covering the years 1890–1930 for Montreal, Winnipeg, and Vancouver, and a cursory reading of the 1930s and 1940s directories for Detroit and Cleveland, point to a parallel use of large office buildings by a few large and very many small establishments. Additional work should focus on determinants of built form touched on here but not fully explored, especially land values, land ownership (and possibilities or obstacles regarding lot consolidation), functional linkages, and accessibility for labour. Although these dimensions may be governed to some extent by "independent" forces, they are not independent of demand or of the operating characteristics of offices at a specific time. Land values, for instance, are not only the result of transportation technology but are also due to demand for agglomerative advantages and/or easy access to the office labour force, the ability of the latter to reach offices being dependent in turn on the wage structure and other characteristics of the companies attempting to find space. The move of insurance companies out of the downtown district, especially the Manufacturers Life Insurance case discussed here, is illustrative of the changing conditions and the possibility to substitute land for a large amount of floor space on a small lot. Building density and built form thus are linked to demand characteristics on several levels of mediation.

A further discussion of demand factors and other factors derived from these does not rule out a consideration of technological and political-institutional forces, or the symbolic content of the high-rise form of these offices. Bylaws restricting height were used in Toronto and elsewhere with varying success,[43] the adoption of the telephone played a role in making some face-to-face linkages redundant, and height, among other architectural symbols, was certainly used to communicate the advent of a new economic system.[44] Further studies of the high-rise office building will have to rely on a synthesis of these principal factors.

The study presented here and future work on the emergence of high-rise office buildings are necessary elements in attempts to link broad economic and social change with the emerging built environment. In all morphological studies, it is not sufficient only to juxtapose the two; rather it is necessary and rewarding to uncover the detailed and yet important connections.

Notes

1. See, for example, Carl W. Condit, *The Chicago School of Architecture: A History of Commercial and Public Buildings in the Chicago Area, 1875–1925* (Chicago: University of Chicago Press, 1964); Winston Weisman, "A New View of Skyscraper History," in *The Rise of an American Architecture*, ed. Edgard Kaufmann (London: Pall Mall, 1970), 115–62; and William H. Jordy, *American Buildings and Their Architects: Progressive and Academic Ideals at the Turn of the Twentieth Century* (New York: Doubleday, 1972).

2. Thomas Bender and William R. Taylor, "Culture and Architecture: Some Aesthetic Tensions in the Shaping of Modern New York City," in *Visions of the Modern City: Essays on History, Art and Literature*, ed. William Sharpe and Leonard Wallcock (New York: Columbia University Press, 1983), 185–215.

3. See, for example, W.C. Clark and J.L. Kingston, *The Skyscraper: A Study in the Economic Height of Modern Office Buildings* (New York: American Institute of Steel Construction, 1930); and George B. Ford, *Building Height, Bulk and Form* (Cambridge, MA: Harvard City Planning Studies II, 1931).

4. Jean Gottman, "Why the Skyscraper?" *Geographical Review* 20 (1958): 190–212.

5. Francis Duffy, "Office Buildings and Organizational Change," in *Buildings and Society: Essays on the Social Development of the Built Environment*, ed. Anthony D. King (London: Routledge and Kegan Paul, 1980), 255–82.

6. See, for example, M.R.G. Conzen, *Alnwick, Northumberland: A Study in Town*

Plan Analysis, Institute of British Geographers publication no. 27 (London: Institute of British Geographers, 1960); Conzen, "The Plan Analysis of an English City Centre," reprinted in *The Urban Landscape: Historical Development and Management, Papers by M.R.G. Conzen*, ed. Jeremy W.R. Whitehand (London: Academic Press, 1962), 25–53; and Jeremy W.R. Whitehand, "Commercial Townscapes in the Making," *Journal of Historical Geography* 10 (1984): 174–200.

7.   David M. Gordon, "Capitalist Development and the History of American Cities," in *Marxism and the Metropolis: New Perspectives in Urban Political Economy*, ed. William K. Tabb and Larry Sawers (New York: Oxford University Press, 1978), 53, 93.

8.   Leslie Hannah, *The Rise of the Corporate Economy*, 2nd ed. (London: Methuen, 1983), 116

9.   Christopher Tunnard and Henry H. Reid, *American Skyline* (Boston: Houghton Mifflin, 1953), 118.

10.   François Lamarche, "Property Development and the Economic Foundations of the Urban Question," in *Urban Sociology: Critical Essays*, ed. C.G. Pickvance (London: Tavistock, 1976), 98

11.   Jeremy W.R. Whitehand, "Land-Use Structure, Built Form and Agents of Change," in *The Future of the Central Core* (London: Institute of British Geographers, 1983), 42–43.

12.   Gunter H.K. Gad and Deryck Holdsworth, "Building for City, Region and Nation: Offices in Toronto, 1834–1984," in *Forging a Consensus: Essays on Historical Toronto*, ed. Victor L. Russell (Toronto: University of Toronto Press, 1984), 272–321; and Gad and Holdsworth, "Large Office Buildings and Their Changing Occupancy, King Street, Toronto, 1880–1950," *Bulletin, Society for the Study of Architecture in Canada* 10 (1985): 19–26.

13.   Hannah, *Rise of the Corporate Economy*.

14.   Alfred D. Chandler, *The Visible Hand: The Managerial Revolution in American Business* (Cambridge, MA: Belknap, 1977).

15.   Paul A. Baran and Paul M. Sweezy, *Monopoly Capitalism: An Essay on the American Economic and Social Order* (New York: Monthly Review Press, 1966).

16.   Sidney Pollard, *The Genesis of Modern Management* (London: Penguin, 1965), 127–85.

17.   Harry Braverman, *Labor and Monopoly Capital: The Degradation of Work in the Twentieth Century* (New York: Monthly Review Press, 1974), 296–98; and Graham S. Lowe, *Women in the Administrative Revolution: The Feminization of Clerical Work* (Toronto: University of Toronto Press, 1987), 222.

18.   Braverman, *Labor and Monopoly Capital*, 304.

19.   David F. Noble, *America by Design: Science, Technology, and the Rise of Corporate Capitalism* (New York: Knopf, 1977), 124–25.

20.   Gad and Holdsworth, "Building for City, Region and Nation," 277–91.

21.   Donald P. Kerr, "Metropolitan Dominance in Canada," in *Canada: A Geographical Interpretation*, ed. John Warkentin (Toronto: Methuen, 1968), 531–55.

22.   Downtown district or "old" business district refers to the area primarily occupied by CBD land uses such as retail, wholesale, and offices by 1951. Since the 1890s, government offices and other offices mostly related to final consumer demand such as medical offices had appeared outside of the downtown district. The density of CBD land uses outside the downtown district, however, was low and the few office buildings were found amid houses, apartments, factories, schools, or university buildings. Only after 1951 did office development in this mid-town district develop to the extent that it could be considered as part of the CBD. The "new" CBD is one that incorporates both these formerly peripheral zones and the "old" business or downtown district, in which

many of the buildings of 1891–1951 discussed in this paper were redeveloped with office structures of up to 72 floors.

23. Bender and Taylor, "Culture and Architecture."

24. Manfredo Tafuri, "The Disenchanted Mountain: The Skyscraper and the City," in Giorgio Guicci, Francesco Dal Co, Mario Manieri-Elia, and Manfredo Tafuri, *The American City: From the Civil War to the New Deal* (London: Granada, 1980), 389–483.

25. The clearest indicators of demand are employment growth figures and the detailed organization of the growing numbers of office employees within the buildings. Unfortunately, employment data and detailed descriptions of the changing deployment of the office workers by rooms and floors are largely lost. It is possible, however, to analyse the ways in which demand was met: occupancy by floor and/or room is documented in city directories and municipal property tax assessment records (Gad and Holdsworth, "Looking inside the Skyscraper: The Measurement of Building Size and Occupancy of Toronto Office Buildings, 1880–1950," *Urban History Review/Revue d'histoire urbaine* 16, 2 (1987): 176–89).

26. Robert M. Haig, "Towards an Understanding of the Metropolis," *Quarterly Journal of Economics* 40 (1926): 427.

27. R.C. Brown and Ramsay Cook, *Canada 1896–1921: A Nation Transformed* (Toronto: McClelland and Stewart, 1974), 90–94; and Ernest A. Epp, "Cooperation among Capitalists: The Canadian Merger Movement" (Ph.D. diss., Johns Hopkins University, 1973).

28. R. Keith Semple and W. Randy Smith, "Metropolitan Dominance and Foreign Corporate Ownership in the Canadian Urban System," *Canadian Geographer* 25 (1981): 4–26; and Deryck W. Holdsworth, "Dependence, Diversity, and the Canadian Identity," *Journal of Geography* 83 (1984): 199–204.

29. Victor Ross, *A History of the Canadian Bank of Commerce* (Toronto: Oxford University Press, 1922), 2:497–505.

30. Ibid., 351.

31. Duncan Donald, "The Why and Wherefore of the New H.O. Building," *The Caduceus: Staff Magazine of the Canadian Bank of Commerce* 2, 1 (1930): 21–22; and Anne M. Logan, *From Tent to Tower* (Toronto: Logan, 1974), 62–63.

32. Neil Quigley, "Bank Credit and the Structure of the Canadian Space Economy, c. 1890–1935" (Ph.D. diss., Department of Geography, University of Toronto, 1986), 177.

33. Joseph Schull and J. Douglas Gibson, *The Scotiabank Story: A History of the Bank of Nova Scotia, 1832–1982* (Toronto: Macmillan, 1982), 148–52; and Quigley, "Bank Credit," 175–222.

34. Schull and Gibson, *The Scotiabank Story*, 192–93.

35. A.S. Mather, "The Bank of Nova Scotia," *Journal of the Royal Architectural Institute of Canada* 28 (1951): 317–37.

36. Canada Life Assurance, *Since 1847: The Canada Life Story* (Toronto: Canada Life Assurance, 1967), 34.

37. Canada Life Assurance, *Toronto Landmark Celebrates Silver Jubilee* (Toronto: Canada Life Assurance Archives, c. 1956).

38. Manufacturers Life Insurance, *Annual Salary Lists, 1893–1936* (Toronto: Manufacturers Life Insurance Archives, n. d.).

39. Ibid.

40. Manufacturers Life Insurance, *The First Sixty Years: A History of the Manufacturers Life Insurance Company* (Toronto: Manufacturers Life Insurance, 1947), 78.

41. Gunter H.K. Gad, "Die Dynamik der Burostandorte: Drei Phasen der Forschung," *Munchner Geographische Hefte* 50 (1983): 29–59.

42. Basil Skodyn, *The Permanent Story* (Toronto: Canada Permanent, 1980).

43. Gad and Holdsworth, "Building for City, Region and Nation," 307.

44. Ibid., 300.

BUILDING "SELF-RESPECT AND HOPEFULNESS": THE DEVELOPMENT OF BLUE-COLLAR SUBURBS IN EARLY VANCOUVER*

DONNA MCCRIRICK AND GRAEME WYNN

In April 1886, Granville Townsite, one of three sawmill settlements on Burrard Inlet established in the mid-1860s, was incorporated as the City of Vancouver. Thirteen months later, the Canadian Pacific Railway's first transcontinental train reached the city.[1] For almost a decade, migration, new transportation and service functions, and an active land market fuelled economic expansion and urban growth. Development slowed during the economically depressed years of the mid-1890s, but the Klondike gold rush of 1897–98, mining development in the Kootenay Mountains of British Columbia, and the growing market for lumber created by Prairie settlement, brought new prosperity by the end of the century. In 1900, Vancouver's commercial and wholesale functions were firmly established and the city had replaced Victoria as the provincial centre of banking, trade, and transportation.[2]

The city grew steadily, but not remarkably, until 1905. Then the promise of improved waterborne access to markets in eastern North America and Europe via Panama, a swelling migration from central and eastern Canada, heavy immigration from Britain, and much smaller influxes of people from continental Europe and Asia, produced unparalled growth in the city. Between 1906 and 1911, Vancouver's population rose from almost 50 000 to over 100 000. There was an extravagant land boom in the city. Building construction surged. Large new buildings—two of them proclaimed, in turn, the tallest of their day in the British Empire—were built in the city centre. Industrial activity expanded along the

---

* This paper was written for this volume by Graeme Wynn, based on research reported in Donna McCririck, "Opportunity and the Workingman: A Study of Land Accessibility and the Growth of Blue Collar Suburbs in Early Vancouver" (M.A. thesis, University of British Columbia, 1981), and reviewed in draft form by Ms. McCririck.

Burrard Inlet waterfront and around False Creek. New homes spread east and south of the city core.[3] By 1914, Vancouver's metropolitan functions were well established and its suburbs were open, if not yet filled.

The new city on the Pacific was strikingly distinct from the overcrowded, often squalid industrial cities of Britain which Charles Dickens described as so many "Coketowns."[4] Vancouver was also very different from the older cities of eastern North America. Created almost overnight, it had virtually no aged, run-down housing. Soon it was widely known as "the city of homes." The city spread rapidly away from its centre, and by 1914 its suburbs ran across some 75 to 80 square kilometres. Real estate development seemed to dominate the Vancouver economy, as eastern Canadian cities reported acute shortages of reasonably priced accommodation. In Montreal and Toronto, the price of urban land rose and tenancy rates increased. When four in every five Montreal families were said to be renters, the forest that surrounded Vancouver was opened for settlement and clusters of wood-frame cottages rose over the rough-cleared landscape between Burrard Inlet and the Fraser River.[5] By one account, early twentieth-century Vancouver led all major Canadian cities "in the proportion of people employed in the building trades and in loan, trust and real estate companies as brokers and clerks." [6]

To contemporaries, the process of suburban growth appeared remarkable, profitable, and chaotic. None could deny its contribution to the dramatic transformation of the urban fabric. By 1913, Vancouver evinced a thoroughly modern morphology. New immigrant groups from the Orient and eastern Europe had moved into modest housing on the fringe of the city centre; new suburbs grew on the periphery of an expanding core; urban space was differentiated by function and by the ethnicity and socio-economic status of its inhabitants.

Clear enough in broad outline, this transformation was an enormously complex process in detail. It affected different areas, groups, and individuals in the city in countless ways. Still, most recent studies of the city have followed contemporary rhetoric in seeing Vancouver as a place of economic opportunity for every man and woman, although the experiences of working people in the early city have received little scrutiny. Nor have there been any detailed studies of suburban land development which might throw light on the extent to which a frenetic land market opened the door to property ownership among those at the lower end of Vancouver's economic spectrum.[7] This study explores these questions, and illuminates the nature of residential expansion on the periphery of rapidly growing early twentieth-century cities by considering the patterns and processes of development in Hillcrest and Grandview, two of the several working-class suburbs of Vancouver opened up in the years before 1914 (figure 1).

Hillcrest

At the turn of the twentieth century, Hillcrest was a semi-rural area with scattered clusters of working people's homes, southeast of the Vancouver city core. It adjoined the city boundary on 16th Avenue, extended a kilometre or so to the south, and was approximately twice as extensive east and west. The southern part of this area lay in the municipality of South Vancouver, but the northern half, known as D.L. 301, remained under provincial jurisdiction until annexation to the city in 1911.

Owned by the wealthy New Westminster merchant, Henry Edmonds, D.L. 301 was subdivided in 1890, at the same time that Edmonds incorporated the Westminster and Vancouver Tramway Company. The company's interurban line would serve the district a year later.[8] Initially, Edmonds offered about 60 percent of the lots in the district for sale. Most of the remainder were reserved for himself and a few business associates. They included almost all of the land along the tramway line and the main road through the district. Lots that followed Westminster Avenue in a two-block wide strip occupied the highest ground in the district, possessed sweeping mountain views, and constituted the best residential land in the area.[9]

Land sales were relatively slow in the early 1890s but by the end of 1896, approximately half the district was owned by the English-based Bank of British Columbia. It had taken title to properties lodged as securities for earlier loans, on which payments had not been met during the economic downturn of the preceding years.[10] Edmonds retained about 15 percent of the district's land in his own name and through his real estate firm, Edmonds and Webster. The remaining quarter of the district was owned by a handful of settlers and small investors. The latter typically held between six lots and a full block each. Only in the northwest corner of D.L. 301—that part of the district nearest to Vancouver—had much district land

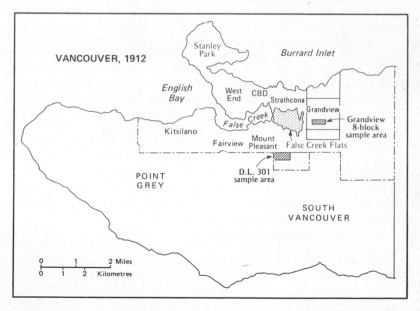

FIGURE 1

passed to those who might properly be called suburban settlers. There, between fifty and sixty landowners held one or two lots each.

Five years later, in 1901, the Yorkshire Guarantee and Securities Corporation took over all of Edmonds' property in the district. Two years later, it acquired a large part of the Bank of British Columbia's holdings in the area. This gave the corporation title to more than a quarter of the district's 127 blocks. Co-incidentally, it acquired a major financial interest in Edmonds' former tramway company.[11] A further 40 to 45 percent of the land in the district was divided about equally among the B.C. Land and Investment Agency and two private investors, Vancouver financier J.W. Horne and James Adams, a Vancouver wholesaler. Their holdings were spread throughout the district. The rest of D.L. 301 was in the hands of small investors and a growing but still limited group of settlers. The thirty or so city blocks of land owned by this group were divided in almost equal proportions among six or fewer property owners, seven to twelve owners, and more than a dozen owners. Approximately 30 percent of these owners appear to have lived on their land.[12] Residents of the district were largely blue-collar workers and, to a lesser extent, small farmers and market gardeners.

Ownership patterns changed substantially in the five years after 1904. In 1910, James Adams was the only large landowner remaining; he held eight blocks. A dozen others owned entire blocks or substantial parts thereof, but most lots in the district were owned individually. Forty percent of ratepayers resided in the area, and the proportion of residents in agricultural occupations had declined. There were more white-collar workers and small business people than in 1904, but about two-thirds of those residents for whom occupations are known were blue-collar workers.

Quite what these changes meant in terms of patterns on the ground is best revealed by closer investigation of land ownership in a fifteen-block sample area in the northwestern corner of D.L. 301 between 1897 and 1910 (figure 2). In 1897, major landowners, in descending order, were: the Bank of British Columbia; Edmonds and Webster; J.W. Horne; and a teamster and a retired logger from the neighbouring suburb of Mount Pleasant, each of whom held one block. The remaining 48 lots belonged to small investors living in the city, and in a few cases outside the province. Only three property owners actually lived in the area.

By 1904, Edmonds and Webster's lands had passed to the Yorkshire Guarantee and Securities Corporation, and the Bank of British Columbia had sold its holdings to five city businessmen. Responding to the rising demand for suburban property, J.W. Horne had sold off a block of his land. Settlement was still very sparse, and buildings stood on fewer than 10 percent of the lots.

In 1910, the last year for which assessment rolls are available, James Adams was the sole large property owner in the area. Most ratepayers owned single lots, almost all of them either 25 or 33 feet in width. A minority held two or three lots of similar size. A few shared title to a single lot. Yet into the second year of Vancouver's land boom, over two-thirds of this centrally located suburb remained undeveloped, and the area was recalled by one resident as "a wild place very sparsely settled up."[13]

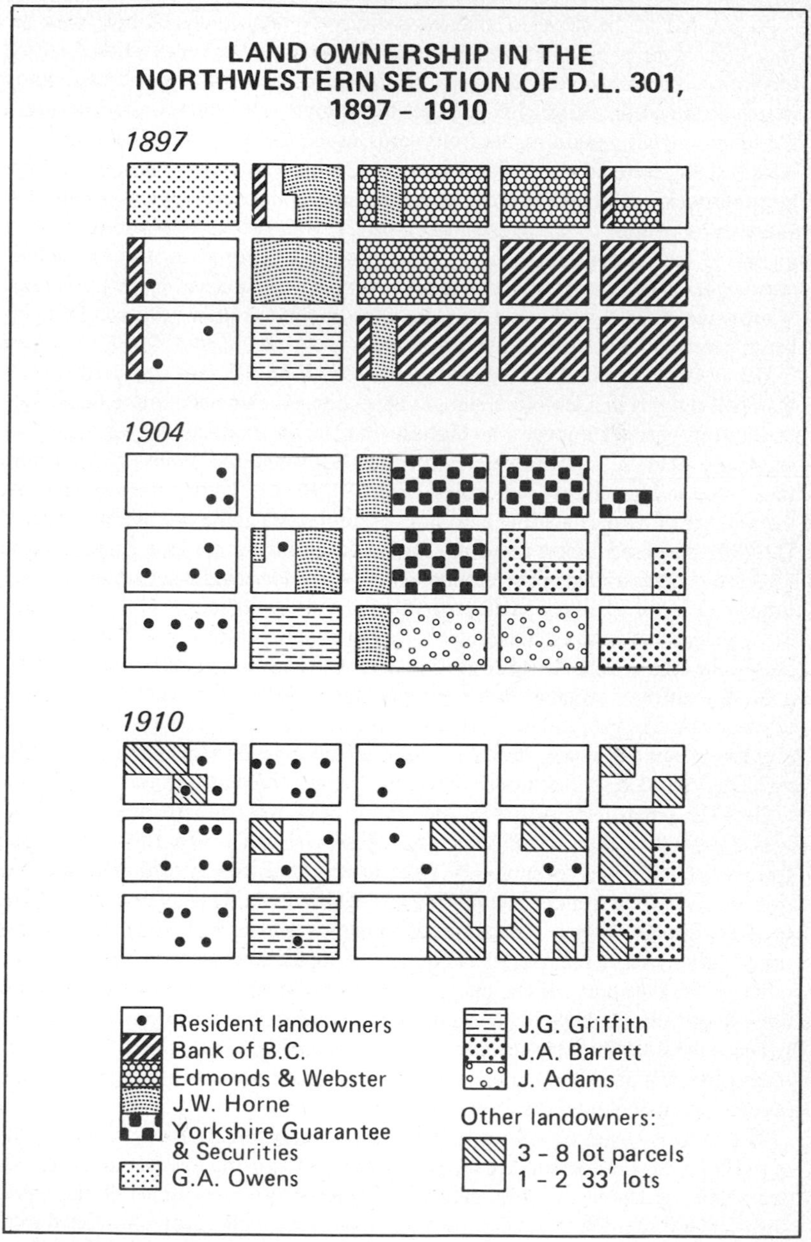

LAND OWNERSHIP IN THE NORTHWESTERN SECTION OF D.L. 301, 1897 – 1910

1897

1904

1910

Resident landowners
Bank of B.C.
Edmonds & Webster
J.W. Horne
Yorkshire Guarantee & Securities
G.A. Owens

J.G. Griffith
J.A. Barrett
J. Adams

Other landowners:
3 – 8 lot parcels
1 – 2 33' lots

FIGURE 2

At the end of the decade, Hillcrest roads were neither graded nor, with the exception of the two main streets in the area, paved. In the centre of the district, blocks were commonly divided into 25-foot lots, upon which stood two-storey houses to the north, and smaller cottages to the south. The setback of houses from the street was fairly uniform, but front yards, especially on those lots where larger houses stood, were minuscule, and most back yards were little larger. The present housing stock in Hillcrest suggests that most residential development occurred in short strips of four to six houses, interspersed with blocks or partial blocks of uncleared lots. Among the houses that survive today, common features include narrow, steep, front steps, above-ground basements, and attics in the larger houses. Narrow wood siding and wood shingles were popular exterior cover, and gingerbread trim was favoured by some owners.

Between 1897 and 1910, land turnover rates in D.L. 301 were moderate. Fewer than half the lots in a ten-block sample area changed ownership more than twice in fourteen years. Turnover was highest (four to six transactions) for those lots originally held by land brokers (including Edmonds and Webster, Yorkshire Guarantee and Securities Corporation, and J.W. Horne). During the same period, the number of owners holding land in the sample area at the northwest corner of D.L. 301 increased almost five-fold. On the face of it, such a broadening of land ownership suggests that opportunities for individuals to acquire suburban property improved. Yet a relatively small proportion of those who bought Hillcrest land in these years settled upon it immediately. In the decade before World War I, a large part of the district was owned by non-residents. According to assessment records, 3 of 35 owners of property in the sample area in 1897 lived there. In 1904, the figures were 15 of 48, and in 1910, they were 36 of 164. For all their unreliability, city directories tell much the same story. In 1910, fewer than a third of the 86 residents recorded for the sample area could be identified as taxpayers.

By 1912, when a voters' list for the recently annexed northern area of Hillcrest was compiled by the City of Vancouver, just over half of the 1 841 lots in the former D.L. 301 were occupied.[14] Titles to this land were spread among 1 265 owners, over 43 percent of whom (549) were absentees. Resident owners (716 in total) were approximately three times as numerous as tenants (249), who thus made up slightly more than a quarter of the area's population. There is, of course, no telling either how many of the lots owned by non-residents had been purchased for their future use, or how many were held as speculative investments. The line between the small investor/speculator and the bona fide suburban settler was by no means fixed. Indeed, the experience of early Vancouver settler Edward Warner reveals just how blurred the distinction could be.

Warner was a teamster who arrived in Vancouver before the incorporation of the city. He purchased a lot and a cabin to the east of Granville townsite in 1885. Six years later, he traded a 25-foot parcel of this lot for an acre of land on the North Arm of the Fraser River. After clearing this property with a span of mules during the depression of the 1890s, he traded both land and animals for a full block of Hillcrest land. This he sold, in turn in 1908, for the tidy sum of $1 500. With the proceeds, he retired to South Vancouver. Certainly many of those who held land in Hillcrest during the first decade of the century derived rental revenues from their properties. Others, who did not build on their suburban lots before 1910, are likely to have gained from the price inflation that characterized the Vancouver land market before 1913.

Grandview

Located north and east of D.L. 301, and subdivided in 1888, Grandview was also opened for settlement by the streetcar. In 1891, the Fairview beltline, which looped through the area south of False Creek, extended service into Grandview along a single spur line that ran east–west from the city core. Two years later, hourly streetcars ran through the area to the eastern limits of the city, and the Westminster and Vancouver Tramway also served the district. By 1907, Grandview real estate agents were anticipating an increase in streetcar service to downtown, which they expected to run at fifteen-minute intervals.

Yet settlement of this eastern fringe of the still-small city was slow for several years. Grandview's first houses were built on creek banks or along the skid-roads used by early logging outfits in the area. So sparse and scattered was the district's population that it was not enumerated in the city directory until 1905, and for a decade and a half a network of footpaths sufficed to link dwellings to the streetcar stops. Early residents recalled the area as, "all trees and logs lying on top of one another and buried—awful place," and as

> a wilderness. . . . [S]tumps, stones, humps and hollows were every-where; only a few streets were opened; none were graded and macadamized. Sidewalks, where there were any, were of the 3 plank variety and at night a solitary electric light at Venables and Park Dr. lighted the whole district.[15]

In 1904, there were approximately 250 households dispersed over the ragged landscape of the suburb. In the next eight years, however, as Vancouver's population more than tripled from 34 000 to about 110 000, the number of households in Grandview climbed above 1 700. Early in these boom years, boosters looked forward to the paving of streets, the introduction of electric light, and the construction of a sewer system, all of which, they proclaimed, would "add much to the comfort of the people." The area gained a reputation as a suburb for skilled workers.

Development was, nonetheless, very uneven. In almost any quarter of the district it is possible to identify blocks that remained completely empty until at least 1910, although others, close by, were almost fully built up by 1907. Even in 1911, Grandview was less than half settled (figure 3). Scarcely 15 percent of the blocks

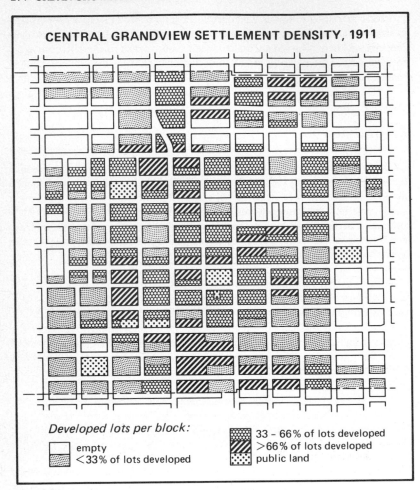

FIGURE 3

in the central part of the district had buildings on two-thirds or more of their lots. Well over half (57 percent) of all blocks in the area had buildings on fewer than a third of their lots. Nor were these the only contrasts. Rooming houses and a few tenements stood in northern Grandview, and there were at least half a dozen apartment houses to the south. Yet there were about fifty vacant houses in the suburb. In western Grandview, small cottages stood on 25-foot lots, along rough dirt roads that rose abruptly from the False Creek flats. To the north and east, blocks were commonly divided into 33-foot lots, and many houses were larger and superior to those found in most other working-class areas of the city (figure 4).

These patterns and contrasts owed much to the activities of those who speculated in and developed Vancouver real estate. In this respect, Grandview differed little from other areas on the periphery of the city during these years. Profiting from real estate seemed simplicity itself in early Vancouver: purchase cheap on the fringe of the urban area; sit tight; sell at a tidy advance.[16] The economic busts that interrupted boom cycles derailed the expectations of many individual speculators, but hardly deflected the general process.

Consider, for example, the results of an 1896 tax sale of Mount Pleasant and Grandview property. This was brought on by the economic downturn that began in 1893, and was described as a "poor man's sale" because of the low selling prices. Many lots were listed at less than $250, yet few lots were sold singly. The city's leading landowner, J.W. Horne, bought almost 40 percent of the 284 lots on offer. Most of the remainder went to a dozen other bidders. Among them were David Oppenheimer, sometime mayor of the city, president of the Vancouver Improvement Company, and a real estate magnate in his own right; J. Barfield, a realtor, who added 38 lots to the many small parcels of land he already owned in Mount Pleasant and Grandview; and Edward Odlum, another real estate dealer, who increased his stock of area land by at least two dozen properties.[17]

As land prices climbed after 1897, such speculators were quick to stress the opportunities for profit upon which they hoped to capitalize. In 1901, for example, a block of Grandview land was offered for sale at $1 500, with the promise that "a quick profit of $2 000" awaited the buyer who subdivided it. As the market heated up, so did the claims of vendors. In 1909, the Vancouver *World* advertised "Grandview money makers! 4 50′ lots $6 000. We will show you how to make a nice turnover on this property." In the frenzy of rising expectations, prices climbed, until by 1910, according to the *Labour Gazette*, most land sales in Vancouver and its suburbs were "by speculators to speculators."[18]

Rising suburban property prices affected the socio-economic mix of Grandview residents. Among a sample of 232 residents drawn from an eight-block area in the middle of the suburb between 1904 and 1913, over 80 percent of those identified before 1910 were blue-collar workers; entrepreneurs and others in white-collar occupations accounted for 14 percent. Between 1910 and 1913, blue-collar workers made up slightly more than 60 percent of all residents, while fully a third were white-collar workers and entrepreneurs.[19]

Unlike Hillcrest, Grandview quickly developed a distinctive identity. More populous and more fully integrated into the developing city than D.L. 301, the area was readily identified by contemporaries. Residents shopped along a commercial ribbon that ran down Park Drive in the centre of the district, and supported two schools, four churches (Methodist, Presbyterian, Anglican, and Roman Catholic), and a community hall. Yet the significance of this institutional infrastructure should not be exaggerated. Only the schools involved a large proportion of the people.[20] Grandview Methodist, the oldest and largest of the four churches, recorded 280 members for 1912. Only a fraction of this number attended regularly.[21] The churches' importance probably lay in their symbolic roles as community

FIGURE 4   Grandview Homes, Decorated for the Coronation of George V, 1911

SOURCE: P. Timms, photograph, Vancouver Public Library, Historic Photos Collection, no. 7461.

anchors and in their provision of social activities for the men, women, and children of the area. Similarly, fraternal organizations such as the Grandview Lodge of the Odd Fellows, had very small memberships. Among the 39 Odd Fellows listed for 1910, just over a third actually lived in the Grandview area; the others came from surrounding suburbs, downtown, and more distant points. The Grandview Rate-payers Association was organized by the area's leading residents to pressure city hall for local improvements, but membership was not large.

The small numbers of residents involved in community organizations reflected both the temporary and the recent nature of much settlement in the Grandview district, as well, perhaps, as the "special strain of individualism" that historian J.M.S Careless discerned in the urban development of the Canadian West.[22] Certainly the family of Joseph Schell, a C.P.R. conductor who moved to the city from Ontario in 1910, gave voice to what may well have been a widespread attachment to privacy and independence when they sniffed at the cultivation of "too much familiarity with the neighbours."[23]

Although Italian and Chinese people had begun to move into the fringes of Grandview by 1912, a substantial proportion of area residents were Canadian-born and had lived elsewhere in Vancouver before moving to Grandview.[24] Among 228 families and individuals known to have moved into the sample area bounded by Woodland Drive, Grant Street, Victoria Drive, and Gravely Street in the ten years between 1904 and 1913, fully 128 (56 percent) were identified at another city address prior to their move (figure 5). Directory canvassers might have missed a further 5 or 10 percent of newcomers to the sample area already resident in the city. A similar proportion who lived with family or friends before moving to Grandview might also have escaped enumeration in the directories. By these estimates, then, barely a quarter of Grandview residents made their first Vancouver home in the area. Almost half (48.4 percent) of those known to have moved into the sample area from a previous city address came from the city's oldest residential areas in Strathcona and the neighbouring downtown core. In short, Grandview was largely settled by people moving away from the rapidly expanding downtown area, from the influx of single men and European families who sought housing near the city core, and from the city's expanding Chinatown.

Yet approximately a quarter of those who moved into the sample area did so from within Grandview. Most of these moves were short—from no more than, say, three blocks away—and many of them were part of a sequential chain of local relocation. The movements of miner and surveyor Roger Pratt illustrate this form of attachment to place. Pratt arrived in Vancouver in the early years of the century, and rented a cabin on the 1400 block of Grant Street, just above the False Creek marsh. In 1907, he moved two blocks east to a piece of land that he had purchased. A year later he bought another property and moved another block east. Then, in 1910, he made his third purchase and fourth move in Grandview, which carried him three blocks south.

Despite the tendency of Grandview residents to remain in the area, the turnover of residents on individual blocks was high. Among 187 households recorded in the

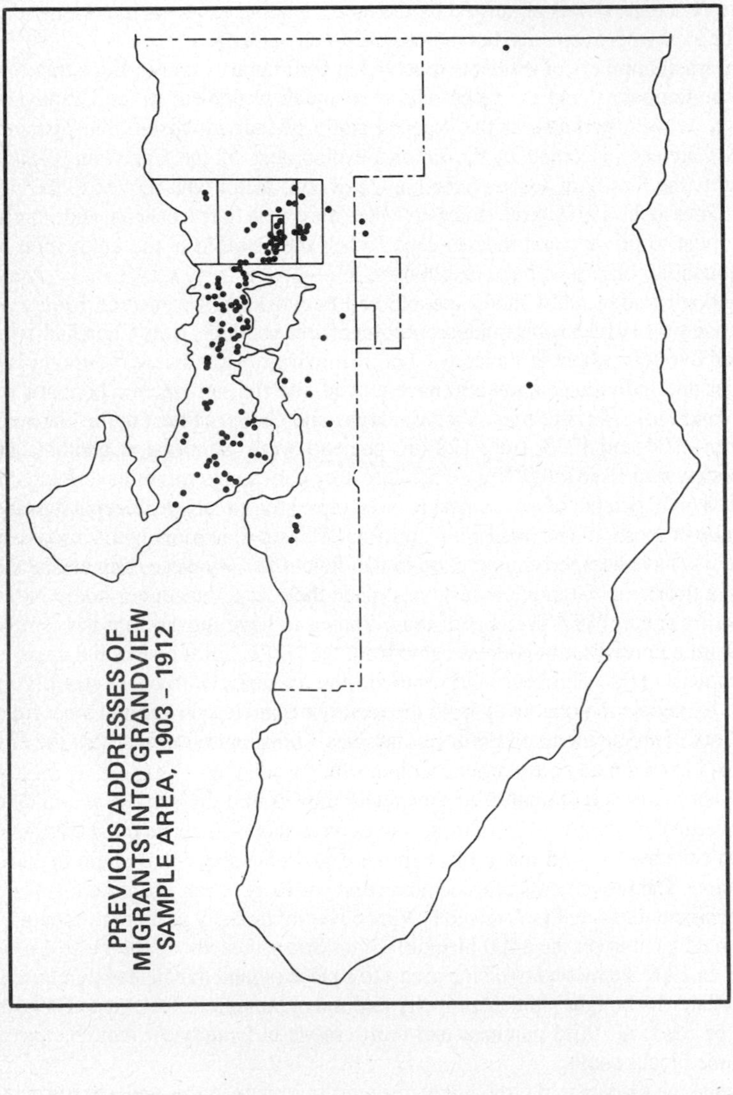

PREVIOUS ADDRESSES OF
MIGRANTS INTO GRANDVIEW
SAMPLE AREA, 1903 – 1912

FIGURE 5

sample area between 1904 and 1912, two-thirds had moved on to new homes by 1913. Approximately 40 percent of these 125 families and individuals could not be traced in later directories and appear to have left the city and its surrounding municipalities.[25]

The remaining 74 households resettled elsewhere in the city or in the municipality of South Vancouver. Again, the tendency for people to remain close to their old neighbourhood was strong (figure 6). Over half of those who could be traced were found in Grandview or the adjacent blue-collar area of Mount Pleasant. Almost a quarter had moved into the downtown peninsula, evidence that the dynamic of urban population movement in the early city was not a simple one-way process of suburban flight. The soon-to-be-entrenched division between a middle-class west and working-class east of the city is reflected in the relative paucity of moves (under 10 percent) from Grandview to suburbs west of Main Street. Yet surprisingly few of those leaving Grandview appear to have relocated in the working-class municipality of South Vancouver. Possibly such a move offered Grandview residents few advantages in terms of cheaper land, accessibility to the city centre, or available rental accommodation during this period. Overall, those who moved differed little in their occupations from those who stayed. For all occupational groups, the ratio of movers to stayers was approximately 2:1. Renters, however, were twice as likely as homeowners to leave the area.

Without assessment records, housing tenure is difficult to determine, but the correlation of directory listings for sample area residents with Vancouver voters' lists reveals that almost a third of those who lived in the area between 1904 and 1913 were not enumerated for electoral purposes. Among the 150 residents whose names were on the voters' lists, almost half identified themselves as tenants. On the reasonable assumption that non-voters were more likely to be tenants than were voters, it appears that more than half of those who lived in the Grandview sample area between 1904 and 1913 did not own their own homes. Within this framework, it is also clear from the records that tenancy increased after 1909. Further, because these figures represent cumulative totals of owners and tenants in the area over a decade, rather than cross-sectional snapshots of residents in the sample area at a particular moment, the proportion of tenants in these eight blocks at any particular time was clearly considerably less than 50 percent.[26]

Conclusion

Suburbs of an "instant metropolis" at the western terminus of a major trans-continental rail line, Hillcrest and Grandview had no precise equivalents in the North America of 1913. Innumerable factors had differentiated them one from another and from the tracts of new housing that surrounded every major city of North America in the early twentieth century. Among these conditions were details of site and situation, climate and vegetation, politics and population. In addition,

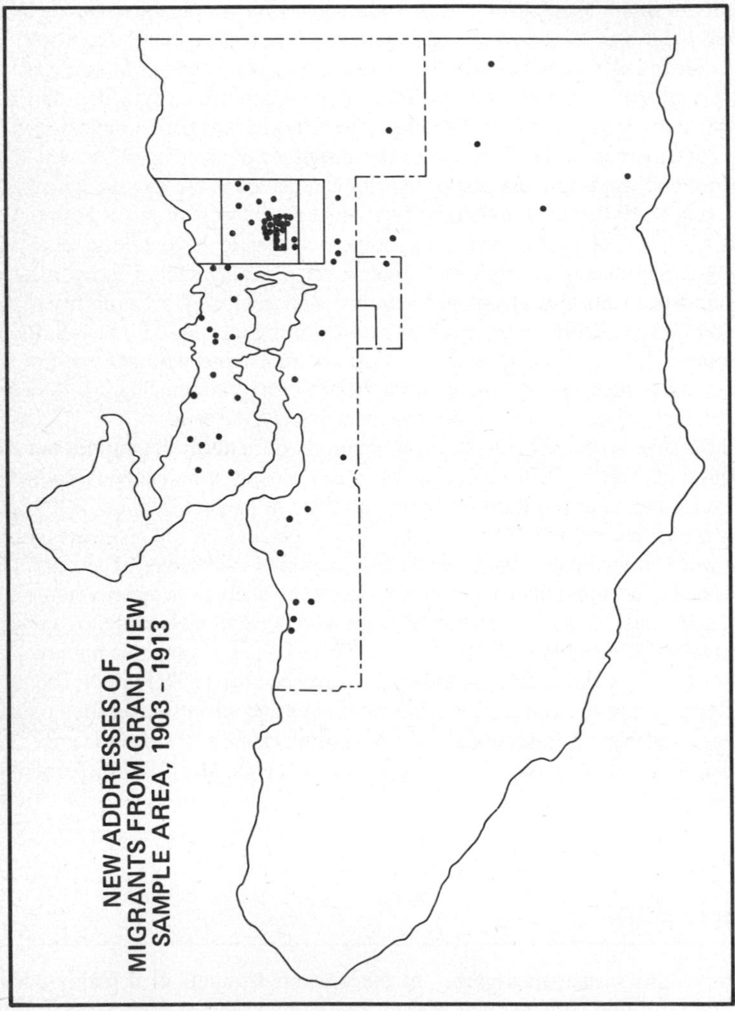

NEW ADDRESSES OF
MIGRANTS FROM GRANDVIEW
SAMPLE AREA, 1903 – 1913

FIGURE 6

the timing of the suburbs' development, prevailing fashions in housing design, the patterns of national and provincial economic growth, and the local courses of streetcar development, land speculation, and rapid urban expansion all imprinted their marks.

Nevertheless, Hillcrest and Grandview were not entirely singular places. In Vancouver, as in Chicago, Philadelphia, Boston, Toronto, Montreal, and countless other urban centres across the continent, mass transportation had opened up vast areas of unoccupied land for residential expansion in the late nineteenth century, and everywhere the results were much the same. Driven by the expectation of handsome profits, scores, hundreds—in the largest cities, even thousands—of large and small investors bought, sold, and developed suburban real estate. Enormous numbers of potential building sites were platted in anticipation of almost endless growth. In Chicago, developers opened 800 000 residential lots in the thirty years after 1890. This was land enough to accommodate more than five million people. As Hillcrest and Grandview were subdivided and settled, Vancouver boosters set their sights on a population of half a million by 1917.

Created, for the most part, in anticipation of demand rather than in response to it, the new suburbs had to be sold. Local newspapers were full of advertisements intended to set developments apart from each other and to attract buyers to them. Acting individually, and for the most part in their own interests, real estate speculators and developers touted the virtues of their "Scenic Heights" and "Workingmen's Paradises." Yet they gave little attention to the co-ordination of their speculative endeavours, to the provision of basic services (with the exception perhaps of the streetcars that made their land accessible), or to aesthetic considerations.

Although a relatively consistent grid of streets imposed a basic order upon the landscapes of D.L. 301 and, to a lesser extent, Grandview (compare figures 2 and 3), in both these areas parcels of various sizes came on the market in dribs and drabs. Some were built on; some were held for later sale. Quickly, the new suburbs assumed a snaggle-toothed appearance that would persist for many years. Within them though, there were soon clusters and occasionally entire streets of similar dwellings. At one level, these small groups of houses reflected the piecemeal way in which development had proceeded but at another they mirrored wider forces. They had been shaped by supply, in the form of land and construction costs, building technology, and the dictates of pattern books; and by demand, in the form of house buyers' preferences. Together, the houses helped to define the character of particular neighbourhoods and revealed the nature of urban life in the early twentieth century.[27]

However modest the houses built in Hillcrest and Grandview before 1914, however ragged their settings, however limited the financial means of their occupants, the new suburbs to which they gave form marked the realization of a new urban order. In Vancouver, as elsewhere, specialization and the fragmentation of urban space accompanied the peripheral expansion of the city. Most of those who lived in the new suburbs depended upon employment beyond their boundaries, and work and home were separate spheres. With this division came a new residential ideal. In Britain, Ebenezer Howard focussed attention on the benefits that would flow from the "joyous union" of town and country; in the United States, dozens of commentators celebrated the small houses and gardens of suburbia for the opportunity they provided to "touch... the freer, sweeter life" of the country. This dream of a single-family dwelling in semi-rural surroundings also had a powerful hold among the population of turn-of-the-century Vancouver,[28] and meshed with the optimistic forecasts of the city's boosters.

In this context, it was probably of little consequence that a quarter or more of those who lived in Vancouver's blue-collar suburbs of Hillcrest and Grandview before 1914 were tenants. In some respects, the difference between owning and renting was less important than the suburban address itself, with all its connotations of "middle class." Moreover, many of those who had yet to buy surely had reason to believe that their prospects of doing so in the rapidly growing new city were better than those offered residents of late nineteenth-century Boston (where approximately a quarter of suburban families owned their homes), of turn-of-the-century Montreal, of early twentieth-century Toronto, or of large English cities in 1914 (where a mere 10 percent of dwellings were occupied by their owners).[29]

Indeed it seemed to visiting Fabian socialists Sidney and Beatrice Webb that a sense of "self-respect and hopefulness" characterised all cities of western Canada. If some found the future less auspicious than the morrow of their dreams, and if the straggling suburbs were almost invariably less picturesque than the places of booster rhetoric, this hardly dented the pervasive enthusiasm of early Vancouver-ites for urban growth. Buoyed by the claims of real estate developers and by the spread of houses across space in this rapidly growing metropolis, they found it relatively easy to believe that suburban homes, surrounded by "yards for people to play in, and gardens" in locations where "sunshine and fresh air" met, were within reach of one and all in early twentieth-century Vancouver.[30]

Notes

1. The early development of the city is treated in R.A.J. McDonald, "City Building in the Canadian West: A Case Study of Economic Growth in Early Vancouver 1888–1893," *BC Studies* 43 (1979): 3–28; N. MacDonald, "The Canadian Pacific Railway and Vancouver's Development to 1900," *BC Studies* 35 (1977): 3–35; and N. MacDonald, "A Critical Growth Cycle for Vancouver, 1900–1914," *BC Studies* 17 (1973): 26–62.

2. L.D. McCann, "Urban Growth in a Staple Economy: The Emergence of Vancouver as a Regional Metropolis, 1886–1914," in *Vancouver, Western Metropolis*, ed. L.J. Evenden (Victoria, 1978), 17–41.

3. P.E. Roy, *Vancouver: An Illustrated History* (Toronto: James Lorimer & Co., 1980).

4. Dickens's characterization, in *Hard Times*, has been elaborated upon by L. Mumford, *The City in History* (Harmondsworth, Middlesex: Pelican, 1966), 508–12.

Note the starkly suggestive comparison of, for example, Roy, *Vancouver*, with
R. Roberts, *The Classic Slum. Salford Life in the First Quarter of the Century* (London:
Pelican, 1973), H.B. Ames, *The City below the Hill* (Toronto: University of Toronto
Press, 1972), T. Copp, *The Anatomy of Poverty* (Toronto: McClelland and Stewart,
1974), and M. Piva, *The Condition of the Working Class in Toronto, 1900–1921*
(Ottawa: University of Ottawa Press, 1979).

5.   Copp, *Anatomy*, 70.

6.   Roy, *Vancouver*, 66.

7.   E.M.W. Gibson, "Lotus Eaters, Loggers and the Vancouver Landscape," in
Cultural Discord in the Modern World, ed. L.J. Evenden and F.F. Cunningham, B.C.
Geographical Series no. 20 (Vancouver: Tantalus Research Ltd., 1974), 57–74; and
D.W. Holdsworth, "House and Home in Vancouver: Images of West Coast Urbanism,
1886–1929," in *The Canadian City: Essays in Urban History*, ed. G.A. Stelter and
A.F.J. Artibise (Toronto: McClelland and Stewart, 1977), 186–211. R.M. Galois,
"Social Structure in Space: The Making of Vancouver" (Ph.D. diss., Simon Fraser
University, 1979) is an exception for its effort to treat working people in the early city.

8.   Edmonds pre-empted D.L. 301 in the 1870s, and paid a dollar an acre for the land
in 1881 (Henry Edmonds, Additional mss. 54, Public Archives of the City of
Vancouver (hereinafter PACV)).

9.   Vancouver Suburban Lands, Assessment Rolls, 1897, PACV. Much of the
analysis that follows in this essay rests upon these assessment rolls (for D.L. 301), and
upon data extracted from *Williams' B.C. Directory* (Vancouver, 1893–1903) and
Henderson's Vancouver Directory (Vancouver, 1904–1913), hereafter referred to
simply as city directories.

10.   V. Ross, *A History of the Canadian Bank of Commerce* (Toronto: Oxford
University Press, 1920), 1:332–50.

11.   P.E. Roy, "The B.C. Electric Railway Company, 1897–1928" (Ph.D. diss.,
University of British Columbia, 1970), 35–40.

12.   The Yorkshire Guarantee and Securities Corporation was the largest single
investor in D.L. 301, Hastings Townsite, and otherwise unidentified "Group I" lands.
James Adams was the third largest landholder in these areas. The B.C. Land and
Investment Agency and the Vancouver Land and Securities Corporation ranked second
and fourth respectively (Vancouver Suburban Lands, Assessment Rolls, 1906). In
estimating the proportion of resident landowners, ratepayers whose given address
coincided with that of their property, as well as those with addresses listed as
"Hillcrest" were assumed to be living on their land. Occupations are taken from the city
directories. Fuller details are available in Donna McCririck, "Opportunity and the
Workingman: A Study of Land Accessibility and the Growth of Blue Collar Suburbs in
Early Vancouver" (M.A. thesis, University of British Columbia, 1981).

13.   For the sample area of 277 lots, the 1904 city directory listed 21 houses and one
business. Quotation from 17th Avenue Additional mss. 54, PACV.

14.   Vancouver Voters' List, 1912, PACV.

15.   Quotations from Mrs. J.D. Cameron and Mr. J. Bennett in Grandview, File 181,
Additional mss. 54, PACV.

16.   McDonald, "City Building," 14; Vancouver *News Advertiser*, 2 Jan. 1910; and
R.J. McDougall, "Vancouver Real Estate for 25 Years," *B.C. Magazine* 7 (June 1911):
597–607.

17.   *News Advertiser*, 30 Nov, 1894, 4 Dec. 1894, 5 Dec. 1894. By 1905, Barfield was
a resident of and developing property in the city's elite West End neighbourhood; see
A. Robertson, "The Pursuit of Power, Property, and Privacy: A Study of Vancouver's
West End Elite, 1886–1914" (M.A. thesis, University of British Columbia, 1977), 266.

18.   Vancouver *World*, May 1901, 15 Apr. 1909; *Labour Gazette* 11 (1910): 589 and 1074.

19.   McCririck, "Opportunity and the Workingman," 115, provides further details.

20.   *B.C. Annual Report of Schools, 1913* (Victoria: Government of British Columbia, 1913).

21.   *Minutes of the Annual Conferences of the Methodist Church* (Toronto, 1912).

22.   J.M.S. Careless, "Aspects of Urban Life in the West, 1870–1914," in *The Canadian City*, ed. G.A. Stelter and A.F.J. Artibise (Toronto: McClelland and Stewart, 1977), 136.

23.   D. McCririck interview with the daughter of J. Schell, Dec. 1979. Further detail regarding this paragraph can be found in McCririck, "Opportunity and the Workingman," 105, 116.

24.   Place of birth data drawn from Grandview Methodist Church, Marriage Register, 1906–13, United Church Archives, Vancouver reveal over half Canadian-born, and approximately one-third British-born.

25.   City directories for the three years following an individual's departure from Grandview were checked for subsequent residence in the city.

26.   City of Vancouver, Voters' Lists, 1904–1912.

27.   There is a sizeable literature on the wider context of suburban development, especially in the United States. H.P. Chudacoff and J. E. Smith, *The Evolution of American Urban Society*, 3rd ed. (Englewood Cliffs, NJ: Prentice Hall, 1988), 87–101 provides a useful brief summary. S.B. Warner Jr., *The Urban Wilderness: A History of the American City* (New York: Harper and Row, 1972); K.T. Jackson, *Crabgrass Frontier: The Suburbanization of the United States* (New York: Oxford University Press, 1985); and S.B. Warner Jr., *Streetcar Suburbs: The Process of Growth in Boston, 1870–1900* (Cambridge, MA: Harvard University Press, 1962) are also important.

28.   E. Howard, *Garden Cities of Tomorrow* (London: Faber and Faber, 1965); F.C. Howe, *The City: The Hope of Democracy* (New York: C. Scribner and Sons, 1905), 204. The phrase from Howe is actually from his wider commentary on the suburban ideal, but neatly summarizes his essential message: "The great cities of Australia are spread out into the suburbs in a splendid way. For miles about are broad roads, with small houses, gardens, and an opportunity for touch with the freer, sweeter life which the country offers." See also D.W. Holdsworth, "House and Home," and Holdsworth, "Cottages and Castles for Vancouver Home-Seekers," *BC Studies* 69–70 (1986): 11–32.

29.   Warner, *Streetcar Suburbs*; Copp, *Anatomy*; Piva, *Condition*; D. Englander, *Landlord and Tenant in Urban Britain, 1838–1918* (Oxford: Clarendon Press, 1983), 2. It is worth noting in this comparative vein that British socialists Sidney and Beatrice Webb, visiting Canada in 1911, were impressed, even in the east, by the Canadian passion for "lots." City-dwelling workers, they remarked, typically lived in separate houses, "ranging in style from mere wooden 'shanties' or 'shacks' to 'quite charming bungalow cottages or artistic villas' put up by worker-owners on their own 'lots' " (G. Feaver, "The Webbs in Canada: Fabian Pilgrims on the Canadian Frontier," *Canadian Historical Review* 58 (1977): 267).

30.   G. Feaver," 'Self-Respect and Hopefulness': The Webbs in the Canadian West," *BC Studies* 43 (1979): 45–64; *The Province*, Vancouver, 5 July 1906, 7, and 7 Oct. 1912, 17, advertising the Vancouver suburbs of Kensington and Bryn Mawr.

SECTION 5

PLACES AND PATTERNS

To describe and interpret the world—to convey a sense of its diversity and yet discern order in its complexity—these are old but fundamental challenges of geography. Scholars have responded to them in a thousand ways. The geographers of classical antiquity, for example divided the earth into tropical, temperate, and frigid zones. Those at the turn of the century entertained the idea that environments shaped societies. In the 1940s and 50s, geographers defined their subject as the study of "areal differentiation," and fragmented inquiry into specialized sub-disciplines. In the 1960s, they embraced abstraction, isolating various parts of reality conceptually and developing normative models of what ought to be rather than what actually was or is. Each of these responses has met particular needs. Each has offered a framework, whether descriptive, comparative, or analytical, within which to understand something of our setting. Together, they provide a range of perspectives on our world that is almost as heterogeneous as the face of the earth itself. Yet relatively few approaches have been able to identify underlying order or draw wider implications from the startling richness of reality while holding on to the broad compass of geography as the study of environments and peoples in all their intricate, interwoven diversity.

This is not a simple task. Teasing interpretation from the past and identifying pattern and order in human use of the earth is an exercise in careful judgment that must rest on wide knowledge of the topic at hand. It implies a great deal of time-consuming work in archive, library, and field. The successful account of a place also depends upon an intimate understanding of an environment and its inhabitants, a clear vision of the wider significance of that locale, and careful attention to the craft of presenting its character and "story." In recognition of this, accomplished historical geographer and prose stylist H.C. Darby once remarked that it could be an humiliating experience to attempt a description of "even a small tract of country in such a way as to convey a true likeness."

Yet the problems of effective geographical writing are not insurmountable. The essays that follow range in scale from the microscopic to the sub-continental and each conveys a good deal about the places and patterns of the developing country. Collectively, they demonstrate ways of responding to the difficulties that Darby described. They also pull together many of the threads introduced by earlier articles in this collection. In the process, the essays make clear that although the geographer's task of treating people, places, patterns, and processes together is a demanding one, it can yield fresh and distinct perspectives on many facets of the Canadian past—that the game, in short, is worth the candle.

"Those intending to join Lord Selkirk's expedition to the Red River are directed to study carefully the enclosed copy of Arrowsmith's map... of North America which was published earlier in this year of our Lord, 1811." So begins *Beyond the River and the Bay*, the book from which the first selection that follows is drawn. Sub-titled *Some Observations on the State of the Canadian Northwest in 1811 with a View to Providing the Intending Settler with an Intimate Knowledge of That Country*, this evocative account was written in the 1960s by Eric Ross. Ross studied history at the University of New Brunswick and geography at the University of Edinburgh before establishing the only university geography department in his native province, at Mount Allison University in Sackville, where he still teaches. His book is a tour de force of geographical description "in the style of the times." Following the lead of R.H. Brown's *Mirror for Americans* (see the general introduction above), it relies almost exclusively upon books, journals, diaries, maps, and reports in existence in the first decade of the nineteenth century. Even the brief section of the book included here reveals how well this technique conveys a vivid sense of the northwest as it might have appeared to, and been understood by, those Scots who came to settle along the Red River in 1811 under the auspices of Lord Selkirk.

Like Brown, Ross attributes authorship of his manuscript to an imaginary character, in this case Ian Alexander Bell Robertson, a native of Edinburgh and lifelong friend of novelist Walter Scott and Thomas Douglas, Lord Selkirk. Both the style of writing and the cartography are intended to evoke a feeling of the period. Thus we are carried back to a past that is almost palpable, to "Huts [so] ... wretched with smoke" that even Prairie winters were no deterrent to stepping out of doors, to diets leavened with a "black, hard crumply moss" boiled to a gummy consistency in fish stock, and to regions where the mosses and willows that covered the ground could "support only a few straggling moose." This is rich, illuminating description. Sustained throughout the book, it provides a remarkable account of the environment of the northwest, its indigenous inhabitants, the fur trade and its supporting enterprises, the major trading posts on Hudson Bay, transport and communication in the western interior, and regional differences across a substantial tract of territory on the eve of permanent settlement. For all the limitations of cross-sectional period pieces, *Beyond the River and the Bay* is a triumph of geographical description and transcends its constituent detail to re-create the character of a place as it appeared to contemporaries.

The next essay, on the tiny Newfoundland settlement of Point Lance, differs dramatically from the first selection in approach and scale. It is abbreviated from a substantially larger work by John Mannion of the Memorial University of Newfoundland, who has written extensively on Irish merchants and settlers in eastern Canada. In *Point Lance in Transition*, Mannion sets out to understand the forces that shaped and transformed an out-of-the-way place and the lives of its people. The result is a distinctively geographical and satisfyingly coherent microstudy that draws data from human memories and field investigations as much as from libraries and archives.

Point Lance began with the arrival of two Irish brothers in the Avalon peninsula in about 1820, and never much exceeded 150 persons in population. Yet Mannion's account of this place tells us all, as the introduction to the original study noted, "something about where we have been and where we are." The brothers Philip and Ned Careen were participants in the great trans-Atlantic migration that flooded into eastern Canada in the first half of the nineteenth century. Their location was a good deal more remote than most but, with settlers elsewhere, they established roots and descendants in the soil of the new world.* The growing

---

* Cf. Courville, "Space, Territory, and Culture in New France," p.165, above.

population of Point Lance was unusually dependent upon its immediate environment since people lived, for the most part, on what they could raise, catch, or glean locally. They therefore gradually developed an intimate, highly specific knowledge of their surroundings that was more extreme than, but little different in kind from, that possessed by rural dwellers in many other parts of pre-industrial Canada. The Irish accents, practices, and beliefs of Point Lance's first household had their counterparts in innumerable immigrant dwellings across the length and breadth of British North America, but generations of Careens, largely isolated from the world beyond St. Mary's Bay, were able to sustain them far longer than were settlers in more heterogeneous communities. So Point Lance grew, and persisted well into the twentieth century, as a small, intensely local, essentially pre-industrial community.

After 1945, however, the winds of change began to blow through Point Lance. Trucks, radios, and telephones were brought in along the new road from Placentia and St. John's. With them came government plans, social programs, cash employment. Abruptly, and thus more starkly than elsewhere, old ways yielded to new goods, ideas, and technologies. Because the changes were swift and intense in this little place, they illuminate particularly well the nature of their broader impact. Point Lance thus acts, in some sense, as a metaphor for the country: to understand how it took shape and to appreciate the influences and tensions that have re-made it in recent times is to understand something of the common circumstances of those who have occupied this changing land.

The third of the papers that follow is the second of two closely connected articles by the editor of this volume, both treating the late eighteenth-century geography of the region later known to Canadians as the Maritimes. In the tradition of geographical synthesis, it conveys the patterns and textures of a still thinly settled yet intricate region. Thus it considers migration and settlement, charts the growth of the economy, describes the developing countryside and emerging towns, and comments on the ways in which economic and social, but above all geographical, changes in this area reflected broader patterns of North American development.

In the final essay of this section, Cole Harris of the University of British Columbia pulls together the results of years of work on the historical geography of this country in a commentary on the pattern of early Canada. This essay builds upon the argument advanced in "The Extension of France into Rural Canada" (in section 2, above), but has more nuances and is more comprehensive in scope. The essay is worth comparing with its predecessor to see how geographers gradually refine and develop their understanding of the past. Here, Harris extends his earlier interpretation to argue that the distinctive shape of modern Canada rests upon the particular configuration of its emerging human geography. He observes that the idea and apparatus of the modern nation state were superimposed after 1867—not without some difficulty—upon robust foundations laid down in the earlier European encounter with the land of northern North America.

This is a penetrating conceptualization, advanced with clarity and infused with detail. It echoes much that has preceded it in this volume, to focus and clarify a wide range of more circumscribed work on the Canadian past. It also suggests new bases for reflection upon the historical geography of this country. Finally, the essay begins to open up new lines of inquiry by incorporating some of the ideas advanced by historical sociologist Anthony Giddens.*

Clearly, too, the implications of Harris's argument reach far beyond the immediate concerns of the essays in this collection. There are links with those who favour a staples interpretation of Canadian development, with the frontier ideas of F.J. Turner, with Harold Innis's claim that Canada emerged not in spite of geography but because of it, and with the vision of Canada as a community of communities. Harris attempts to ground these bold ideas in a detailed understanding of the past, and to examine more closely than has often been done the ways in which specific processes shape societies, regions, and landscapes. Thus the essay provides a fitting conclusion to this volume, whose contents reveal, to borrow a phrase from Harris's final paragraph, "neither a few stark principles from which...[the country] can be deduced, nor an endless complexity of individual detail." Rather, these pages bind together environment and society, people, and place, process and pattern, in a distinctively geographical perspective that sheds much light on the shaping of this country and its people.

---

* Anthony Giddens, *The Nation-State and Violence* (Berkeley and Los Angeles: University of California Press, 1987) provides a thought-provoking introduction to Giddens's ideas. For further reading, see n. 68 of the general introduction to this volume.

EAST WINNIPEG, MUSKRAT AND ENGLISH RIVER COUNTRIES, AND THE BARREN GROUNDS*

ERIC ROSS

Between Fort William and York Factory on the east, and Lake Winnipeg on the west, is a vast section of the Stony Region known as the East Winnipeg Country (see figure 1). Its inhabitants, Crees and Ojibwas, are not numerous, for the land is incapable of supporting a large population. Though originally rich in animals, the forests are now largely exhausted. Fur animals are very few indeed, and deer are virtually unknown. The natives have come to rely mainly on the fish in the lakes,[1] although some of the Ojibwas have turned to agriculture,[2] while others have chosen to abandon the country and have migrated to the lands of the Assiniboines and Crees to the westward.[3]

Except for a few small outposts away from the main routes, all of the houses in the East Winnipeg Country are now intended as staging points for canoes and boats going to and from the interior, rather than for trading furs. There is Oxford House and Rock Fort on the Hayes, and Rainy Lake House, Rat Portage House and Fort Bas-de-la-Rivière-Winnipeg on the Fort William route (see figure 2). Each is an important supply depot and storehouse.

North of the East Winnipeg Country is the Muskrat Country. It is an area worthy of considerable discussion not so much because of the furs and provisions which it produces (for its production is not great), but because it illustrates so well the complexities of the fur trade in the Northwest, as well as the great difficulties and hardships that face those who are engaged in it.

Strictly speaking, the Muskrat Country comprises only the area east of the Sturgeon-Weir between the Nelson and Churchill rivers,[4] although earlier traders of the region have tended to link it up with the lower valley of the Churchill as far as Reindeer Lake.[5] The term is used here in its wider sense. The maze of rivers and lakes that cover the surface of much of the Muskrat Country are easily accessible

* From *Beyond the River and the Bay* (Toronto: University of Toronto Press, 1970), 109–18.

from the Nelson, Churchill and Saskatchewan rivers. In the early days of the trade, it was these waterways that enabled the Crees and Chipewyans who inhabited the country to take their furs with comparative ease to the bayside factories to trade. Although the country was never rich in furs, the Hudson's Bay Company enjoyed a steady trade from this area for many years. Then came the Canadians, and the

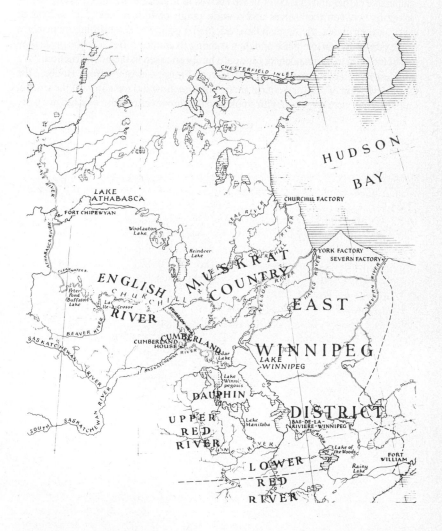

FIGURE 1   Section of " 'Countries' of the Northwest," map 3 of *Beyond the River and the Bay*.

Hudson's Bay Company saw the greater part of the furs go to their rivals for several years. However, in 1793, the English company at last sent people into the Muskrat Country and it soon recaptured much of the trade, which it continues to hold until this day. Because of the short distance its men have to travel and the large quantity of goods it can afford to supply, the company has had little difficulty in underselling its rivals.[6] Moreover, the shorter route has meant that the English traders can arrive earlier and thus commit the natives to trade with them. To assure happy relations between themselves and a wide range of Indian bands, as well as to out-fox their rivals, the English have adopted a policy of establishing themselves for a year or two in one place and then moving to another.[7] Because the posts they build are soon to be abandoned, little care has been taken in their construction. "We built log Huts to pass the winter," wrote Thompson of Bedford House, "the chimneys were of mud and coarse grass, but somehow did not carry off the smoke, and the Huts were wretched with smoke, so that however bad the weather, we were

FIGURE 2 Section of "Fur Traders' Posts," map 6 of *Beyond the River and the Bay*.

glad to leave the Huts."[8] It had been the practice for the men's house to be built some distance from the store-house and the master's house. But when this came to the attention of the governor of Churchill in 1807, he decided that the posts were too vulnerable and immediately ordered that all detached dwellings be immediately taken down and rebuilt attached to the store-house, with the men's quarters forming one end and the master's apartment, the other. Henceforth, no apology or excuse would be accepted "for deviating from this indispensable precaution."[9]

Because of the general scarcity of game animals in the Muskrat Country, it has been even more necessary than elsewhere for the posts to be located near good fisheries. This was the lesson learned at Fairford House during a hungry winter in 1795–6. The house was built on the bank of the Churchill just a mile below the mouth of the Reindeer River. It had been an excellent place for trade but, because of the poor fishery, the men could "barely maintain" themselves and the post soon had to be abandoned. The Churchill is poor for fish and so is generally unsuitable for settlement, although some of the deep lakes, "wholly independent" but discharging into it, have very good fisheries indeed.[10] But even on those lakes, the fishery can unpredictably fail, as did the one on Reindeer Lake during the present winter.[11] Considering it is on the Churchill, Nelson House has enjoyed a reasonable fishery for many years. During the winter of 1810–11, however, the English traders were forced by the Canadians to abandon the spot where they had placed their nets for the past eighteen years. Fortunately, however, they were able to find another place before starvation overtook them, for animals in this area are exceedingly scarce. The mosses and willows which cover the ground can support only a few straggling moose; buffalo are unknown, and seldom do reindeer penetrate from the north.[12] Traders on the Nelson have apparently fared no better. At Sipiwesk Lake House, fish are described as being "very Scarce," but at Split Lake the situation is somewhat brighter. There, fish are caught throughout the year "but not in great numbers nor of the best quality."[13] However, since the post is situated on a deer crossing there is always the hope of supplementing the fish with fresh venison between August and November, and again in April, each year.[14]

Although the climate of the Muskrat Country is far more favourable to vegetation than it is at the factories along the coast, it is far from being equal to that of the more southerly districts of the Northwest; or of situations that are more "remote from the chilling influence of the sea."[15] Agriculture is therefore necessarily limited. At Split Lake, for example, the climate will permit potatoes, turnips, and cabbages to be grown but not corn.[16]

Split Lake House provides an interesting example of the competition not only between the English and the Canadian traders but also of the rivalry within the English company itself. Built in response to Canadian competition in 1790, it was the first Hudson's Bay Company post in the Muskrat Country. Although it was intended to draw furs from the Canadians, there were soon complaints from Churchill that the Indians who traded at the new post were Chipewyans "who never in their lives *saw York Factory* but yearly brought the produce of their hunt to Churchill, and were engaged every spring to kill Geese there." In 1791, another settlement was made on the Nelson and trade at Churchill dropped accordingly. The next year, yet another post was founded and there was a further decrease. But in the following year, 1793, Churchill entered the competition with a post up the Churchill River, and soon her trade began to recover.[17]

This rivalry between company posts undoubtedly delighted the Indians. It tended to raise the prices of their furs and provided a wonderful opportunity for them to escape from their debts at one factory by going to an outpost of the other.[18] In this, they were aided and abetted by some of the more unscrupulous inland traders. To increase their own portion of the trade, they were not above diverting furs from their fellow company men. The injured parties frequently took revenge with similar actions. Tempers rose. Accusations followed counter-accusations, and the situation became increasingly confused. In 1803, the exasperated governor of Churchill complained bitterly to his opposite number at York that one of his men was continuing "his practices upon our Northern [Chipewyan] Indians, intercepting them, seducing them, and villainously deceiving them by propagating false and injurious reports, which would scarcely become a Canadian."[19] As early as 1795, the dispute reached the London Committee room, where David Thompson's charts were unrolled and an attempt made to work out trading areas for each factory. But it was a difficult situation to arbitrate, for even if a trader did refuse to trade with the Indians who came to him because they belonged to another post, there was no guarantee that the Indians would not then go to the Canadians rather than to the other company post.[20]

The rivalry continued at least until last year, when the whole of the Northwest was put under the command of a single superintendent. One of his duties was to end the York–Churchill rivalry and to prevent it from developing elsewhere. At the same time, the Muskrat Country was placed under an inland master responsible to York. But by then the country was largely hunted out and its productiveness so diminished that W. Holmes, the first inland master, does not think it will pay the company to remain in the area even supposing they should gain the whole of the trade.

Years of competition between the Canadians and the English, and between the two English factories, have produced a sellers' market which the Indians have known how to exploit. Liquor is virtually the only thing they will now accept for beaver, the only fur presently in demand on the London market. Even if our goods were "embroidered in Gold," moans Holmes, the Indians will not trade if we "keep back Liquor." And so the liquor continues to flow. But even so, seldom do the Indians repay two-thirds of their credits, small though they usually are.[21] By now, most of the beaver within easy range of the posts have been exterminated. Yet the natives are reluctant to go further afield in search of other beaver areas because they can no longer bear to be far from the source of their liquor. As a result, many of the poor debauched wretches are so reduced in circumstances that during the hard winter of 1810–11 some of them were forced to eat the few furs they did get in order to survive.[22] However, it must be pointed out that the destruction of the beaver has not been entirely of their own doing. Much of the damage has been perpetrated by Indians from Canada who were brought into the Muskrat Country to hunt for the Canadians. Auld has been extremely bitter about the interlopers and claims that wherever there is plenty of food for the intruders' support, there the fur animals will soon be "extirpated" by them.[23] So discouraged are some of the local Indians becoming that they are beginning to migrate towards Cumberland House, where there are more furs and provisions.[24] If the trend continues, it is likely that very few posts will be retained in the area in the future. Already, moderately successful posts like the one belonging to the Hudson's Bay Company at Indian Lake are being closed down. In this particular case, the English post has been getting more of the trade than its rival's establishment near by.[25] But apparently the company does not feel that it is justifying expenses.

The future of the Muskrat Country looks bleak indeed. Not only is it becoming less productive in itself but, with the migration of its natives, there will be fewer middlemen to carry the furs and provisions of richer areas to its trading posts. To the traders, it will seem even more of a barrier between the fur lands of the north and west and the Great Lakes and Hudson Bay.

Above the mouth of the Reindeer River, the Churchill is usually known as the English River, and the area that it drains as the English River District or Department. Although also part of the Stony Region, its climate is more favourable to the "productions of the vegetable and animal kingdoms" than is that of the Muskrat Country. Furs and provisions are produced in considerable quantity but, like the Muskrat Country, the English River is important primarily because of its geographical position. For through it runs the main route to the Athabasca Country, the Eldorado of the fur trade. For several years, the Athabasca Country has been the exclusive preserve of the North West Company. Now it would seem that the English River District may become so as well. For by the end of 1811, as we have seen, through bullying and even through open violence, the Canadians have succeeded in driving nearly all of their English rivals from the district. They know that the English River District is the geographical key to the Athabasca Country and they have been prepared to go to almost any lengths to keep the Hudson's Bay Company traders out of it.

The North West Company brigades bound for the English River District and the Athabasca Country enter the English River near Portage-de-Traite, after coming from the Saskatchewan by way of Cumberland House, the Sturgeon-Weir River and Beaver Lake. Portage-de-Traite takes it name from an event which took place in 1774–5. Joseph Frobisher, a trader from Canada, after having wintered near by, met in the spring a group of Indians making their annual journey to Churchill to trade. He persuaded them to trade with him instead and soon he had all the furs his canoes could carry. Ever since this coup, the carrying-place has been known as Portage-de-Traite. Before that, it had been called Frog Portage from the Crees having placed a stretched skin of a frog there as a sign of derision to the natives of the country, whom they regarded with contempt because, among other things, they were ignorant of how to prepare, stretch and dry the skins of the beaver.[26] As far as the Canadians are concerned, the carrying-place might well be called "Portage Cornucopia" for across it have flowed not only the furs of the Athabasca Country and English River District, but some of those of the Muskrat Country as well. An envious official of the Hudson's Bay Company reported in 1811 that "not less than

1,300 Bundles of furs came over the Frog Portage last year." In 1809, he said, 52 canoes with six or seven men in each went north; but in 1810, there were only 34 with five or six men, "which is a very strange difference."[27] Possibly the difference was not quite as great as the Hudson's Bay man believed, for 38 canoes had been assigned to this area at the annual meeting of the North West Company at Fort William in 1810. Of these, 31 had been apportioned to the Athabasca Country and seven to the English River. In the same year, only three canoes were assigned to the Muskrat Country.[28] These figures illustrate well the relative importance of the three districts to the North West Company.

From Portage-de-Traite, the brigades head up the Churchill, pass through several "lakes" in the river and negotiate 36 portages before they come to a well-built fort on the north side of Lac-Ile-à-la-Crosse, the headquarters of the North West Company's English River Department. The post has an excellent garden. From the lake, the best of white fish are taken throughout the year, and along its banks moose, deer and other game animals are captured.[29] The only Indians who come to trade are the Chipewyans and Crees. Since the peace arranged by Matonabbee, the Chipewyans have been allowed by the Crees to hunt on their lands south of the Churchill, but not without exacting contributions when they occasionally meet them. Failure to pay can bring punishment with arms. The contributions are often levied when the two tribes meet at the trading posts and are usually in the form of rum, which the Chipewyans readily part with since they seldom drink it themselves.[30] Relations between the two peoples seem to be good on the whole and from the Crees, the Chipewyans are now learning how to build canoes and in other ways to adapt themselves to the living conditions of their new lands.[31]

About the turn of the century, the Hudson's Bay Company had built beside the North West Company at Lac-Ile-à-la-Crosse,[32] but from the beginning, this distant outpost of the English company met with unusually fierce opposition because of its strategic position in relation to the Athabasca Country. Any further expansion of the English in this area is to be prevented. Last year, for instance, when the Hudson's Bay Company tried to buy a few canoes to go up the Beaver River to settle at Green Lake, the Canadians forbad the Chipewyans to sell them any.[33] Green Lake is situated on the edge of the Stony Region. Beyond it, the Beaver flows through the Great Plains and in one place, near Lac d'Orignal [Moose Lake], approaches the Saskatchewan. From the plains, buffalo can be procured and from the Saskatchewan, dried meat and pemmican, which can be easily carried across to Beaver River by way of Lac d'Orignal and brought down the river to Green Lake. Thus, a post on Green Lake would have given the Hudson's Bay Company the provision depot it needed if it were to extend its operations into the Athabasca Country. A similar depot has been operated by the North West Company for several years. In fact, it is the provisions from this post that have enabled the canoes each year to speed down the English River with the minimum of delay. During a period of expansion about the turn of the century, the Hudson's Bay Company did manage to build a post on Green Lake called Essex House, but it flourished for only a short time.[34] After the Canadians had prevented the Chipewyans from selling them the canoes they required last year, the English efforts to re-establish themselves upon the lake took on a rather pathetic air, as Mr. Sutherland began to saw in two the company's small boat at Ile-à-la-Crosse to lengthen it by four feet.[35] But before the enlarged boat could be used in an advance towards Green Lake, the Canadians had succeeded in driving the English from their base at Ile-à-la-Crosse, and forced them to retreat down the English River towards the Muskrat Country.[36]

From Ile-à-la-Crosse, the annual brigades of the North West Company paddle northwestwardly through Buffalo [Peter Pond] Lake to Methye Lake and finally to the Methye Portage, the most famous portage of them all. This enables the brigades to cross the great divide which separates the rivers draining into Hudson Bay from those flowing northward into the Frozen Ocean. It is a long portage—eight miles and fifteen hundred yards, according to Turnor[37]—but, because the plateau-like divide is level and thinly wooded, the road is good. From a high hill near the western end of the portage, the traders may catch a breath-taking view of the promised land of the fur trade, the Athabasca Country.[38]

A far more arduous route to the Athabasca Country lies across the Barren Grounds. Although used by some of the natives, this route is never travelled by the traders because of its difficult waterways and the scarcity of food. Its rivers and lakes are less useful for transportation than elsewhere in the Northwest because of their arrangement and the fact that they are frozen over much of the year.[39] The vegetation consists largely of mosses and lichens which support the reindeer [caribou], which, in turn, make possible the little human habitation that exists there.[40] These animals travel in vast herds and, because of the sparseness of vegetation, are nearly always in motion. According to Hearne, their direction is usually either from east to west, or west to east, depending upon the season, and the prevailing winds. "From November till May," he wrote, "the bucks continue to the Westward, among the woods, when their horns begin to sprout; after which they proceed on to the Eastward, to the barren grounds; and the does that have been on the barren ground all the Winter, are taught by instinct to advance to the Westward to meet them, in order to propagate their species."[41]

The natives of the Land of Little Sticks bordering onto the Barren Grounds are all of the same [Athapaskan] group. The most important of them are the Chipewyans who, as already seen, occupy the strategic area north of the Churchill between the fur lands of the west and Hudson Bay. To the north and west of them are the tribes from whom they obtain many of the furs which they trade to the Europeans. These are Yellow-knives, Hares, Dogribs, and Slaves. Like the Chipewyans, the Yellow-knives and Hares follow the reindeer out onto the Barren Grounds during the summer. The Dogribs, however, make only quick sorties onto the Barren Grounds, while the timid Slaves prefer to remain under the cover of the trees.[42] All of these tribes of the northern Stony Region travel on foot and use their tiny canoes only for crossing rivers and narrow lakes, or for hunting reindeer. The reindeer provide their main subsistence, as well as their clothing and many other useful articles. But sometimes the reindeer suddenly and inexplicably disappear. On these occasions the Indians can often fall back, for food at least, upon the rich fisheries of the lakes and rivers, and, if they are very lucky, capture a few water-birds as well. Some of the marshes produce several kinds of grasses which grow very rapidly but are "dealt out with so sparing a hand as to be barely sufficient to serve the geese, swans, and other birds of passage, during their migrations in the Spring and Fall, while they remain in a moulting state." Alpine hares are also "pretty plentiful" in some parts of the Barren Grounds as well as some herds of musk-oxen. To the westward among the woods, there are rabbits and partridges. But should these, as well as the birds and fish, fail as well, there is always the black, hard crumply moss growing upon the rocks. It is far from appetizing in appearance but, when boiled to a gummy consistency, is actually quite palatable. In fact, Hearne said that most people grow fond of it. It is "remarkably good and pleasing when used to thicken any kind of broth," he wrote, but it is "generally most esteemed when boiled in fish-liquor."

Yet in spite of this apparent abundance of food on the Barren Grounds, Hearne found that half of the inhabitants, and perhaps the other half as well, are frequently in danger of starving to death, partly, as he observed, "owing to their want of economy." Scenes of distress, he wrote, have been particularly common during the long dangerous journeys to Churchill when, presumably, the Indians have been more intent upon reaching their goal than following the reindeer, or in seeking out the best fishing areas along the way. For the more distant tribes there is, as already discussed, the additional hazard of falling prey to the depredations of their kinsmen, the Chipewyans, who are always ready to relieve them of their furs, goods, women, and, sometimes, even of their lives.[43] In this way, the Chipewyans have ruthlessly guarded their one big asset in the trade, *their geographical position*. During recent years, however, now that they have largely turned their attention to the fur lands of the Crees to the south of them, they seem to have missed, or even to have ignored, the small bands of Indians from the Northwest who are again coming to Churchill to trade.

In a similar way, the Eskimos immediately north of Churchill assume the position of middlemen in the trade with their relations living further to the north. When the more northerly tribes travel to the factory to trade, they must pass through the lands of their southern relations. While doing so they are filled with all sorts of malicious rumours about the white traders and generally discouraged from going any further. At the same time, the southerners offer to take their furs off their hands for a mere trifle. This having been done, the southerners proceed to the factory where they exchange them for trading goods and are then ready to journey to the northward to go into business for themselves. For many years, the Hudson's Bay Company has tried to persuade the nearer tribes to come to the factory to hunt whales, and to leave the fur trade to the more distant Eskimos. But as late as 1811, these efforts had met with little success.[44] It is to enable the northern Eskimos to avoid their grasping neighbours, as well as the depredations of the Chipewyans, which has caused the company annually to send a boat northward to trade with the Eskimos along the west coast of the bay. As far as is known, the Eskimos live only near the sea-coast.[45] They apparently never venture inland and, unlike the Indians, remain on the Barren Grounds throughout the year.

There are no trading posts on the Barren Grounds; its limited trade is conducted from posts along its periphery. There is Churchill in the east and a number of North

West Company posts in the west. Among the latter are Fort Chipewyan, Slave Fort, Fort Providence, Great Bear Lake House, Fort Norman and Fort Good Hope. All of them are approached by way of the Great Plains, and from the plains come much of the provisions which enable the posts to exist.

Notes

1. J.B. Tyrell, ed., *David Thompson's Narrative of his Explorations in Western America, 1784–1812* (Toronto, 1916), 181.
2. D.W. Harmon, *Sixteen Years in the Indian Country*, ed. W. Kaye Lamb, (Toronto, 1957), 211.
3. L.F. Masson, *Les Bourgeois de la Compagnie du Nord Ouest* (Quebec, 1889–90), 2:308.
4. That is, the area where the shield disappears under the broad marine terraces of the bay.
5. A.S. Morton, *History of the Canadian West to 1870–71* (London, 1939), 440. It includes the whole of the region forming a low saddle in the shield between the bay and the prairies.
6. Sir Alexander Mackenzie, *Voyages from Montreal, on the River St. Lawrence, through the Continent of North America to the Frozen and Pacific Oceans, in the Years 1789 and 1793* (London, 1801), *lxxvi*.
7. Morton, *History of the Canadian West*, 449.
8. Tyrell, ed., *Thompson's Narrative*, 153.
9. Churchill Correspondence Book (1806–7), Circular Letters to Officers and Traders Inland from Churchill Factory by W. Auld, fall of 1807, B. 42/b/50, f. 23, Hudson's Bay Company Archives (hereinafter HBCA). Even to this day, as a legacy of the need for defence, the Hudson's Bay Company posts have a very compact form.
10. Tyrell, ed., *Thompson's Narrative*, 133–36.
11. W. Auld's (Churchill) Correspondence Book (1811), J. Charles, Inland Master, Clapham House, Deer Lake, to W. Auld, 7 Feb. 1811, B. 42/b/55, f. 6d, HBCA.
12. Ibid., f. 10d.
13. York Factory Report (1815), W.H. Cook to T. Thomas, dated York, 1 Sept. 1815, B. 239/e/1, ff. 4–4d, HBCA.
14. Ibid., f 4.
15. Ibid., f 5.
16. Ibid., f 4. Ice coming down stream at the deltas and mixing with off-shore pack ice at the bay, helped to delay the spring and shorten the growing season.
17. Churchill Miscellaneous (1797–1803), "Reasons for preferring Churchill River, to York River, for conducting the Northward Trade," London, 29 Nov. 1797, B. 42/z/1, f. 48d, HBCA.
18. York Factory Correspondence (1802–3), from W. Auld to the Chief at York, B. 239/b/68, f. 25, HBCA.
19. Ibid., ff. 24d–25.
20. York Correspondence Book (1794–1809), Colen and Council at York to the London Committee, York Factory, 16 Sept. 1795, B. 239/b/79, f. 10, HBCA.
21. W. Auld's (Churchill) Correspondence Book (1811), extract of private letter to W. Holmes, Inland Master of Rat River, dated Bedford House, 12 Feb. 1811, B. 42/b/55, f. 5d, HBCA.

22. W. Auld's (Churchill) Correspondence Book (1811), extract of Letter from Mr. Snoddie, dated Nelson House, 24 Feb. 1811, B. 42/b/55, f. 10, HBCA.

23. Ibid., W. Auld's remarks (undated) on the above letter, ff. 10d–11.

24. Cumberland House Report (1815), report on the Cumberland District by Alexander Kennedy, addressed to Thomas Thomas, Gov. of Northern District, B. 49/e/1, f. 4d, HBCA.

25. Peter Fidler's Ile-à-la-Crosse Journal, dated 8 June 1811, B. 89/a/2, unnumbered, HBCA.

26. Mackenzie, *Voyages, lxxvi–lxxvii.*

27. W. Auld's (Churchill) Correspondence Book (1811), extract of private letter from W. Holmes, Inland Master of Rat River, dated Bedford House, 12 Feb. 1811, B. 42/b/55, f. 6, HBCA.

28. W.S. Wallace, ed., *Documents Relating to the North West Company* (Toronto, 1934), 264–65.

29. Harmon, *Sixteen Years*, 113–14.

30. Mackenzie, *Voyages, lxxxi.*

31. Tyrell, ed., *Thompson's Narrative*, 539.

32. Morton, *History of the Canadian West*, 453.

33. Peter Fidler's Ile-à-la-Crosse Journal (1810–11), dated June 1810, B. 89/a/2, f. 1d., HBCA.

34. Morton, *History of the Canadian West*, 451–52, 453.

35. Peter Fidler's Ile-à-la-Crosse Journal (1810–11), dated June 1810, B. 89/a/2, f. 1d, HBCA.

36. Ibid., June 1811, f. 36d.

37. J.B. Tyrell, ed., *Journals of Samuel Hearne and Philip Turnor* (Toronto, 1946), 446.

38. Harmon, *Sixteen Years*, 114.

39. Samuel Hearne, *A Journey from Prince of Wales Fort in Hudson's Bay to the Northern Ocean 1769, 1770, 1771, 1772*, ed. R. Glover (Toronto, 1958), 210.

40. Mackenzie, *Voyages*, 404; Hearne, *Journey to the Northern Ocean*, 210–11.

41. Hearne, *Journey to the Northern Ocean*, 129.

42. Diamond Jenness, *The Indians of Canada*, 3rd ed. (Ottawa: Queen's Printer, 1955), 392–93.

43. Hearne, *Journey to the Northern Ocean*, 210–12, 116–17.

44. W. Auld's (Churchill) Correspondence Book (1811), Auld at Churchill to Thomas Thomas at Albany, 16 Aug. 1811, B. 42/b/55, ff. 15d–16, HBCA.

45. Tyrell, ed., *Thompson's Narrative*, 16–17.

POINT LANCE IN TRANSITION*

J.J. MANNION

Point Lance is located near the southwest corner of the Avalon Peninsula, on the southern side of the peninsula that divides Placentia Bay from St. Mary's Bay (figure 1). The hamlet nestles at the foot of a steep slope on the western edge of a broad valley drained by a river and a brook. One mile to the east, another ridge skirts the valley and both ridges jut out into the Atlantic to form a picturesque, south-facing cove (figure 2). Point Lance is connected by gravel road to Placentia, a small service centre sixty miles away, and is 125 miles from the provincial capital, St. John's. With the exception of St. Brides, the settlements along the Cape Shore road between Point Lance and Placentia are little different in size or character from Point Lance, which had a population of 135 people (24 households) in 1974. All originated early in the nineteenth century, not as commercial fishing communities, as was the case with the vast majority of Newfoundland outports, but as settlements devoted to commercial cattle raising.

These settlements were established by the Sweetmans, a southeast Irish Catholic family with lands in south Wexford and mercantile businesses in Waterford and Placentia. According to local tradition, the Sweetmans brought out young men from southeastern Ireland and placed them in the unsettled coves along the shore for the purpose of raising cattle and crops to feed the Irish labourers and fishermen in Placentia. Before this time, Placentia had been supplied mainly from Waterford, and the Sweetmans hoped these new agricultural settlements would provision their Placentia operations more cheaply.

Point Lance received its first permanent settlers around 1820. Two brothers, Philip and Ned Careen, worked for a summer or two as "shore-men" for the Sweetmans in Placentia, and then were moved to Point Lance to establish a stock farm. The Careen brothers were part of a large annual exodus of young, unmarried Irish men who migrated seasonally to exploit the summer fishery in Newfoundland. After 1800, many decided to stay, and settled especially along the coast from

* Adapted from *Point Lance in Transition: The Transformation of a Newfoundland Outport* (Toronto: McClelland and Stewart, 1976).

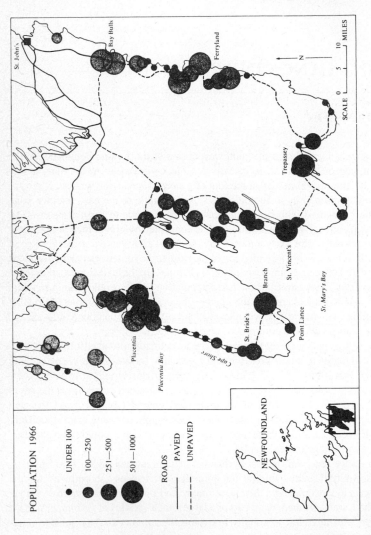

FIGURE 1

SOURCE: All maps by J.J. Mannion, drawn by David Hunter.

St. John's to Placentia, where they became the dominant—in most cases, the exclusive—ethnic group. Philip Careen married a woman of Irish-born parents from Red Island, inner Placentia Bay; Ned remained single. During their lifetimes, their nearest neighbours were two other nuclear families located three miles along the coast on either side of Point Lance.

In these remote locations, social isolation was partially but slowly offset by the influx of wives from other settlements, by large families, and by the fact that few if any adult men left the area. In Point Lance, all sons inherited property and none left the community to live elsewhere until after 1950. Moreover, all persons born in Point Lance after 1820 were descended from the first family, most of them in the male line. Through five generations, the society of Point Lance was dominated by Careen men. Almost all Point Lance women left the community when they married, until marriages within the community began amongst second cousins in the fourth generation. Only through marriage ties did other males ever settle in Point Lance after the arrival of the first Careens.

For five generations most Point Lancers found their spouses in nearby settlements, especially Branch and St. Brides, in certain settlements in east St. Mary's Bay (from where people traditionally travelled to Point Lance for the summer fishery), and in a few settlements along the old cattle droving route from Point Lance through southeast Placentia to Holyrood and St. John's (figure 3). There was a distinct tendency for Point Lancers to form alliances with certain families: the Nashes and Englishes of Branch, the McGraths of Gull Cove, and the Conways and Lundrigans of St. Brides. There was, in addition, a fairly even balance or rate of exchange between the Careens and these families in terms of the number of departing and incoming female spouses. Traditionally, marriages in Point Lance were romantic rather than mercenary, in the sense that the initiative in choosing a mate was taken by the young people themselves and not arranged by the parents or old folk, although young couples valued encouragement from the older people. In the traditional economy daughters were far less useful economically than sons and were encouraged to marry early; this was all the more possible because of the scarcity of women of marriageable age. Because women received little in the way of capital or goods, the Careens and certain neighbouring families may have encouraged a reciprocal exchange of daughters.

Except for the youngest (or only) son, marriage meant leaving the parents' home and setting up a new household. Rigid rules of inheritance persisted through the generations. By tradition, cleared land was divided equally among all sons. Few sons remained single and the key to the expansion of settlement was the number of sons in a family and the availability of marriageable women nearby. Sons married women from other outports, brought them back to Point Lance, and settled on their portion of the cleared land. In this way, the number of households increased from one to five to thirteen to eighteen in four generations, and the fifth generation so far has added a further seven households.

One of the major characteristics of Point Lance over the generations has been the consistently large size of families. Large families reflect more than simply a

FIGURE 2   Point Lance. The hamlet is at the foot of a steep slope on the western edge of a broad valley.

Catholic attitude: the familial household was the basic unit of economic production; and all the children were employed in household production at a very early age. Under the old regime of a simple, manual technology, the larger the family—especially if there was a preponderance of boys—the more economic muscle the head of the household commanded. Girls tended to marry young, thereby increasing the possibility of large families, and the population of Point Lance grew apace. Early in the 1870s, the settlement had 30 residents; by 1911, 60. In 1935, there were 90 people in Point Lance, and in the early 1960s numbers exceeded 150. This pattern of population growth was typical of other outports along the Cape Shore and elsewhere in Newfoundland.

Living frugally in a harsh, isolated, and in many ways uninviting environment, the Point Lancers developed a remarkable resilience. Their present commitment to this place can only be understood in the light of their history, and especially of the many strategies they adopted to enable them to survive. It was the goal of all Point Lancers to become as self-sufficient as possible as soon as possible, and to produce a surplus for sale. Isolation induced a remarkably diversified and complex yearly round of activities on land and sea. Cattle, horses, sheep, and pigs were raised on the land, together with domesticated ducks, geese, and hens; potatoes, turnips, cabbages, oats, hay, and a variety of other vegetables and fruits were planted; cod, capelin, and kelp were taken from the sea; foxes, muskrat, and rabbit were trapped; caribou, eiderducks, shags, loons, turres, and other sea-fowl, as well as partridges, were shot; bakeapples, blueberries, partridge berries, and cranberries were gathered; natural meadows were grazed and harvested, and lumber was cut in the woods. In addition, Point Lancers built their own houses, outbuildings, fishing premises, and boats almost totally from local materials; made their own nets; and produced their own clothes and shoes as well as most of their household furniture and farm implements.

In general terms, the settlement of Point Lance comprised an extended family occupying a small hamlet strategically located in relation to scattered local resources. This type of settlement was found in many of the maritime areas of Europe from Brittany to Norway, and was transferred to Newfoundland from Ireland, where the Gaelic custom of inheritance entitled each son to an equal share of all land resources, and sons often built their dwellings close to the ancestral home. Clusters evolved, as in Point Lance, around the home of the father. Such settlements were typically small, and institutionally simple. In contrast to the large villages of mediaeval manorial tradition in continental Europe, they generally lacked formal buildings. The settlements housed primary producers and job specialization was rare. These communities were isolated and tight-knit; they emphasized co-operation and self-sufficiency, and regulated their affairs informally through custom, consensus, and patriarchal advice. Without school, church, and larger institutions, and built around the patriarchal extended family, the community of Point Lance exemplified in many ways the traditional social structure of the hamlets facing the seas of the northern North Atlantic.

The layout of these hamlets appears loose and haphazard, in contrast again to the compact and orderly morphology of many European villages. The apparent disorder is deceptive, however, for numerous factors impinge on the decision to locate a dwelling or any other structure in strategic relation to exploited or exploitable resources. Some are disposed linearly along the axis between good and marginal land, or in a circular pattern around an infield area, while others are more tightly clustered, as in Point Lance. The spatial structure of traditional Newfoundland fishing settlements ideally comprises a range of wharves and stages along the shore, backed by a tier of structures devoted to storing and curing fish, then lines of dwellings, farm outbuildings, gardens, and meadows. Property lines run back from the shore, transecting these linear patterns and forming long, segmented family plots with each family enjoying water frontage and a share of the valuable land close to shore. In reality, this geometry is usually considerably modified, however, and in Point Lance it scarcely exists. The beginnings of a linear patterning of fishing structures did emerge, but Point Lancers continued to build their houses a mile away in the lee of the ridge, close to the valuable meadowlands and gardens. Point Lancers followed the agricultural tradition of the first generation, rather than locate on the exposed slopes of the ridge behind the "rooms." The beach area was unsuitable for fish landings and the fluvial terraces around the beach were unsuitable for farmstead sites. As a result, family plots were carved out along the

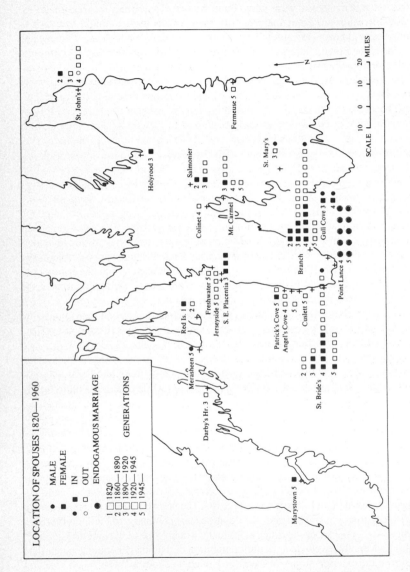

FIGURE 3

brook in a highly fragmented manner, rather than in long, narrow compact lots running to the shore.

In the traditional outport economy, where a combination of scattered natural resources was exploited seasonally, mobility was important. Some communities shifted three times in a year: from the home gardens to the fishing "rooms" in summer, back to the gardens to harvest crops in the fall, and inland to the woods in winter to trap and to log. In Point Lance, apart from the cod, all exploited resources lay within daily travelling distance from the hamlet and, apart from the seasonal shift of men to the "rooms," Point Lancers' domiciles remained fixed by their meadows. This reflects the importance of farming in the traditional economy of the hamlet.

Farming in Point Lance

Unlike most European immigrants in pioneer settings in northeastern North America, the Careens did not confront formidable stands of deciduous and coniferous forests. Balsam fir and black spruce, rarely exceeding fifteen feet in height, grew along the valley sides fifty feet above sea level, but the broad valley floor, which was to form the core of improved land in Point Lance, contained only patches of low alder and willow scrub. In the low plateau country surrounding the settlement, vegetation was equally stunted and patchy. Pockets of coniferous scrub and small trees were found in the sheltered, stream-eroded valleys, but elsewhere in this exposed and wind-swept headland a rolling treeless terrain covered with dark brown moss heath and underlain with bog was characteristic. To the first settlers, the "barrens" of the Point Lance country must have appeared strikingly similar to the open hill masses of their homeland.

By far the most notable environmental contrast between Ireland and Point Lance was the climate. In the new world, the winters were harsh and spring was very late. Southeast Ireland enjoys a mild, temperate climate with mean January temperatures of 6°C, compared to -4°C in Point Lance. July mean temperatures in both areas were between 13°C and 16°C, but in Point Lance the growing season is restricted to around 120 days, commencing in May, whereas in the homeland, frost is rare and growth almost continuous through winter. Considerably more fodder was needed to feed cattle through the long Newfoundland winter and hay has remained the main crop in Point Lance from the early days of settlement. A high annual precipitation (1 400 mm) favoured grasses, but frequent fog and rain retarded haymaking as well as the drying and curing of fish in the fall. Moreover, the heavy rainfall and low evaporation rates combined to produce highly leached, acidic, podzolic soils. High winds sharply curtailed the fishing season and in sharp contrast to southeast Ireland, the cool, damp climate placed Point Lance beyond the margins of easy cereal cultivation.

The first settlers of Point Lance adjusted quickly to the new conditions and established an economy similar in many ways to the traditional peasant economy they had in Ireland. Hill country and other marginal agricultural areas were widely used for summer grazing in Ireland and the Careens would have been familiar with some of the skills required to establish a commercial stock farm in an environment like Point Lance. The natural meadows along the brook and river afforded good summer grazing, but cattle could not survive on bent and fescue grasses alone. The Careens cleared off patches of scrub on the fluvial terraces along Conway's Brook, drained the deep soils, and sometimes planted a crop or two of potatoes on the newly enclosed ground before returning it to permanent hayland. Timothy hayseed was probably planted to augment the native grasses. Trees were levelled with small axes or hatchets and scrub roots removed with picks and mattocks. Much of the refuse of the clearings was burned and the ashes sprinkled over the ground as fertilizer, although brush and light timbers were used for fences and the better timber was salvaged for construction and for fuel. The farmstead was located strategically in the lee of the western ridge, between the more or less continuously cultivated potato garden and the more expansive meadows along the brook (figure 4). All the meadows were just above the high water line, but the garden and farmstead sites were on slightly more elevated and drier ground at the base of the ridge.

Despite the absence of dense forests, the rate of land improvement in Point Lance was inordinately slow by North American standards. After four decades of settlement only twenty acres or so had been improved and the average rate of clearing per household declined after the first generation. Over much of frontier North America land was plentiful and cheap, whereas labour was scarce and expensive. In these conditions it was economically advantageous to clear land as quickly as possible and to adopt an extensive system of agriculture. However, the pioneers of Point Lance, the Cape Shore, and indeed much of Newfoundland, cleared ground slowly and worked their acres intensively, much like the peasants in the land-hungry regions of Europe. This intensive mode of farming was less a transfer of agrarian attitudes from the old world than an adaptation to local environmental and economic constraints. Soils were too poor and the climate too inclement to sustain a commercially viable, arable economy.

The major incentive for clearing extra land in Point Lance was not to grow vegetables but to produce hay for feed. As the numbers of livestock increased, the area of improved land expanded and Point Lancers combined an intensive and extensive pattern of pastoral husbandry. Improved meadows were enclosed, heavily manured, and worked intensively, but such land was rarely reserved as pasture. Livestock were grazed from May to November in the open country or "commons" beyond the home fields, and wild meadows were harvested to supplement the hay grown on improved meadows. Such practices meant that there was little pressure to clear much land.

As was common in the most marginal parts of peasant Ireland at the time of the migrations, improved land in Point Lance was normally divided equally among all sons. To ensure an egalitarian division in Ireland, each son would usually inherit a portion of each type of land and this custom was maintained to some extent in the first transfer of land in Point Lance. All six sons of Philip Careen received equal

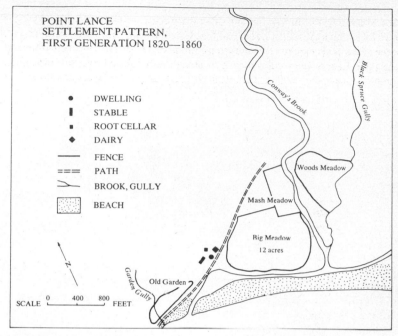

FIGURE 4

shares of the cleared section of the Big Meadow, the oldest and largest meadow on the farm (figure 5). After each son married he occupied his share and built a house and outbuildings so there was a gradual dispersion from the parental household. Ned, the first to marry, built as close as possible to the parental dwelling, out on the meadow. There was no room for farmsteads along the base of the ridge beside the old house, however, and the other sons seemed unwilling to locate on the flats. Like their father, they selected sites along the base of the ridge, as close as possible to the ancestral dwelling. Four sons moved "downalong" to occupy the "Old Garden," some distance from their meadows but strategically located in relation to the fishing premises or "rooms." One of these, Dick, did not marry, and lived with Micil and his family. Only one son, Jim, moved "upalong," strategically located in relation to his meadows and gardens but at considerable distance from the fishing "rooms."

Ned married at least a decade before any of his brothers, and fenced off his shares; the other subdivisions in the old fields were marked but not fenced. Each household worked its share separately, but after the hay was gathered, the open plots were grazed jointly. Extra land was cleared by each new household and these clearings were enclosed and farmed individually. Most of the new plots were located on the well-drained slopes along the western ridge and served mainly as

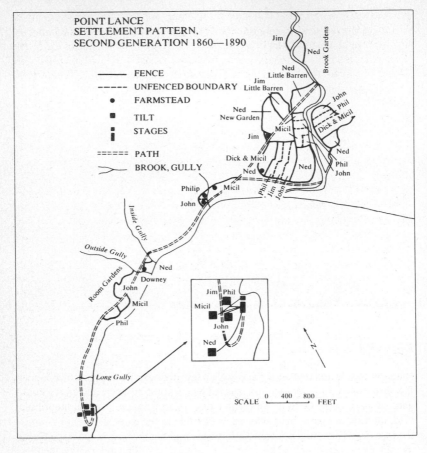

FIGURE 5

potato gardens. Ned expanded along the brook, north from his dwelling, and with the aid of six sons cleared more land than any of his brothers. Jim cleared parcels next to Ned's, while the three households "downalong" eventually used the "Old Garden" solely for buildings and carved out new gardens on the bank along the pathway to the "rooms."

The old open fields were further fragmented in the third generation, but because of the tiny size of plots it was impractical to continue the tradition of allocating shares of each plot to all sons. Shares in the "Big Meadow" and the "Mash Meadow" doubled in numbers in this generation, although only one plot was subdivided in the "Woods Meadow" (figure 6). Ned's and Jim's children expanded north onto the parental gardens under the lee of the western ridge and some sons established new farmsteads in the "Old Garden," but the latter area could not accommodate all heirs and two moved "upalong" and built on their shares in the "Mash Meadow." Over twenty parcels of new ground were enclosed and improved by the third generation, mainly on the fluvial terraces on either side of the brook. Each new garden was worked privately by the individual household and some were cleared through a government "bonus" incentive at the end of the last century.

While the practice of splitting up land among male heirs continued through the fourth and fifth generations, the dividing of ancestral meadows and gardens became less common. Indeed, some adjoining parcels were amalgamated through exchange, as in the "Big Meadow," where the number of plots dropped to seven. Only in three cases were parental plots split among heirs and these were all for farmstead sites (figure 7). Settlement intensified along the foot of the ridge, in Ned's and Jim's gardens, and spread onto the flats on the west bank of the brook. Good farmstead sites were becoming scarce around the old settlement nucleus and in the fifth generation settlement expanded across the brook along the new road. Despite another government-subsidized agricultural scheme in the 1930s, the average rate of clearing per household declined and the number of improved acres per household fell to an average of 3.5 by 1935.

During the depression, farming was revitalized on the Cape Shore through a Commission of Government scheme and more land was cleared in Point Lance between 1936 and 1940 than in any previous decade. Clearing continued northward along Conway's Brook, eastward across the flats past Point Lance river, and southward along the pathway to the fishing "rooms" (figure 7). A considerable portion of extra land was cleared by three men who married Point Lance girls and received little more than building lots when settling there. Including farmstead units, over one hundred individual parcels of land were occupied by twenty-one households at the end of the fourth generation. By 1974, only six sons of the fifth generation had established houses; each of these received shares of the ancestral lands and cleared parcels on his own, across the river and out beyond the fishing "rooms."

Improved land was the major item of inheritance in Point Lance. Considerable labour was expended in clearing a garden on the slopes and even a meadow on the river flats required a lot of attention before it reached full productivity. Sons helped their fathers clear extra land and were rewarded by a share of the family property, and at no time in the history of land succession in Point Lance was a son excluded from the patrimony. Each division of the land weakened the family property but uncleared land lay all about and cost only the price of the labour invested in clearing it. Through the generations, almost every heir added land to his inheritance and fathers often continued to clear land after transmitting shares to the older sons. In the crowded lands of Ireland this pattern of inheritance implied a permanent diminution of family property, but the land resource was always replaceable in the frontier environment of Point Lance. Land availability is an important factor in understanding succession and settlement patterns over the generations. Inheritance of a part of his father's land meant more, however, than simply an economic reward for the labour expended by a son on the family farm. It gave each son a start and a

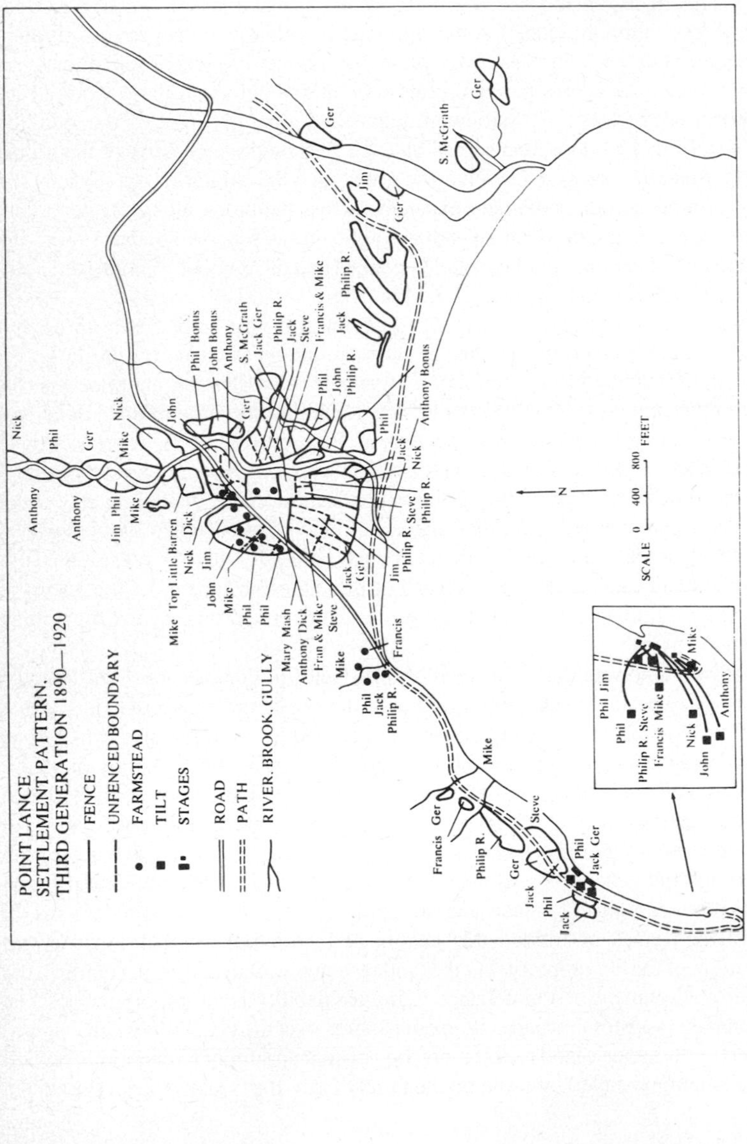

POINT LANCE
SETTLEMENT PATTERN,
THIRD GENERATION 1890—1920

FENCE
UNFENCED BOUNDARY
FARMSTEAD
TILT
STAGES
ROAD
PATH
RIVER, BROOK, GULLY

SCALE 0 400 800 FEET

FIGURE 6

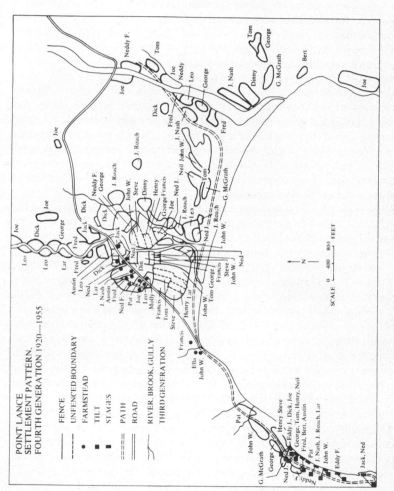

POINT LANCE
SETTLEMENT PATTERN.
FOURTH GENERATION 1920—1955

——————   FENCE
- - - - - -   UNFENCED BOUNDARY
●   FARMSTEAD
■   TILT
═══   STAGES
═ ═ ═   PATH
═══   ROAD

〜〜〜   RIVER, BROOK, GULLY

THIRD GENERATION

SCALE   0   400   800   FEET

FIGURE 7

stake in the community, a recognition of his right to "make a stand" in the place, and most important, recognition of his acceptance by his immediate male relatives and the community in general. With this initial stake, all he required was a pair of strong arms and the help of some sturdy sons to win complete economic independence for his household.

In Point Lance, the nuclear family has always been the basic unit of subsistence production. This individualism was most manifest in farming, where a labour force larger than the single family was rarely required. The major task of the householder was to feed his family and from the beginning of settlement the dietary staple in Point Lance and other Cape Shore coves was the potato. Other vegetables, notably cabbages and turnips, had a place in the traditional subsistence arable economy but the potato provided more calories daily than any other item of diet. Environmental and economic conditions and cultural preferences favoured the potato above other foods. Although it was susceptible to frost and blight it thrived in the cool, damp conditions of the Cape Shore. For a minimum of labour it provided a bountiful harvest, required little ground, and produced more calories per acre than any other crop. It had been, of course, the main food of the Cape Shore Irish in their homeland and was also useful as a colonizing crop, with each new field beginning its career with a summer or two under potatoes.

Work in the gardens started around the first of May and potatoes were the first crop planted. In the first generation, over one hundred barrels (2 250 bushels) were grown in Point Lance, but later the relative importance of potatoes declined as other foodstuffs, particularly fish, became important and as the numbers of pigs raised began to decline. Potatoes were planted in ridges or "lazy-beds," each two and a half feet wide and separated by a trench or furrow one and a half feet in width. Ridges were fashioned with a long, narrow-bladed southeastern Irish spade and the craft of ridgemaking was transferred from the homeland. Furrows were dug to a depth of around twelve inches, the soil heaped on the ridges to raise the bed above the water table. Potatoes were preferably planted on sloping ground and furrows ran upslope to aid drainage. Deep digging with the sharp spade not only ensured that extra nutrients in the deeper layers were brought to the surface of the beds but also unearthed rocks and roots which were cleared away. Each successive year, ridge was alternated with furrow and this helped to work up the ground.

The gardens grouped along the slopes of the western ridge, extending almost two miles from the "rooms" to the fluvial terraces along Conway's Brook, were worked intensively and were extremely productive. Kelp was the staple fertilizer and up to fifty cartloads were dumped on half an acre. Stable manure was seldom used because it brought weeds to the gardens, but fish offal was often substituted for kelp and sometimes a compost of offal, kelp, and manure was made. As were the infields of many Atlantic-European hamlets, the gardens of Point Lance were cropped continually, some for as long as twenty consecutive seasons. Sometimes, however, the small subsistence arable plot was shifted around the "ley" every few years to reduce weeds and disease and to keep the ground well worked. Cabbages, turnips, and the other vegetables, notably carrots and beets, were planted in wider beds, often beside the potato patch. The gardens were tended by the women during summer and harvested by the men in the fall, and the produce was stored in long, narrow pits outdoors or in specially constructed root cellars near the dwelling. Gardening in Point Lance was a highly labour-intensive operation that changed little over the generations.

Oats were sown on arable patches being converted into ley, but the crop did not ripen easily and was usually fed green to the livestock. Local tradition asserts that wheat was once raised, but it would ripen only in exceptional summers. Flour has always been the most important imported food, in contrast to the homeland where wheaten and oaten bread and porridge were made from the produce of the fields. In the homeland, oats and straw supplemented hay as winter feed for livestock, but Point Lancers depended almost solely on the latter crop to tide their cattle, sheep and horses through winter. Hay occupied over 90 percent of the cleared ground. A horse or cow can consume over two tons of hay in a winter and in the last century, the Careens kept an average of over a dozen cattle, a dozen sheep, and a pair of horses per household (table 1).

Haying began traditionally on Lady Day (August 15) but was often deferred until September, depending on the weather or the demands of the fishery. The crop was mowed with the scythe until the advent of horse-drawn mowing machines through government aid in the 1930s. In the inclement and uncertain weather of Point Lance, hay-making was always a hurried operation that summoned the labour of the entire family. Men cut and women and children spread the hay and it was stored in stable lofts or in barns and the surplus stacked outdoors. Timothy hay grown on improved ground was supplemented by wild hay harvested along brooks and rivers late in the fall.

From May to November, cattle, sheep, and horses were grazed in the un-enclosed, unimproved "commons" beyond the farms. Good grazing was found along the cliffs and up the rivers, and herds wandered up to ten miles from the settlement, especially as the numbers of livestock increased. Each householder branded his stock, but care of these herds was a shared responsibility, usually undertaken by boys who combined trouting or berry picking with the weekly task of checking the livestock. Cows were grazed in open areas close to the home fields and folded in a "pound" by the stable after milking each evening. This practice of communal summer grazing resembled in some ways traditional Irish trans-humance, but none of the salient features of the latter system was reproduced in Point Lance or anywhere on the Cape Shore. In the homeland, rights to graze the mountain pastures were reckoned by the amount of land or the number of ridges a family held in the infield and were just as jealously guarded, an indication of extreme land pressure. Each family in an Irish hamlet had rights of access to all local land and marine resources but this meticulous subdivision or allocation was unnecessary in the new setting, where the local resources were comparatively abundant. Restricted grazing, for example, was unnecessary in the under-exploited territory around Point Lance, and there was plenty of wood and fish and game for all. Young folk moved and stayed with their herds all summer in Irish trans-humance tradition, but such labour in Point Lance could be far more profitably invested in clearing land, farming, and fishing.

TABLE 1 *Point Lance Agriculture, 1857–1970*

	Houses	Improved acres	Barrels of potatoes	Tons of hay	Barrels of turnips	Cows	Cattle	Horses	Sheep	Pigs	Poultry	Eggs by the dozen	Lbs. of butter	Lbs. of wool
1857	1	12	100	20		6	15	3	17	7			500	
1869	2		80	20	3	13	11	5	26	19			300	
1874	3	28	160	42	4	18	17	6	28	10			500	
1884	5	29	140	31	33	13	16	6	37	19			760	
1891	6	32	96	45	50	17	17	7	28	6	26		1332	171
1901	9	42	235	46	46	24	26	11	47	6	47		1000	70
1911	11	68	203	70	44	33	36	16	82	7	57	180	1650	234
1921	10	49	105	43	20	51	11	11	90		76	215	1840	360
1935	17	58	320	83	58	26	38	14	85					
1945	22	88	400	112	450	34	15	25	116	3	89		2086	493
1970	21	135	50	195	200	14	17	15	120		74			
1974	24	135	180	140		10	14	9	100		50			

During the first generation of settlement, cattle provided the major cash income in Point Lance. Over twenty head were kept and beef and butter were marketed in Placentia and later in St. John's and Holyrood. In supporting a petition in 1845 for the improvement of the Cape Shore road, an inspector noted the agricultural emphasis in the area and suggested that the number of cattle driven from there to St. John's would double if road improvements were made, a proposition confirmed a few years later. Over 1 000 lbs. of butter were produced each summer for the local market. Butter was made in traditional Irish churns and was salted and stored in the dairy in homemade tubs or firkins until fall, when it was shipped out by schooner. Dry cattle, usually two or three years old, were driven each fall along the Cape Shore road to market. There was no regularly scheduled, European-style fair in Newfoundland, but butchers and farmers did congregate near the wharves in St. John's at certain times and the butchers paid cash for the livestock.

Throughout the nineteenth century each household slaughtered a few mature cattle late in the fall and the beef was stored in the dairy for domestic consumption. Point Lancers relied on the cold winter to preserve their meat, and whatever remained in the spring was salted. Hides were tanned and turned into leather for shoes, usually made by one man in the community. Mutton was an equally important item of diet and most families killed up to a dozen lambs in the fall. Traditionally, the first lamb was killed on Lady Day and mutton was eaten fresh or fresh frozen until spring, when the surplus was salted.

The local market for salt mutton was poor and sheep could not be driven easily over the rough terrain to Placentia, Holyrood, or St. John's; it was not until the introduction of motor-truck transport in the 1930s that commercial sheep-raising developed along the Cape Shore and slaughtering for local consumption declined. Sheep were shorn every June, the wool washed, carded, and spun into yarn by the women, who would spend winter nights knitting socks, sweaters, mitts, dresses, and underwear. Pigs were raised only for home consumption. A thriving market for salt pork existed in St. John's but the Careens and other Cape Shore settlers could not compete with the homeland in supplying this demand. Pigs would not thrive in the commons and required a diet of grain and potatoes all year. The land in Point Lance was inhospitable to grain, and potato cultivation was labour-intensive. Consequently, pigs were considered costly to raise and disappeared altogether in the twentieth century. Domesticated ducks and geese were also sources of food and their feathers were used to stuff pillows and mattresses. Each household kept enough hens to supply eggs during summer and fall. In the traditional subsistence economy of Point Lance, the horse was widely used and every household kept at least one. The horse performed a variety of tasks: drawing kelp, capelin, offal, and stable manure to the fields; hay and other crops to the yard; and wood from the forest; and transporting people (by slide) to neighbouring settlements in winter.

Farming practices in Point Lance grew out of those of the Irish homeland, although considerable adaptation was required by the very different environmental and social conditions. The climate was more rigorous and the soils were poorer than those of Ireland, and land improvement proceeded very slowly by North

American standards. Because of this, land was always in short supply and agricultural practices tended to be intensive in nature. The increase of improved farmland was encouraged by the system of inheritance, in which land was divided among all sons. As the original plots were subdivided and each holding became smaller, there was a great incentive to open up new areas elsewhere. Nonetheless, suitable land is limited in Point Lance, and increasing population soon made it necessary to look to the sea for additional resources.

Fishing in Point Lance

Although they lived beside one of the richest inshore fishing grounds in New-foundland, the first generation of Careens never fished commercially. Several species of fish, including herring, haddock, mackerel, capelin, salmon, and lobster and other shellfish, are found in the waters off Point Lance but cod is the only species Point Lancers have ever caught commercially. Each spring, the cod spawn in the cold, deep waters offshore and having eaten little during spawning, begin to feed ravenously on their favourite source of food, the tiny, silvery capelin. In June, the capelin swarm in millions towards the beaches of Newfoundland to spawn and are pursued by the cod, which remain close to shore during summer.

Point Lance was well located in relation to this annual movement of capelin and cod, and the inshore waters along the headland from Point Lance to Cape St. Mary's attracted hundreds of fishermen from Placentia and St. Mary's bays long before the Careens entered the fishery. Some of these summer visitors cleaned and dried their fish on shore and lived in small "tilts" until the end of the season. It was through contact with these migrant fishermen that the second generation of Careens learned the value and craft of the fishery and around 1850 turned to the sea as a major source of commercial production. It soon gained a pivotal place in the traditional economy.

Lance Cove is far from ideal for landing fish. It is wide open to the strong southeasterlies and many a boat moored in the cove has been smashed off the rocky coast or off the treacherous nobs and shoals that form the core of the fishing grounds. Whenever a storm threatens, large boats have to race for shelter in North Harbour, thirty miles away in inner St. Mary's Bay. At least six feet of water is required to land fish comfortably and the Careens initially used small "punts" to transfer the catch from their large skiff to the shore. The skiff was around forty feet long, ten feet wide at the centre and was capable of carrying over thirty quintals of fish. It had five rowing oars and a scull oar and was manned by the six Careen brothers.

In the mid-nineteenth century, seining and jigging by hand with hook and line were the dominant catching techniques in the Newfoundland inshore fishery. The typical seine was a huge wall of hempen mesh, often 200 feet long, sixty feet deep in the centre, and tapering toward the ends. The Careens waited for a school of fish to come inside the cove, circled the school, dropping off the seine, and then hauled it into the skiff. Sometimes they fastened one end of the seine to a fixture on shore and dragged the cod onto dry beach. After fish were landed they were pitched (or "pewed") up the cliff on a series of platforms to the top stage-head where they were split, gutted, headed, washed, salted, and then stacked in the "stage" beside the splitting table.

In dry, windy weather, when the sea was too rough for fishing, the salt cod were transported in handbarrows along a circuitous path to the top of the cliff, where they were placed on "flakes" to dry. Curing or drying was a laborious and time-consuming task. Fish had to be taken in each night to the "store," or covered with rind (bark) to protect them against rain or fog, and it took several weeks of sunshine or wind before the cod were fully cured. It was often late in November before fish were taken to market, and curing continued up to this date. Oil, an important commercial by-product, was extracted from the cod liver.

Fish were landed about a mile from the hamlet, on the western shore of Lance Cove. Fishermen lived during summer in "tilts" in the fishing "rooms." The "tilts" were substantial wooden structures, usually one room each, equipped with a fireplace for preparing meals, and bunks for the crew. Women sometimes assisted in curing the fish but never stayed overnight in the "rooms"; fishermen usually returned to their houses each weekend.

By August, the capelin and cod had retreated from inshore waters. The seine was put away and Point Lancers jigged with hook and line until September. There were great fluctuations in catches, but fifty quintals of dried cod per fisherman was considered a good annual yield. Like other kin groups along the Cape Shore, the Careens purchased a brig or schooner, weighing some forty tons and capable of carrying up to 800 quintals of fish to the market. Following the decline of the Sweetmans, no other merchant of consequence settled in Placentia or along the Cape Shore, and the Careens took their fish directly to the Water Street merchants in St. John's. Initially they dealt with the Catholic Irish firm of Sheas, and later with Jobs, Bowrings, Rendells, and Munroes. The fish were graded on the wharf, weighed, and after the merchant had deducted the amount spent the previous spring for the season's "fit out" and the amount spent for winter provisions, the surplus was paid in cash. Frequently, there was little cash but rarely did Point Lancers "fall behind"; that is, fall into a state of continuous debt to the merchants.

Point Lancers did not change their methods of curing fish until after 1950, but they did replace the old seine by home-knit hempen nets around 1875, and this change reflected new directions in the evolution of society and settlement in Point Lance. The new nets were around 300 feet long, but only seven feet deep with four-inch meshes to trap and strangle the cod. The deep "fish-holes" inside the cove, ideal for the seine technology, were now abandoned for the nobs, ledges, and shoals beyond Bull Island Point where cod congregated in the shallow waters. These nets were best operated by a crew of two men, using a locally built thirty-foot skiff equipped with a mainsail, foresail, jib, and a pair of oars. Each crew normally set two or three nets every evening and hauled next morning, but when cod were plentiful nets were often set twice a day. The new technology improved the catch per fisherman, involved less labour than the seine, and was far more consistent through the season, but the breaking up of the old kin-based crew destroyed much of the closely knit communal and patriarchal nature of Point Lance society. The eldest brother, who was skipper of the old crew, retired from the fishery, the second eldest "shipped" men until his son was old enough to fish, and the four remaining brothers split into two two-man units.

There were strong pressures for splitting up at this time. Two brothers had married and had children and two others were about to marry, so too many people were dependent on the produce of a single seine and skiff. Cod may also have been scarce inside the cove in the 1870s. Since then the dominant fishing unit has been a pair of men, usually two brothers or father and son. This was an egalitarian unit with the partners pooling their limited capital to maintain their collectively owned gear and to share the catch. Two brothers normally split up only after one had a son old enough to fish with him, had accumulated sufficient gear, and was satisfied that his brother had found an acceptable partner. Economically, it was most desirable that the crew should be from a single household. Crews were sometimes formed of cousins, or of an uncle and nephew, but the three initial crews evidently influenced the subsequent pattern of recruiting: the descendants of Ned never formed a lasting alliance with fishermen descended from the members of the other two crews, and there was little cross-recruitment between the descendants of James and Philip on the one hand, and John and Micil on the other.

The shareman, who usually lived with the skipper and family during the summer, worked in the gardens and meadows, helped catch and cure fish, and received one-quarter to one-third of the total catch in the fall, was an important element in the composition of fishing crews after 1870. Even in the days of the seine, men (and sometimes women) were "shipped" to help cure fish during summer, but few of these labourers ever fished until after the old seine crew had broken up. It was potentially more profitable for a fisherman who could provide gear to hire a shareman as fishing partner, but the skipper always ran the risk of losing his gear. Few Careens ever worked as sharemen in Point Lance, but men who had married into the community did, as well as in-laws from neighbouring outports. The majority of sharemen, however, were from outside the family. Some remained for several seasons, working for different members of the Careens, while others stayed only for a summer or two.

After 1875, cod nets were set in the shallow waters just outside Lance Cove. There were three distinct areas within two miles of the stages: Bull Island Point and the Frothy Sunker, Delaney's Rock, and the Bull, Cow, and Calf. These grounds varied in productivity and each crew usually set a net in each area to cover possible fluctuations in the supply of cod and to minimize the risks of a poor season's catch. As long as the stocks remained, crews continued to fish in the same places each season. An intimate knowledge of the sea-bottom, the direction of currents, tides, and winds, and the migratory habits of cod was required to locate good berths, and it often took several years of trial and error before a crew discovered the better locations. Over the decades, knowledge of the inshore increased but cod frequently shifted ground and berths were abandoned. A system of visual triangulation with marks on shore was used to locate berths each morning; the geometry often remained the secret of the crew and was passed on orally to their successors. Initially, there was little pressure on the resource, but with the proliferation of crews in the third generation, competition for good berths became intense and prime berths were retained by a crew or skipper for a lifetime and then transmitted to the heirs.

Tenure or inheritance of berths was never as fixed or rigid as it was with fields, but any encroachment by a Point Lance crew on a local berth was considered by the mass of Point Lancers to be as reprehensible as an intrusion by outsiders. In some larger outports, where competition at sea was even more intense and society less cohesive, territorial fishing rights were re-allocated each year under a formal drawing system intended to ensure a more egalitarian distribution. In the small and intimate society of Point Lance, any serious inequities were informally discouraged. True, Point Lancers respected individual opportunism and skill at sea, and the spirit of competition and even economic envy were important stimuli, but economic aggression was decried because it led to social discord.

The stages, stores, flakes, and tilts, as well as boats and nets, were fixed items of property transmitted from father to son in a pattern closely related to the transmission of land, houses, outbuildings, and livestock. Initially, all six brothers used a single stage, store, flake, and tilt, but with the breaking up of the crew, all but the stage were inherited by the youngest son, who also inherited the ancestral dwelling, outbuildings, and livestock. This pattern of inheritance by the youngest son has persisted through the generations. The old stage, a substantial wooden structure one hundred feet by eighteen feet, was used by the three crews after 1876 but one crew later built a stage beside it (figure 5). Both stages were divided among sons in the third generation and conditions became increasingly congested, especially in the ancestral stage, where eight crews operated for a time (figure 6). All shared a single wharf and landing stage and had to await turns landing and "pewing" up fish to the common stagehead. There was room for only one extra stage on the old site and after 1900 some crews relocated in the "Inside Cove," a process accelerated by the loss of the old stages in a storm in 1935 (figure 7). It was much more difficult to land fish in the shallow waters of the "Inside Cove" but boats were more sheltered and the cliff was lower, factors which eased the arduous task of "pewing" fish to the stageheads. Most of these new stages were divided among sons of the fourth generation, but were too small to accommodate more than three crews.

Stages commanded access to the sea and were the only structures consistently divided among heirs. Other facilities were usually passed on undivided to the youngest (or only) son and most fishermen, when starting out on their own, built their boat, store, flake, and tilt and purchased their own nets. Although the basic fishing technology in Point Lance has changed little since 1875, several improvements have been made. Late in the last century, the dory became the dominant inshore craft in Point Lance as elsewhere along the south coast. This was a smaller, lighter boat, and much more manoeuvrable than the skiff. It was easier to build and beach and was rowed by a single pair of oars, but unlike the skiff it did not have sails. Around 1940, the oars were replaced by an outboard motor, but despite mechanization Point Lancers continued to fish in their traditional grounds. Cod nets continued to dominate, but the material changed from hemp to cotton and more recently to nylon. In this century, some fishermen also used trawls. Despite these improvements, catch averages increased little and this may be explained, in part, by the rapid proliferation of crews in the fourth generation after 1920, and by the depletion of inshore stocks. The average income per fisherman remained extremely low and Point Lancers were no better off financially after a century of fishing. Few two-man crews have ever salted over 200 quintals of cod and prices have until recently been below $10.00 a quintal. Even with a motor dory, 100 quintals was considered a good catch and $500.00 a good return for a fisherman over the season.

For more than a century, however, the fishery has remained the pivot of the Point Lance economy, bringing in the bulk of whatever cash was accumulated. Point Lancers fear and respect the sea, and its many moods are a common topic of conversation, especially in summer. The marine outlook is reflected in the frequent use of nautical terms describing land-based activities, in the woods, in the fields, and through the hamlet. For more than a century, all other exploitative strategies have been interwoven with, but supplementary to the exploitation of the sea.

Supplementary Activities: Trapping, Shooting, Gathering, and Lumbering

Although they contributed only in a trifling way to the commercial economy of Point Lance, trapping, shooting, gathering, and lumbering held an important place in the traditional subsistence economy. The trapping of foxes was an exception, at least early in this century, when pelts fetched up to $30.00 each in St. John's. Red and patch foxes are found around Point Lance, but few settlers ever set more than half a dozen steel traps and rarely caught more than two per trap in a season. Foxes normally dwell inland but travel frequently to the coast to feed on various littoral deposits, especially fish. Traps were placed close to the cliff and were covered with moss. Skins were scraped and stretched over a board to dry and were sold to St. John's buyers in the fall. Foxes were not nearly as numerous as in other parts of the island, and Point Lancers trapped along the entire south coast of the headland, from Cape St. Mary's to Gull Cove. Furring declined as prices slumped in the European market. The only other species caught consistently and sold for its fur was muskrat. These were plentiful locally, frequenting the numerous ponds and gullies around the hamlet. Muskrat were trapped in the fall and spring within a five-mile radius of Point Lance. Each trapper set between one or two dozen traps and usually caught between fifty and one hundred muskrat. In any generation, however, only a few Point Lancers were involved, and trappers never received more than $2.00 for a pelt.

Every householder traditionally kept guns, which were used to supplement the meat store. Products of the hunt were rarely if ever sold. In the early days, caribou were taken, and later moose and rabbit, but gamebirds were the most popular target, especially eiderduck and ptarmigan or "partridge." Eiderducks arrive in September and stay until May. They remain on salt water but come close to shore at dawn to feed on shellfish. Traditionally, two men in a boat constituted a hunting crew. Using "muzzle-loaders," as many as twenty ducks might be taken in a good outing. Ducks weigh about 5 lbs. each and are usually baked or stewed and the feathers used for pillows and mattresses. The tiny partridge never became popular in the traditional diet of Point Lancers, but was a delicacy in St. John's even in the last century. Point Lancers have traditionally acted as guides for St. John's sportsmen but also took partridge for sale.

Bakeapples, blueberries, partridge berries, and cranberries were gathered in late summer and fall by the women and children, for local consumption and occasionally for sale. Patches of unimproved land near the hamlet were burned in the spring, diminishing the natural complexity of the flora but allowing a recolonization by berries. Unless the patches were burned over again after a few years, however, the old plant associations revived.

From the beginnings of settlement, timber was vital for buildings, fences, fuel, and a wide array of tools. In the homeland, timber was a rare resource and the first Point Lancers had little or no expertise in building with wood. Irish peasant houses, outbuildings, and fences were fashioned traditionally with mud or stone and buildings were roofed with straw (thatch) or sods. The only wood in Irish folk architecture was the frame of the roof. Building with wood was far less time-consuming than building with stone or mud. Consequently, on the frontier, where labour was at a premium, the first Careens quickly adapted to the Newfoundland tradition of wooden structures. Using local timber they built houses similar in form and layout to the traditional abode of the fairly substantial southeast Irish peasant farmer. In Point Lance, the walls of dwelling houses, outbuildings, and fishing premises were built with vertically placed and abutting timbers, called "studs"; floors and doors were made of boards cut locally with the pit-saw; and the wooden roof frames were covered with horizontally placed boards and home-made wooden shingles, although oral tradition maintains that the first houses were thatched.

A vast quantity of timber was required over winter to heat the substantial dwelling houses with their enormous stone fireplaces and chimney flues, and all the cooking was done over the open fire until the introduction of the wood stove late in the last century. The fishery was also extremely demanding on the forest resource: tilts, stores, stages, flakes, wharves, barrels, barrows, and boats were all made of wood and some of these items had to be repaired or replaced every season. A variety of hand-tools and transport vehicles used on the farm, in the woods, and in the fishery were basically of wooden construction and most items of household furniture, including benches, chairs, tables, dressers, cradles, bed frames, and many containers were made from local timber.

Initially, the timber cleared off the gardens and taken from the stands surrounding the improved lands satisfied most of the local demand, but with the inception and expansion of the fishery, and the proliferation of houses after 1870, Point Lancers were forced to travel further afield for timber. As far back as local memory extends, timber was cut in several stands one to four miles' distance from the hamlet; local tradition also asserts that these sites have been exploited for at least a century. Half a dozen well-worn slide paths lead radially inland from the settlement, some begun in the first generation by "winter men," whose major task was the provision of timber for fuel and building. Their names are commemorated in the place names of these inland areas.

Within living memory, almost every adult male spent a good part of the winter in the woods. Beginning in November, after the crops and fish were stored away, men went alone or in pairs into the woods and cutting continued in a piecemeal manner until March. Trees were cut most easily during frosty weather, when brittle, and were hauled home over the frozen ground by horse and slide. Sometimes the timber was floated on rafts down Point Lance river, but the river was usually frozen during the logging season. There was no strict delineation of timber areas among different families, and householders could shift cutting locations annually. Timber was plentiful in the sheltered valleys and there was never any intense pressure on the resource; consequently there was no sense of proprietorship and no efforts were made to regulate its use.

Occupational pluralism was a deeply rooted facet of life in Point Lance. Each household normally exploited a number of local natural resources and endeavoured to be as self-sufficient as possible. Different activities dominated different parts of the year but there was considerable overlap and occupations were sometimes cleverly combined—shooting and fishing on the one hand, or logging, trapping, and shooting on the other. In the annual round of Point Lancers, there were periods of relative calm and periods of stress when several tasks demanded completion. One of the major talents of the head of household was the ability to deploy skilfully the labour force at his command. Since the breaking up of the old fishing crew, the individual household has supplied the bulk of the labour required to support itself. Farming, shooting, trapping, logging, and building did not normally require a labour force larger than the nuclear family and even fishing crews often comprised a father and son or two brothers from the same household. Within the household, there was a division of labour between the sexes: women tended the gardens, the poultry, and the cows, and helped to cure fish, make hay, and pick potatoes and berries, in addition to completing their domestic duties; men fished, hunted, trapped, cut wood, and performed the heavy work in the fields. The entire family came together for certain tasks in periods of stress, and if they could not cope, less pressured neighbours were expected to lend a hand. Mutual exchanges of labour and goods between householders in times of need was a basic characteristic of Point Lance society.

The Winds of Change

Following World War II and Confederation with Canada in 1949, the traditional social and economic framework of Point Lance has crumbled in the face of several new pressures. These have included new sources of cash income, the breakdown of isolation, the influence of outside planning, and the decline in the exploitation of traditional resources. All have combined in one way or another to produce changes in Point Lance that are analogous to the changes that have taken place in small communities elsewhere in Newfoundland, and in Canada.

Alternative seasonal employment for wages became available with the building of a road to the settlement in 1938–40 and the construction of a major American military base near Placentia during and after World War II. Following Confederation, the expanding urban-industrial sector of the provincial economy provided seasonal work for young Point Lancers in Labrador and in the woods of western Newfoundland, while periodic employment for wages also became possible in Point Lance. Work became available for road maintenance and bridge construction, the building of a large community stage and federal wharf, and the installation of electricity, water, and sewers. There is steady employment in education, the transportation of goods and personnel, the running of a store, the staffing of a new oil exploration station one mile from the hamlet, and in the operation of a new fog horn.

In addition to wage employment, other sources of cash became available after Confederation. Before this time, the only government payment made in Point Lance was a small pension, based on a means test, for people over seventy. After Confederation, family allowances, unemployment insurance benefits, social assistance, an enlarged pension, and other payments flowed from Ottawa to Point Lance and other Newfoundland outports. These payments had a profound effect on the traditional economy— such payments reduced the necessity of many people to farm or fish, and provided a cushion in difficult times.

Following the completion of the road, Point Lance became accessible to entrepreneurs operating with trucks once weekly along the Cape Shore. Under the old mercantile system of exchange, Point Lancers traded no more than twice each year, while after the road, goods could be bought or sold much more frequently. A store was established in the hamlet, and a wider range of consumer goods became available. Regular wages and high fish prices during the war, and then government disbursements, enabled Point Lancers to purchase more and more goods. Moreover, Confederation removed the tariffs on Canadian goods and as a result, the volume and range of packaged goods coming into Point Lance expanded. Point Lancers had postal services in the nineteenth century, and a telegraph station was installed in the 1920s, but radios became popular during the war, and more recently, television and telephones were introduced. With the road came the automobile and the end of excessive isolation. The young people now drive to dances as far away as Placentia; they attend high school in St. Brides; and a few have reached Memorial University in St. John's. The people of Point Lance are aware, as never before, of the larger, outside world. This awareness draws many of the young away from Point Lance and its traditions.

Decisions about Point Lance have been and are being taken by government planners. Until recently, planners were not very familiar with Point Lance, so they paid little attention to the views of Point Lancers, and their decisions did little to perpetuate local traditions. Some, indeed, have tended to do the reverse. Faced with the enormous cost of providing facilities such as water and sewers, electricity, telephones, roads, schools, and medicine in isolated communities, the provincial government began a resettlement scheme in 1954. A sum of $600.00 was to be allocated to each householder provided all families in a particular community agreed to move, and by 1965 a total of 185 communities had been relocated through government aid.

Point Lancers resisted community relocation, but after the government revamped its resettlement program in 1965, by increasing moving expenses and dropping the requirement that the entire community must move, four Point Lance families moved to St. Bride's. The settlement programs have hastened the transformation of a traditional way of life, by making it possible for people to consider moving away as a reasonable alternative.

Probably as a result of overfishing by the international fleet, cod stocks dropped dramatically in the late 1960s and early 1970s. Cod are still fairly plentiful beyond the traditional inshore zone, five miles away, but a shift to new grounds not only meant relinquishing ancestral fishing berths, but the loss of an intimate knowledge of the old grounds, gleaned over generations. Some crews have moved to the more distant grounds, but only after several consecutive seasons of poor fishing, while others have abandoned the fishery. In 1960, sixteen boats fished out of Point Lance; in 1973, only four boats remained. With the influx of packaged foods, land clearing ceased and gardening declined. The majority of Point Lancers no longer supply their own meat, milk, butter, or eggs. Oil has replaced wood in most kitchens. Hunting and trapping have disappeared and shooting is now a sport.

Thirty years ago, Point Lance was a self-supporting community. A delicate balance between households and the exploitation of local natural resources had evolved over generations of experiment and adjustment. Today, the old economy has virtually collapsed and Point Lancers derive the bulk of their cash income from government disbursements and work in local services.

In the Newfoundland context, Point Lance is rich in human and natural resources. Capital for initial investment is scarce, however, and the issue of local representation in the search for outside aid is a major problem. Isolation, colonialism, and the social egalitarianism of Point Lancers have traditionally discouraged strong local leadership and there is no tradition of formal community representation. Links with external institutions such as the church, school, banks or other commercial institutions, the law, and various branches of government have been perfunctory in the past. Throughout the nineteenth century, Point Lance was a basically illiterate society and illiteracy continued up to Confederation, despite the construction of a small school after 1920. Child labour was needed on the land and in the fishery, and school days were often restricted to winter. Occasionally, the clergy articulated community grievances—the local priest played a major role in the revival of land clearing and farming along the Shore during the Depression—but there has never been a resident priest in Point Lance. The most enduring links with the outside were with the merchants, but contacts were personal and informal and different crews often dealt with different merchants in St. John's. Co-operative bargaining was unknown.

Confederation ushered in a system of political patronage that now pervades the community. Jobs and projects are usually recommended and distributed on the basis of party affiliation, not on merit, and considerable internecine discord has resulted. From a tradition of low political representation, lobbying for government favours has now become excessive; the traditional paternalism of the mercantile regime has been replaced by that of the government. Countless pre-election ploys and empty promises have instilled a sense of suspicion and fatalism among Point Lancers. However, there has been some change in recent years. Social and economic planners now strive for total community involvement, emphasizing the outport traditions of self-help and self-reliance. Participation of the people is not only more democratic, but community representations are generally more effective than the representations of individuals or planners. The recently revived Cape Shore Development Association (CSDA) is an example of the rising local interest in local improvement. Each outport has its own development association, with sub-committees appointed to appraise different aspects of resource potential, and elects members to the central Cape Shore committee. This structure involves many people, tends to discourage traditional rivalry between communities, and lays the foundations for an integrated economic development policy.

Oldtimers like to point out that if present production could match the average household level of the old economy, there would be considerable prosperity in Point Lance. The older people place great faith in the potential of local natural resources and emphasize the virtues of hard work and occupational pluralism. The future of Point Lance, however, can no longer be guided by the older generations. The traditional patriarchal system of authority has crumbled and young people are now making their own decisions. With the advent of wage labour, the family household is losing its position as the basic unit of economic production. Young unmarried members of a household want their own bank accounts, and this individualism is alien to the social traditions of Point Lance. Generalized reciprocity of labour and goods is largely a thing of the past. Compulsory education provides the community with an increasingly articulate voice in representing grievances to the outside, but weans children from their role in the traditional economy.

Fewer and fewer of the younger generation subscribe to the traditional way of life. In part, the blame for this new disparity between young and old resides with the older generation, who abandoned the old economy. In the past, young men inherited lands and other property and skills to continue in a traditional way, but the disintegration of the old way of living means the present generation have little to transmit to their children. Lacking the initial capital and resources so essential to become a successful farmer-fisherman, the disillusioned youth have turned to the quick profits of wage labour that takes them away from home. Some young Point Lancers accumulate enough capital in seasonal work away from home to finance themselves in the fishery but are reluctant to do so. They regard the fishery as an unclean, miserable occupation with long, irregular hours and uncertain economic rewards. Most of these youth would prefer to live in Point Lance if they could find local jobs for wages. For most of them, such a prospect is highly unlikely. A portion of Point Lance's youth—probably a minority—support the notion of a revived economy and appear committed to living and working in Point Lance. Fish and farm prices were never better, and there is government support for such efforts. It is on the shoulders of these young people that the future of Point Lance rests.

The problems that presently beset Point Lance are found in varying degrees across rural Canada. Social and economic pressures have resulted in mass movement to the cities. Rural incomes and living standards are distinctly lower than urban incomes and standards. In some ways, rural depopulation has increased social isolation in the countryside, despite modern communications. As contacts between city and countryside multiply, there is a growing urbanization of rural society, particularly amongst the young. Considerable social as well as economic planning is needed to improve the quality of rural life and help reduce the disaffection of young rural Canadians. The aspirations of young Point Lancers are little different from those of young people elsewhere in rural Canada. The fate of Point Lance is an integral part of the fate of rural Canada.

Note

Much of the information on which this study rests was derived from interviews in the community, and the author is pleased to record his gratitude to the people of Point Lance for all their help. Among archival records that were most useful were the Roman Catholic Parish Register, Placentia, 1840–1900 (Provincial Archives, St. John's); the Saunders and Sweetman Letter Book, 1788–1804 (Arts and Culture Centre Library, St. John's); and the Sweetman papers, 1780–1850 (Private mss. Placentia, Newfoundland). Road reports in the appendix of the *Journal of the House of Assembly, Newfoundland*, the *Census of Newfoundland* (1836, 1857, 1869, 1874, 1884, 1891, 1901, 1911, 1921, 1935, 1945, 1966), and *McAlpines Newfoundland Directory* were also useful. Point Lance is described in the Report of Captain Milne, *Public Ledger*, 9 Dec. 1841. For more detail on the Sweetman family, see J.J. Mannion, "Irish Merchants Abroad: The Newfoundland Experience, 1750–1850," *Newfoundland Studies* 2 (1986): 127–90.

A REGION OF SCATTERED SETTLEMENTS AND BOUNDED POSSIBILITIES: NORTHEASTERN AMERICA 1775–1800*

GRAEME WYNN

With three-quarters of its population New Englanders, and numerous ties of trade and sentiment to the line of British colonies that ran from Newfoundland to the Bahamas, pre-Revolutionary Nova Scotia was part of a wider economic and cultural unit, only a fraction of which seceded from Britain between 1776 and 1783.[1] If, in historian John Bartlett Brebner's vivid metaphor, the fires of rebellion burned less fiercely there than they did at the centre of the colonial arc, they glowed sporadically for all that. Nova Scotians protested the Stamp Act with their Boston cousins and celebrated with them its repeal in July 1776. Unexplained fires damaged the Halifax naval yard and destroyed hay consigned from the city to the British garrison in Massachusetts. And a few Nova Scotian merchants refused to handle East India Company tea.

But provincial opinion was far from unanimous. Halifax tea imports increased 26-fold and more in 1770, precisely at the time that non-importation agreements raised tea prices in New England. Large numbers of provincial vessels engaged in contraband trade with neighbouring colonies, but while some Nova Scotians were "hearty in the Cause," others denounced the Revolutionary leaders as demagogues.[2] In the end, neither side mounted a decisive action. Beyond Halifax, where officials, the navy, and British coin demonstrated the reality and benefits of colonial dependence, most Nova Scotians were preoccupied with survival. Their settlements were isolated, they lacked capital, industry, and significant, autonomous, merchant communities. Influenced by the revivalist preaching of Henry Alline, which flourished on the psychological unease of a migrant, still rootless people forced to recognize a new division between themselves and residents of

* The Canadian Geographer/Le Géographe canadien 31, 4 (1987): 319–38.

their former homeland (and in which the war became God's retribution for the corruption of London and Boston), the "weak and exposed" majority of Nova Scotians opted for neutrality.[3]

This was no shield from turmoil. American privateers raided almost every substantial settlement in the province except Halifax between 1776 and 1782. If bloodshed was rare, the spoils were often considerable. Ships, provisions, and valuables were carried away, "neutral Yankees" were taunted, and some were drawn to the American side. Machias-based raiders disrupted the provision trade between Fundy settlements and British troops, and in 1775 they burned abandoned Fort Frederick at the mouth of the St. John River. The next year a small force under Jonathan Eddy laid seige to Fort Cumberland in Chignecto.[4] Earlier, the principal officers of the Island of St. John had been removed by an unauthorized raiding party. To defend the Saint John valley, Fort Howe was built in 1778 on a cliff at the mouth of the river. In Halifax, the defences "were extensive but hardly imposing." Yet commerce there was, invigorated by the presence of wealthy exiles from the American colonies, military officers, and troops with money to spend.[5] The cargoes of condemned vessels were auctioned in the prize court. Prices rose, and suppliers and landlords benefited.[6] In contrast, many poorer citizens probably fared badly during the periodic shortages of food.[7]

Early in the 1780s, it was clear that substantial numbers of civilian refugees and disbanded soldiers (Provincials)—collectively Loyalists—who had taken the British side in the Revolution were to be settled in British North America. Prior to their arrival, negotiations with the Americans established the St. Croix River (rather than the St. John or Penobscot) as the western limit of Nova Scotia. From the source of the St. Croix, the boundary was drawn through little-known territory northwards to the highlands separating the St. Lawrence and Atlantic drainage basins. Later both the identity of the "St. Croix" and the precise meaning of this demarcation were to be debated in territorial disputes between New Brunswick and the United States and between New Brunswick and Quebec; but in the short term the boundary agreement secured the "back part" of Nova Scotia for Loyalist occupation.[8]

To facilitate settlement of the Loyalists, almost 1.5 million acres of land, granted between 1752 and 1774 but still unoccupied, were escheated between 1783 and 1788. Added to the enormous area of Nova Scotian Crown land that remained beyond the handful of naval timber reserves established earlier in the 1770s, this made available a vast estate for distribution to the newcomers in free grants. Purchase fees (hitherto 10 shillings per 100 acres) and those for surveying and registering grants were waived to ensure that Loyalists received land without charge. Each family head was entitled to 100 acres, with a further 50 acres for each member of his household; those with the "desire and ability to cultivate" more could apply for up to 1 000 acres of extra land; commissioned and non-commissioned officers received additional quantities according to their rank, ranging downwards from the 1 000 acres allowed field officers. Under these terms, approximately 4 750 Loyalist grants, amounting to an estimated 700 000 acres, were made in peninsular Nova Scotia during the 1780s; in New Brunswick, divided from the peninsula as a separate, largely Loyalist colony in 1784, some 476 000 acres passed into Loyalist hands before 1790.[9]

Quite how many Loyalists arrived in Nova Scotia and its neighbouring islands will never be known with certainty. Many departed without acquiring land or being enumerated in any of the several musters organized by harried authorities; more relocated—some twice or thrice—within the region; there were spurious applications for land; and the administrative challenge posed by so large a group of newcomers created its own confusions. By most estimates the Loyalist influx amounted to some 35 000 persons. It transformed the geography of the region. Returns of those Loyalists entitled to government provisions in the late fall of 1785 recorded totals of almost 15 000 for Nova Scotia, almost 11 000 for New Brunswick, 420 for the Island of St. John, and 121 for Cape Breton.[10] The number of Loyalists actually settled in these areas was certainly greater. In all, 6 220 Loyalists received Nova Scotian grants. Although slightly more than 700 of those were subsequently escheated, it is likely that the Loyalists added some 19 000 persons to the permanent population of the province. For New Brunswick, the equivalent figure is 15 000, some 85 percent of whom are estimated to have "remained in New Brunswick until the end of their lives."[11] In broad terms, then, Loyalist migrations approximately doubled the population of the Nova Scotian peninsula and virtually quadrupled that of the "mainland." Some 500 Loyalists went to the Island of St. John (Prince Edward Island after 1798), but many were transients, and probably no more than 200 remained in 1786. Cape Breton, created as a separate colony in 1785,[12] received a similar increment, but more stayed to play a significant role in its settlement, social development, and politics.

Drawn from all walks of life, and from each of the 13 former colonies, the Loyalists shared little but the experience of exile and the uncertainty of their prospects in British North America.[13] Before the Revolution, some had been persons of wealth and stature. Edward Winslow, who traced his American roots back to the *Mayflower*, was a graduate of Harvard, clerk of the General Sessions in Plymouth, and prominent Boston tory; John Saunders and Beverly Robinson were sons of rich and powerful Virginia families; an ordained Anglican minister and medical doctor, Jonathan Odell of New Jersey was outstanding among loyal satirists of the 1770s; Dr. Azor Betts was "a well known practitioner of physic in New York... noted for his success in inoculation" before he went to Nova Scotia; Mather Byles was the great-grandson of Increase Mather and minister of Christ Church, Boston; John Wentworth had succeeded his uncle as governor of New Hampshire and surveyor-general of the King's Woods in North America and held those offices for a decade before being proscribed by the Continental Congress.[14]

But for all their prominence in late eighteenth-century Nova Scotia and New Brunswick, such individuals were the merest fraction of the Loyalist population. The overwhelming majority of their fellow migrants were men and women of modest circumstances, tradesmen, labourers, farmers, and their families, accustomed to hard work and simple comforts. Yeomen, carpenters, and cordwainers outnumbered gentlemen, esquires, and merchants four to one among the 530 persons given the freedom of Saint John at its incorporation in 1785, and the disproportion was almost certainly greater in the New Brunswick countryside.[15]

Educated, relatively well-to-do Loyalists may have been drawn to established settlements such as Halifax and Annapolis, but these places also had large numbers of impoverished exiles. Public buildings sheltered scores of destitute newcomers through the Halifax winter of 1783; in the harbour a group, mainly women and children from the southern colonies, lived aboard a vessel "crowded like a sheep-pen"; in the city as a whole, hundreds died and thousands survived on meagre rations of codfish, molasses, and hard biscuit.[16] In Annapolis, too, all available buildings were used to accommodate the newcomers, but many lacked shelter and several families had to make do with "a single apartment built with sods, where men, women, children, pigs, fleas, bugs, mosquitoes and other domestic insects, mingle[d] in society."[17]

Evidence assembled by the British Commission for Enquiry into the Losses, Services, and Claims of the American Loyalists confirms the essential elements of this picture. In all, 280 Nova Scotian and 308 New Brunswick claimants received awards; they averaged £552 and £364, respectively. Only 8 percent of New Brunswick Loyalists (and a smaller proportion of those in Nova Scotia) sought restitution for their losses. On a per capita basis, they claimed at barely half the rate of all Loyalists. Their claims were also relatively modest. Sixty percent sought less than £500, and fewer than 70 claimed more than £1 000, although the average value of all Loyalist claims exceeded £1 580.[18] Their submissions recounted their "Low Sercumstances" and told of families "in Great Poverty and Distress."[19] Countless others who left little behind, who could not prove their losses, or who lacked the skill, time, and money to set down and pursue a claim were not heard from.

Information about Loyalist origins is most complete for New Brunswick (figure 1).[20] Fully 90 percent of those who settled in the new province were American born, and most were from families long established in the 13 colonies. Less than a quarter came from New England (Connecticut 12.9 percent; Massachusetts 6.1 percent; Rhode Island 1.9 percent; and New Hampshire 1.2 percent). Almost 70 percent were from the middle colonies (New York 40 percent; New Jersey 22 percent; Pennsylvania 7.7 percent). Maryland, Virginia, and Delaware counted 3.6 percent, the Carolinas 3.1 percent, and Georgia a bare 0.3 percent. Surnames reflected something of the ethnic composition of the populations from which the migrants came and included at least 200 of Dutch derivation (from New York and New Jersey), 80 of Huguenot origin, and perhaps half as many German names, borne by Pennsylvania "Dutch" families. Overall, peninsular Nova Scotia may have received a larger proportion of Massachusetts Loyalists than did New Brunswick and likely had fewer exiles from New Jersey. But an analysis of the origins of some 700 family heads among the Shelburne Loyalists confirms the dominance of the middle colonies as a source area. New Englanders were a less significant proportion of Shelburne than New Brunswick Loyalists, but both the Chesapeake and the Carolinas contributed an appreciably greater fraction to the population of the town than the province.[21]

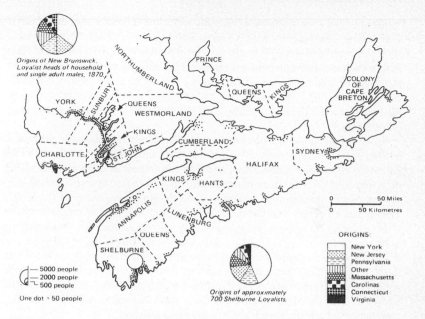

FIGURE 1   Origins and Distribution of Loyalists in Nova Scotia, New Brunswick, Cape Breton, and the Island of St. John, 1785

SOURCES: General Returns of Loyalists, MG23 D1(1), vol. 24, Public Archives of Canada; E.C. Wright, *The Loyalists of New Brunswick* (Moncton: Moncton Publishing, 1972); A.H. Clark, *Three Centuries and the Island* (Toronto: University of Toronto, 1959); and R.J. Morgan, "Orphan Outpost" (Ph.D. diss., University of Ottawa, 1973).

Black Loyalists comprised fully a tenth of those who went to greater Nova Scotia.[22] Most were runaway slaves from Virginia and South Carolina, and, judging from the slim evidence of two lists enumerating 216 individuals, many (over 40 percent) were skilled men; their numbers included blacksmiths, carpenters, coopers, and tailors. But rarely were their hopes of freedom and independence realized in British North America. For a few, skills learned in slavery or servitude were the foundations of later autonomy: Boston King was a carpenter in Shelburne; Willis caulked vessels in Simeon Perkin's Liverpool shipyard; others were masons, coopers, blacksmiths, and blockmakers.[23] Often they toiled for less than white workers and —as in the "Extraordinary... Riot" of 1784 in Shelburne, when disbanded soldiers "Drove the Negroes out of the Town"—suffered the resentment of their fellow Loyalists.[24]

Generally, black Loyalists fared poorly in comparison with whites. Some survived by fishing to supplement the produce of small gardens. Hundreds became day labourers, servants, or tenants. Many, realized one sensitive critic, were "obliged to live upon White-mens property which the Governor has been liberal in distributing—and for cultivating it they receive half the produce so that they are in short in a state of Slavery."[25] In the difficult climate and on the thin soils of Nova Scotia, such arrangements held few prospects but indigence. Denied several of the privileges of white citizens, and frequently treated with cruel severity before the law, black Loyalists "were regarded as little more than physical beings whose function was to fill the lowest levels of the labour force" in late eighteenth-century Nova Scotia.[26]

Nova Scotian land-grant procedures were hopelessly inadequate to the task of settling so many newcomers. To secure a grant, individuals had to petition the governor, either for a specific tract or for an assignment of the acreage to which they were entitled. The governor referred the request to the surveyor-general, who conducted or commissioned a survey. Then the surveyor-general of the King's Woods had to certify that the timber on the land was neither required by nor reserved for the Royal Navy. All being well, the provincial secretary would prepare a draft grant for the signature of the attorney-general before the actual grant was drawn up. Once that had been signed by the governor and the applicant had sworn the oath of allegiance, the land was his or hers. Although disbanded regiments were generally settled together under one petition and groups of civilian Loyalists could apply for land in conjunction, the system soon bogged down. Nor was that established in New Brunswick appreciably more efficient.

By 1784, a very small proportion, indeed, of the Loyalists were on their lands. "Discontent and uneasiness" were reported in several settlements.[27] There were too many applicants, too few surveyors, too many administrative delays, and, in the climate of confusion, too many individuals jockeying for particular advantage, for the allocation of land to proceed without dispute and injustice. In Shelburne there was much strife over matters of property; in Annapolis County, Loyalists impatient at delays moved on to common and glebe land; black Loyalists in both locations waited longer than most to receive land, and those who eventually received it generally got smaller holdings; in 1791, a small group of Pictou Loyalists threatened to return to the United States if they did not soon receive their grants, and many Digby Loyalists waited until 1800 for clear title to their properties.[28]

By 1785, there were Loyalists in most parts of peninsular Nova Scotia. Generally they added little to the population of established agricultural districts, where free land was scarce. Horton and Cornwallis townships mustered fewer than 250 Loyalists, Windsor but a few dozen more; at most 1 000 Loyalists settled about the fertile Minas Basin. Along the indented, rocky shore east of Halifax, and westward from Canso to Chignecto, by contrast, there were few pre-Loyalist settlers; provision musters enumerated over 3 000 newcomers in these areas. Halifax, according to Governor Parr, had approximately 1 200 Loyalists. Few of them received the royal bounty which, by contemporary account, was intended neither for the wealthy nor "the vicious & indolent," but not all were merchants and placemen; some 200 of the city's Loyalists were sustained by charity. Beyond the capital there were four significant nodes of Loyalist settlement: a thousand and more clustered near the head of Chedabucto Bay; almost double that number settled in the Annapolis Valley, especially in the Granville, Wilmot, and Clements districts; Conway, renamed Digby in February 1784, had approximately 1 300 Loyalist settlers; and Shelburne, formerly Port Roseway, rose from insignificance to become, briefly, the fourth largest town in America, with some 10 000 residents. Within this matrix there developed three all-black settlements—Birchtown on the outskirts of Shelburne, with 1 500 inhabitants in 1784; Brindley Town near Digby (with perhaps 200 residents); and at Tracadie Harbour near Chedabucto. There were also significant concentrations of black Loyalists in Halifax (which had 422 blacks among its 1791 population of 4 897) and neighbouring Preston.[29]

Shelburne was the most spectacular achievement and greatest failure of the Loyalist resettlement. The town was built with astonishing rapidity. The survey of the site began in late April 1783. Two weeks later, the first Loyalists arrived. By late July, the tent-town had a population of 7 600. In December, Governor Parr reported 800 houses built in Shelburne and 600 more "in great forwardness." Early in the new year residents celebrated Queen Charlotte's birthday with dancing, tea, and cards "in a house which stood where six months ago there was an almost impenetrable swamp." Within nine months of the first arrivals the town had 1 127 dwellings, 80 of them temporary, 231 framed, and the remainder of logs. According to the *London Chronicle* of 4–7 December 1784, "the inhabitants vie[d] with each other in making fine appearances."[30] But the pretensions of its citizens, the wharfs and stores of its waterfront, its three newspapers, and its fine harbour could not compensate for Shelburne's rocky, infertile hinterland, its failure to develop a firm economic foundation, and the fact, recognized by Governor Parr, that "the generality of those who came [t]here, were not much burthened with Loyalty, a spacious name which they made use of."[31] In 1785, the *Port Roseway Gazetteer and Shelburne Advertiser* offered substantial properties for sale: Peter Lynch thought his large, elegant two-storey house with 4 rooms per floor, cellar, adjoining kitchen, and large yard and garden "in high cultivation" "entirely proper for a merchant." Others simply sought let, lease, or sale arrangements.[32] The majority of residents, observed a contemporary, were "as poor as Rats in an empty house." By 1790, upwards of two-thirds of the town was uninhabited; some 700 families (say 3 000 persons) made up the population of Shelburne and its vicinity. By 1818, the town had fewer than 500 occupants.[33]

Across the Bay of Fundy, Parrtown and neighbouring Carleton (incorporated as the city of Saint John in 1785) rivalled Shelburne in rapidity of development, if not size. Fewer than 425 persons (including a garrison of 118) occupied a site one Loyalist considered "the roughest land... [she] ever saw" when the first exiles arrived in May 1783.[34] By July, there were about 400 houses built; by September, 700, almost all of them in Parrtown. By March 1784, the settlement comprised "about fifteen hundred framed Houses, and about four hundred temporary ones constructed of hewn logs." By 1788, it had "near 2 000 Houses" and had become, in Edward Winslow's judgment, "One of the best cities in the new world."[35] Functionally, this new town was a funnel, a point of disembarkation through which Loyalists would move to lands in the interior. But with the finest harbour on the north side of the Bay of Fundy and the extensive, fertile St. John valley as its hinterland, it retained an importance that Shelburne did not. Although Fredericton was proclaimed the provincial capital, Saint John accounted for 2 000 of the near 11 000 New Brunswick Loyalists enumerated in the final provision muster of 1785 and was the largest urban centre in the province. Six years later a visitor described a "well-planned" town "of about five hundred houses, all of timber, well painted... and some of them even elegant."[36]

By design intended to ensure colonization of the back country, civilian and military Loyalists were directed to different areas of New Brunswick. Loyalist regiments were assigned lands along the St. John River above Fredericton; civilians were to settle in the lower St. John and Passamaquoddy districts. But this plan was hardly realized. Several regiments refused their allocated blocks, and only a fraction of the officers and men in those regiments that accepted grants settled the designated lands. Most soldiers remained in the lower St. John valley among the civilian refugees. In 1785, Fredericton had approximately 650 bounty claimants, the area up-river about 850; rather more than 5 000 were enumerated along the 90 miles of the St. John River (and the lower reaches of its major tributaries) between Fredericton and Saint John. Passamaquoddy, the southwestern corner of the province, was the other important focus of settlement, with approximately 1 900 Loyalists; there were a few in the marshland district of Westmorland county and a handful on the lower Miramichi.[37]

For most Loyalists, strenuous exertion was necessary for survival in the wilderness of northeastern America. Hardship and privation were common. For some, such as Filer Dibblee, once a representative in the Connecticut Assembly, who committed suicide in 1784, they were intolerable. For most, they were burdens to be borne in hope of future comfort, but even "the most industrious farmers," realized clergyman Jacob Bailey, faced several years of struggle before they could "raise provisions sufficient for their families."[38] After a year or two on their grants, most Loyalist families might have had a rough dwelling and 2 to 4 acres of cultivable land. With continuing effort, and good health and fortune, such a beginning might be turned into the comfortable property described in the mid-1780s by William Cobbett as comprising "a large and well built log dwelling house... on the edge of a very good field of Indian corn, by the side of which was a piece of buckwheat just then mowed."[39]

Several fared far worse than these New Brunswick settlers. Poor soils, inclement weather, and wheat blight dimmed the prospects of farmers in the late 1780s and early 1790s. Settlers of the Bear and Moose river districts of Nova Scotia described themselves as "real objects of Charity" in their "excessive distress"; in a petition for medical aid, Loyalists in Digby recounted their suffering from "hard labor, incommodious Lodging open Huts Long Fastings and Unwholesome Provisions." And clergyman Jonathan Wiswall drew a sorry picture of the disbanded soldier settlements of Aylesford and Wilmot in 1791. "This part of the Province is very thinly settled by persons of all discriptions in general extremely poor & scattered over the country in all directions, they chiefly live in Hutts little if anything superior to the Cabins in Ireland—and can scarcely be said to have even the bare necessarys of life. They have been for so long a time habituated to what may be called a savage life, that it is extreme difficult to bring them off from it to a civilized state."⁴⁰

These were not the rewards of dreams. In Annapolis, Jacob Bailey found himself "continually molested with the disappointments—the chagrin the complaints—the manners, the distresses of the loyalists."⁴¹ Disillusioned, many sought yet another new start on life by relocating, either to join friends, relatives, or co-religionists, or because of inadequacies in the initial hurried survey and allocation of land. Others moved simply in hope of greater advantage elsewhere. Diffuse and idiosyncratic as these movements were, they are difficult to chart, but Edward Winslow offered a telling observation when he remarked that "the strange propensity [of Americans] to change their situations" was far exceeded in his province.⁴²

Trans-Atlantic migration to British North America virtually ceased during the Revolution, but began again, in a sporadic way, after 1783. Among the first arrivals from England—several hundred in number—were Loyalists disappointed at their prospects in the Mother Country. They were joined by smaller numbers of traders and fortune seekers and, to the annoyance of Nova Scotian officials, at least one group of transported convicts.⁴³ But the major influx was of Highland Scots, who gravitated to the small Scottish settlements in Pictou and the Island of St. John. More than 300 migrants from Moidart, Morar, and neighbouring Clanranald lands sailed for the island in 1790, and 1 300 emigrants from the Western Highlands and islands entered the Gulf in 1791. At least 650 of the latter group who landed in Nova Scotia depended upon government assistance to survive their first American winter, but in 1792 the Catholics among them moved east to Antigonish, and by 1800 both they and the Presbyterians who remained in Pictou were well established. Affluent enough to pay their passages, they migrated to preserve a traditional way of life and, as some contemporaries recognized, carried a considerable sum in goods and money across the Atlantic with them. Yet changing circumstances in Scotland and war with France slowed this migration to a trickle after 1793; in total it brought no more than 2 000 people—the vanguard of important nineteenth-century migrations—to the region between 1784 and 1800.⁴⁴

These gains were more than offset by departures. According to some, whose dislike of the American republic was manifest, a large and deplorable exodus of Loyalists occurred once the government issue of provisions ceased; by these accounts several thousand returned to "the Country of Traitors." Whether they "sold their Lotts... for a Gallon of New England rum and quit the Country without taking any residence," as many men in the Cumberland Regiment were alleged to have done, or went "back to Egypt after living so long in idleness on the King's provisions," these migrants raised doubts in the minds of those who stayed.⁴⁵ But it is difficult to gauge their numbers with confidence. One observer put departures from Nova Scotia at "Some Hundreds of Families in the 18 months before October 1787" and suggested that "some Hundreds more" were "preparing for removal." A careful analysis of the New Brunswick record concludes that fewer than 600 of 6 000 families who remained in the province long enough to be identified there returned to the United States. Certainly the movement was substantial; equally it failed to "unpeople these provinces," as one critic feared it might.⁴⁶ More significant in its impact upon the demographic structure of Nova Scotia was the exodus, in January 1792, of almost 1 200 black Loyalists bound for Sierra Leone and the prospects of land, independence, and security that they had failed to achieve as marginal members of a predominantly white society.[47]

Across the region, however, population growth was sustained by early marriages, a high birth rate, and low mortality. If it was more extreme than characteristic, the experience of one New Brunswick missionary who married 48 couples, baptized 295 infants, and buried 17 persons between 1795 and 1800 suggests the dynamics that drove the population of Nova Scotia, New Brunswick, Cape Breton, and the Island of St. John (Prince Edward Island after 1798) upwards by some 35 percent (a rate of approximately 2 percent per annum) between 1785 and 1800.[48]

The impact of the Loyalist migrations on the Nova Scotian economy was dramatic. With the demand for housing, provisions, lumber, and other supplies overwhelming, price inflation was steep. According to one account, Nova Scotian prices for necessities doubled between 1775 and 1782, and they undoubtedly escalated further in the months that followed with "the scarcity daily increasing by the daily increase of the number of the distressed starving Loyalists." By 1783, costs in Annapolis were said to be three times those in New York. In Halifax, government officials complained at the rents demanded for "very indifferent" accommodation, and one newcomer to the Fundy side of the province wondered how he might afford to build "a small Hut, such as other unhappy fugitive Loyalists generally creep into."[49]

Imports of foodstuffs and lumber from the United States eased immediate shortages, and fine flour and grains continued to come in from the south under vice-regal proclamation after 1786, but both demand and prices remained high and stimulated local production. From farms established on the Fundy borderlands in the 1760s and 1770s, livestock, butter, and cheese moved in unprecedented quantities to new urban and (at least for the first few years after 1783) rural markets in the region. Small sawmills cut lumber for local needs, and some soon found an export market for their product. In Nova Scotia, 25 sawmills were built between 1783 and 1785; in the two years that followed, when the government offered a bounty for mill construction, several more were erected. New Brunswick, with only a handful of mills in 1784, had 20 or more sawmills in Charlotte County alone by 1800. Shipbuilding also expanded.[50] Paying a bounty of 10 shillings per ton on new-built vessels of 40 tons or more, the Nova Scotian government disbursed approximately £1 000 in 1786 and 1787.[51] By 1793, some 160 sloops, schooners, and square-rigged vessels had been built in New Brunswick alone.[52]

Late in the 1780s, some Loyalist farms yielded their occupants "bread enough & potatoes of their own raising & Hay sufficient to winter their small stock."[53] Fish were taken from river and sea for local consumption and export. Settlements such as Sissiboo seemed to adumbrate the rapid progress and bountiful prospects of the region. There, reported Samuel Goldbury in 1785, Loyalists had found good lands and excellent timber. Four mills had been built, and more were under construction; 1 000 black cattle, as well as horses and sheep, grazed the fields; cod, taken from

"Log canoes and small Boats," had been consumed in "considerable quantity" by the settlers and provided 1 200 quintals for export to the West Indies in the settlement's 120-ton sloop and 80-ton brig. Well might these "generally Poor but industrious" individuals have contemplated regaining "those agreeable Circumstances they sacrificed in consequence of the Late War."[54]

But the foundations of such optimism were fragile. The fertility of new-cleared soils was soon exhausted; too few Loyalists were experienced fishermen or farmers; once the provision bounty ceased, the real difficulties of survival became apparent. Overland communication was difficult and costly. Loyalists from Remsheg mustered at Cumberland incurred costs of 5 shillings a hundredweight in transporting their provisions across the Chignecto Isthmus.[55] And despite considerable expenditure and effort on the opening of roads, little was achieved. Ways cut through forest soon grew back to scrub. Although communities were linked by water, connections were often circuitous and dangerous. Sawmills built near coastal settlements soon exhausted the good accessible timber of the spruce-fir forests in their immediate hinterlands, and several ceased operation as the costs of bringing trees from further afield became prohibitive. Recognizing that the rural economy was faltering, a group of prominent Haligonians formed the Society for Promoting Agriculture in Nova Scotia in 1789, and in 1791 both Nova Scotia and New Brunswick added lumber to the list of those articles allowed into the provinces from the United States for "the supply of the Inhabitants."[56]

External trade also fell short of expectations. With the Navigation Acts excluding American commodities from the British West Indies after 1783, Nova Scotian merchants hoped to assume an important place in trade with the islands.[57] Yet they were poorly equipped to do so: shipping was scarce, and local consumption left little for export in the first years of peace. By orders in council of 1783, American wood, livestock, and other provisions were allowed into the British West Indian islands in British ships; this left the fish and salt meat trade to the British North American colonies.

But the Nova Scotian fishery simply could not meet West Indian demands. American vessels continued to work northern waters in great numbers. In the summer of 1784, it was estimated that they would take at least 30 000 quintals along the Nova Scotian coast; larger vessels, some with 8 to 10 boats, fished the Gulf shore; and Nova Scotians cured the catch of New England fishermen as they had before the Revolution.[58] Several years later, Nova Scotian exports barely exceeded this American take from local waters. In 1787, the province exported 44 723 quintals of dried cod. In the same year, Cape Breton—more involved in the trans-Atlantic trade—shipped 36 736 quintals, and New Brunswick and the Island of St. John together exported 2 203 quintals.[59] Dried cod exports from Newfoundland were almost nine times greater than those from the four provinces combined.

By the end of the decade, fish and other enumerated items were being admitted to the West Indies in American vessels. In fast-declining Shelburne, the leading citizens recognized the obvious when they acknowledged that American experience in the trade (and, they argued, the "liberal indulgences" of the peace treaty) had "hitherto precluded" them from rivalling their southern competitors in "this valuable branch of Commerce."[60] When Britain and France went to war in 1793, privateers disrupted such trade as there was between northeastern America and the British West Indies. The subsequent opening of British Caribbean ports to American shipping dealt commerce a further blow. In the 1790s, observers found the trade of Annapolis "very trifling" and reported that both the river and sea fisheries of Nova Scotia were in decline.[61]

In this context, payments from the British government to individual Loyalists were of enormous significance to fledgling British North American communities in the 1780s and 1790s. As compensation for losses sustained or as "half-pay" pensions for military service, these remittances to Nova Scotia and New Brunswick Loyalists may have amounted to £475 000 between 1783 and 1800.[62] Not all of this money was spent in the colonies. After 1787, when military pensions were allowed to those resident beyond the empire, several recipients left for the United States; by one—likely high—contemporary estimate, £5 000 per annum crossed the border from New Brunswick in the early 1790s.[63] But whether consumed in the development of a country estate, invested in an inn or tavern, or filtered into the local economy month by month over the years, compensation and pension payments contributed a significant leaven to pioneer economies. If few Loyalists were willing to tenant farms, many depended, in the first years of settlement, upon the casual employment offered by Loyalist officers and gentlemen. The departure of such individuals, feared one observer, would have a catastrophic effect upon their communities: "tis these Men's Pay we depend upon" he wrote, "to keep our poor alive by finding Employment for labouring men. . . . If they go the poor must follow them or starve."[64]

In Halifax, at least, the economic difficulties of the late 1780s and early 1790s were quickly dissipated by the war with France. A garrison of 600, the newly formed Royal Nova Scotia Regiment, the navy, and privateers bringing prizes into port put cash in circulation. When fears of French invasion heightened after the capture of St. Pierre and Miquelon by men from the Halifax garrison, some 1 500 militiamen were embodied in the town. In 1796, a further 1 000 or so were called into the city from outlying districts. Five of ten batteries built to defend the harbour before the Revolution, but long in ruins, were reconstructed, and two new works were erected. In the next few years, considerable sums were spent improving and strengthening these structures, and the stone Prince of Wales Tower was built on Point Pleasant to secure the rear of the defences.[65] The presence of Prince Edward, Duke of Kent, as commander of the British troops added to the social cachet of Halifax society, the upper echelons of which participated in a vigorous round of drinking, dining, and social calls.[66]

By 1801, Haligonians contemplated raising £100 000 to establish a bank, and the provincial legislature allocated funds for the paving of city streets. Despite the narrow blocks and small lots of the original survey, the élite concentrated in the centre of the city. Government House, St. George's Church, and several substantial town houses were built in this area in the 1790s and reflected both its prestige and the expansive mood of these years.[67]

By this time, too, the benefits of prosperity in Halifax were percolating into other parts of the colony. Money from provincial coffers was being turned to road building. Bay of Fundy farmers received good prices for their surplus, and with militia obligations and the enlistment of provincials, a shortage of manpower raised the price of labour. Reflecting these developments, Loyalist storekeeper Henry Magee of Horton Corner (now Kentville) did a vigorous trade in the last years of the century. Although payment in kind was often recorded in his ledgers, some 80 percent of his customers appear to have settled their accounts with cash. In 16 months of 1795–6, Magee took almost £3 000 in gold and silver, much of which he (literally) salted away, recording in his day book quantities of "gold put by in the apel box," "silver in the wheat," and "gold in the salt."[68]

New Brunswick, in contrast, was a backwater. With the war, troops were withdrawn to Halifax and the West Indies, and with them went their salaries and their contracts for fuel and provisions. The colony lacked the strategic importance of Nova Scotia, its annual revenue was barely a tenth of that colony's and the province was regarded, in official eyes, as a satellite of its neighbour.[69] Commercially, its chief importance lay in the rich pine forest brought under imperial jurisdiction early in the eighteenth century, but the quantities of New Brunswick wood entering trade were small. Masts were the most valuable of local commodities; annual shipments rarely exceeded 2 000 in number. In the 15 years to 1800, ton-timber and lumber shipments approximately doubled from their low 1785 levels of 2 000 tons and 2 million feet respectively.[70] Much of this material came from the southwestern corner of the province, where the American boundary was barely recognized by lumbermen and others who prosecuted a contraband trade in fish and gypsum (from the head of the Bay of Fundy) on "the lines." While the late 1790s brought prosperity to Nova Scotia, New Brunswick Loyalist Amos Botsford reported that the West Indies trade of his province "ha[d] been reduced by frequent captures, shipbuilding ha[d] decreased, and exports of timber to the British market... [were] entirely decreased."[71] By 1800, emigration from the province was discernible.

The islands of Saint John and Cape Breton also shared little in the prosperity of war. In 1797, when the former colony had a population of 4 300, a mere 36 families occupied 35 of its 67 townships. Half the population was Scottish, 15 percent Acadian. In 1789, the island had neither school nor church, and the disruptive legacy of the preceding decade or so continued to stunt development into the nineteenth century. Although there were 18 grist and sawmills by the end of the century, there was little nucleated settlement.[72] Charlottetown was a muddy village of large lots, wide streets, and 70 dwellings. According to Lord Selkirk, Princetown and Georgetown were "rotten boroughs" of three houses each.[73] Most settlers occupied small farms where arms of the sea ran deep into the island along the Malpeque–Bedeque and Hillsborough–St. Peters axes. Herring and cod were taken along the north shore. Cattle were shipped to Newfoundland occasionally, and little vessels maintained frequent connection with Halifax, but the balance of trade in this underdeveloped colony was clearly inward.

Small as it was, Cape Breton held more economic importance. A centre of the migratory Jersey-based fishery that had expanded in the Gulf of St. Lawrence since 1763, the island attracted approximately 100 Channel Islanders each summer.[74] At Arichat and Cheticamp they worked alongside resident Acadians to produce the prime merchantable fish for southern European markets that made up perhaps two-thirds of the colony's cod exports. Three-quarters of Cape Breton's population probably depended upon the resident fishery. Its product was generally inferior to that of the Jerseymen, and most of it went to West Indian markets through Halifax. Neither fishery returned very much to Cape Breton's inhabitants. Profits and wages from the Jersey enterprises accrued to Great Britain; resident fishermen—largely Acadian, with a few Irish from Newfoundland—depended on credit from local merchants, and, like their counterparts elsewhere in the fishery, many were deeply in debt. Coal from primitive mines on the north side of Sydney Harbour provided a second export commodity, but the costs of extraction and transport to markets in Halifax and St. John's limited the trade: it never exceeded 10 000 tons per annum before 1800, and no more than 50 or 60 men worked in the mines. Farming supported 120 to 150 Cape Breton families. Most of them were Loyalist, few had more than 10 or 15 acres in cultivation, and the small surpluses they produced generated only a sporadic trade with Newfoundland. Sydney, never more than a shadow of the pretentious capital planned in 1785, supported a cluster of salaried officials and hangers-on amid the forest; by 1795, many of its wharfs and buildings were in ruins.[75]

By 1800, the four maritime provinces of British North America were markedly diverse in economy, society, settlement patterns, and landscapes. Perhaps 75 to 80 000 people lived in the region. Halifax, with a fifth of Nova Scotia's population, and Saint John, with a tenth of New Brunswick's, were the only cities. Shelburne ranked third among the region's urban centres, but it was little bigger than Fredericton, a capital village of 120 to 150 houses, "scattered," according to the wife of a military officer, "on a delightful common of the richest sheep pasture I ever saw."[76] Despite their administrative functions, Charlottetown and Sydney were tiny places, and few other agglomerations were more than hamlets.

Along the rocky Atlantic shore of Nova Scotia and on the coast of Cape Breton (type 1 areas in figure 2), kitchen gardens and fish provided a meagre subsistence for residents of isolated fishing settlements whose catch entered Atlantic commerce. In detail, this was a complex trade. Liverpool fishermen took salmon in Newfoundland and Labrador and cod, mackerel, and herring along the Nova Scotian coast. Halifax merchants organized cargoes drawn from scattered outports. Pickled fish (salmon/herring) was exchanged for provisions and marine supplies in the mid-Atlantic states, and salt cod for salt, sugar, rum, and molasses in the West Indies. But life in the fishing settlements was simple; a scattered group of merchants apart, their residents had little contact with the world beyond. There was little geometric order to these places, the accretive growth of which was shaped by

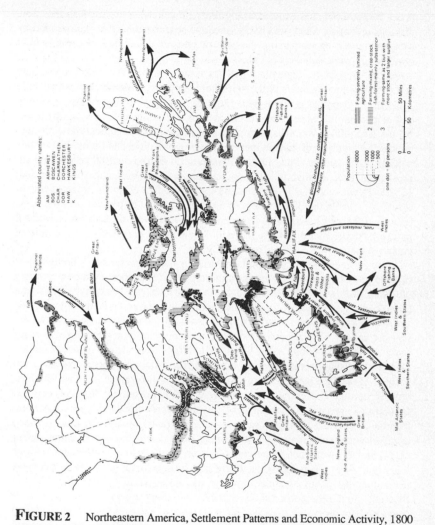

FIGURE 2 Northeastern America, Settlement Patterns and Economic Activity, 1800

SOURCES: Poll tax returns, RG1, vol. 443, 444, 444½, Public Archives of Nova Scotia (PANS); F.B. MacMillan, "Trade of New Brunswick with Great Britain, the United States and the Caribbean 1784–1818" (M.A. thesis, University of New Brunswick, 1954); H.H. Robertson, "The Commerical Relationship between Nova Scotia and the British West Indies 1788–1828: The Twilight of Mercantilism in the British Empire," (M.A. thesis, Dalhousie University, 1975); Duties and trade of Nova Scotia 1801–1828, RG13, 7, vol. 40, PANS; and *Royal Gazette* (Saint John), *Gazette* (Halifax), various issues, 1790s.

beach room, topography, and consanguinity. Dwellings were modest, their furnishings utilitarian. Sheds and flakes lined the strand; cabins were surrounded by irregular fences, encompassing the acre or two of rock-bound soil from which families supplemented diets of fish.[77]

Generalizing from fragmentary poll-tax returns of the 1790s, we can estimate that possibly three-quarters of the households in these communities owned cattle or horses.[78] Over half of those with cattle kept only one or two beasts; very few had more than five. Sheep were less numerous than cattle and were kept by fewer people, a handful of whom had flocks of 10 or more. Cattle numbers were less than double the numbers of taxable men in these communities, and most individuals paid the minimum head tax. In the Guysborough district over 80 percent did so; mechanics made up slightly less than 10 percent of taxables, and only 13 among 163 were enumerated as physicians, attorneys, vendors of goods, or recipients of annuities. Among the 300 taxables of Queens County, 70 percent paid the basic poll tax. Mechanics made up 14 percent of the total, vessel mates and masters 8 percent, and merchants and shopkeepers 7 percent. In Guysborough, the ratio of cattle to taxables was 1.47, in Queens, 1.26.

Away from the fishing ports, mixed farming was characteristic. Through most of the region, farms were the means and purpose of existence. Potatoes, a variety of grains, peas, and turnips were grown. In those areas designated type 2 in figure 2, surpluses were generally small and sporadic; when they entered trade it was, first and foremost, to sustain relatively high levels of local self-sufficiency. Again, poll-tax returns indicate something of the economic structure of these communities. On a per capita basis, livestock holdings were clearly more substantial than in the fishing settlements. In broad terms, cattle and horses exceeded the number of taxables by a factor of three or four. In some areas, such as Windsor, with an unusual concentration of relatively well-to-do settlers, horses accounted for almost 25 percent of this total; generally they were considerably less important. Several individuals kept 8 or more neat cattle (and some 25 or more). Sheep numbers were substantial and in some areas exceeded the number of cattle; flocks of 20 and 30 were not uncommon, but as in the fishing settlements, fewer households kept sheep than cows. Here, as in most farming settlements, there was a considerable range of circumstances. By the standards of the day, "Mount Pleasant" on the Kennebecasis River was a fine property, with 130 cleared acres (most of them intervale); it yielded 80 to 100 tons of hay each year.[79] More typical were two St. John valley properties offered for sale near the turn of the century: one had "15 acres of interval and about 20 acres cleared ready for the plough"; the other—an "agreeable" farm—"about 13 acres under improvements, a handsome two story Dwelling House ... [and] an excellent Garden of about three-quarters of an acre, well enclosed with a pale fence."[80] Yet others had a bare 5 or 6 acres under cultivation, and their occupants practised "a crude catch-as-catch-can sort of agriculture."[81]

Only a few parts of the region (designated type 3 in figure 2) contributed regularly to the regional trade in foodstuffs. From older-settled districts on the productive Fundy marshlands, livestock went to Halifax and Saint John. From Lunenburg, roots and other supplies accompanied shipments of firewood to the provincial capital, and hay, at least, moved downriver from the immediate hinterland of Saint John. In the Fundy settlements, farmers grew a variety of grains and other crops on marsh and upland, but American flour was stiff competition in the region's urban markets, and these were mainly for local consumption. Livestock offered better returns, and large areas of dyked and undyked marsh were turned to hay as economic connection prompted product specialization. Numbers of cattle and horses exceeded the number of taxables five- or six-fold in many parts of this district during the 1790s, and William Trueman surely followed a familiar line of trade when he made two trips from Chignecto to Halifax in the summer of 1802, the first with 30 oxen and the second with 24 cattle for sale.[82]

Landscapes revealed rather more of the social geography of the area. Contrasts and incongruities were many: a few large, well-established farms pointed up how little cleared land most settlers had; finely coifed ladies in "pink and lilac high-heeled shoes" picked their ways over the "rugged rocky paths" of Saint John; hard-scrabble fishing settlements bore little resemblance to the well-cultivated marshland fringes of the Bay of Fundy; the social world of the Halifax élite was a vast remove from the humble settings of countless provincial lives.[83] For every farm family comfortable upon the surplus of productive acres, there were many more squeezing a meagre subsistence from a rudimentary agriculture on thin, stump-strewn soils.

Through much of settled New Brunswick and southwestern Nova Scotia, building forms revealed the American origins of the settlers. The Cape Cod house—with its approximately square plan, low walls, tight eaves, large central chimney, one-and-a-half-storey height, and shingle-clad exterior—was an established form on the Atlantic coast of Nova Scotia, as it was along the shores of Maine and Massachusetts (figure 3a).[84] A second recognizably American house type was also common by 1800 (figure 3d). Larger and more expensive, this symmetrical dwelling with central hall and two chimneys has generally been associated with Loyalist settlement in the region.[85] Houses of this type (modelled on American Georgian or "Colonial" models that were widespread before the Revolution) and Cape Cod cottages were among those erected in Shelburne. They were also built in the Annapolis and Minas basins, in Passamaquoddy and the St. John valley, and in other south shore towns. Clapboarded, they differed only slightly in appearance (albeit more in floor plan) from the houses of earlier New England settlers in the Fundy townships. Barns, where built, were generally of wood, free standing, and apparently of the English two-bay type, although the common northern New England practice of connecting dwelling, barn, and service buildings may have been followed in parts of New Brunswick before the nineteenth century.[86]

Gravestones were another indicator of cultural ties between New England and Nova Scotia. Traditional death head motifs, more fashionable in early than in late eighteenth-century Massachusetts, decorated gravemarkers shipped from Boston

(a)

The Cape Cod cottage of the Atlantic coast

(b)

Death head motif, Lettice Doane grave marker, Barrington, Nova Scotia

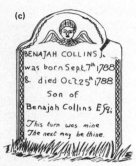

(c)

Cherubim motif, Benajah Collins grave marker, Liverpool, Nova Scotia

(d)

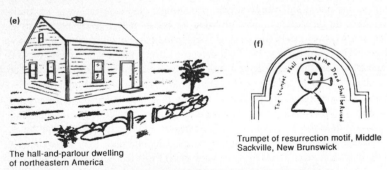

(e)

The hall-and-parlour dwelling of northeastern America

(f)

Trumpet of resurrection motif, Middle Sackville, New Brunswick

FIGURE 3   Cultural Landscape Elements. All sketches by the author.

to the south shore communities between 1765 and the 1780s (figure 3b).[87] Angel-heads, or cherubim, carved on late eighteenth-century gravemarkers, still stand in the graveyards of Liverpool, Cheboque, and Halifax; many have close stylistic counterparts in Salem and neighbouring Massachusetts towns (figure 3c). Death heads are absent from Connecticut-settled Horton and Cornwallis; the cherub on a stone shipped there from New London differs from those characteristic of the south shore, and here local carvers developed their own variants of the winged-head motif after 1783. Other symbols vied with cherubim in the 1790s. Angels sounding the trumpet of resurrection were perhaps most common in areas touched by evangelical Protestantism (figure 3f); urns—reflections of the neo-classical revival in the United States—appeared on imported and local stones by the turn of the century.

Elsewhere, distinctive cultural imprints on the landscape were less obvious. German inscriptions and simple floral designs distinguished the gravestones of Lunenburg. In Pictou, sandstone gravemarkers generally recorded the origins of the deceased but were rarely ornamented with more than a thistle or two. York-shiremen in Chignecto had begun to replicate in brick and stone, as well as wood, the Georgian and hipped roof forms of dwellings in their native county.[88] Through much of the Gulf shore, Prince Edward Island, and Cape Breton, however, the recency and economic marginality of settlement stamped a utilitarian similarity on the landscape. Crude cabins, hall-and-parlour dwellings, and simple log structures with two or three rooms were frequently home to returned Acadians and the first permanent shelters of immigrant families. Found throughout the region in 1800, and characteristic of settlement frontiers the length of eastern North America, they remained a persistent type in the lexicon of regional folk architecture (figure 3e).[89]

Yet the basic ethnic divisions that marked the region through the nineteenth century—an English/American south and west, a Scottish Gulf, Germans in Lunenburg, Irish in Halifax and the Cobequid area, and a cluster of Acadian enclaves in Madawaska, northeastern New Brunswick, western Prince Edward Island, southeastern Cape Breton, and St. Mary's Bay— were already coming into focus at the end of the eighteenth century. So, too, were the associated patterns of religious differentiation.[90] And the essential and persistent patterns of economy and settlement in this overwhelmingly intractable region were clear: most people occupied modest farms or clustered in sea-girt villages; their distribution was basically peripheral; fingers of population followed the region's major valleys inland.[91]

At the turn of the nineteenth century, the Maritime colonies remained an unconsolidated amalgam of families and small communities. In most things, the reach of colonial institutions was limited. Although common backgrounds provided a measure of coherence among many groups of settlers, there had been little time for the settling of people into place. The flux of population continued. The considerable task of establishing, and maintaining, a subsistence threshold pre-occupied the majority of the region's settlers. In these respects, as in the under-development of manufacturing, the poor quality and slender articulation of overland transportation, the lack of an urban network, and the inchoate pattern of intellectual life, the Maritime colonies bore more resemblance to the back country of the U.S. south and the northern hill country of New England than they did to the older colonial hearths from which so many of their people had come and to which they remained connected by trade.[92]

In 1800, as in 1755, these four colonies accounted for an insignificant proportion of the wealth and population of America. Yet economic, social, and, above all, geographical changes in this corner of the continent during the last half of the eighteenth century reflected broader patterns of North American development. The migratory fishery of Cape Breton shared a great deal with the trade that shaped landscapes and settlements in Newfoundland and much of the Gulf of St. Lawrence for better than three centuries. Essentially static in technology and organization, it turned "surplus" European labour to the extraction of New World resources. Closely controlled by powerful merchants, and integrating the western Atlantic littoral into a complex international trading network, it made that area a distant work-place for several thousand young men from the farms and villages of Ireland, southern England, France, and the Channel Islands, but returned little to local, North American economies.

The essential characteristics of the region's resident fishery—which was more widely dispersed and employed far more people than its migratory counterpart— were repeated the length of the coast, from Twillingate to Martha's Vineyard. Few prospered in this enterprise. In Nova Scotia, even more than in New England, the industry was "delicately balanced between profit and loss." Catches were variable, the cure was unreliable, and, as Ralph H. Brown recognized long ago, those engaged at all levels of the trade were caught up in "a relentless battle on an economic front that included all countries of the North Atlantic basin."[93] For the individual fisherman, the results were all too often debt and impoverishment. "Who ever knew a Fisherman thrive?" asked New Brunswick Loyalist William Paine in 1788. "I am persuaded that a coast calculated for fishing is so far from being a benefit, that it really is a *curse* to the Inhabitants. . . . [They] will ever be *poor* and *miserable* . . . . At Salem, Marblehead and Cape Ann . . . [fishermen] are the most wretched of the community."[94]

Although colonial rather than European merchants dominated the resident fishery, and although its connections to the West Indies were stronger than those of the Mediterranean-oriented migratory fishery, the commercial spheres of the two enterprises overlapped and interlocked. Together they sketched, in outline, the complex web that bound the North Atlantic into a triangle of trade. But with few forward, backward, or final demand linkages, neither migratory nor resident fishery was an effective motor of local economic growth in the Maritime colonies. Even the profits and multipliers generated for Nova Scotia by the resident fishery tended to concentrate in Halifax. Beyond, harsh toil on the rugged Atlantic coast yielded a meagre subsistence for scattered families.

In New Brunswick, Loyalist dreams of creating a stable, ordered, hierarchical society—an exclusive Elysium in the north—had faded through 15 years of settlement.[95] For all Edward Winslow's hope that his new province would be "the most Gentlemanlike one on Earth" and the very "envy of the American states," regardless of John Saunders's belief that education and rank should entitle young men to privilege and position, and despite the handful of extravagant estates financed by payments from the Loyalist Claims Commission, most colonists exhibited a sturdy independence while struggling to make their way in the new land.[96] Few, indeed, shared the social conceptions of the élite. For most New Brunswickers, pedigree was a thin claim to privilege, and tenancy was unpalatable. When 55 gentlemen petitioned for 5 000-acre grants on the basis of their "most respectable Characters" and former status, 600 ordinary settlers refused to recognize the claimants' superiority in anything but "deeper Art and keener Policy." When Col. Kemble sought to rent properties on his "Manor," he soon learned that "no man... [would] become a tenant" and that "even the best cultivated farms" could not be leased "to any valuable purpose." For Governor John Parr, such signs were evidence that many Loyalists had inherited "a deal of that Liver, which disunited the [Thirteen] Colonies from their Mother Country."[97] But prevailing attitudes were as much the product of conditions in New Brunswick as they were of convictions shaped in the old colonies.

In New Brunswick, as on countless New World frontiers, land had little intrinsic worth. Its value was created by the hard labour of forest clearance and cultivation. And where readily available land allowed men to work for themselves, they would rarely toil for others. Thus large land holdings brought few economic benefits. Gentlemen of education and refinement were obliged "to undergo all the drudgery of farming"; servants were hard to come by; hirelings insisted on sharing their masters' tables; and British soldier William Cobbett, who had never thought of approaching a "Squire without a most respectful bow" in England, found himself, "in this New World," ordering many "a Squire to bring me a glass of Grog and even to take care of my knapsack."[98] Abhorred as they were by Loyalist leaders, the levelling democratic tendencies of North American settlement could not be excluded from New Brunswick. Around the indulgent islands of splendid houses, fine wines, and social pretensions sustained by military pensions and aristocratic conventions, most turn-of-the-century New Brunswickers inhabited an essentially egalitarian world. Recent and relatively remote, defined in opposition to the United States, and without a vigorous commercial outlet, their society bore a thin veneer of traditional English conservatism on its democratic New World core.[99]

Settlement in the four colonies had proceeded largely by chance. If, as Jacob Bailey adduced, many Loyalists were impelled by "a passion for novelty and a love of rambling" rather than by "any virtuous attachment to their royal masters," most other inhabitants of the area were there for equally capricious reasons: for many, the region had provided tolerable alternatives to unpromising or difficult circumstances in their former homelands; for some, it had offered prospects of real advantage; to few had it yielded substantial wealth or comfort. In 1800, as in the decades that followed, the eastern colonies of British North America formed a region of scattered settlements and bounded possibilities. Although much land remained to be taken up, although the economy would be invigorated by the early nineteenth-century timber trade, and although the face of the country would be further transformed by ongoing settlement and development, the essential patterns of land and life in the Maritime provinces were clearly outlined in the half-century after 1755. Here and there across the region, newcomers might find, for a time, a modest niche for themselves and their families. Whether that niche were in narrow valley, along rocky shore, or on upland plateau, hard work, ingenuity, and versatility—to say nothing of good fortune—were generally required to take advantage of it and to survive. And within a generation or two (at most), the limits of local resources would be met. As contexts changed, so new adjustments were made. But always sons and daughters would move on, in the late eighteenth century, to occupy new pockets of land and limited opportunity in the region, in the late nineteenth, to find work in Boston, and in the late twentieth, to seek their fortunes in Toronto and Alberta. Simply to recognize as much is to conceive the experience of settlement in these provinces as an important variant of a recurrent facet of life in the Canadian archipelago.[100]

Notes

1. This point has been made recently in two important treatments of the colonial seaboard colonies: J.P. Greene and J.P. Pole, eds., *Colonial British America: Essays in the New History of the Early Modern Era* (Baltimore: Johns Hopkins University Press, 1984); and J.J. McCusker and R.R. Menard, *The Economy of British America 1607–1789* (Chapel Hill, NC: University of North Carolina Press, 1985).

2. J.B. Brebner, *North Atlantic Triangle* (Toronto: McClelland and Stewart, 1966), 56–57; D.C. Harvey, "Machias and the Invasion of Nova Scotia," Canadian Historical Association (hereinafter CHA), *Report* (1932), 21; *Nova Scotia Gazette* and the *Weekly Chronicle*, 10 Sept. 1776, cited in *Revolution Rejected 1775–1776*, ed. G.A. Rawlyk (Scarborough, Ont.: Prentice Hall, 1968), 27; J.B. Brebner, *Neutral Yankees of Nova Scotia* (Toronto: McClelland and Stewart, 1969), 264–65.

3. J.M. Bumsted, *Henry Alline, 1748–1784* (Toronto: University of Toronto Press, 1971); G. Stewart, "Socio-Economic Factors in the Great Awakening: The Case of Yarmouth, Nova Scotia," *Acadiensis* 3 (1973): 18–34; G. Stewart and G.A. Rawlyk, "Nova Scotia's Sense of Mission," *Histoire sociale/Social History* 2 (1968): 115–17; Stewart and Rawlyk, *A People Highly Favoured of God: The Nova Scotia Yankees and the American Revolution* (Toronto: Macmillan, 1972); G.A. Rawlyk, *Ravished by the Spirit: Religious Revivals, Baptists and Henry Alline* (Montreal: McGill-Queen's University Press, 1984); Brebner, *Neutral Yankees*, 275.

4. J.D. Faibisy, "Privateering and Piracy: The Effects of New England Raiding upon Nova Scotia during the American Revolution, 1775–1783" (Ph.D. diss., University of Massachusetts, 1972). Considerable attention has focused on the reasons why Nova Scotia did not join the American Revolution. The debate is summarized in *Revolution Rejected*, ed. Rawlyk. With a few exceptions, the perceptive regional and biographical studies called for there have yet to appear.

5. J. Greenough, "The Defence of Halifax 1783–1825" (unpublished paper presented to the CHA, Halifax, 1981), 2.

6. L.R. Fischer, "Revolution without Independence: The Halifax Merchants and the American Revolution, 1749–1775" (unpublished paper presented to the CHA, London, Ont., 1978), 28–31.

7. P.M. Gouett, "The Halifax Orphan House 1752–87," *Nova Scotia Historical Quarterly* 6 (1976): 281–91.

8. N.L. Nicholson, *The Boundaries of the Canadian Confederation* (Toronto: Macmillan, 1979), 27–30.

9. M. Ells, "Clearing the Decks for the Loyalists," CHA, *Report* (1939), 56–58; M. Gilroy, *Loyalists and Land Settlement in Nova Scotia*, Genealogical Committee of the Royal Nova Scotia Historical Society publication no. 4 (1980). The Nova Scotian acreage estimate is based on a 5 percent sample of grants. See R. Fellows, "The Loyalists and Land Settlement in New Brunswick, 1783–1790: A Study in Colonial Administration," *Canadian Archivist* 2, 2 (1970–74): 5–15.

10. Campbell to Sydney, 30 Nov. 1785, RG1, sec. 4, vol. 107, Public Archives of Nova Scotia (hereinafter PANS); N. Mackinnon, "The Loyalist Experience in Nova Scotia, 1783–1791" (Ph.D. diss., Queen's University, 1975), 182–85; E.C. Wright, *The Loyalists of New Brunswick* (Moncton: Moncton Publishing, 1972), 249–50; General Returns of Loyalists, MG23, D1(1), vol. 24, Public Archives of Canada (hereinafter PAC).

11. M. Ells, "Settling the Loyalists in Nova Scotia," CHA, *Report* (1935), 105–9; A.G. Condon, *The Envy of the American States: The Loyalist Dream for New Brunswick* (Fredericton: New Ireland Press, 1984), 2–3; A.H. Clark, *Three Centuries and the Island* (Toronto: University of Toronto Press, 1959), 58.

12. W.S. MacNutt, "Fanning's Regime on Prince Edward Island," *Acadiensis* 1 (1971): 37–53; Clark, *Three Centuries*, 57–58. Still this period was of vital importance in shaping the pattern of eighteenth-century development in PEI. See J.M. Bumsted, "The Patterson Regime and the Impact of the American Revolution on the Island of St. John 1775–1786," *Acadiensis* 13 (1983): 47–67; R.J. Morgan, "The Loyalists of Cape Breton," *Dalhousie Review* 55 (1975): 5–22; R.J. Morgan, "Orphan Outpost" (Ph.D. diss., University of Ottawa, 1973).

13. Or, as Jacob Bailey described the Annapolis Valley Loyalists: "a collection of all nations, kindreds, complexions and tongues assembled from every quarter of the Globe and till lately equally strangers to me and each other" (cited in MacKinnon, "The Loyalist Experience," 241). Additional recent work on Loyalists in the "Maritime region" includes: H.C. Hazen, "The Story of New Brunswick's Black Settlers 1700–1820," *Journal of New Brunswick Museum* (1979): 44–53; G.C.W. Troxler, "The Migration of Carolina and Georgia Loyalists to Nova Scotia and New Brunswick" (Ph.D. diss., University of North Carolina at Chapel Hill, 1974); C. Troxler, " 'To Get out of a Troublesome Neighbourhood': David Fanning in New Brunswick," *North Carolina Historical Review* 56 (1979): 343–65; W.S. MacNutt, "The Loyalists: A Sympathetic View," *Acadiensis* 6 (1976): 3–20; N. Mackinnon, "The Changing Attitudes of the Nova Scotia Loyalists to the United States 1783–1791," *Acadiensis* 2 (1973): 34–54; N. Mackinnon, "Nova Scotian Loyalists, 1783–1785," *Histoire sociale/Social History* 4 (1969): 25–38; J.W.St.G. Walker, "Blacks as American Loyalists: The Slaves' War for Independence," *Historical Reflections* 2 (1975): 51–67; and R. Nason, "Meritorious but Distressed Individuals: The Penobscot Loyalist Association and the Settlement of the Township of St. Andrews, New Brunswick, 1783–1821" (M.A. thesis, University of New Brunswick, 1982). Two important books have appeared since this article first went to press: J.M. Bumsted, *Land, Settlement, and Politics on Eighteenth Century Prince Edward Island* (Montreal: McGill-Queen's University Press, 1987); and N. Mackinnon, *This Unfriendly Soil: The Loyalist Experience in Nova Scotia 1783–1791* (Montreal: McGill-Queen's University Press, 1986).

14. Condon, *The Envy*, passim; C. Moore, *The Loyalists: Revolution, Exile, Settlement* (Toronto: Macmillan, 1984); Wallace Brown, "Mather Byles," in *Dictionary of Canadian Biography* (hereinafter *DCB*) (1983), 5:127–28; A.G. Bailey, "Jonathan Odell," *DCB*, 5:628–31; J. Fingard, "Sir John Wentworth," *DCB*, 5:848–52; A.G. Condon, "Edward Winslow," *DCB*, 5:865–69.

15. Wright, *The Loyalists*, 161.

16.   J.S. Macdonald, "Memoir of Governor John Parr," Nova Scotia Historical Society (hereinafter NSHS), *Collections* 14 (1910): 54–56; PAC, *Report* (1894), 412–18.

17.   C.W. Vernon, *Bicentenary Sketches and Early Days of the Church in Nova Scotia* (Halifax: Chronicle Printing, 1910), 145. See also W.O. Raymond, ed., *The Winslow Papers, 1776–1826* (Saint John: Sun Printing, 1901), 264.

18.   H. Temperley, "Frontierism, Capital and the American Loyalists in Canada," *Journal of American Studies* 13 (1979): 5–27; Wright, *The Loyalists*, 165–66; J. Eardley Wilmot, *Historical View of the Commission of Enquiry. . .* (London, 1815).

19.   Wright, *The Loyalists*, 166.

20.   Ibid., 151–67.

21.   L. Sabine, *Biographical Sketches of Loyalists of the American Revolution* (Boston, 1864). Sample of approximately 700 Shelburne family heads. Mackinnon, "The Loyalist Experience," 252–53.

22.   J.W.St.G. Walker, *The Black Loyalists: The Search for a Promised Land in Nova Scotia and Sierra Leone, 1783–1860* (New York: Africana Publishing/Dalhousie University Press, 1976) is the standard work on which much of this discussion depends.

23.   J.W.St.G. Walker, "Boston King," *DCB*, 5:468–69.

24.   H.A. Innis, D.C. Harvey, C.B. Fergusson, eds., *The Diary of Simeon Perkins* (Toronto: Champlain Society, 1958), 2:238; W.O. Raymond, "The Founding of Shelburne and Early Miramichi: Marston's Diary," New Brunswick Historical Society, *Collections* 3 (1907): 265.

25.   John Clarkson, cited in Walker, *The Black Loyalists*, 46.

26.   Walker, *The Black Loyalists*, 57.

27.   Province of Nova Scotia, Proclamations 1748–1807, Document 88, 22 Jan. 1784, RG1, section 2, vol. 346, PANS; Col. R. Morse, "Report on Nova Scotia, 1784," Canada Archives, *Report* (1884) *xli*; Wright, *The Loyalists*, 35; John Parr to Lord North, Enclosure, 21 Oct. 1783, MG2, vol. 103, PAC.

28.   Raymond, "The Founding of Shelburne," 234; Muster Rolls of Loyalists and Military Settlers, Annapolis, Digby, RG1, vol. 376, PANS; John Robinson to Edward Winslow, 16 Sept. 1784, MG23, D1(1), vol. 24, PAC; I.W. Wilson, *A Geography and History of the County of Digby Nova Scotia* (Halifax, 1950), 50–51.

29.   Gilroy, *Loyalists and Land Settlement*; Mackinnon, "The Loyalist Experience," 183; Raymond, ed., *Winslow Papers*, 248; Walker, *The Black Loyalists*, 21–32. Expansion of settlement pushed indigenous peoples of the region back to more remote territory and deprived them of land. In New Brunswick, at least, there were concerted efforts to anglicize and Protestantize the Indians. See J. Fingard, "The New England Company and the New Brunswick Indians 1786–1826: A Comment on the Colonial Perversion of British Benevolence," *Acadiensis* 1 (1972): 29–42; L.F.S. Upton, *Micmacs and Colonists: Indian–White Relations in the Maritimes, 1713–1867* (Vancouver: University of British Columbia Press, 1979); W.D. Hamilton, "Indian Lands in New Brunswick: The Case of the Little South West Reserve," *Acadiensis* 13 (1984): 3–28.

30.   M. Robertson, *King's Bounty: A History of Early Shelburne* (Halifax: Nova Scotia Museum, 1983); Raymond, "The Founding of Shelburne"; Mackinnon, "The Loyalist Experience," 124, 154–56; Moore, *The Loyalists*, 158–60.

31.   Parr to Shelburne, 9 Oct. 1789, typescript, Vertical mss file: Shelburne, PANS.

32.   *Port Roseway Gazette and Shelburne Advertiser* (Shelburne), 7 Feb., 6 June 1785.

33.   S.S. Blowers to W. Chipman, 13 May 1786, MG23, D1(1), vol. 1, PAC; Parr to Shelburne, 9 Oct. 1789, Vertical mss file: Shelburne, PANS; Journal of Bishop Charles

Inglis, 1785–1810, vol. 4, 2 Aug. 1790, Inglis Papers, MG1, PANS. Inglis's estimate of 3 525 is too high because it takes no account of the single men (perhaps 15 percent of the population) in applying a multiplier to the number of families (Raymond, "The Founding of Shelburne"). A parallel case is well recounted in T.H. Raddall, "Tarleton's Legion," NSHS, *Collections* 28 (1947): 1–50.

34. W.O. Raymond, ed., *Kingston and the Loyalists of the Spring Fleet of AD 1783* (Saint John: Barnes, 1889).

35. D.G. Bell, *Early Loyalist Saint John: The Origin of New Brunswick Politics, 1783–1790* (Fredericton: New Ireland Press, 1983), 48–49; Raymond, ed., *Winslow Papers*, 354.

36. Wright, *The Loyalists*, 249–50; P. Campbell, *Travels in the Interior Inhabitated Parts of North America in the Years 1791 and 1792* (Toronto: Champlain Society, 1937 [1791]), 25.

37. Wright, *The Loyalists*, 177–83, 249–50; T.W. Acheson, "A Study of the Historical Demography of a Loyalist County," *Histoire sociale/Social History* 1 (1968): 53–65; Condon, *The Envy*, 72–96.

38. For Filer Dibblee and his family, see W. Brown, *The Good Americans: The Loyalists in the American Revolution* (New York: W. Morrow, 1969), 140–41, 206–7. Jacob Bailey cited in Mackinnon, "The Loyalist Experience," 211.

39. G. Wynn, "The Assault on the New Brunswick Forest 1780–1850" (Ph.D. diss., University of Toronto, 1974), 64–70; W. Cobbett, *Advice to Young Men and (Incidentally) to Young Women* (London: Anne Cobbett, 1837), 137–39. Further detail about the patterns, achievements, and hardships of Loyalist settlement can be pieced together from a series of M.A. theses completed at the University of New Brunswick, including: T.W. Acheson, "Denominationalism in a Loyalist County: A Social History of Charlotte, 1783–1940" (1964); T.M.F. Kilbride, "The Process of Growth and Change in Carleton County, 1783–1867" (1969); W. Moore, "Sunbury County, 1760–1830" (1977); B.D. Pilon, "Settlement and Early Development of the Parish of Kingsclear, York County, New Brunswick, 1784–1840" (1966); C.A. Pincombe, "The History of Moncton Township (ca. 1700–1875)" (1969); and W.A. Spray, "Early Northumberland County, 1765–1825: A Study in Local Government" (1963).

40. Mackinnon, "The Loyalist Experience," 462–64.

41. Jacob Bailey to Samuel Peters, 7 Nov. 1786, Peters Papers, 1–2 mfm, MG1, PANS.

42. Raymond, ed., *Winslow Papers*, 468.

43. Mackinnon, "The Loyalist Experience," 193–94.

44. J.M. Bumsted, *The People's Clearance: Highland Emigration to British North America, 1770–1815* (Edinburgh: Edinburgh University Press, 1982); D. Campbell and R.A. MacLean, *Beyond the Atlantic Roar: A Study of the Nova Scotia Scots* (Toronto: McClelland and Stewart, 1974), 7–75.

45. J. Wentworth to J. Parr, 5 Mar. 1788, RG2, vol. 49, PANS; Mackinnon, "The Loyalist Experience," 500.

46. Roger Viets to Samuel Peters, 12 Oct. 1787, RG2, vol. 4, PANS; Wright, *The Loyalists*, 212; Mackinnon, "The Loyalist Experience," 486.

47. Walker, *The Black Loyalists* 115–44.

48. Wright, *The Loyalists*, 223.

49. Sir A. Hammond to —, 1782, MG30, D62, vol. 15, PAC; Mackinnon, "The Loyalist Experience," 120–21, 210.

50. G. Wynn, "Late Eighteenth Century Agriculture on the Bay of Fundy Marshlands," *Acadiensis* 8 (1979): 80–89; Jacob Bailey to Dr. Maurice, 28 Oct. 1785 and 12 May 1786, Bailey Papers, mfm, MG1, vol. 14, PANS; J. Parr to Sydney, 31

Dec. 1785, CO 217, vol. 58, PAC; Mackinnon, "The Loyalist Experience," 444;
G. Wynn, *Timber Colony: A Historical Geography of Early Nineteenth Century New Brunswick* (Toronto: University of Toronto Press, 1981), 20.

51. This is a best estimate on the basis of conflicting evidence. Cf. Mackinnon, "The Loyalist Experience," 444, 448.

52. F.B. MacMillan, "Trade of New Brunswick with Great Britain, the United States and the Caribbean, 1784–1818" (M.A. thesis, University of New Brunswick, 1954), 45–46.

53. Mackinnon, "The Loyalist Experience," 459.

54. Samual Goldbury to Edward Winslow, 1 Mar. 1785, in *Winslow Papers,* ed. Raymond, 270–71.

55. C. Stewart to Col. Winslow, 29 Sept. 1784, 148, MG23, D1, series 1, vol. 24, PAC.

56. Roads in this country "covered with woods" and "much intersected by waters" remained in very poor state a decade after the Loyalists' arrival (Report of 20 Dec. 1794, RG2, vol. 48 #120, PANS; and material in RG16). Carleton to Grenville, 15 July 1791, MG11, NBA5, 28–32, PAC. A comparison with D. McCalla, "The 'Loyalist' Economy of Upper Canada 1784–1806," *Histoire sociale/Social History* 16 (1983): 279–304, the most useful survey of the Upper Canadian economy during these years, is revealing.

57. D.A. Sutherland, "Halifax Merchants and the Pursuit of Development, 1783–1850," *Canadian Historical Review* 59 (1978): 1–17. See also Macmillan, "Trade of New Brunswick"; H.H. Robertson, "The Commercial Relationship between Nova Scotia and the British West Indies, 1788–1828: The Twilight of Mercantilism in the British Empire" (M.A. thesis, Dalhousie University, 1975).

58. William Shaw to Col. Winslow, Canso, 15 June 1784, MG23, D1, series 1, vol. 25, 251, PAC.

59. Wet cod shipments—of 13 363 barrels from Nova Scotia and 18 103 from the four colonies—increased the total quantity somewhat. Dry cod exports from Newfoundland in 1787 were 732 216 quintals (wet-cod shipments totalled 3 865 barrels). Mackinnon, "The Loyalist Experience," 444–45.

60. Memorial of Leading Citizens of Shelburne, 20 June 1791, RG1, vol. 221, PANS.

61. Mackinnon, "The Loyalist Experience," 456–57, 403; W. Dyott, *Dyott's Diary, 1781–1845: A Selection from the Journals of William Dyott, Sometime General in the British Army and Aide-de-camp to His Majesty King George III*, ed., R.W. Jeffrey (London: A. Constable, 1907), 68; G.S. Graham, *Sea Power and British North America, 1783–1820: A Study in British Colonial Policy* (Cambridge, MA: Harvard University Press, 1941); W.S. MacNutt, *New Brunswick: A History, 1784–1867* (Toronto: Macmillan, 1963), 70–72, 96–97.

62. This is my own calculation, based on data and statements in Temperley, "Frontierism." Compensation for losses sustained can be estimated at £266 000. A figure of £200–210 000 for half-pay receipts stems from assumptions that two-thirds of payments before 1813 were made before 1800, that the "take-up" rate was 66 percent, that slightly more than half of all payments went to North America, and that the 56 percent of North American payments accounted for by Nova Scotia and New Brunswick in 1810 approximated the earlier distribution.

63. Observations on the Province of New Brunswick, Enclosure in Daniel Lyman to Lord Hawkesbury, 9 Mar. 1793, MG11, NBA #6, 30, PAC.

64. P. Campbell, *Travels*, 282–84; H. Temperley, ed., *Gubbins' New Brunswick Journals* (Fredericton: Kings Landing Corporation, 1980); Roger Viets to Samuel Peters, 11 Aug. 1789, Peters Papers, MG1, vol. 4, PANS.

65. Greenough, "The Defence of Halifax."

66. Dyott, *Dyott's Diary*. Such patterns were not unknown earlier, among wealthy Loyalists. See Mackinnon, "Nova Scotia Loyalists," and Raymond, ed., *Winslow Papers*, 141–42, 150, 252, 288.

67. G.A. Stelter, "The Political Economy of the City-Building Process: Early Canadian Urban Development," in *The Pursuit of Urban History*, ed. D. Fraser and A. Sutcliffe (London: Edward Arnold, 1983), 179; L.B. Jensen, *Vanishing Halifax* (Halifax: McCurdy Printing, 1968), n.p.

68. K.B. Wainwright, "A Comparative Study in Nova Scotian Rural Economy, 1788–1812: Based on Recently Discovered Books of Account of Old Firms in Kings County, Nova Scotia," NSHS, *Collections* 30 (1954): 78–119.

69. In its economic vigour, Westmorland County, in Chignecto, was perhaps more akin to the Fundy settlements of Nova Scotia than to the rest of New Brunswick.

70. Wynn, *Timber Colony*, 11–25.

71. Amos Botsford to Provincial Agent, 5 Mar. 1796, MG11, NBA 5, 25, PAC.

72. Bumsted, "The Patterson Regime," 67; Clark, *Three Centuries*, 58–65.

73. P.C.T. White, *Lord Selkirk's Diary, 1803–4* (Toronto: Champlain Society, 1958), 7–10.

74. Cf. R. Ommer, "All the Fish of the Post: Property Resource Rights and Development in a Nineteenth Century Inshore Fishery," *Acadiensis* 10, 2 (1981): 107–23; and R. Ommer, "From Outpost to Outport: The Jersey Merchant Triangle in the Nineteenth Century" (Ph.D. diss., McGill University, 1979). D. Lee, *The Robins in Gaspé* (Toronto: Fitzhenry and Whiteside, 1986) is of general relevance.

75. S. Hornsby, "An Historical Geography of Cape Breton Island in the Nineteenth Century" (Ph.D. diss., University of British Columbia, 1986), is a significant contribution to the geographical literature. I am grateful to Hornsby for considerably sharpening my understanding of the island in 1800. Other items of relevance include J.M. Bumsted, "Scottish Emigration to the Maritimes, 1770–1815: A New Look at an Old Theme," *Acadiensis* 10 (1981): 65–85; Campbell and MacLean, *Beyond the Atlantic Roar*; and B. Kincaid, "Scottish Immigration to Cape Breton 1758–1838" (M.A. thesis, Dalhousie University, 1964).

76. Mrs. Hunter to Elizabeth Bell, 7 Aug. 1804, typescript, MYO/H/76, Provincial Archives of New Brunswick.

77. For similar patterns, see J.J. Mannion, *Point Lance in Transition* (Toronto: McClelland and Stewart, 1976), reprinted in this volume. F.P. Day, *Rockbound* (Toronto: University of Toronto Press, 1973) is an evocative Nova Scotian source treating a later period (ca. 1900–14).

78. Poll tax returns are in RG1, vol. 443, 444, 444 1/2, PANS, also available on microfilm. Some have been printed, viz. T.M. Punch, "Assessment Rolls of Halifax County, 1792–93," *Genealogical Newsletter of the Nova Scotia Historical Society* 15 (1976): 14–23; T.M. Punch, "Lunenburg County, Nova Scotia: Poll Taxes of the 1790s," *Canadian Genealogist* 1 (1979): 103–4. As with all following estimates from these returns, this is a very broad guess. Some 50 to 65 percent of taxables had cattle and horses (an enumeration category—horses were scarce in these settlements), but extended family households and a proportion of taxable men living with their parents have to be allowed for.

79. *Saint John Gazette* (Saint John), 6 Apr. 1798.

80. *Royal Gazette* (Saint John), 7 Dec. 1803; *Saint John Gazette*, 25 Feb. 1791.

81. Clark, *Three Centuries*, 63.

82. Stephen Jarvis to Munson Jarvis, 31 July 1805, Jarvis Papers 1801–19, New Brunswick Museum (hereinafter NBM); Wynn, "Eighteenth Century Agriculture"; Col. R.E. Morse, "Report on Nova Scotia, 1784," Canadian Archives, *Report* (1884), *xxxvi*;

J[ohn] K[eillor] to T. Millidge, 9 Nov. 1804, Westmorland County Documents and Correspondence 1783–1859, 70b F-30, NBM; Diary of William Trueman, 5 May 1802–Apr. 1809, Mount Allison University Archives.

83. Wynn, *Timber Colony*, 24.

84. P. Ennals and D. Holdsworth, "Vernacular Architecture and the Cultural Landscape of the Maritime Provinces: A Reconnaissance," *Acadiensis* 10 (1981): 86–106, reprinted in this volume; P. Ennals, "The Yankee Origins of Bluenose Vernacular Architecture," *American Review of Canadian Studies* 12 (1982): 5–21.

85. Ennals and Holdsworth, "Vernacular Architecture," 94–95; Ennals, "Yankee Origins," 10–12.

86. Robinson and Rispin, *Journey through Nova Scotia Containing a Particular Account of the Country and its Inhabitants* (York: C. Etherington, 1774), 21; W. Zelinsky, "New England Connecting Barns," *Geographical Review* 84 (1958): 540–53; Ennals, "Yankee Origins," 7.

87. This discussion of the cultural landscape derives in large part from my own field observations. D. Trask, *Life How Short, Eternity How Long: Gravestone Carving and Carvers in Nova Scotia* (Halifax: Nova Scotia Museum, 1978) is a useful first study of gravemarkers in the region, although the text is brief. For New England, see A.I. Ludwig, *Graven Images* (Middletown, CT: Wesleyan University Press, 1966); E. Dethlefson and J. Deetz, "Death's Heads, Cherubs and Willow Trees: Experimental Archeology in Colonial Cemeteries," *American Antiquity* 31 (1966): 502–10; J. Deetz and E. Dethlefson, "Death's Heads, Cherub, Urn and Willow," *Natural History* 76 (1967): 28–37; and P. Benes, *The Masks of Orthodoxy: Folk Gravestone Carving in Plymouth County, Massachusetts, 1689–1805* (Amherst: University of Massachusetts Press, 1977).

88. Trask, *Life How Short*, 24–27; Ennals and Holdsworth, "Vernacular Architecture," 94; Memorandum of 16 Aug. 1790 between John Wheldon Esq. and Charles Cairns and Frederick McGuire (masons), Westmorland County Documents and Correspondence, 1783–1859, 70b F-30, NBM; Westmorland County Petitions (Duplicates), Agreement between John Fawcett and John Harris, 7 Apr. 1802, C6, NBM.

89. Ennals and Holdsworth, "Vernacular Architecture," 88–89; P.F. Lewis, "Common Houses, Cultural Spoor," *Landscape* 19 (1975): 1–22; H. Glassie, *Pattern in the Material Folk Culture of the Eastern United States* (Philadelphia: University of Pennsylvania Press, 1968), 80–81.

90. A.H. Clark, "Old World Origins and Religious Adherence in Nova Scotia," *Geographical Review* 50 (1960): 317–44; G. Wynn, "The Maritimes: The Geography of Fragmentation and Underdevelopment," in *Heartland and Hinterland: A Geography of Canada*, ed. L.D. McCann (Scarborough, Ont: Prentice-Hall, 1982), 167–68; R.C. Harris and J.Warkentin, *Canada before Confederation* (Toronto: Oxford University Press, 1974), 169–231. The religious patterns are reviewed in G.S. French, "Religion and Society in Late Eighteenth Century Nova Scotia," *Acadiensis* 4 (1975): 102–11, which is in part a review of J. Fingard, *The Anglican Design in Loyalist Nova Scotia, 1783–1816* (London: SPCK, 1972). See also G. French, "The Papers of Daniel Fidler, Methodist Missionary in Nova Scotia and New Brunswick 1792–1798," *The Bulletin: Records and Proceedings of the Committee on Archives of the United Church of Canada* 12 (1959): 3–18, and 13 (1960): 28–46. See also J.M. Bumsted, "Church and State in Maritime Canada 1749–1807," CHA, *Report* (1967), 41–58.

91. There are several published descriptions of parts of the region in the first years of the nineteenth century, among them: G.O. Bent, "New Brunswick in 1802," *Acadiensis* 7 (1907): 128–48; D.A. Muise (intro.), "A Descriptive and Statistical Account of Nova Scotia and its Dependencies in 1812," *Acadiensis* 2 (1972): 82–93;

J.B. Gavin (intro.), "An Extract from the Memoirs of Alexander Drysdale," *Acadiensis* 5 (1975): 146–49; A.H. Clark, "Titus Smith Junior and the Geography of Nova Scotia in 1801 and 1802," *Annals of the Association of American Geographers* 44 (1954): 291–316; Temperley, *Gubbins'*; Wynn, *Timber Colony*, 11–25.

92.   J.M. Bumsted, "Puritan and Yankee Rediviva: Recent Writings on Early New England of Interest to Atlantic Scholars," *Acadiensis* 2 (1972): 3–21 makes a similar point and touches on some of the links discussed below. P.S. Saxton, "The Paragon of Localism in Nova Scotia 1760–1783" (M.A. thesis, Saint Mary's University, 1975); R.R. Beeman, *The Evolution of the Southern Backcountry: A Case Study of Lunenberg County, Virginia, 1746–1832* (Philadelphia: University of Pennsylvania Press, 1984).

93.   R.H. Brown, *Historical Geography of the United States* (New York: Harcourt, Brace and World, 1948), 111.

94.   W. Paine to John Wentworth, 1 Mar. 1788, Wentworth Papers, MG1, vol. 940, PANS.

95.   MacNutt, *New Brunswick*, 11, 12, 42, 92; A.E. Morrison, "New Brunswick: The Loyalists and the Historians," *Journal of Canadian Studies* 3 (1968): 39–49; F. Cogswell, "Literary Activity in the Maritime Provinces, 1815–1880," in *Literary History of Canada*, ed. C.F. Klinck (Toronto: University of Toronto Press, 1965), 103.

96.   Condon, *The Envy*, passim; Moore, *The Loyalists*, 139–54.

97.   Wright, *Loyalists*, 175–77; Condon, *The Envy*, 42, 89–90, 108. Various items relating to Kemble's Manor are in the Ward Chipman correspondence, MG23, D1, PAC; J. Parr to Nepean, 3 Sept. 1784, CO217, vol. 59, PAC. Similarly, B. Marston spoke of the "cursed republican town-meeting spirit" in Shelburne (Raymond, "The Founding," 268).

98.   Temperley, *Gubbins'*; W. Reitzel, ed., *The Autobiography of William Cobbett* (London: Faber and Faber, 1933), 28.

99.   Broader theoretical statements of the interpretation offered here can be found in R.C. Harris, "The Simplification of Europe Overseas," *Annals of the Association of American Geographers* 67 (1977): 469–83, and R.C. Harris, "European Beginnings in the Northwest Atlantic: A Comparative View," in *Seventeenth-Century New England*, ed. D.G. Allen (Boston: Colonial Society of Massachusetts, 1985), 119–52. A broadly similar argument about the development of New Brunswick, based on very different foundations, is in E.C. Wright, "The Settlement of New Brunswick: An Advance Toward Democracy," CHA, *Report* (1944), 60.

100.   Cf. J.M. Bumsted, "Settlement by Chance: Lord Selkirk and Prince Edward Island," *Canadian Historical Review* 59 (1978): 170–88. Bailey cited by Mackinnon, "The Loyalist Experience," 242. D.A. McNabb, "Land and Families in Horton Township, Nova Scotia" (M.A. thesis, University of British Columbia, 1986); A.A. Brookes, "The Golden Age and the Exodus: The Case of Canning, Kings County," *Acadiensis* 11 (1981): 57–82; R.C. Harris, "Regionalism and the Canadian Archipelago" in *Heartland and Hinterland*, ed. McCann, 458–84. In arguing thus I seek to illuminate one important strand of regional experience rather than to deny (for example) the important struggles and achievements of Maritimers in the 1880–1930 period.

THE PATTERN OF EARLY CANADA*

R. COLE HARRIS

As Europe reached across the Atlantic to the vast territory that became Canada, it sent capital and labour to create work camps or trading posts in the wilderness, and then, in time, began to reproduce the two most fundamental elements of the human geography of pre-industrial Europe: town and countryside. As in Europe, towns became the loci of power, while the countryside became the place where most people lived. Neither town nor countryside, the work camps of staple trades were perched in the wilderness where a resource and the means to transport it were both available. These different types of settlements, none exactly like their European progenitors, were the building blocks out of which Canada was slowly composed, a composition always constrained by the physical and political limitations of space. By 1800, the pattern of Canada that we know today was established in many of its essentials. The idea of Canada and the modern nation-state that followed it would not begin to emerge until the 1860s.[1]

This essay describes the three basic types of settlement in early Canada, the space in which they emerged, and the composition that, in sum, they made by 1800.[2] In conclusion, it comments on other attempts to identify the pattern of Canada, suggests that they are partial, and holds that the distinctiveness of Canada—compared to Europe from which it sprang or the United States with which it shares a continent—is bedded in the particular configuration of its emerging human geography.

Types of Settlement

Work Camps

Staple trades in slightly processed primary resources are the oldest and have been the most enduring non-native economies in Canada.[3] French and Portuguese fished

---

* The Canadian Geographer/Le Géographe canadien 31, 4 (1987): 290–98.

in waters around Newfoundland by 1500. In the 1530s, Basques hunted whales along the Labrador coast and rendered the blubber ashore. Soon hundreds of ships and thousands of men—more than went each year to the Spanish Main—crossed the Atlantic to seasonal work camps in eastern Newfoundland, along the Strait of Belle Isle, and at the tip of the Gaspé peninsula.[4] Before the end of the sixteenth century, the fur trade detached itself from the fishery and began to move westward along the St. Lawrence River, the earliest conduit for the furs of the continental interior. By the 1680s, French fur traders had built posts around the Great Lakes, on the Mississippi River, and well into the Canadian Shield north of Lake Superior; farther north, the Hudson's Bay Company had established several river-mouth posts on James and Hudson Bays.

Located in the wilderness at points of resource extraction or trade, these first European settlements in Canada were bound to distant sources of capital and labour, and to distant markets. Settlements came into existence as resources became known, the skills and capital to exploit them became available, and systems of long-distance transportation were put in place.

Life in these settlements turned around the specialized work that procured the resource and the particular system of transportation that carried it. The rhythms of work and transportation, adapted to the extremes of a continental climate, divided time; and the hierarchy of command in the staple trade dominated social relations. These cells of specialized work were not bounded, as they would have been in Europe, by Europeans about other pursuits, but by wilderness, ocean, and native North Americans. In the early years, they were units of European production or trade abstracted from Europe; eventually they became outliers of an expanding North American economy. Built as quickly and as cheaply as possible to perform a specific task, they were starkly utilitarian settlements, most of which would disappear when local resources were exhausted or when technologies of production or transportation changed.

In the work camp there was neither the constraint of tradition nor, usually, of alternative employment. Capital acquired a particular leeway. There could be no recourse to village custom in new settlements perched in the wilderness; rather, trading companies or ship captains imposed their own rules. Distance from markets and forbidding environments eliminated alternative economies. Were land available for family farms, it would bid up the price and increase the independence of labour, but in most of Canada rock and growing season excluded this possibility. To the degree that labour was insulated from agricultural land, the societies associated with staple trades in primary resources would be sharply stratified by position in the productive system. They would come closer than other European settlements in early Canada to creating a proletariat, and eventually, on both sides of the Atlantic, they would make some wealthy men. Social stratification in the work camp would lose its European nuances and would be tied to position in a single system of production.

Initially composed of migratory male workers, these settlements became more rooted with the arrival of women and the creation of families. Where people came from the same source region and had few contacts with others in the New World, isolation protected some local European traditions—accent, for example—that were independent of the staple trade itself. In this way, elements of regional European cultures could long survive within settlements dominated by the technique and routine of specialized work. If such settlements endured, distinctive folk cultures, reflecting the settlers' background, the work of a staple trade, and the local environment, would emerge.

Towns

In the 16th century, all the work camps in Canada depended on towns on the other side of the Atlantic. Rouen, St-Malo, Nantes, La Rochelle, Bordeaux, San Sebastian, Oporto, Lisbon, Exeter, Dartmouth and dozens of other European ports managed the early transatlantic fishery. The landward momentum of the fur trade, in contrast, soon required year-round bases of operation in the New World. Quebec, established as a trading post in 1608, and Montreal, established as a mission in 1642 but almost immediately a centre of trade, accumulated commercial, administrative, and military functions and emerged as small towns, the first in Canada, late in the 17th century. By this time in Newfoundland some fishermen and fish merchants were overwintering and a few women and families had appeared; but at the end of the 17th century, Plaisance, the largest French settlement in Newfoundland, and St. John's, the largest English settlement, were little more than garrisoned fishing camps. A century later, 300 years after the cod fishery began, the Napoleonic Wars finally drove the principal British fish merchants across the Atlantic and firmly established the towns of eastern Newfoundland. In what is now Nova Scotia, military considerations prompted an earlier urbanization. Louisbourg, a French garrison town superimposed on a fishing camp, was built on Cape Breton Island after 1717 and became a focus of trade in the northwestern Atlantic; Halifax, a British response to Louisbourg, was another garrison town that became a busy port. The Loyalist migrations in the 1780s created several town surveys, one of which, Saint John, New Brunswick, became a town by 1800.

These small towns were transplanted foci of European power.[5] Like towns in Europe, they concentrated the administrative and military apparatus of the state, commercial capital, and ecclesiastical organization. All but Montreal were located on defendable deep-sea harbours; Montreal, a river town, was at a point of trans-shipment along the St. Lawrence. Garrisoned and usually walled, these towns figured prominently in the struggle between France and England for control of North America; they were seats of colonial administration; and they handled almost all external trade.

Occupationally, they were far more diverse than other settlements in early Canada. Government officials, military officers and men, merchants, and clerics lived there. In Montreal and Quebec, some 40 percent of heads of households were artisans representing all the basic trades associated with a port, construction, and the provision of common consumer goods.[6] In Louisbourg, where more consumer goods were imported, the occupational range was narrower, as it was in St. John's, which was even more dependent than the other towns on imports and a single export. Socially, urban populations were sharply stratified by occupation, income, and many fine social distinctions transplanted from Europe. Compared to European towns their size, the social range had perhaps contracted a little. The aristocracy was often absent, there had been less time for a generational accumulation of wealth, and there was an outlet for the urban poor wherever agricultural land was available nearby.

Early visitors wrote disparagingly of the Canadian towns; later they compared them quite favourably to their European equivalents. The towns looked European, minus the legacy of centuries. Montreal was an approximate grid that was pallisaded in the 1680s. Halifax was planned in precise Georgian proportions. St. John's to be sure, emerged out of the ramshackle constructions of the fishery, early trails, and the haphazard boundaries of farms. Institutional buildings in all the towns reflected the national architectural tastes of the day. French Baroque lines appeared in Quebec and Montreal, followed after the conquest by the first English Georgian and classical revival buildings. The common internal urban geography of power in the pre-industrial European city, a lower town given to commerce and a fortified and more institutional upper town, emerged in each of the early Canadian towns and was particularly pronounced in Quebec. There the lower town, pressed against the cliff, was congested before the end of the seventeenth century, while the upper town was a spacious array of gardens and institutional buildings.

Outliers of European power, these towns were fairly comprehensive transplantations from Europe that performed much the same functions as towns of similar size in France or England, housed fairly similar societies, and looked like newish versions of them.

Countryside

Most of the work camps and some of the towns of early Canada were located where gardens might survive but farming was out of the question. However, there were pockets of potential farmland around the Bay of Fundy, in the St. John River valley, along much of the south shore of the Gulf of St. Lawrence, and in the St. Lawrence valley. Agriculture began in these areas, usually a somewhat inadvertent by-product of the fishery or the fur trade.

Colonists were sent, but never very many because trading companies were not interested in such expensive, unprofitable undertakings; nor, after a time, was the Crown. Few individuals would accept the costs and risks of emigration to heavily forested land near the climatic margin for agriculture. A few dozen families comprised the founding Acadian population. Only some 9 500 immigrants, most of them demobilized soldiers or indentured servants, settled along the lower

St. Lawrence during the entire French regime. After the deportations of the Acadians during the Seven Years' War, New Englanders and a few people from Yorkshire settled the former Acadian marshlands and adjacent uplands. Loyalist migrations in the 1780s brought 35 000 immigrants to four colonies in the Maritimes (Nova Scotia, New Brunswick, Prince Edward Island, and Cape Breton Island) and about 12 000 to the British side of the Upper St. Lawrence River and Lower Great Lakes. The staple trades could not employ these people and their descendants, and nor could the towns. The great majority turned to farming or associated trades. In 1755, virtually all the 14 000 Acadians were farmers, as were at least 60 000 of the some 75 000 people along the lower St. Lawrence.

The establishment of a farm in early Canada entailed the transplantation of European sentiments of family and property, European peasant techniques, and, to a degree, a European relationship between town and countryside, to land near the northern climatic margin of North American agriculture. Although patches of land suitable for farming were available, the local market for farm products was small and the export market was non-existent until the 18th century. No agricultural export staple was established anywhere in British North America before 1800.

In these circumstances, farming developed primarily in response to the needs of farm families. A farm was an unspecialized, mixed operation that provided as much as possible for domestic consumption and some surplus for sale. Along the lower St. Lawrence its basic components were a kitchen garden, in which a wide variety of vegetables, tobacco, and perhaps a few fruit trees were grown; ploughed fields, which were planted primarily in wheat but also in legumes, barley, and oats; some meadow and pasture; and, depending on the age of the farm, more or less forest. Pigs, sturdy animals that could fend for themselves most of the year, were kept for meat. Cattle were kept for meat and milk, and oxen as draught animals. Sheep were raised for their wool. By the 18th century, there were horses on most farms, used for hauling. Every farm had poultry. The nominal censuses reveal little market specialization. Large farms produced more of the same things than smaller ones. With 5 hectares cleared there was hardly a surplus for sale; with 15 cleared there usually was: some wheat, a cow or two, perhaps a pig or some piglets, perhaps a few tubs of butter. No farm family wanted to be self-sufficient. There were rents and tithes to pay, and some manufactured goods to be purchased: iron tools, some kitchenware, some items of clothing, and, if it could be afforded, an iron stove made in the ironworks near Trois-Rivières. Most payments were made in kind.[7]

Elsewhere, farming was much the same. The basic unit of work was the nuclear family; production was diversified and largely but never exclusively for domestic consumption. Excavations of Acadian farm houses along the Annapolis River[8] reveal small wooden structures, presumably thatched, in which there were some imported iron tools and kitchenware—what might be expected from a domestic economy that was never closed. By the end of the eighteenth century, farms on some of the best land around the Bay of Fundy were a little more specialized, a little more oriented towards the market,[9] as were increasing numbers of farms on the Montreal plain. In early Ontario, military spending, the capital accompanying settlers, and the markets they generated, created more market opportunity than had been available to pioneer farmers elsewhere in Canada. Overall, the domestic economy overwhelmingly prevailed in the countryside. The small log or timber-frame house on a farm lot was a measure both of a New World opportunity and of its limitations.

In a weak commercial economy there were no wealthy farmers, no counterparts of the few yeoman farmers or *laboureurs* who often rented most of the land of an English or French village. As long as new farmland was available there were few landless families or beggars in the countryside. Farms of equivalent age were usually fairly similar; recently established farms were small, older farms were larger. Eventually, the timely inheritance of land gave some young farm families an edge over others. Once established, early Canadian farms provided the basics: enough to eat, rough clothing, shelter, fuel in winter, some surplus for sale. As long as there was an opportunity to establish such farms, the farming population along the lower St. Lawrence married younger, had more children, and lived longer than most French peasants.[10]

The common sources of power in rural Europe—state, landlord (usually within the seigneurial or manorial system), church, and merchant—variously penetrated these early Canadian countrysides. The Acadian settlements were particularly detached: some merchant connections with New England and, later, Louisbourg; a few parish priests but no effective seigneurs and no consistent enforcement of state power. In the 17th century, Acadia alternated between French and English control; the English, who took Acadia for the last time in 1710, largely ignored its French-speaking peasantry. The Acadians were left to their own devices, supported for a time by marshland farms and detached from the institutions that burdened peasant life in France, but exposed by this very detachment and vulnerable to their eventual, horrible fate: deportation. Along the lower St. Lawrence, external power diffused more consistently through the countryside. There were no royal taxes, but farmers were required to perform road work and, in wartime, to fight in the militia. The land was divided into seigneuries, and the rents and charges for the long-lot farms the seigneurs conceded added up to a considerable burden for people largely dependent on subsistence farming. They paid reluctantly, prevaricating as they could. By the 18th century, the seigneurial manor, still small by European standards, was usually considerably larger than the habitant house. The tithe to support the parish priest, 1/26th of the grain harvest, was another charge that had to be paid. Merchants from the town were also active in the countryside, particularly from the 1720s, when the colony began to export foodstuffs to Louisbourg and the French sugar islands. The merchants bartered and extended credit; many habitants were in debt to them. In such ways the common sources of power in rural France penetrated the relatively undifferentiated countryside along the lower St. Lawrence.[11]

Quite absent, of course, was the power of the modern nation state. In early Canada, the state reached into the countryside to punish or conscript, sometimes to count, but not to regulate the pattern of daily lives or to impose a national culture. The means to do so were not at hand, either in Canada or in Europe.[12] In Europe, the limitations of state power on the one hand, and the oral traditions, rootedness, and substantially regional economies of the peasantry on the other, sustained a mosaic of local regional cultures. Approximately similar circumstances in Canada encouraged the rapid emergence of regional cultures, none of which would reproduce more than some elements of any particular European peasant culture.

The regional cultures of France and England in the 17th and 18th centuries depended on common memories that were difficult to reassemble overseas, then difficult to maintain in new environments that exerted strong selective pressures. Sometimes almost all the people in a new settlement were from the same regional background, but more often they were not. Then different sets of memories converged, and none survived unaltered. Common assumptions—for example, about the importance of land, the primacy of the family, and the need for frugality—would be transferred. For the rest, an unconscious selection of remembered ways would reinforce particularly common memories or memories that were especially relevant to life in a new setting. Without the support of numbers, differences in language and dialect among a group of settlers would quickly disappear, and a new dialect, unlike any in the mother country, would emerge. The common log or timber-frame house of the Acadian and St. Lawrence settlement was not associated with any particular region of France. Rather, it drew on building techniques that had been common in early medieval Europe when the forest was at hand, had largely lapsed when it was cleared, and re-emerged, never entirely forgotten, when migration suddenly returned some French people to the forest.[13] In effect, some memories were reinforced by migration and resettlement and others were lost. Overall, European memories were being recombined and supplemented by New World experience. Vigorous, distinctive regional cultures were emerging.

The territorial extent of these new cultures depended on the migration fields, generation after generation, of the young brought up in them. Where land was available locally, most of the young would marry and settle close to parental farms, creating homogeneous patches of New World culture. In the longer run, such land would not be available, and the destinations to which the young migrated and the people they met there would largely shape the result: whether a particular regional culture would expand; whether another culture, born of another mixing of peoples in another environment, would emerge; or whether the migrants would be absorbed by a culture already in place.

The Territory

Drawn by fish and furs, the French outreach to North America entered the continent near or beyond the northern limit of agriculture. Fishermen encountered a rock-bound coast, unsuited for farming, that stretched from Labrador to southern Nova Scotia. Jacques Cartier found a land of "horrible rugged rocks"—perhaps the land God gave to Cain—when he entered the Gulf of St. Lawrence via the Strait of Belle Isle in 1534. As he sailed southward, the aspect of the land improved. The St. Lawrence valley, which Cartier visited the following year as far as Montreal, seemed lush and bountiful in summer, an assessment reiterated by the next

European to make this reconnaissance and write about it, Samuel de Champlain in 1603. As the fur trade was drawn towards the continental interior, France became committed to the St. Lawrence valley and the Gulf. To the north, rimming both, was the severe, pre-Cambrian Canadian Shield. To the south, not much further away but somewhat gentler, were the Appalachian Highlands. Between was a strip of land in the St. Lawrence valley suitable for the crops and livestock of north-western Europe. Far to the east of this valley was the Atlantic face of northern North America, attractive only for its fisheries, and behind that face some patches of land, such as the marshes around the Bay of Fundy, that could be cultivated. To the west was the territory of the fur trade, Indian territory, reached late in the 17th century by canoe routes to trading posts as far west as Lake Superior and the upper Mississippi. Such, in the 17th century, was the French position in North America.

In the 18th century, French activity in North America became even more dispersed and exceedingly difficult to consolidate. A new colony, Louisiana, was established along the Mississippi River; traders from the St. Lawrence built posts on the Saskatchewan River some 3 000km from Montreal; a garrison town, Louisbourg, was built on Cape Breton Island to counteract the loss of much of mainland Acadia; and French agricultural settlement began in the Illinois country, that is, in the upper Mississippi valley. Father Vivier, the Jesuit who served the Illinois settlements in the 1750s, described a bounteous land (corn, he said, yielded 3 000-fold) that was connected to a market in the French Antilles by the Mississippi and New Orleans. France had reached the future agricultural heartland of North America, but too late and with too few people to hold it. The 3 000 French-speaking people in the Illinois country when New France fell in 1760 would soon be engulfed by the tide of American settlement. After the American Revolution and the treaty of 1783 that created most of the eastern half of the border between Canada and the United States, Britain was left, conservatively and ironically, with the 17th-century French position in North America plus Newfoundland and Rupert's Land (the lands bordering Hudson Bay)—that is, with an Atlantic fishery, the Gulf of St. Lawrence, the Bay of Fundy, the St. Lawrence valley, and canoe routes to trading posts in the interior. The border settlement excluded from British North America territory south and west of the Great Lakes that France had claimed and traded in but had hardly occupied. The soon-to-be-realized agricultural poten-tial of these rich, continuous, agricultural lands—and with them a different and more abundant direction of North American development—passed to the United States. British North America was dominated by rock that could yield some primary resources and included some patches of land suitable for crops—the Canada that Cartier, looking for gold, had seen something of in the 1530s and that French traders, officials, and settlers had lived with throughout the French regime.

The Pattern of Settlement in 1800

In Canada in 1800, two old staple trades exploited quite different primary resources in different ways and in different areas. Towns, foci of colonial administration, defence, and trade, were integrated parts of the British imperial system but had little to do with each other. Farming turned on the domestic economy and maintained distinctive, bounded regional cultures in patches of land along the northern margin of North American agriculture. Wilderness sparsely inhabited by native people was nowhere far away.

In Newfoundland, along most of the Atlantic coast of Nova Scotia, and around the northern and western Gulf of St. Lawrence, life was still dominated by the cod fishery. A migratory French fishery continued to northern Newfoundland, but the English migratory fishery was rapidly declining and most fishermen lived in tiny, ramshackle fishing settlements perched along a rock-bound coast. Daily life in such settlements turned around the fishery, the weather, subsistence activities of the domestic economy (such as gardening and wood cutting), and the local community. External connections were controlled by merchants. Although the techniques of catching and processing cod, the merchant system, and the poverty of the fishermen were everywhere much the same, isolation supported different ethnic communities. In some Newfoundland outports, one or two surnames accounted for all families. On the Gaspé, different ethnic groups were more likely to mix. Overall, ethnic isolation was characteristic. An Irish dialect of English was spoken in some settlements, a dialect from Devon or the south of England in others. The Lunenburgers, south of Halifax, spoke a dialect of German. Acadians on Cape Breton Island and French Canadians on the Gaspé spoke different dialects of French.

In 1800, fish merchants operating along the Labrador shore still traded for a few furs. Otherwise these two staple trades, which still dominated the Canadian export economy, were separate. By 1800, the reach of the St. Lawrence fur trade was almost transcontinental; trading posts were well established in the drainage basin of the Mackenzie River, more than 4 000km by canoe from Montreal. The Hudson's Bay Company had expanded inland from its forts around the perimeter of the Bay to compete with the Montrealers in both the Petit Nord (between Lake Superior and Hudson Bay) and the Grand Nord (northwest of Lake Winnipeg). Supplies and trade goods carried inbound by canoe from Montreal and by river boat from the posts on Hudson Bay were destined for dozens of posts (some 320 were built between 1790 and 1805 alone) scattered through the boreal forest and parkland. Furs and some hides, carried outbound to the Bay or to Montreal, were shipped to London in a few bottoms a year—the sole export from Hudson Bay in 1800 and easily the principal export (by value) from the St. Lawrence.

Montreal traders hired about 1 000 men in the interior, the Hudson's Bay Company about half as many at its posts. A polyglot population of whites and natives occupied most trading posts, the social hierarchy dominated by the hierarchy of command in the fur trade. White men took "country" wives, and by 1800 there were many half-breeds.

Away from the trading posts in most of the Canadian Shield and on the northern plains, natives were usually the only people, their numbers much reduced by the introduction of European diseases (against which they had little immunity) and firearms (which increased the scale and intensity of native warfare). Long before 1800, the hunting of fur-bearing animals for trade had been incorporated into the seasonal rounds of native life. European goods were sought for their convenience, but natives were probably only dependent on muskets—needed to ward off enemies so armed.[14] For some native groups, a more invidious dependence, born of the shortage of food, was emerging by 1800. In some areas, big game, hunted for the provisioning trade, had become scarce; then, during cyclical downturns in populations of small game, natives might starve. As the fur trade expanded and competition intensified between traders from Montreal and those from Hudson Bay, the ecological basis of native hunting and fishing economies was slowly being undermined. In Newfoundland, European fishermen had finally penetrated the north central coast and the few remaining Beothuk, cut off from their summer fisheries, were starving.[15]

The different staple trades depended on towns, not all of them in 1800 in British North America. The St. Lawrence fur trade was tied to Montreal and Quebec, the Hudson Bay trade to London, England. The British fishery in Newfoundland largely depended on merchants in St. John's, Carbonnear, Harbour Grace, and Trinity; the migratory French fishery on towns in the Gulf of St-Malo. Merchants based in Halifax, New England, and the Channel Islands dominated the fisheries along the Atlantic coasts of Nova Scotia and Cape Breton (then a separate colony). Merchants from Quebec, Bristol, Dartmouth, the Channel Islands, and New England competed for the fisheries in the Gulf. Each of the port towns on the Atlantic, principally Saint John, Halifax, and St. John's, was the focus of a separate coasting trade that distributed imports and assembled exports. Quebec received imports for the St. Lawrence settlements and shipped some wheat, as well as furs, overseas. All the towns of British North America in 1800 were bound by trade and administration to London; within British North America, there was no system or hierarchy of towns.

As during the French regime, the towns were administrative and military as well as commercial centres. After the conquest, the British destroyed Louisbourg but the other towns of New France remained, their functions intact, their elites largely replaced. Occupationally these towns were diverse, as they had always been, and socially they remained sharply stratified, their most important citizens colonial officials, military officers, and merchants—more of one than another in different towns. Society tended to be expatriate and imitative, but the ethnic compositions of these towns had no close British equivalents: the Newfoundland towns were primarily English and Irish; Montreal and Quebec were predominantly French Canadian, with additions from Britain, New York, and New England; Saint John was composed of Loyalists from several former colonies plus immigrants directly from Britain; Halifax was a mix of New Englanders, English, and a few Scots, Irish, Acadians, and blacks.

These small, pre-industrial towns accounted for less than 10 percent of the some 350 000 people who lived in the seven British North American colonies in 1800. Quebec and Halifax, the two largest towns in British North America, each had some 8 000 inhabitants, and Montreal some 6 000. St. John's, with 3 000 people, was growing rapidly as commercial control of the British fishery shifted across the Atlantic during the Napoleonic Wars. Saint John, a creation of Loyalist settlement along the St. John River, also had about 3 000 people. Away from the towns, almost everyone in Newfoundland and the great majority of people along the Atlantic coasts of Nova Scotia and Cape Breton Island and around the Gaspé peninsula depended directly on the fishery. The few whites in the Canadian Shield or on the northern Plains were employees of the fur trade. In all other patches of European settlement, farming dominated.

Farming still took place fairly close to the climatic margin on land that was bounded, rarely far away, by rock and soils that could not be cultivated. The largest patch of arable land was in the lower St. Lawrence valley where, in 1800, the rural population was over 200 000. A distinctive regional culture, French in most details but not any particular French culture, had emerged there long since. Because farming developed within broadly similar environmental and economic constraints from one end of the lower St. Lawrence to the other, and because part of the population was remixed generation after generation as young adults moved from areas where all agricultural land was occupied to others where it was still available, the rural culture of early Canada was expansive and probably fairly uniform.

By 1800, settlement was expanding rapidly inland, away from the river, occupying all arable land in many seigneuries and spreading rapidly across the Montreal plain, the last large reservoir of agricultural land in the lower St. Lawrence valley. As land became scarce its value rose. In some areas, family land was again held as tenaciously as in France.[16] Seigneurial revenues increased as the population rose and the local market economy expanded. Villages became more common, small service centres for farmers nearby. Here and there, especially near the towns, a few farms were much larger and more specialized than the rest. Wheat, flour, and meat were exported. Overall, the agricultural economy remained unspecialized, still oriented much more to the immediate needs of farm families than to the market. The domestic economy and the distinctive rural culture that had evolved along the lower St. Lawrence when farmland was widely available and agricultural prices were low were still viable, still expanding, still supporting a people within the St. Lawrence valley.

Another distinctive regional culture, formed on the marshes and within the migration field around the Bay of Fundy, had been uprooted when British officials deported the Acadians during the Seven Years' War. Reassembled from near and far, the 7 000 Acadians in British North America in 1800 were mostly fishermen who practised a little farming and lived in tiny settlements from Cape Breton to Gaspé. Most farmers in the Atlantic colonies were English-speaking, recent arrivals from New England, Yorkshire, or Scotland, and settled on patches of marsh, intervale, or upland where agriculture was feasible. For most of these people, as for the Acadians before them, agriculture was primarily for domestic consumption, with a small surplus for sale. The ethnicity of settlements around southern Nova Scotia and the Bay of Fundy and along the St. John River was strongly influenced by New England, whereas the south shore of the Gulf was Scottish with Acadian enclaves, patterns that would endure.

There were also 15 000 to 20 000 English speakers in rural Quebec, settled along the Richelieu River, near the towns, or in the townships newly laid out between the seigneurial lands of the St. Lawrence valley and the American border. There, at the end of the century, the northern edge of the American settlement frontier was beginning to spill into British North America. In Ontario, where settlement spread discontinuously along the upper St. Lawrence River and the north shore of Lake Ontario and Lake Erie, there were perhaps approximately 35 000 people: 3 000 French speakers along the St. Clair River opposite Detroit, 3 000 Gaelic-speaking Highlanders just established 800km away near the border with Quebec, some 2 000 Indians who had settled in the 1780s on reserves in the Grand River valley, and perhaps 23 000 Loyalists, late Loyalists, and their descendants, most from upstate New York. In some of these early Ontarian settlements, British military spending, capital brought by settlers, and the availability of good land had created a vigorous agricultural start. Wheat exports were beginning.

These different rural peoples, in what had been New France and had become the several colonies of British North America, were isolated by rock and distance. Except locally, overland transportation was virtually non-existent. There was nothing like a continuous, expanding agricultural frontier to mix peoples of different backgrounds. Quite the contrary, as patches of land filled they admitted few newcomers. The young who left these settlements often went to the adjacent United States, a destination that was usually closer, more familiar, and provided more opportunity than other patches of British North American settlement. With such migration patterns, the settlements left behind would maintain distinctive local cultures for generations.

Conclusion

Eventually, the idea of Canada and the apparatus of the modern nation-state were superimposed on the fragmented, discontinuous human geography of the several British colonies spread along, or beyond, the northern edge of the North American agricultural ecumene. The enlarged power of the state coupled with economic expansion behind protective tariffs worked to integrate Canadian space. A sense and, to a degree, an experience of Canada emerged alongside more local identifications.[17] Yet the realities of an earlier Canada complicate in countless ways the bureaucratic, technological, and emotional surfaces of contemporary Canadian life, and affect, in good measure, the ways that Canadians are able to conceive of themselves.

The Turnerian idea of the frontier which so long captured American popular and intellectual imaginations could not, for example, take similar hold in Canada.[18] The Canadian land was far too bounded, too niggardly; there was no continuous, expansive frontier as there was across much of the United States. In its more abundant context, the American imagination could fashion an American type, the frontiersman, as the Canadian imagination, confronted with the patchwork reality of Canada, could not. Similarly, the liberal vision of freedom inherent in the Turnerian frontier was undoubtedly encouraged by an ongoing relationship with a forthcoming land, and would be much more pinched in Canada where landed opportunity soon ran out, authority was not far away, and the unmanaged penetration of the recesses of Canadian space was virtually impossible. If, in Turnerian metaphor, immigrants shed some of their European clothing in Canadian countrysides, they did not create American frontiersmen—nor quite the myth and ideology associated with them—because, essentially, their landed opportunity was so constrained and discontinuous.

The Canadian imagination would turn more readily to the northern wilderness and the staple trades that penetrated it. The Laurentian vision, expressed monumentally in canvasses by the Group of Seven, theoretically in the political economy of Harold Adams Innis, and more colloquially in a great deal of Canadian literature and political rhetoric, sustained a long generation of English Canadian nationalism, and undoubtedly reflected elements of Canadian reality. Innis was right that staple trades were the early motor of Canadian development; right that Canada could not be explained by theory intended to interpret European or American experience; right that in the New World equation of land, labour, and capital, land was the most distinctive variable (in this Innis and Turner agreed); right that Canada was the outgrowth of the European penetration of a northern land, and that the border between Canada and the United States is not a geographical absurdity. Innis almost argued, as his most prominent student, Marshall McLuhan, might have put it, that the land itself had become the medium of social formation. But Innis left out an enormous amount: the towns, except as nodal points in transportation systems; the countryside, except so far as it bore (as it rarely did) on export trades; and much of Canadian society and culture. In the end, he had not constructed an interpretation of Canada, but rather of some elements of Canadian experience. Eventually, only a small fraction of the scholarship on early Canada would be able to work within his ideas, while the Canadian public, comfortable in its towns, would not quite recognize itself within the stark outlines of the Laurentian vision.[19]

Rather, and in contrast to the spare, comprehensive grandeur of the Laurentian vision, it became popular to emphasize the limited identities of Canadian life.[20] Canada came to be seen as a mosaic,[21] at most as a community of communities, a country characterized by variety and essentially ungeneralizable. This vision, too, is grounded in elements of long-standing Canadian reality, particularly in the patchy distribution of agricultural land, the wide scatter of other resources, and the processes of settlement and migration that encouraged the formation and perpetuation of regional cultures. But variety is a fact of many national societies, and the metaphor of the mosaic, by itself, eventually seems rather lazy. It identifies none of the particular characteristics of this particular mosaic, and it discounts elements of order—such as those Innis discerned—within the manifest variety of Canadian life. It provides no account of the emergence of Canada and little enough of the particular reality of this country in relation to the two societies with which it has been most engaged: Northwestern Europe and the United States.

It is, I think, to the human geography of early Canada that we have to turn to bring these different elements of Canadian reality into some measure of common focus. The outreach of Europe to Canada embodied an encounter with a new land,

and as Europeans penetrated this new land and fitted themselves to it, the pattern of European life changed. This process can be followed at different scales; it is revealed, more or less, within each of the different types of settlement of which early Canada was composed, and in the whole geographical composition of early Canada, a composition that was, in sum, a unique spatial arrangement of approximately European elements. Put most abstractly, European social formations were bent in Canada by non-European space. To the south of Canada was very different non-European space, far less rock- and winter-bound, more welcoming, larger. European life was bent there too, but not as in Canada. Different national societies eventually evolved, each of the New World, each expressed in, and in considerable degree created by, their own evolving human geographies.

The general outline of the human geography of early Canada can now be discerned. It reveals neither a few stark principles from which, as it were, early Canada can be deduced, nor an endless complexity of individual detail. Rather, as I have tried to suggest in this essay, the pattern of early Canada was a complex but clearly discernible composition of a small number of distinctive forms in a particular spatial arrangement. In sum, the composition was unique, and therein is the underlying originality of Canada.

Notes

1. By the idea of Canada I mean, simply, the idea that there could be a transcontinental state north of the United States. This use of the phrase is considerably simpler, therefore, than Leslie Armour's in *The Idea of Canada*, (Ottawa: Steel Rail Publishing, 1981).

2. This essay is a considerably reworked version of a presidential address to the Canadian Association of Geographers, published in *The Canadian Geographer* 31, 4 (Winter, 1987): 290–98. That address, written in the exhausting months before publication of volume 1 of the *Historical Atlas of Canada: From the Beginning to 1800* (Toronto and Montreal: University of Toronto Press/Les presses de l'université de Montréal, 1987), needed some reconsideration, and I appreciate this opportunity to publish it in revised form. The subject of the essay had been in mind for years—parts of it are in some of the essays published in the *Historical Atlas*, parts in my essay "European Beginnings in the Northwest Atlantic: A Comparative View," in *Seventeenth-Century New England*, ed. David D. Hall and David Grayson Allen (Boston: The Colonial Society of Massachusetts, 1984)—but this is the first outline of the whole argument. Such an outline would not have been possible without volume 1 of the *Historical Atlas*, and my dependence on the many authors of that volume is surely obvious. The cartographic evidence upon which, in good part, this essay rests is in the *Atlas*.

3. Harold Innis was right about this. The early development of Canada cannot be understood apart from staple trades, a fact that is sufficient to set the economic development of Canada and Europe apart, and even, because of the different availability of land for individual initiatives, the development of Canada and the United

States. The problem with Innis's basic ideas about Canada is, essentially, that they generalize about a country on the basis of one of its characteristic parts. See the conclusion.

4. Work by Laurier Turgeon reveals the scale of the 16th-century fishery particularly clearly. See "Pour redécouvrir notre 16me siècle: les pêches à Terre-Neuve d'après les archives notariales de Bordeaux," *Révue d'histoire de l'Amérique française* 39, 4 (Spring 1986): 523–49; and also "Le temps des pêches lointaines. Permanences et transformations," in *Histoire des pêches Maritimes en France*, ed. Michel Mollat (Toulouse: Editions Privat, 1987).

5. In Anthony Giddens' terminology, cities were the "power-containers" in absolutist states, whereas in the modern nation-state, power is much more evenly distributed through the whole territory of the state. See Giddens, *The Nation-State and Violence* (Berkeley and Los Angeles: University of California Press, 1987), chap. 4

6. These comments on artisanship have been much sharpened by discussion and correspondence with Louise Dechêne.

7. Again, this description of habitant indebtedness relies on comments by Louise Dechêne in response to an early draft of this essay.

8. David J. Christianson, "Belleisle 1983: Excavations at a Pre-expulsion Acadian Site," Curatorial Report no. 48 (Halifax: Nova Scotia Museum, 1984).

9. Graeme Wynn, "A Region of Scattered Settlements and Bounded Possibilities: Northeastern America 1775–1800," *The Canadian Geographer* 31 (1987): 319–38, reprinted in this volume.

10. Hubert Charbonneau, *Vie et mort de nos ancêtres: étude démographique* (Montreal: Les presses de l'université de Montréal, 1975). See plate 46 of the *Historical Atlas of Canada* for a more current demographic graph of the early Canadian population.

11. I argued this differently in *The Seigneurial System in Early Canada*, (Madison: University of Wisconsin Press, 1966, republished in 1984 by McGill-Queen's University Press) and, to a lesser degree, in my other essay in this volume. Other studies have shown, however, that seigneurial charges accumulated year by year to become a substantial burden on many peasants, and that other traditional forms of power in absolutist states could and did penetrate a countryside in which, compared to rural France, the economic range was short. Since its publication, the dominant study of the Canadian peasantry during the French regime has been Louise Dechêne, *Habitants et marchands de Montréal au XVIIe siècle* (Montreal: Plon, 1974). Another major evaluation of habitant life is Allan Greer, *Peasant, Lord and Merchant: Rural Society in Three Quebec Parishes, 1740–1840* (Toronto: University of Toronto Press, 1985).

12. There were many careful nominal censuses of the early Canadian population, particularly during the first four decades of royal government (after 1663). But it was one thing to reach into the countryside to count, and another to disseminate a national culture there. In the 17th and 18th centuries, the former was possible, but hardly the latter. See the essay by Serge Courville in this volume,, and, for a more theoretical statement of the problems, Anthony Giddens, *The Constitution of Society* (Berkeley and Los Angeles: University of California Press, 1984), especially 253–62.

13. George-Pierre Léonidoff, "The Wooden House," *Historical Atlas of Canada*, vol. 1, plate 56.

14. This summation of the effects of the fur trade on native peoples is Conrad Heidenreich's. The comments on this topic in the essay, "Inland Expansion," in volume 1 of the *Historical Atlas of Canada* are his.

15. Ralph T. Pastore, "Fishermen, Furriers, and Beothuks: The Economy of Extinction," *Man in the Northeast* 33 (1987): 47–62.

16. For example Jacques Mathieu, Celine Cyr, Guy Dinel, Jeanine Pozzo, and Jacques Saint-Pierre, "Mobilité et mariage dans le gouvernement de Québec au XVIIIe siècle," in *Evolution et éclatement du monde rural*, ed. Joseph Goy and Jean-Pierre Wallot (Montreal: Les presses de l'université de Montréal, 1986), 305–13.

17. Some of this is elaborated in my essay "The Emotional Structure of Canadian Regionalism," *The Walter L. Gordon Lecture Series*, vol. 5 (1980–81), reprinted as "Regionalism and the Canadian Archipelago," in *Heartland and Hinterland: A Geography of Canada*, ed. L.D. McCann (Scarborough, Ont.: Prentice Hall, 1982), 458–84.

18. But it did take some hold, particularly in the 1920s and 1930s. My Ph.D. thesis, written in the early 1960s and published as *The Seigneurial System in Early Canada*, has obvious Turnerian overtones as, more faintly, do parts of this essay. In detail, Turner is no longer analytically useful, but the primary question he raised—the influence of the relative availability of land on European social structures—remains as fundamental as ever. A central problem with Turner's answer, besides his mystical vagueness and his American zeal, is that he claimed far too much for a particular form of the European connection with the New World. Yet in the United States, where agricultural land was abundant, the frontier was large and wide. The American imagination was conditioned by such plenitude, and Turnerian exaggeration would be less evident than in more pinched Canadian circumstances. A useful survey of Turnerian thought in Canada is still Michael S. Cross, ed., *The Frontier Thesis and the Canadas: The Debate on the Impact of the Canadian Environment* (Toronto: Copp Clark, 1970).

19. See the chapter on Innis in Carl Berger's *The Writing of Canadian History: Aspects of English-Canadian Historical Writing, 1900–1970* (Toronto: Oxford University Press, 1976) for a shrewd appraisal of the man and his intellectual context; and W.L. Morton, *The Canadian Identity* (Toronto, University of Toronto Press, 1972), chap. 1, for a late and eloquent example of the Laurentian voice.

20. J.M.S. Careless, " 'Limited Identities' in Canada," *The Canadian Historical Review* 50, 1 (March, 1969): 1–10.

21. A classic consideration of the metaphor of the mosaic in Canadian thought is Allan Smith, "Metaphor and Nationality in North America," *Canadian Historical Review* 51, 3 (1970): 247–75.

An honest attempt has been made to secure permission for all material used, and if there are errors or omissions, these are wholly unintentional and the Publisher will be grateful to learn of them.

Conrad E. Heidenreich, "The Natural Environment of Huronia and Huron Seasonal Activities," from *Beitrage zur Kulturgeographie von Kanada*, ed. C. Schott (Marburg: Marburger Geographische Gesellschaft e.V., 1971), 103–16. Reprinted with the permission of the publisher.

D. Wayne Moodie, "Indian Map-Making: Two Examples from the Fur Trade West," An earlier version of this paper appeared in the *Bulletin* of the Association of Canadian Map Libraries and Archives, Number 55 (June 1985), pp. 32–43. Reprinted with permission.

Arthur J. Ray, "Diffusion of Diseases in the Western Interior of Canada, 1830–1850," *Geographical Review*. 66 (April 1976): 139–57, © The American Geographical Society. Reprinted with the permission of the Society.

R. Cole Harris, "The Extension of France into Rural Canada," from *European Settlement and Development in North America*, ed. J.R. Gibson (Toronto: University of Toronto Press, 1978), 27–45. © University of Toronto Press, 1978. Reprinted by permission of University of Toronto Press.

Stephen J. Hornsby, "Scottish Emigration and Settlement in Early Nineteenth Century Cape Breton Island." Reprinted by permission of Acadiensis Press from Kenneth Donovan, ed., *The Island: New Perspectives on Cape Breton History* (Fredericton: Acadiensis Press, 1990).

John C. Lehr, "Kinship and Society in the Ukrainian Pioneer Settlement of the Canadian West," *The Canadian Geographer/Le Géographe canadien* 29, 3 (1985): 207–19. Reprinted with the permission of The Canadian Association of Geographers/L'Association Canadienne des Géographes.

Serge Courville, "Space, Territory, and Culture in New France: A Geographical Perspective," D'abord paru sous la titre "Espace, territoire et culture en Nouvelle-France: une vision géographique," dans *Revue d'histoire de l'Amérique française*, 37, 3 (hiver 1983): 417–429. Reprinted with permission.

Peter Ennals and Deryck Holdsworth, "Vernacular Architecture and the Cultural Landscape of the Maritime Provinces: A Reconnaissance." Reprinted by permission from *Acadiensis*, Vol. X, no. 2 (Spring 1981) pp. 86–105.

Thomas F. McIlwraith, "The Adequacy of Rural Roads in the Era before Railways: An Illustration from Upper Canada," *The Canadian Geographer/Le Géographe canadien* 14, 4 (1970): 344–60. Reprinted with the permission of The Canadian Association of Geographers/L'Association Canadienne des Géographes.

"Damaged and Efficient Landscapes in Rural Southern Ontario, 1880–1900," by Kenneth Kelly, first appeared in *Ontario History*, March, 1974, published by The Ontario Historical Society, 5151 Yonge Street, Willowdale, Ontario, M2N 5P5 and is reprinted with their permission.

L.D. McCann, "Metropolitanism and Branch Businesses in the Maritimes, 1881–1931." Reprinted by permission from *Acadiensis*, Vol. XIII, no. 1 (Autumn 1983) pp. 112–25.

Gunter Gad and Deryck Holdsworth, "Corporate Capitalism and the Emergence of the High-Rise Office Building," *Urban Geography* 8, 3 (1987): 212–31. Reprinted with the permission of V.H. Winston & Son, Inc.

Donna McCririck and Graeme Wynn, "Building 'Self-Respect and Hopefulness': The Development of Blue-Collar Suburbs in Early Vancouver." Adapted and rewritten from Donna McCririck's "Opportunity and the Workingman: A Study of Land